BEYOND THE COLOR LINE AND THE IRON CURTAIN

New Americanists ¦ *A Series Edited by Donald E. Pease*

BEYOND THE COLOR LINE AND THE IRON CURTAIN

Reading Encounters between Black and Red, 1922–1963 ⦙ *Kate A. Baldwin*

DUKE UNIVERSITY PRESS ⦙ DURHAM AND LONDON 2002

© 2002 Duke University Press All rights reserved
Printed in the United States of America on acid-free paper ∞
Designed by Rebecca Giménez Typeset in Adobe Minion by
Keystone Typesetting, Inc. Library of Congress Cataloging-in-
Publication Data appear on the last printed page of this book.
Parts of chapters 3 and 4 appeared originally in a different
form in *Cultural Critique* 40 (fall 1998): 103–144; and
Diaspora 9, no. 3 (winter 2000): 399–420.

FOR BRIAN AND OLIVER

CONTENTS

ACKNOWLEDGMENTS

Like its subject matter, this book is the product of influence and support that spans three continents. Throughout their travels, its multiple tracks of interest have been guided by generous minds. The book's earliest routes were sketched in the town of Amherst, Massachusetts, where I had the good fortune to encounter and learn the pleasures of the Russian language and Russian literature from such teachers as Stephanie Sandler, Dale Peterson, Stanley Rabinowitz, Jane Taubman, and Joseph Brodsky; and to see these pleasures buoyed, challenged, and reconfigured through the acumen of Andrew Parker. My interest in Russian literature continued down the road, in New Haven, Connecticut, under the generous tutelage of Monika Greenleaf and Michael Holquist. Simultaneous to these Russian inflections, my thinking was sharpened by the critical insights of Jennifer Wicke and Shoshana Felman, and the imprint of two Americanists, Hazel Carby and Wayne Koestenbaum, whose work and examples of professorship I take as models for my own. They sustained the possibility of a Russian–African American dialogue, and I am indebted to their friendship, intellectual rigor, and muselike inspiration. They are pathbreakers who sent me on my way. During a brief semester at Duke University, I gained from the divinity (and good food) of Eve Sedgwick and Michael Moon, and the interlocutions of Henry Louis Gates Jr. Though now dispersed, these three have continued to exert their supple influences.

Together, these collective voices encouraged me to take my interests abroad. And in Leningrad and Moscow I benefited from the insights of numerous friends and colleagues. I am especially thankful to Lena Petrovsky, Sasha Ivanov, and Valery Podoroga for the sustenance, intellectual and otherwise, they have provided me throughout the years. I also owe a debt of gratitude to the Russian Academy of Science's Institute of Philoso-

phy for its repeated invitations to me to pursue my research and participate in its seminars in Moscow. The routings of this project led me to
Africa as well, and my work there was sustained by the keen insights and
good comradeship of longtime friends in Morocco. Sadik Rddad and
Ouafae Elattaoni generously opened their home and new intellectual avenues to me; Khalid Bekkaoui and Taieb Belghazi invited me to give seminars in Fez and Rabat. Together, their comments helped me to resituate
the question of "Africa" in U.S. discourse, and negotiate intersections
between feminism and Islam. I am grateful to the Moroccan Cultural
Studies Center at Sidi Mohammed Ben Abdallah University for the opportunity to present and discuss materials on Hughes and the veil.

Institutional support for this project has been abundant, and my work
has benefited from an array of dynamic academic settings. A postdoctoral
fellowship at Brown University's Pembroke Center offered the means,
time, and inspiration to distance myself from graduate school and fathom
this project. Conversations with Ellen Rooney, Neil Lazarus, Elizabeth
Weed, and Nancy Armstrong undoubtedly inform this work and make it
better. A Mellon Fellowship at Johns Hopkins University's Women's Studies Program and Humanities Center enabled me to pursue the idea, bringing me into contact with the helpful advice of Judith Walkowitz and Jeffrey
Brooks. Much of the initial writing of this book was done at the Mary
Ingraham Bunting Institute. Radcliffe's tradition of "sister fellows" pro-
vided unparalleled comradeship and nourishment for the early stages of
this work. In particular, I thank Meg McClagan, Neta Crawford, Rachel
Manley, Christina Shea, Jill Reynolds, Carol Mason, Maggie Keane, Sheila
Pepe, and Brian Larkin for their contributions to the emerging product.
Funds from a Notre Dame Institute for Scholarship in the Liberal Arts
faculty research grant allowed me to take an extended research trip to
Moscow in 1998 to work in the newly accessible archives there. This archi-
val research was extended into 1999 through the technological wizardry of
Michael Workman and patient responses to my distant queries by Irina
Silyatitskaya. I am also grateful to the archivists and librarians at Rossiiskii
gosudarstvennyi arkhiv literatury i iskusstva (RGALI [the Russian State
Archive of Literature and Art]) and Rossiiskii tsentr khraneniia i izu-
cheniia dokumentov noveishei istorii (RTSKHIDNI [the Russian Center for
the Preservation and Study of Documents of Recent History]) in Moscow;
Alfred Mueller of the Beinecke Library in New Haven; Linda Seidman,

head librarian of the Du Bois Papers at University of Massachusetts at Amherst; the Special Collections at Notre Dame's Hesburgh Library; and the support staff in my department at Notre Dame—notably, Nancy Mitchell for her clerical assistance and good humor.

The bulk of *Beyond the Color Line and the Iron Curtain* was written throughout the time I have been at Notre Dame. Friends and colleagues I have met and learned from here leave their mark on this book in various forms. For their kindnesses and generous expenditure of intellectual energy on my behalf, I thank Kathy Psomiades, Ewa Ziarek, Hilary Radner, Jessica Chalmers, Julian Dibbell, Grail Bederman, Valerie Sayers, and Joseph Buttigieg. Christopher Fox and Julia Douthwaite committed their administrative acumen and largesse to my project. Among other interlocutors who have commented on portions of the text, with inestimable erudition Robyn Wiegman and Robert Reid-Pharr offered early support, Kevin Platt elaborated insights at the end, and with discerning vision Siobhan Somerville read many drafts and provided fresh as well as invaluable feedback.

I would also like to thank Duke University Press, in particular the steadfast support of Ken Wissoker and his staff, especially Katie Courtland and Christine Habermaas, assistant managing editor Justin Faerber, my copy editor Cindy Milstein, and Nancy Zibman for her assistance with the index. I am grateful as well to the anonymous readers who evaluated the manuscript and offered helpful advice on how to revise it.

I also offer my appreciation to the other people who embarked on this journey unbeknownst to them. They include my long-distance friends, Adrie Kusserow and Jessica Lerner, who continue to sustain and inspire me with their laughter, loyalty, and poetry in motion. Barbara and Thomas Campbell welcomed my peregrinations to and from Ghent where I found rejuvenation in the friendships of Tom Campbell, Mark McGurl, and Henry Blodget. Eileen Byrne generously created a home away from home for my son, Oliver. And with perfect pitch throughout, Ric Menck composed the soundtrack. To my extended family on both the Edwards and Baldwin sides—in particular Barbara Baldwin, Henry Blume, Rosanne Herbert, Ann Edwards, and Ken Edwards—I am grateful for unerring support. I am especially indebted to my parents, Mary Burt Blume and Joseph Lyle Baldwin, and my sisters, Pamela Baldwin and Elizabeth Baldwin, from whom I continue to learn how to be a better person.

Finally, this book is dedicated to the persons who have made the trip worth taking, Brian Edwards, whose labor and love are reflected in each page, and Oliver Baldwin Edwards, who instills the pleasures of interpretation with newfound delight each day.

Because many of the readers of this book will not know Russian, I have translated original Russian passages and provided the Russian transliteration in the notes. The modified Library of Congress system is used, except in the case of well-established English spellings of names and nouns, such as Dostoevsky and czarist.

I am grateful for the kind support of Mary Louise Patterson, who generously granted me access to and permission to use citations from the unpublished memoir of her mother, Louise Thompson Patterson. A grant from the Notre Dame Institute for Scholarship in the Liberal Arts generously helped to subsidize the cost of reproducing the images herein.

INTRODUCTION

The Demand for a New Kind of Person:
Black Americans and the Soviet Union, 1922–1963

In Russia the darker peoples were serfs without land control [whose history]
paralleled that of American freedmen.—W. E. B. Du Bois, *Russia and America*

The history of the Russian peasant closely parallels that of [the] Negro
peasant in America.—Paul Robeson, interview in *The Observer*

The historical affiliation between the Russian peasant and the American
black as involuntarily indentured servants who were emancipated from
servitude at roughly contemporaneous moments is an affiliation that has
sparked the interest of some of the twentieth century's most influential
African American intellectuals. Not only did Claude McKay, Langston
Hughes, Paul Robeson, and W. E. B. Du Bois comment on this parallel
history at different points in their careers, they each also spent concentrated periods of time in the Soviet Union exploring the fertile territories
of comparison.[1] All of them produced significant work while traveling in
the Soviet Union and all wrote about their experiences. At the same time,
as public figures, each was the subject of Soviet media attention and
cultural production, and had reciprocal influence on the way the questions of "Negroes" and by extension Africa were thought about in the
Soviet Union.[2] Despite the importance of the relationship of the Soviet
Union to these men, their work and Soviet responses to them—together
what I call the Soviet archive of black America—have been largely overlooked or read in isolation from their larger oeuvres, pushed to the sidelines of their careers. As a result, many of the texts that I address in this

book remain unpublished; others have been left out of standard anthologies. Much of the Russian material I consider has heretofore not been translated into English.

This book retrieves and rethinks routes of influence between Moscow, Tashkent, and Harlem. Beyond its focus on these four African Americans, this study is about an extended moment—from 1922 to 1963—when the Soviet Union and Soviet Communism drew scores of African Americans beyond the color line and across the East/West divide to visit the experiment under way in the USSR. The turn in Russian history from czarism to Bolshevism (and later to Stalinism) seemed to offer black Americans not only a means of contesting the exclusionary practices of citizenship and national belonging on which their understandings of identity were based. In the name of an international movement poised to challenge Western domination, Soviet Communism established an interracial alliance between "blacks" and "whites," and it was this cross-racial affinity between Russians and blacks as marginalized, world historical "others" that enabled, in part, the belief that the Soviet alternative was preferable to that of the United States. The records that document such traversals are significant because they offer not only a sense of Russia's receptiveness to these figures but a sense of how these crossings had reciprocal effects—both in terms of specific policy and cultural perception. In retrieving the chronicles of these interactions, the book examines them as products of interracial exchange made possible by arguably parallel routes of subordination to "the West" and put forth as alternatives to accounts of political modernity that reiterated the dominance of Western paradigms. *Beyond the Color Line and the Iron Curtain* explores how these figures used their encounters with the Soviet Union as a means of transforming exclusionary patterns into an internationalism that was a dynamic mix of antiracism, anticolonialism, social democracy, and international socialism.

In recent years, the emerging field of diaspora studies has helped to illuminate the cultural, social, and systemic links between geographically distant peoples. Paul Gilroy's 1993 book *The Black Atlantic: Modernity and Double Consciousness* navigated the route for one region within this field that has challenged existing paradigms used to understand the cultural production of a black diaspora.[3] In the wake of Gilroy's study, interrogations of the relationship between the historical event of the middle passage and wave of cultural production with which black modernism is identified have solidified the argument for a black transatlantic tradition. Rewriting the conventional configuration of "black" identity as primarily national in content, these assertions have questioned African American exceptionalism and widened the context in which black American cultural production is interpreted. The idea of black internationalism has played a key, if sometimes unpredictable role among the variety of forces at work in this reconfiguration. Although in the twentieth century the concept of the "international" has distinct links to Soviet rhetoric, the interplay between black American culture and the Soviet Union in the formation of internationalism has not been sufficiently explored.[4] Retrieving the Soviet archive provides a fuller picture of the patterns of "nation" in which Soviet internationalism was etched.

Outlining the dynamism of the cultural, social, and racial pulls behind the involvement of these black Americans with the Soviet Union, this book argues that a phrase like "black internationalism" cannot be understood without documenting the specific interaction between Soviet ideology and black American aspiration toward racial liberation and a society free of racism. The fruits of this interaction—the various ways in which these black authors negotiated between ideology and aspiration—established paradigms that affected black modernism and persisted through the early cold war period. The period under consideration here, 1922–1963, encompasses an era that stretches from the meeting of the Third International in Moscow to the decline of Nikita Khrushchev's reign, from the rise of black cultural production associated with the Harlem Renaissance to the death of Du Bois. This book offers a genealogy of "the Negro question" as it emerged in dialogue between the Soviet Union and these black Americans, and demonstrates how thinking through this question in the 1960s linked back to its earlier associations established in the 1920s. At the same time, I maintain that the occlusion of this dialogue bears a crucial relation to the exclusion of race in debates over the meaning of "nation" and "national identity" that affected some historiography of the 1970s and 1980s.[5] It is largely due to enduring paradigms that marginalize the important relationships between race and radicalism that there is less awareness of the Soviet archive of black America than there might be. The writings of McKay, Hughes, Du Bois, and Robeson reveal how the conceptual aid of internationalism enabled an exposure of the ways in which the major antagonisms with which the early Cold War period was associated—a fear of Soviet imperialism—had a genealogy in U.S. attitudes toward race. A fear of blacks transgressing the racial status quo of white supremacy characterized by Jim Crow was restated as fear of outside infiltration and contamination of the national polity during the 1950s. It is both the specificity of the Soviet-inspired black challenge to U.S. conceptions of national belonging and citizenship and its occlusion in standard accounts of a black transnationalism that arise from the black Atlantic model that this book seeks to reconsider.

Discounting the significance of the Soviet archive reflects a tendency to disregard both the international impulse put forth by these authors and the Russian language in which this impulse sometimes found its voice. In this guise, black internationalism does not equate itself with an easy mobility that cancels out national boundaries but rather with a framework in which to contemplate linkages between peoples of the African diaspora and their nonblack allies—those bound together by a shared sense of exclusion from the nation-state, from citizenship. Internationalism conceived of in this manner stresses the connectedness between nations, thereby allowing the specter of nation to hover ambiguously. This ambiguity was key to the interest of black Americans who by joining the cause of internationalism, were nonetheless reluctant to throw away national belonging with the proverbial bathwater of the "nation-state." Their interests in the internationalism of these theoretical underpinnings brought them to the Soviet Union as journalists, writers, activists, and performers. My book thus argues against a marginalization of the international—whatever its native tongue—in black American authorship. In this sense, the question of the translation of these authors' works and their images into Russian is viewed not simply as a function of a Soviet imperialist project, of Sovietization through the Russian language. Rather, the fact and availability of textual production in Russian facilitated types of resistance unavailable to these men in the United States.

The figures under consideration here spoke varying levels of Russian: Robeson achieved near fluency, but Du Bois mustered only a few words; McKay's and Hughes's proficiency fell somewhere in between. McKay expressed a desire to return to Russia and "study the 'ochen krasivy' [very beautiful] Russian language."[6] Hughes picked up both Russian and Uzbek phrases during his several months of traveling and study. Nonetheless, the materials that comprise the Soviet archive of black America include many texts written in Russian. For example, there are Russian translations of speeches and articles written by McKay while in the Soviet Union for which the original English version has been lost; correspondence between Robeson and the Union of Soviet Writers; media coverage of Du Bois in such periodicals as *Pravda* and *Ogonek*; Soviet political cartoons depicting Robeson; and Comintern files documenting McKay's participation in deliberations over the so-called Negro question. These materials have rich implications for black internationalism because they indicate the reception these writers, as public figures, received in the Soviet Union. Their reception, in turn, affected their perception of the Soviet Union, their sense of status, place, and belonging. Together, these elements produced a dialogue that was key to the formulations of black internationalism that emerged from these encounters. Reclaiming the transnational routings of this black radicalism, I assert that the authors' interest in the boundary-challenging formations put forth by the promise of Soviet internationalism—as by definition a multilingual and hybrid project—led these men to the Soviet Union in the first place and to contemplate U.S. race relations from a new perspective. While in the Soviet Union, these figures tinkered with alternate myths of self-consciousness, of being, that traversed the boundaries separating black and white as surely as they themselves had trespassed the borders delineating "East" and "West."

The material offered here owes a debt to work that has preceded it. In the field of black radicalism, the scholarship of Mark Naison and Robin D. G. Kelley has offered historical accounts of black/red relations that countered prevailing cold war assessments of black involvement with communism as necessarily a relationship of the deceived to the deceiver. Picking up from the important inroads made by Nell Painter, Naison's and Kelley's work connected the personal experiences of black Party members with the political agenda of the Communist Party of the United States of America (cpusa), emphasizing the varying degrees of black autonomy and agency within Party lines. More recently, scholars such as William J. Maxwell and James Smethurst have drawn on this historicist approach to contribute assessments of the relationships between black agency and Communist doctrine in terms of the literary production of periods prior to World War II. Maxwell sees the relation between black modernism and communism as a reciprocal one of give-and-take; Smethurst is more interested in the formal strategies and thematic concerns with which the resulting texts were imbued. But whatever the specific point of entry into the dialogue, each of these critics makes a case for the importance of communism to African Americans (whether in terms political or aesthetic, or both) as a function of the newness of the paradigm at hand. As Naison puts it, "Because of its links to an international revolutionary movement and efforts to encourage integration within its entire sphere of influence, the Party represented something decisively new in Afro-American life."[7]

It is not so much on the question of "newness" per se that my work departs from that which has preceded it but on the specific derivation of this decisive novelty. Although as evidenced in the quotes that open this introduction, Du Bois and Robeson both noted the parallelism between Russians and African Americans, the territory on which this internationalist stake was claimed has not been thoroughly explored in previous studies. For instance, in his study of depression-era black poetry, Smethurst stresses the communist-inspired representation of the folk voice as linked to "romantic assessments of African-American rural culture based in no small part on European valorizations of peasants, soil, and blood. . . . [T]his approach, which saw African Americans as an integral part of the United States and yet culturally distinct, had a huge impact on black poetry and its audience."[8] While Smethurst credits the Comintern for its contribution to this cultural model, he determines that its basis was singularly European. In point of fact, however, the Europeanism of the Soviet movement was at issue from the Bolshevik get-go: it was precisely the non-Western or anti-Western aspect of the call to the proletariat that helped to form the basis of its mass appeal. The Bolshevik promise of a global internationale offered a means of contesting Western paradigms of identity, subjecthood, and relatedly, nation—models with which Russians had for years struggled to come to terms, either through triumph or disdain. Imbued with this spirit of dissent from prevailing norms, the international revolutionary movement did not simply promise something new, nor did it offer a European reflection of emancipation. Rather, this movement had a specific genealogy in Russian cultural paradigms and models for shaping the (inter)nationalist project.

An inability to account for the persistence of the appeal of the Soviet project to black intellectuals throughout the decades spanning 1920–1960 can, I believe, be linked to this oversight of the specificity of the nation-building project at hand. Even though Maxwell and Smethurst have challenged the periodicity of earlier accounts—Maxwell arguing for the integration of the 1920s and 1930s, and Smethurst for that of the 1930s and 1940s—scholars have yet to interrogate the continued attraction of Soviet internationalism for African Americans through and beyond World War II. While the appeal of the Soviet Union was historically specific and modified throughout the decades, its ability to maintain a continued allure seems to come back to a Soviet advocacy of integrationist internationalism combined with a rudimentary populism based in non-Western national identification.

As early as the nineteenth century, theorists of Russian national identity were jockeying for a place on the scale of world historical progress established by their Western counterparts. Having been all but dismissed by German idealist philosophy, marginalized by Hegelian and Herderian accounts of the *Geist* of global evolution, Russian intellectuals were determined that their national essence was a more universal one, befitting eventual global leadership if not domination. However differing in opinion on the particulars of Russia's role, nineteenth-century Russian thinkers agreed that Russia had a unique and providential role to play in world historical progress. Vladimir Lenin parlayed this thinking into his theories of the nation in which he left ample space for ambiguity between the terms of unity and consolidation he used to distinguish between populist and colonialist approaches. Support for self-determination, under Lenin's guiding gaze, went hand in fist with an advocacy of Sovietization, but as the saving grace from Western domination. Although Lenin would certainly not have put it this way, the Soviet Union became the twentieth-century space in which previous models of the nationalist project fell apart. One could perhaps be emergent and benevolently unifying at the same time, in Lenin's vision.

This idea of unity in multiplicity is, of course, a centuries-old Russian notion taken from Russian orthodoxy. And it is into theorizations of Russian nationalism that I interject this spectacle of black internationalism. By placing accounts of black involvement with the Soviet Union in conversation with those of the Russian nationalist project, the question of communism's specific lure to African Americans can not only be opened up but it can also offer a counter to assessments of the Soviet nationalist project as singularly constraining. Liah Greenfeld, in her work on Russian nationalism, identifies ressentiment as the defining mechanism behind

Soviet assertions of statehood. Greenfeld's argument is that although leading up to the Bolshevik period there were two dissenting camps that theorized Russia's position vis-à-vis European concepts of national identity—Slavophiles and Westernizers—both groups were effectively sprung from the same seed and linked together by pangs of ressentiment. Whatever the particular typos within this larger wave of feelings—negative or positive—for the West, Russian intellectual elites imagined the West as a locus of progress. This sense of inferiority persisted into the twentieth century with compelling force. Claiming that "in his very advocacy of the sudden Russian internationalism, Lenin clarified the national sentiment behind it," Greenfeld sees nationalist ressentiment masquerading as global goodwill at the root of the Bolsheviks' internationalist project.[9] In maintaining that Russians were self-destructively blinded by the lure of this sentiment, Greenfeld contends that its impact could be only negative. So intense was the desire for recognition from Europe that "to gain self-respect," Russia "took upon itself the burden of the world's salvation," sacrificing themselves in the process. A singular focus on the costs to Russia of Soviet internationalism diverts attention from the importance this kind of agitation provided for emergent nationals such as McKay, Hughes, Du Bois, and Robeson. It distracts from internationalism's potential to trigger others' national self-consciousness, however blindsided by the universal motto of Russia. Greenfeld is not the only critic to be skeptical about the opportunity afforded Russia's others by Soviet internationalism. Andrew Wachtel, for example, in his theorization of the relationship of Russian nationalism to translation seems to agree with Greenfeld that little good came out of the Soviet project; it was either self-destructive or devolved into Stalinist debasement. In part, I too agree with these conclusions. But my contribution here is to point out how the Soviet work of McKay, Hughes, Du Bois, and Robeson opens up such assessments, offering specific instances of textuality that challenge the idea that internationalism was necessarily negative in its effects. If Soviet internationalism is interpreted as primarily definable by its destructiveness to Soviets, it is occluded as a narrative of possibility for non-Soviet others.

Moving away from the European paradigm also affords an opportunity to reconsider the illuminating account of black modernism provided by Gilroy in *The Black Atlantic*. Putting Russia into this configuration changes its shape precisely because Soviets were theorizing "transnationalism" under the guise of internationalism long before contemporary theory provided the impetus. The absence of Marxism in Gilroy's study has been noted before, but it seems particularly apt to mention it again in the context of Russian cultural dualism—the persistence of a kind of double consciousness not theorized by, but certainly applicable to Greenfeld's account of ressentiment. In fact, ressentiment seems to contain all the markings of double consciousness—an observation further confirmed by Gilroy's own deployment of the term.

Gilroy's black Atlanticism draws on Du Bois's notion of double consciousness to extrapolate a structure of subjectivity that in spite of its indebtedness to modernity, cannot be reduced to the official, master narrative of modernity based as it was in practices of exclusion and normalization. This double consciousness, in Gilroy's words, "emerges from the unhappy symbiosis between three modes of thinking, being, and seeing. The first is racially particularistic, the second nationalistic in that it derives from the nation state in which the ex-slaves but not-yet-citizens find themselves rather than from their aspiration towards a nation state of their own. The third is diasporic or hemispheric, sometimes global and occasionally universalist."[10] Gilroy argues that the intellectual heritage of the West since the Enlightenment informs the writings of black intellectuals who formed a counterculture of modernity against the ethnic absolutism of Western nationalist discourses. Through webbed networks informed by the processes of exclusion from the nation-state, black intellectuals challenged the rigid bounds of ethnic particularity, using their encounters with Europe and imbrication in Western models as a means of reworking these paradigms, thereby refashioning them toward transcultural models "in which anti-imperialism and anti-racism might be seen to interact if not fuse."[11] Key to Gilroy's formulation are the conceits of mobility and travel, and the ways in which black experiences of elsewhere—in particular Western Europe—changed their understandings of race to preclude binary oppositions between national and diasporic perspectives.

For all of Gilroy's discussion of the relationship between national discourses and international ones, his occlusion of the Soviet Union—the nation most invested in a dual rhetoric of national and multinational federations—is surprising. My book thus extends Gilroy's analysis to Russia and demonstrates how the frame of the Soviet Union alters the black Atlantic model. Because Russia's own position vis-à-vis Europe and the

West was historically vexed, Russia cannot be easily appended onto Europe, and its own intellectual heritage cannot be uniformly traced to Western models without some difficulty. Captive to nationalist ressentiment, Russia was neither "European" nor was she removed from the influence of occidental thought. This duality is pointedly apparent in the intellectual genealogy of Lenin, whose Marxian-derived theory of internationalism became the launching pad for a Soviet directive intended to entice black Americans to renounce the color line for a communist one. Lenin's internationalism encouraged both the self-determination of peoples united by culture and yet oppressed by a national unit that excluded them, and the transnational alliance of peoples similarly excluded by ethnic absolutism—under the mantle of world internationalism. For McKay, Hughes, Robeson, and Du Bois alike, the ambiguity between the support for black self-determination and the call to disband ethnic particularity through affiliated countercultures to combat imperialism and racism was an enabling one. Despite the turns in Soviet policy away from these endorsements in the postwar years, the galvanizing effect of this early Leninist thinking held firm. Thus, in the Soviet Union's formulation of a world internationalism one sees some of the more subtle points of Gilroy's black transnationalism made explicit. And yet, the occlusion of the Soviet Union from Gilroy's book has been significant not so much because the USSR radically alters his schematic but because the black Atlantic model has become common parlance for negotiating the webbed, international genealogies of black modernism. As the sourcebook, the book that seeks routes instead of roots, Gilroy's model has come to be synonymous with the study of black transnationalism. A consideration of Russia extends the geographic confines of Gilroy's mapping, moving it beyond Anglophone archipelagoes and resisting the continental confines of a Europe-Africa-U.S. triangulation. Whereas Gilroy uses black Atlanticism to rethink modernity, black internationalists, from McKay to Robeson, used Marxism to focus on the worlding of capitalism. In the words of Neil Lazarus, who decries Gilroy's occlusion of "countervailing or alternative theories of transnationalism or globalization"—namely, Marxism—"the only form of politics capable of presenting a decisive challenge to the globalism of actually existing capitalism is an internationalist socialism."[12]

I am not the first to call attention to the resonant affinities between the sense of marginalizations with which some Russian and African American

cultural practices are imbued. Drawing on the affiliation established famously in Nikolai Gavrilovich Cherneshevsky's *What Is to Be Done?* Dale
Peterson's *Up from Bondage* focuses on a parallel sense of "soul" that he
articulates as carved from the experience of historical peripheralization
and conducted into emergent expressive cultures. Peterson's book aptly
links the counterdiscourses of Russian and African American soul. But
positioning some of his insights alongside Gilroy's offers an opportunity
to open up Gilroy's admittedly limited formulation to consider other
routes of slavery and subordination that gave rise to similar kinds of
challenges to the dominance of the West. Coupling these works enables
one to pursue the question of how these individually powerful alternative
cultural and political expressions *interacted*—a topic that neither critic
examines.[13] To this end, Gilroy's project of disrupting modernity, or traversing its specifically racialized axis, is more in keeping with my own.[14]
Unlike Peterson's study, my book offers an account of internationalism in
order partially to reframe Gilroy's discussion of transnationalism by taking up related areas prominently absent from *The Black Atlantic* (and *Up
from Bondage*): Marxism, the Soviet Union, and the alternate theorizations of the international that were so important to some black American
intellectuals of the twentieth century. If, as Peterson contends, a "kinship"
between Russian and African American literatures has been forgotten, I
would remind readers that it has been forgotten with a purpose.[15] A
sedimented ideological structure of separation has contributed to the
maintenance of boundaries between Russian and African American studies, and to the forgetting of the field in which actual crossings and cross-
pollenization did occur: that of black radicalism.[16] I offer the Soviet work
of McKay, Hughes, Robeson, and Du Bois as ciphers for an "internationalist socialism" that understood social formations from a perspective that
criticized capitalism's determining role in shaping modernity.

In gathering together the materials for this book, both here and in the
ex–Soviet Union, I learned many lessons about the relationship between
the archival and theoretical that the nexuses between race and the legacy of
the Cold War invariably summon. The complexities of this relationship
were at no time better outlined for me than during one of my routine visits
to the microfilm department of a U.S. library where I planned to pick up
copies of manuscript materials I had ordered a few days earlier. While
filling out the forms that would finalize the transaction, I overheard a

student worker express confusion as she sat at the microfilm copier. Aware that this student was engaged in duplicating materials I had requested, I listened. Apparently stymied by the contents of the frame before her, she asked a coworker, "Do you think she really wants this? It's just a bunch of scribble." "Well," the coworker responded, stepping over to assess the projected frame for herself, "you never know." The student shrugged her shoulders as she pressed the green button labeled "print."

Russia no longer holds the cloak-and-dagger allure for students that it once did prior to 1991, when Boris Yeltsin mounted the tanks outside Moscow's White House and declared the passing of Mikhail Gorbachev's glasnost along with the death of the Soviet era. From 1980 to 1990, years dominated by Ronald Reagan's evil empire rhetoric, there was an 86 percent increase in enrollments in Russian language courses at the college level. By 1995, after the Cold War had officially been declared won and the evil empire vanquished, enrollments had dropped 44.6 percent from their 1990 numbers.[17] Government funding of Russian scholarship has slowed with the cutbacks of recent years, and the cancellation of funding for areas once designated "strategic" or "critical" such as the former Soviet Union have continued to dull opportunities for U.S.-based scholars of Russia and Eastern Europe. Similarly, there is very little work in the humanities that engages Russian and American cultural production comparatively.[18] For U.S. departments of Slavic studies, this lack of work can be attributed to an entrenched sense of disciplinary boundaries as well as the historically heavy influence of Soviet and East European émigrés, few of whom had fond associations with Marxism and thus did not warm to the incursions of Marxist-infused analytics into their milieu. For the interdisciplinary field of American studies, translation problems of a different order have stymied comparative work. Simply put, the demands of Ph.D. requirements have not encouraged graduate students in American literature and American studies to pursue foreign languages such as Russian, and older comparative literature programs have not privileged African American literature as a "national literature." Even when the war on everyone's mind was a cold one, and Russian language was correspondingly "hot," there was still a paucity of comparative work in Russian and U.S. cultures. In spite of Reagan's injunction that Gorbachev "tear down that wall," the kind of American exceptionalism that characterized the Reagan era affected the larger trends of U.S. historiography in which walls of a different type were not denounced but reinforced. Although this era saw the pro-liferation of cross disciplinarity that gave rise to cultural studies, the challenging of disciplinary boundaries did not extend to Slavic departments. More often than not, the result—like Reagan's reproof—was not intended to equalize access to resources but to establish one side as the dominant zone through which contact would be monitored and superior goods exported.

With the wall gone and the precipitous decline in enrollments in Russian language courses intact, I suspected that neither of these young women in the microtext department had encountered handwritten Cyrillic before. Because the materials I had ordered included large portions of handwritten documents in Russian, I guessed that the student worker was somewhat mystified about the viability of some part or another of Russian text I had requested. And although seemingly cavalier, her response highlights the theoretical stakes of my book. Easy readability and transparent immediacy—and our own desire to seek out these qualities as readers of the past—are what this book works against. Even though many people are aware that a relationship existed between the Soviet Union and some of the most prominent black American intellectuals of the twentieth century, few assessments of these relationships have refused to place them in a framework of perfectly defined choices between "good" and "evil." The Soviet work of McKay, Hughes, Du Bois, and Robeson has been cast as misguided and for the most part understood as regrettable missteps in otherwise illustrious careers. This book attempts to rectify some of this imbalance.

Without retreating to the shell of a reductive motto, it would be fair to say that *Beyond the Color Line and the Iron Curtain* pursues what the student in the microfilm department described as "scribble." In seeking out that which appears indecipherable at first glance, that which has been situated in the background of our attention, this book argues that the archive of materials linking McKay, Hughes, Du Bois, and Robeson to the Soviet Union must be kept open. Rather than forcing these materials into a preordained model safeguarded by the contemporary pressures of hindsight, this book uses them as a departure, as a means of unlocking a past that has heretofore been silenced and/or obfuscated. Yet in spite of the fact that they have been consistently ignored, these stories are no less valuable than the more familiar ones. This is not an attempt to replace one narrative with a better or more accurate one but rather to exhibit how, as Michel-Rolph Trouillot has taught us, "presences and absences embodied in sources or archives are neither neutral nor natural."[19] A refusal to repeat the mistakes of the past by placing materials retrospectively in a seamless continuum offers instead an investigation of the seams, irresolutions, and complexities of this extensive archive. The questions that this book poses are: Can one recapture the moments in which the energy of alternate myths of subjecthood offered by the Soviet Union found their way into the imaginative minds of McKay, Hughes, Du Bois, and Robeson? Can one read the texts that display this imaginative synergy without pressing them into a foregone conclusion of closed debate based on a superior vantage point? Despite efforts to consolidate the past into a fluid running narrative of the Cold War as "won," can the efforts made to counter the early Cold War fictions of East/West binaries be recalled while maintaining some of the more sobering facts of U.S. and Soviet doublespeak, tyranny, and suppression of dissent?

THE MAGIC PILGRIMAGE

Beginning with McKay's journey to attend the congress of the Third International in Moscow in 1922, many blacks endeavored to make the "magic pilgrimage" to the Soviet Union during the early years of the Communist regime.[20] A system that claimed to condemn racial segregation along with class stratification was something that many African Americans felt they needed to see and experience firsthand. Oftentimes, the sustenance offered by the Soviet project was not only ideological but material as well. But the black Americans who ventured to Russia and other Soviet republics were not credulous dupes strung along by empty rhetoric and vacuous enticements as the standard account of black involvement would imply. Rather, they were active participants in the shaping of the Union that was evolving, and their imprint lingered in arenas ranging from party policy to consumer culture. Some prominent examples: Corretti Arle Tietz, Harry Haywood, Lovett Fort-Whiteman, and Otto Huiswood were four of the first black Americans to make the eastward journey. Arle Tietz toured Russia with a theater group just before 1917 and stayed to partake in the Revolution; Haywood and Fort-Whiteman arrived as scholarship students at the Comintern's Communist University of the Toilers of the East

(KUTVa), and both later shaped Comintern policy on the Negro question.[21] Huiswood was a CPUSA delegate who greeted McKay when he arrived. Du Bois made the first of his four trips to the USSR in 1926. And in 1932, twenty-one black Americans traveled along with Hughes to Russia to make the ill-fated film *Black and White*. Organized by the politically active Louise Thompson and arranged under the auspices of the Meschrabpom Film along with the U.S.-based Friends of the Soviet Union, the group included Wayland Rudd, Loren Miller, Matt Crawford, Homer Smith, Dorothy West, and Lloyd Patterson.[22] This enterprising group of young students, journalists, social workers, writers, and actors was surprised to find what Hughes later called a "colony" of African Americans residing in Moscow, and even more startled to discover a similar settlement of black Americans headed by the agricultural expert Oliver Golden in the Central Asian town of Yangiyul. Soon after, in 1934, Paul and Eslanda Robeson would make their first journey to the Soviet Union, and like Hughes, spent time with Golden outside Tashkent. In the late 1940s, the Robesons deposited their son Paul Jr. with his grandmother and uncle (Eslanda's brother Paul Goode) in Moscow for elementary schooling. Paul Jr. was in a community with a number of African Americans who had settled permanently in the Soviet Union. Wayland Rudd became a member of Meyerhold's Moscow theater and Lloyd Patterson worked as a set designer for Meschrabpom. Homer Smith was enlisted to help modernize the Soviet postal system.[23] Under the pen name of Mary Christopher, Dorothy West wrote about her experiences for the first issues of her journal *Challenge*, using titles such as "Room in Red Square" and "Russian Correspondence."[24] But following the surge of pilgrimages in the 1920s, 1930s, and 1940s, the Khrushchev revelations of 1956 led to a slackening of black interest in the USSR. As black Bolshevism dropped to an all-time low in the 1950s, Du Bois and Robeson strengthened their ties. In the wake of their undaunted support, Angela Davis and Audre Lorde each made journeys to the Soviet republics in the 1970s, attesting to an ongoing fascination of radical blacks with the Soviet promise that Lorde described as a "mythic representation of that socialism which does not yet exist."[25]

While there were a number of black Americans who traveled to the Soviet Union, producing a variety of responses and written accounts, this book focuses on four. This stress enables a concentrated engagement with the ways in which the inspiration and failures of the Soviet promise of a new society filtered through the work of some of the twentieth century's most influential black American cultural producers. Thus, this book is not a comprehensive account of black involvement with the Soviet Union from its inception to its demise. I have instead chosen to study McKay, Hughes, Du Bois, and Robeson because they were the primary shapers in two cultural contexts—the USSR and the United States—of representations of black America.

Without reifying the category of "experience," this book maintains that the experience of the Soviet Union as elaborated by each of these authors was crucial to the identifications and perceptions of the Soviet Union that influenced their formulations of black internationalism, and in turn, influenced the Soviets' associations with the Negro question. Although the analytic apparatus of Marxism and communist adages were important to these figures, the trips were the events that altered and reconfigured their thinking. Following his 1926 trip to Russia, Du Bois wrote, "My mental outlook and the aspect of the world will never be the same."[26] In the works of these authors, experience becomes a site of intervention and theory, a place where dialogue between Soviet reception and black identity proceeds, a location where specific crossings materialize into alternative myths of black self-consciousness. Hence, other prominent black authors who were attracted to communism during the period—most notably Chester Himes, Ralph Ellison, and Richard Wright—are outside the scope of this book, since despite an interest in and involvement with communism, they did not travel to the Soviet Union. The slippage between communism generally conceived and the Soviet Union as terra firma often has enabled the difference between the two to be elided. But in my account the terms become detached, so that traveling to the Soviet Union is not trivialized as a logical conclusion to an interest in communism. At the same time, the relatedness of the aspirations housed in a turn toward communism and the Soviet Union is not dismissed but rather seen as a starting point from which to discuss the accounts that these travels conspired to reveal. While the investigations of communism penned by Ellison, Wright, and Himes are beyond the parameters of this book, it is hoped that this study will serve as a springboard from which to better assess the involvement (and eventual disillusionment) of each with communism.

Of these three writers, the case of Richard Wright is the most difficult to dispense with without an additional mention. This book was originally structured to include a chapter on Wright and the trip not taken. When I began to do research in the Soviet archives for materials on Wright, however, I found a thin file. Although there was expressed interest in Wright visiting the Soviet Union as a guest of the Union of Soviet Writers, and even an expectation that he would come in 1940, Wright's failure to do so resulted in an abruptly foreclosed dialogue. The materials that would help construct an argument about the Soviet influence on Wright's concept of internationalism, and Wright's influence on Soviet policy, simply do not exist. This is not to say that Wright did not leave an impression on the Soviets, though. As Ella Winter remarked in her 1945 *I Saw the Russian People*, in addition to the popularity of Hughes's work, Wright's *Native Son* was "a best-seller in Russia" that "every farmer, worker, and schoolchild knows."[27] Like *Native Son*, *Black Boy* was also translated in 1945, and clippings of various articles by Wright that appeared in the *Daily Worker* and *New Masses* can be found housed under the archival auspices of the Foreign Commission of the Union of Soviet Writers at RGALI. Nonetheless, his refusal to visit the Soviet Union foreclosed the possibility of Soviet media coverage or a public reception, and the response of Soviets to his work did not shape his own thinking about communism or internationalism in the way it did the work of McKay, Hughes, Du Bois, and Robeson. Neither Wright nor Ellison nor Himes effected anything like the kind of popular influence on Soviet accounts of "Negroes" and "Africa" that McKay, Hughes, Du Bois, and Robeson did.[28]

My decision to focus on four men and not include a chapter on, say, Louise Thompson Patterson, Eslanda Robeson, or Shirley Graham, all of whom did visit the Soviet Union, was the result not so much of limited archival materials but the limited influence that women, sadly, had on Soviet awareness of black America. It was indeed part of Soviet short-sightedness and doublespeak on women's issues that these women received peripheral notice during their visits to the USSR. While the Soviets may have been remiss in their attention to women, however, Eslanda Robeson and Shirley Graham received more positive media coverage there than they did in the United States in the 1940s and 1950s.[29] An interpretation of these dialogues is reserved for another, future project. Still, throughout this study, I've been influenced by a commitment to feminist methodologies and indebted to feminist work that precedes my own.

Hazel Carby has written that contemporary feminism's greatest challenge is to transgress the boundaries of previous feminist inquiry and write about "constructions of gendering across the board." And in her compelling *American Anatomies,* Robyn Wiegman specifies such inquiry, instructing her readers about the importance of acknowledging the differential ways in which black masculinity is gendered. This is a crucial point and one that with small exception often gets overlooked.[30] Following Carby's and Wiegman's leads, in its earlier chapters my own work investigates the pairing of political commitments deemed unconventional with racial marginalization. Its later chapters also explore how black masculinity has been gendered in its association with communism. While it is certain that a pivotal aspect of the attraction of Soviet ideology was its emphasis on the "new" people under construction there, it is also possible that this very stress enabled enthusiasts to believe that gender inequities would be subsumed in and solved by the formation of the new *chelovek.*[31] Thus, as I discuss in chapter 1, the masculine contours of reformulated Soviet citizenship often went undetected even as the necessity for outlining linkages between racial and women's emancipation was being pronounced. At the same time, the works of McKay, Hughes, Du Bois, and Robeson each highlighted the centrality of sexual emancipation to racial liberation. Each author addressed this issue differently and with varying degrees of urgency in his Soviet work. For example, Du Bois subsumed his outward appreciation for women's equality beneath a rhetoric of male exceptionalism, whereas Hughes staked out territories in which he challenged a compulsory heterosexuality encoded in the "veil" of black masculine consciousness. In this manner, my book attends to the place of women and the feminine in each of these authors' works, from McKay's engagement with miscegenation and the "woman question" and Hughes's fascination with Uzbek unveiling, to Shirley Graham's rephrasing of portions of Du Bois's autobiography and Eslanda Robeson's alliance with her husband's political/aesthetic goals. A focus on black masculinity therefore becomes an opportunity for thinking through gender's links to racial difference, and interrogating the presumed neutrality of a category like "men."

This book, then, is neither a full account of nor an apologia for African American involvement with the Soviet Union. Rather, it is an attempt to weave back into the larger tales of these particular authors' aesthetic and political attachments the marginalized place of the Soviet Union, demonstrate how this marginalization threatens to be renewed in contemporary accounts, and establish the stakes of such potential reproduction. Two of the authors willingly turned away from their earlier involvements with Russia; the other two did not. Some readers may wish that Robeson and Du Bois had renounced the Soviet Union, as did many members of the CPUSA, following Khrushchev's 1956 denunciation of the Stalinist purges of the 1930s. But the correcting of past errors is not this book's aim. This book instead shifts our knowledge about these figures' Soviet attachments, and in so doing, not only repositions their work but also wages against a historical hegemony that would keep these particular collusions of radicalism and desire silenced.

The absence of the Soviet Union from the black Atlantic routes is at once hard to critique and necessary to announce. A specific configuration of a black Atlantic to the exclusion of other geographic regions and hemispheres enacts its own silencing of the past. Even though the Cold War era is over, its vestiges remain. On Du Bois's death in 1963, the *Wall Street Journal* commented, "You really have to forget about the last years of Du Bois's life"; this request now threatens to become a historiographical reality.[32] Such fusions of past and present in which one seems to be inescapably immersed in a mind-set of years gone by are not necessarily attributable to an irremediable prolongation of a "Red scare" mentality. Rather, these convergences emerge due to an academic ambivalence that corresponds to a lack of resources and research in areas that appear to have become superannuated. While the problem is institutional and broad based, its influence targets specific areas and threatens to foreclose on histories about which one is not aware one knows nothing. As Trouillot remarks, "The past—or, more accurately, pastness—is a position."[33] Differential access to the means of historical production are reflected and reproduced in the retrieval of sources in which those differences are themselves housed. As a contemporary of the past, then, one is also engaged in the intertwined processes of inclusion and exclusion. It is this fact that the prior silencing of the Soviet archive—and the various mechanisms and forces that conspired to keep it so—makes explicit. Thus, rather than boasting a superior vantage point or more trustworthy tale, this narrative stakes as its ground the claim that in as much as archives assemble, they also dissemble in performing this authority. This is particularly true in the case of Russian archives, where the very means and conditions of preservation are themselves under siege.

Over the last few years, archives in the former Soviet Union that were once inaccessible to scholars have opened their doors and materials. But even the most enterprising researcher will find that this very openness forces one to come to terms with a redefinition of "access." For example, my own interests led me to a number of different state-run archives, including RTSKhIDNI and RGALI, both in Moscow. While the elaborate procedures through which one must navigate in order to find oneself legitimately poised in a Russian *chitatel'nyi zal'* or "reading room" will not sound unusual to anyone familiar with the process of doing research in Eastern Europe, some of the labyrinthine ways bear mentioning.

The researcher must first establish her legitimacy as a scholar. If she is not emerging from an immediately recognizable institutional genealogy— that is to say, not conducting research through the conventional arm of a government-sponsored program such as International Research and Exchanges Board (IREX), Social Science Research Council (SSRC), or a Fulbright grant—then the researcher must first find a way of obtaining a nontourist visa to enter Russia. Once in the country, she must establish an *otnoshchenie* or official "relation" with a Russian institution willing to vouch for the validity of the project. With otnoshchenie in hand, the researcher makes her way to the designated archive for an interview to establish the combined legitimacy of the person and their project. At this point, she receives a *propusk,* a card that verifies who the researcher is and the length of time for which that individual will be granted admittance to the archive, sometimes including the days of the week and hours during which she will be admitted as well. Most materials are uncataloged so depending on the archive, one is left with two options: as I did at RTSKhIDNI, to either describe the kinds of materials one is seeking to a librarian and hope that the librarian likes the project and feels sympathetic enough to be helpful; or, if (as is now the case at RGALI) one can gain admittance to the card catalog room, plow through the musty stacks of index cards on which handwritten notations from various years, hands, and it seems, classification systems suggest possible *fond,* or collections, in which one might look. From here on, it is another delayed process of ordering materials (no more than three at a time) and waiting an unpredictable amount of time (a day or two usually) for the designated files to surface. Once the documents are in hand, there are the difficulties of inconsistent policies regarding laptops, maximum quotas on copying, and prohibitively exorbitant costs for reproducing materials. Unpredictably foreshortened summer hours or an impromptu, month-long closing of the archive for an annual "cleaning of the pipes" can leave even the most intrepid scholar feeling discouraged, if not distraught, particularly when visas are not easily extended.

These challenges aside, the results of recent research in the ex–Soviet Union have produced exciting new reassessments in fields from policy studies to art history. These newly available resources, however, have not yet affected our reading of those black American writers who spent significant time there. Bringing together well- and lesser-known materials, each of the following chapters relocates a figure in light of such reassessment. The Soviet work of each of these men reflects a dialectic of displacement in which an imaginary and actual elsewhere furnishes a space to rethink crucial aspects of social and cultural life at home. Against Western claims of unrealized universality, Soviet rhetoric offered something new. The promise of Soviet internationalism did not entail reshaping old relations but as Hughes put it, transforming selfhood "from the ground up." The figures I discuss saw connection with the USSR as a means of escaping old oppressive affiliations and establishing in their place new liberating ones. Although this book spans several decades, the emphasis on the newness of the Soviet project, of society reconfigured, continued as a linking strand of "mythic representation" throughout the years. "The Soviets are making a new people," Du Bois wrote in the late 1950s.[34] At the same time, Russia promised that national longings—the desire to adhere in a community— would not be left behind, and offered an opportunity for multinational, international federation while nurturing a sense of national separateness and self-determination for blacks in the U.S. South. Thus, while "there can be no doubt that a socialist society demands a new kind of person/man," as Robeson reported to *Pravda* in 1960, the desire to renounce the old in favor of the "new" also revealed how the constraints of nation were not easily escaped.[35]

Still, what Russia offered black Americans was different from the paradigms and experience of Europe. As Hughes noted in "Poor Little Black Fellow," written in Moscow in 1933, Europe was only the beginning. The construction of a new Soviet citizen in the 1920s drew Left-leaning individuals in the United States to the Soviet Union to explore a national identity putatively free of class, gender, and racial biases. Unlike the repositioning of self in a territory of relatively familiar class, gender, and to a purportedly lesser degree racial inequities offered by expatriate experiences of Europe, the new Soviet citizen, dubbed the *novy Sovetsky chelovek,* advanced a breathtaking reconfiguration of selfhood, a reconfiguration of inner and outer subjectivity. For Louise Thompson, a journey through six of the fifteen Soviet republics in 1932 was a revelation. In a still-unpublished manuscript, Thompson writes,

> My Soviet journey had an enormous personal and political impact on me and shaped my life for many years to come. . . . I had seen more and learned more in the Soviet Union than I ever had before in such a short span of time. What I had witnessed, especially in Central Asia, convinced me that only a new social order could remedy the American racial injustices I knew so well. I went to the Soviet Union with leftist leanings; I returned home a committed revolutionary.[36]

After the 1929 stock market crash, the Soviet alternative appeared all the more attractive, and hundreds of black Americans migrated east to see the Soviet experiment for themselves. Following World War II and the unraveling of the wartime alliance between Russia and the United States, linkages between anti-communism and racism that had begun to appear in the Red scares of the 1930s reemerged more forcefully. For some black Americans, communism became more attractive, and for others, as I discuss in chapter 4, patriotism took center stage. The extent of the anticommunist fervor of the 1950s is well documented; the connection to black internationalism less so.

Beyond the Color Line and the Iron Curtain traces this history of anti-internationalism to 1922 and the appearance of McKay at the Third International in Moscow. Chapter 1 examines McKay's Russian texts, *Negry v Amerike* (*Negroes in America*) and *Sudom Lincha* (*Trial by Lynching*)—for which his English-language manuscripts have been lost and the available English editions are posthumous translations back from the 1923 and 1925 Russian translations. I argue that these works provide key critical lenses through which to explore the specific ways in which McKay's nationalist and internationalist politics, his aesthetic and social aspirations, shared common concerns. Rather than advocating a theory of black self-determination that Soviet bureaucrats eagerly incorporated into policy, McKay's work challenged Bolshevik positions on the issue of self-determination. Illustrating the interwoven dilemmas of sexual and racial disenfranchisement in the United States, McKay's work disputed the Soviet reduction of women's issues to those of class, highlighting the connectedness between the Negro and woman questions. Readings of Russian and English versions of McKay's participation in Moscow, including previously classified Comintern documents, map out ways McKay's function as a "stand-in African" set the stage for black visitors who followed. I investigate how McKay's embodiment of "Africa" began to disembody Africa—that is, how an idea of the representative "Negro" seemed to offer a more easily understood alternative to the racially imbued political instability of Africa. This mis-embodiment would reemerge forcefully with the appearance of Robeson in the Soviet media in the late 1950s, when cold war animosities would lead Soviet bureaucrats back to Africa.

Chapter 2 reclaims portions of Hughes's account of his trip to the Soviet Union that he removed from his memoir, *I Wonder as I Wander.* I target the complex identificatory processes at work in Hughes's unanthologized writings about Uzbekistan, and how these configurations carry over into his better-known work from the 1930s. Marked by a preoccupation with the unveiling of the Muslim Uzbek woman, these writings exhibit how Hughes rephrased the emancipatory potential of "unveiling" through the prism of a different discourse of "the veil"—that of black American male consciousness. His Soviet work reflects the importance of the feminine to this remapping of subjectivity as well as the way Soviet institutional reconfiguration of identity on a public scale provided Hughes with a means of articulating a liberated racial selfhood on a more private scale. Such rephrasings of subjectivity reappear in Hughes's anthologized work from the 1930s, in particular the short stories he wrote following his return from Uzbekistan to Moscow, and collected in *The Ways of White Folks.*

The third chapter iterates how pressures resulting from political animosities between the United States and Soviet Union contributed to censorship of the work of Du Bois. While McKay and Hughes officially renounced their early ties to the Soviet Union, Du Bois and Robeson suffered for their refusal to do the same. The *Wall Street Journal's* comment that Du Bois's last years should be forgotten is a sentiment that has, with small exception, functioned as a mandate in establishing critical perceptions of Du Bois's leftward turn late in his life. Focusing on Du Bois's post–World War II redrawing of the color line, this chapter addresses overlooked volumes of Du Bois's late writings, including the unpublished, book-length manuscript *Russia and America: An Interpretation.* Tracing out connections between Du Bois's reformulations of his politics and his later autobiography, including *Dusk of Dawn, In Battle for Peace,* and *The Autobiography of W. E. B. Du Bois,* this chapter negotiates between Du Bois's commitment to the Soviet Union as an expression of the will to dissent, and the ways his dissident opinions have been dismissed by popular recollections of Du Bois's life and his aesthetic output.

My fourth chapter looks at both U.S. and Soviet popular and bureaucratic perspectives on Robeson's trips to the Soviet Union in the 1940s and 1950s. This chapter charts how the fissures created by Robeson's articulation of being "at home" in Russia can best be attended to by sifting through not only U.S. investments in a postwar global and cultural security but also through the Soviet mythos of "*Robson.*" I demonstrate how investigating Robeson's political agenda alongside Soviet manipulation of Robeson's image offers a framework with which to understand how the Soviet model provided a mobilizing discourse for Robeson's internationalism. I negotiate the complexities involved in Robeson's attempts to counter U.S. anti-communism by making use of the lessons of Soviet internationalism and focusing on "the folk" as an authentic source of national self-understanding. At the same time, I elucidate how Robeson's performance of folk ballads both played into and resisted U.S. and Soviet racializing agendas.

Throughout the Soviet era, U.S. and Soviet conceptions and fantasies of blackness served as competing fronts, and yet in discussions of superpower jockeying, little consideration has been paid to the embattled black bodies across which much of this competition was waged. The overriding strength of such falsely oppositional categories as West and East, good and evil, and capitalism and communism, has obscured the very real hopes and utopian aspirations that Soviet Communism once held for various black Americans. Throughout the book I attend to these silences, and the related pressures to edit and excise, in hopes that the agendas behind the mutual appeal of mythic representations can be interrogated, and in so doing, open the archive into a space for a newly wrought resistance.

CHAPTER ONE

"Not at All God's White People": McKay and the Negro in Red

What is a Russian? A Russian is one who is not an American. We agree.
—Gertrude Stein, "This One Is Serious"

In McKay's 1928 novel *Home to Harlem,* the author's alter ego ponders his relationship to writing. He asks himself how he survived the preceding period of world upheaval to outlive his literary "masters" who "marched with flags and banners . . . into the vast international cemetery" of the twentieth century. The character wonders if he could, after all, create art: "Art around which vague incomprehensible words and phrases stormed? What was Art anyway?" In answer to this monumental question, McKay's narrator offers up a conspicuous model: "Only the Russians of the late era seemed to stand up like giants in the new. Gogol, Dostoevsky, Tolstoy, Chekhov, Turgenev." These Russian writers stood the test of time because they were preserved by "the soil of life"; "they were so saturated, so deep-down rooted in it," the narrator proclaims admiringly.[1]

McKay's description of the particularity of Russian literature uses the terminology of a school of nineteenth-century Russian writers and intellectuals who adopted the moniker "*pochvenniki*" ("native soil thinkers") from the word *pochva* (soil). Led by such figures as Fyodor Dostoevsky and Apollon A. Grigor'ev, *pochvennichestvo* was founded in part as a response to the Westernization of Russia that began with the reforms of Peter the Great in the eighteenth century. Against the mounting influence of European culture, pochvennichestvo sought to reconcile Westernism with the communalism of the folk. It was believed that Russia was uniquely poised to conduct such a reconciliation, based in part on an enduring momentum of populist messianism that mandated that Russians were positioned to leap past their European counterparts on the path of historical progress.

McKay's predilection for Russian literature "of the late era" indicates that the Russian model of particularism favored by Dostoevsky offered him a compelling counterpart to the European example. By European convention, Africans and Russians alike were excluded as nonhistoric peoples, marginalized in the narrative of world progress and civilization. McKay may have been drawn to a Russian prototype as a counter to enforced peripheralization by Western philosophies of identity and Enlightenment thinking, to which formative differentiations between white and black, historic and nonhistoric peoples were not incidental.[2] But what is most interesting about McKay's articulation of admiration for Russian literature is not so much the fact that it establishes a counter to European standards but the cross-racial allegiances it establishes in so doing.

Suggesting an interracial, cross-national affinity between two distinct, arguably non-European literary models, the passage anticipates a caution that David Lloyd and Abdul JanMohamed pose in their work on "minority discourse." Acknowledging that subjects often respond to enforced nonidentity by transforming that position into a positive one so as to critique the mechanisms of domination, the authors advise that

> the nonidentity experienced by minorities as the oppressive effects of Western philosophies of identity is the strongest reason that a rigorously critical minority discourse, in its positive transformation of the discourses emerging from that nonidentity, should not merely fall back on the oppositional affirmation of an essential ethnic or gender identity. In minority discourse the abstract philosophical questions of essence and ethics are transformed into questions of practice: the only meaningful response to the questions "what is or ought to be" has to be the question "what is to be done"?[3]

The phrase used by Lloyd and JanMohamed to close their sentence—"what is to be done"—is silently borrowed from the title of a novel by Cherneshevsky, the nineteenth-century Russian populist who publicly compared (and denounced) Russian serfdom and U.S. slavery. Lenin admired Cherneshevsky's novel so much that he adopted its title for his own 1905 essay outlining the party's role in communist revolution. In spite of the fact that they certainly would have objected to the term "minority" to describe their literature, Russian thinkers were contemplating the political efficacy of "minority discourse" long before contemporary criticism provided the nomenclature. A critic of Russian literature, Peter Steiner, elaborates on the uneasy relationship between Russian and Western literary paradigms that may have necessitated such awareness. He argues, "Based on a Western model and functioning in a non-Western milieu, Russian literature was perceived from its very inception as an instrument of social engineering."[4] Steiner's words suggest that because of a perceived difference between model and function, Russian thinkers used culture as a means of fomenting social change. In other words, it was the dualism inherent in the very idea of Russian literature that linked it to an ability to conduct social transformation. On the point of literature's social utility, thinkers as philosophically opposed as Dostoevsky and Cherneshevsky could agree. During the years following the revolution, a Marxist rescripting of populist rhetoric into a folk-based workers' culture benefited from this association. Soviet engineering relied on a sense of cultural doubleness—both Western and non-Western—and likewise enabled both a means of critiquing the exclusivity of Western standards and asserting cultural legitimacy. This approach appealed to black intellectuals and writers who sought to distinguish the particularity of "Negro" cultural patterns, and in some cases, to use the expressive cultures of the folk as a fount of authenticating Negro culture.[5]

But McKay's praise of Russian literature indicates that McKay intuited not only an affinity between Russian literature's relationship to European cultural margins and his own but that he believed this affinity had everything to do with the political potential of black art, of black culture's ability to do the work of "social engineering." Cherneshevsky's novel, subtitled "Tales about New People," was, after all, largely concerned with exploring the sexual politics inherent to a revamping of society along socialist lines, and its author firmly believed that the structural faults within U.S. capitalism could be traced to its ties to slavery. Although Lenin's tract was intended as an homage to Cherneshevsky, he nonetheless marginalized the issues of sex in his essays, apparently preferring to relegate women's issues to the narrativizing concerns of novelistic discourse. Yet just as Lenin removed sex from his essays, McKay's Soviet work demonstrated how thinking through the question of an alternative socialist

"Not at All God's White People" | 27

future necessitated rethinking the relationships among gender, race, and nation, how sexual politics were intrinsic to the construction of a new society. On this point McKay's work, in both essay and story form, is poised to reassert the often-overlooked link between "what is to be done" as a political slogan and attention to literal as well as figurative concerns of sexual politics. McKay's Soviet writings help put the interrelatedness of sex and race back into Lenin's, and indeed more recent, theorizations of socialist reform. McKay's invocation of Russian literature suggests that the tensions involved in a perceived perpetual dualism were the fount of a drive not toward essentialist retrenchment (the "oppositional affirmation" of identity) but a cultural practice that could sustain difference. In other words, McKay's engagement with Russia produced theories about using culture not only as a tool of internationalism but also interracialism.

Six years prior to the publication of *Home to Harlem,* the capacity of a Russian model for social transformation had intrigued McKay so much that he was drawn to the Soviet Union for a period of seven months, from November 1922 to June 1923. At the onset of his trip, the promise of the international for McKay lay as much in the ability to create a new kind of art, one that could transgress national boundaries, as it did in the ability to create new kinds of social and political affiliations, ones that took shape outside the nation as they entered the space of new, internationalist formations. Covering the Third International for the Negro press, McKay, a Communist supporter at the outset of his trip, turned to Russia as a model space for exploring the possibilities of international aspirations, both literary and political. And while in Russia, he solidified his thinking about internationalism's potential on both fronts. McKay's assessment of the promise of internationalism as a political goal along with a related interrogation of U.S. investments in the idea of racial purity and domestic containment appeared in two texts, both of which emerged from McKay's engagement with a Soviet paradigm of anti-Westernism: a group of essays titled *Negroes in America* (1923) and a collection of three stories titled *Trial by Lynching* (1925).[6] Written for a Russian audience, these works were rigorously critical of the hegemonic American national identity emerging out of World War I, and directed this criticism most emphatically toward U.S. anti-internationalism and the false notions of racial purity that bolstered this domestic stance.

In spite of McKay's eventual rejection of Soviet Communism, his Russian work from the early 1920s offers terrain in which to see intersections between his nationalist and internationalist politics, and his aesthetic and social aspirations.[7] Yet because these works have been difficult to access—both because of Soviet archive policies and the peculiar fact that McKay's English manuscripts for the two books written in Russia have been lost—generally they have been discounted.[8] With the exception of one document located in the Comintern files, the closest material to an original document for the bulk of these pieces are Russian translations of the original manuscripts of *Negroes in America* and *Trial by Lynching*, published in 1923 and 1925, respectively, under the titles *Negry v Amerike* and *Sudom Lincha*. As McKay's work from the early 1920s makes clear, such linguistic interracialism has a close affinity to reproductive interracialism—both challenge the notion of a "pure" source through which the authentic black history or black body should appear.[9] It was precisely McKay's interest in the boundary-challenging cultural forms put forth by the promise of Soviet internationalism as by definition a multiracial, multilingual project that led McKay to Russia in the first place, and while in Russia, to write a series of essays and stories about the American Negro. Discounting the importance of McKay's Russian texts reflects a similar logic of discounting the international impulse and the related critique of American mechanisms of whiteness put forth in these works.

But *Negroes in America* and *Trial by Lynching* are significant not simply because they contest McKay's later and better-known version of his Soviet journey recorded in *A Long Way from Home*.[10] They stand independently as texts that elaborate his keen perception of the interrelatedness of race, class, and gender oppressions within the emerging currents of a redefined American national identity following World War I.[11] And together they perform an ambivalent repositioning of black self-determination in the South, leaving open the question of McKay's shaping influence on what emerged from the later 1928 Comintern congress as the "black belt thesis"—the theory that the U.S. South made up a primarily black nation and could under this guise be revolutionized to become a member of a global Soviet. Twelve years after his visit, McKay indicated his assumption that his Russian work spawned a shaping influence over Communist policy toward black Americans.[12] But McKay's assertion should be approached with caution. As indicated by the Comintern files, *Negroes in America* was

"Not at All God's White People" ⦙ 29

heavily indebted to others with more intimate connections to Moscow, such as Otto Huiswood and Sen Katayama, who addressed similar questions. While to be sure McKay took pleasure in the fact that he could be a representative of the oppressed Negro for the Bolsheviks, McKay's ability to take up this position was enabled by a Russian tradition of academic inquiry into Africa, a prehistory to McKay's visit that has not been taken previously into consideration. While McKay was without a doubt a key figure, his position on the resolution on the Negro question—the black belt thesis—becomes indefinite when seen in light of the stories in *Trial by Lynching*. The fact that *Trial by Lynching* links in no uncertain terms the issues of racial and sexual emancipation leads one to question Soviet attentiveness to McKay's postulates. The year of the Soviet endorsement of the black belt thesis, 1928, also spelled the end of open discussion on the place of sexual politics within socialism. Soviet willingness to commit to women's rights on paper, but not in policy is partly related to the iconic status of McKay in Russia. McKay's representativeness of "the new Negro" relied on a privileged relationship between masculinity and the iconography of the "new Soviet."[13] Just as this new Soviet relied heavily on an idealization of masculinity as representative, so too did McKay's link to "the Negro" establish the Negro as male. This idea of a representative masculinity was reinforced by Soviet doctrine that subordinated women's issues to those of class. McKay's challenge to this kind of gender inequity as intimately related to the question of Negro self-determination emerges in both the essays and stories.

Seen in this light, *Negroes in America* and *Trial by Lynching* render unstable the conclusion that McKay was an unambiguous supporter of the notion of black self-determination in the U.S. South. But more important, *Trial by Lynching* extends the critique of whiteness offered by McKay in *Negroes in America* specifically to the visual economy of subjectivity within white supremacy. The stories shift the emphasis of McKay's intervention in Soviet conceptions of American national identity from debates about black self-determination to the inextricability of racial, sexual, and national boundaries in the American imagination. Reading the essays without the stories provides only a partial view of this imagination, and the suggestiveness of the stories is not evident in the often rough analyses provided by McKay's essays. This is not to say that the propaganda propounded by *Negroes in America* was standard Soviet fare, however. Reading the essays alongside *Trial by Lynching* reveals how the stories elaborate on the theoretical claims of *Negroes in America* by exhibiting how such claims are linked with specific figures of representation. McKay's depictions of black life in the United States infiltrate Soviet dogma with abstract formulations of identity, selfhood, and the interrelated configurations of racial and sexual difference. The related symbolic politics at work in both, then, not only permeates the barrier between fiction and nonfiction, the implicit line between Chernevshevsky's novel and Lenin's essay, it also offers an alternative to the white, male-centered accounts of political modernity.

McKay's trip to the Soviet Union occurred during a period of political and artistic experimentation and openness due, in part, to the New Economic Policy (NEP), launched in July 1921 and ending with the first Five-Year Plan of 1928. Distinguished as an era of broad-mindedness and relative tolerance, the NEP years reintroduced to Russia a contained capitalism, and during this period images of the United States abounded in film, journalism, and other routes of consumer culture.[14] Although the United States continued to be condemned as the paragon of evil capitalism, American methods of industrialization and technological advance were supported and admired. Public receptiveness to McKay must be seen in the context of a departure from socialism, the opening of Soviet doors to an influx of market-driven, American images of race and gender, and the waning interest in advancing the cause of Soviet women's rights.[15] At the same time, McKay's warm reception by the Soviets should be approached from a vantage point that admits Russia's own troubled relationship to European paradigms of "whiteness." Indeed, the Soviet Union of 1922 was ripe territory for McKay's desires to establish an alternative to Euroamerican norms. Russian philosophers and intellectuals had for nearly a century been immersed in contesting German idealist philosophy in which they, alongside the peoples of Africa, were positioned as nonhistoric peoples. As Dale Peterson has argued, a perceived exclusion from European cognitive traditions sparked in nineteenth-century Russian philosophers and writers a counterclaim based in an equally valid and yet different sense of self articulated through "soul." Peterson connects the ramifications of this outsider status accorded to Russians by German idealist philosophy to those expressed by African American intellectuals of similarly sequenced periods, demonstrating a solidarity between these groups rejected by the

West's social order, between "similar strivings of Russians and African Americans to give visibility and voice to a native culture that had been hidden from view and held in bondage to narrow Western standards of civility and literacy."[16] Peterson's work is important for my purposes not only because these rich parallels were previously left unexamined but because he brings together distinct, yet affiliated experiences of subjugation that lay the groundwork for the terrain of receptiveness to McKay that the Soviets offered him in 1922.

What McKay's work offers, then, is an opportunity to see what happened when the nationalist affinities between Russian and black American cultural patterns *interacted*. Such traversals are crucial because they provide not only a sense of Russia's receptiveness to McKay but a sense of how these crossings modified and failed to modify the routes of both—in terms of specific policy as well as cultural perception. In spite of McKay's and other concerted efforts to bring attention to rampant racism within the Party, the Comintern records indicate a deep ambivalence toward the eradication of "white chauvinism" in the Communist Party (CP), and an even deeper ambivalence toward attacking its rootedness in the CPUSA.

NEGOTIATING "NEGROES"

The neglect of Soviet–African American crossings is not unusual, although there are strong exceptions to the rule. The approach to the question of red-black relationships has tended to fall into two dissenting camps. On the one hand, the pioneering work of Mark Naison and Robin D. G. Kelley has argued compellingly for the autonomy of black radicals in their relationship to the Comintern and CPUSA.[17] This contention has been a critical rejoinder to the widely held assumption that minorities who participated in communist-inspired or financed agitation for reform were idealist fools, unaware of the duplicity of their purported supporters. This latter view was alleged throughout the period of the Cold War by historians such as Theodore Draper, and has been revivified by recent investigations into the Soviet archive by historians such as Harvey Klehr. Recently, Mark Solomon has made use of archival materials from the former Soviet Union to ascertain a middle ground vis-à-vis the new history of Naison and Kelley as well as the retrenchment history of Klehr.[18] He writes that "the Americans who embraced communism were neither mindless dupes of the

Soviet-dominated Comintern nor the new historians' wily, independent radicals cleverly sidestepping external directives. . . . Looking homeward and looking to Moscow at the same time created a perpetual duality. This sometimes produced tensions but more often than not led to a willing acquiescence to foreign-made decisions that were often applied reflexively in the United States."[19] Reducing the importance of Soviet intervention in African American conceptions of American national identity in the early 1920s to "the crushing burdens of the economic crisis," Solomon pointedly downplays the relevance of cultural and social context. He notes that "cultural history and oppositional culture have often propagated impenetrable abstractions that locate motivations in vague longings and social habits derived from memory and accumulated spiritual goods." Claiming that such critical forays have "obfuscated concrete power relationships," Solomon terms such motivations "secondary."[20]

In looking to the particular history of McKay's involvement with Russia and the texts this interaction produced, my work departs from Solomon's implicit separation of "concrete power relationships" and the cultural abstractions they purportedly produce. In fact, it is my contention that McKay's Russian work provides precisely the framework with which to see how the two are inseparable. Coupling *Negroes in America* and *Trial by Lynching* displays the way that an emphasis on empirical evidence occludes the subtle portraits of selfhood that figures of representation, metaphor, modes of address, and narrative pattern, to name a few, can offer their readers. If motivations are voiced in vague terms, it is because of a history of partially formed desires that learn from proscription to remain "obfuscated" and "impenetrable." In the quote that opened this chapter, McKay describes art as a site of indefiniteness and ambiguity. In a literally minded segregationist nation, McKay's depiction of the stridently racist agenda of American national identity following World War I required subtlety: longings for black selfhood and autonomy were, in a word, unspeakable. By directing these tales to a Russian audience, McKay was able to shape some of this unspeakability into patterns that enabled the burdens of economic crisis to be seen, in part, as not only producing but products of the consciousness of racial, sexual, and national oppressions. It is my intention to restore some of the complexity, and not the Soviet one-sidedness, of the "perpetual duality" between home and Moscow as articulated by McKay in his Russian work.

"Not at All God's White People" ⋮ 33

But before delving into the work McKay produced while in Russia, it is essential to get some sense of the climate surrounding the much-debated topic of the Negro question in 1922. The work of Naison, Kelley, Maxwell, and Solomon has been helpful in unraveling the interest of the Comintern in the Negro question, and the Comintern's impact on the ways in which "race" was understood and implemented in the early stages of Soviet Communism. Prior to their reassessments, a reduction of Soviet policy to the bare-bones stance of "national" self-determination at all costs had proven to be a means of evading both the vast attention Communists paid to the U.S. Negro as a determinant political force and the reciprocal interest of black Americans in communism. This reduction also ignored historical shifts and tensions in the perceptions and mobilizations of the very term "Negro" by both Americans and Soviets. Aided by the archive of the Comintern, my contribution to this critical conversation draws on these mobilizations to provide a portrait of the atmosphere surrounding the Negro question (and its elision of sexual difference) in Russia when McKay arrived in 1922.

The period under consideration here is roughly contiguous with that of the NEP. This is an important contextual locator for McKay's arrival in Russia, because the years 1921 to 1928 were ones of relative openness and flexibility. With the departure from strict state socialism came experimentation in the arts as well as politics. At the same time, however, this period also spelled the waning of government attention to women's issues. Nearly 70 percent of state cutbacks were directed toward organizations supporting women's interests, and the Zhenotdel (the Women's Department established by the Central Committee in 1919) was limited to outreach programs such as the "Sovietization" of rural women.[21] If the Bolsheviks were less interested in pursuing the emancipation of women, they were not receiving signals that might counter this predilection in the influx of materials related to the United States in the 1920s. As Jeffrey Brooks has demonstrated, for Russians in the 1920s, the United States was the locus of contradictory identifications. The myth of America that had blossomed during the turn of the twentieth century was allowed to flourish to some extent, helping to administer what Brooks has called a "romance with America." Although the press was full of perfunctory anticapitalist statements, movie houses continued to boast a plethora of American films, and Hollywood stars were matinee idols. People were more "likely to see 'The

Thief of Baghdad' than a film about Soviet life" because there was no viable alternative; the Bolsheviks had failed to "translate into popular imagery the language and aims of the Revolution."[22] The two sides of the face of the United States did not, however, seem to work against one another in any productive kind of way. The United States was able to represent the land of modernity—encapsulated in the Russian enthusiasm for Taylorism and Fordism—and simultaneously embody precisely the kind of future that good Soviets did not seek. Soviets seemed able to take the trope of America as the model of success and mobility, and dissociate it from the idea of the United States as the bastion of capitalism. America presented both the progress of technological advance and scientific efficiency along with the backwardness of class and racial inequity. It was within this climate that McKay's work was supported and distributed. With this in mind, McKay's work can be read as an attempt to establish an intervention into Soviet dissociation of cultural production and economic buttressing, while endeavoring to establish points of contact or frames of reference for his Soviet audience. In confronting this incongruous projection of the United States, McKay's work sought to intervene in the easy receptiveness of these kinds of contradictions, to provide an alternative "new citizen" without resorting to ideas and images he wanted to unseat.

Historical context is, of course, of equal importance to the U.S. side of this conjuncture. The marginalization of women's issues in the discussion of black self-determination was reflected on both the Soviet and U.S. fronts.[23] Nonetheless, a lack of post–World War I political alternatives made communism as presented by the Soviets particularly attractive to African Americans, both women and men. Contributing to Communism's palatable sheen was the fact that it was the Soviets who agitated sufficiently to rouse interest in racial issues where previously none had existed in the CPUSA. For its own part, the still-underground CPUSA had made only the most token of gestures toward African Americans when it chartered its foundational program in 1919. Included in CPUSA policy was a paragraph stating that the racial oppression of Negroes is simply the expression of their "economic bondage and oppression." But unlike American straggling behind the issue, Soviet interest was keen and insistent, and Lenin commissioned one U.S. delegate to the 1920 Second International Congress to prepare two reports on the "American Negro Problem."[24] The delegate, John Reed (who later became famous for his description of the

"Not at All God's White People" ¦ 35

Bolshevik takeover of the interim Soviet government in October 1917), announced to the Comintern that American Negroes "consider themselves first of all Americans at home in the United States."[25] The influence of Reed's words should not be underrated, for as the first U.S. citizen to speak in Moscow on the issue, Reed held a prominent place in the Soviet introduction to black America. Responding to a request for information about U.S. race relations as they pertained to the Party, in a letter to "Comrade Z" (Zinoviev), Reed provided a detailed historical explanation, and explained his sense that "the Negro leaders who preach to their people submission, patience and patriotism are nothing but traitors to the colored workers and to the workers in general."[26] If Reed's words were on target—and the American Negro was "at home in the United States," but needed to be revolutionized by thinking beyond the strict terms of "patriotism"—then what better way to incite a more general struggle against capitalism than by seizing the potential applicability of the American Negro to the project of a global anti-imperialism?

McKay's visit to the Soviet Union was thus not the first occasion on which the question of the Negro's place in world Communism had been forged in Russia. The sheer scope of Moscow's influence post-1928 during a period of fixed attention on the U.S. South has caused scholars to overlook the earlier period, particularly the Third and Fourth Comintern Congresses, held in 1920 and 1922, respectively. U.S. scholars of Russian history such as Theodore Draper have used Lenin's early mention of the Negro as the basis for the assumption that Moscow's policy toward American "Negroes" was first and foremost based on a doctrine of national self-determination justified by a definition of African Americans not as a "national minority" but rather a "subject nation." This assumption of continuous Soviet support for black self-determination (and male representativeness in contemplating the Negro question), culminating in the resolutions passed in 1928, is based on two early essays written by Lenin: his "Theses on the National and Colonial Question," which he presented to the Second Congress of People's Deputies in Moscow in 1920, and the earlier "The Formerly Slave-Owning South." But in point of fact, Moscow's course of support for self-determination did not include nor even address African Americans specifically as such until 1928. Prior to the decision to promote the black-belt thesis in 1928, Moscow's interest in black Americans was explicitly voiced as an interest in their use value for the liberation of Africa, not their individual political existence as a nation.[27]

In fact, Comintern files indicate that in the period between 1920 and 1928, there existed antagonism toward the very notion of national self-determination, which was described in one file as "owing its origin to the illusion that Negroes can find a promised land where the tentacles of imperialism cannot touch them" (RTSKhIDNI, 495–155–25: 73). During the Third Comintern Congress, the newly established "Eastern Commission" was asked to investigate the Negro question. Likewise, as Zinoviev explained, the Fourth Congress "outlined a detailed program of activity for the party and revolutionary organizations in the Near and Far East . . . to *differentiate* [the program from] the resolution of the Second International Congress of the Comintern."[28] The Third International advocated the "precise application of 'The Theses on the Colonial Question' towards the *Negro problem*" without addressing U.S. Negroes as a subject nation.[29] Although the Third Congress laid the groundwork for the consideration of the Negro question, it was not until the Fourth Congress that the first policies directed explicitly to the Negro problem came into being.

It was to this congress that Reed posted an invitation to his friend and fellow writer McKay (*ALWFH*, 206). McKay arrived in November of 1922 in time for the opening of the Fourth Congress of People's Deputies (also called the Third International). Along with Otto Huiswood, a native of Dutch Guiana who had emigrated to New York, McKay was one of the first politically motivated blacks to visit the Soviet Union.[30] The speech McKay presented to the congress on the Negro question was delivered in English, but appeared the next day in Russian translation in *Pravda,* the party newspaper. Four months later, on 5 January 1923, the *International Press Correspondent* published McKay's English version. There are intriguing discrepancies between the two renditions, and the differently nuanced implications of the Russian and English versions are suggestive of the ways in which the agendas of McKay and the Soviets might have diverged.[31] A comparison of the English-language version of a speech McKay made to the Fourth Comintern Congress and the rendition of this speech published in *Pravda* provides a sense of some of the devices state translators used to finesse interpretation when transmitting McKay's work to the Soviet public.[32] Occlusions and omissions created the building blocks of exchange between McKay and his guests, and may help explain the willful

1. Zinoviev, McKay, and Bukharin in Moscow, 1922. Yale Collection of American Literature, Beinecke Rare Book and Manuscript Library.

attitude of the Soviets toward black Americans as well as McKay's attempts during his Russian journey to educate the Soviets about U.S. racism. In noting the disparities between the two accounts, though, I am not seeking to establish an authentic or correct version. Rather, I am interested in stressing how the occlusion of these Russian texts from McKay's oeuvre has collaborated with the demand that an "authentic" history of African Americans be singularly contained in English.

Similarly, and this is a point to which I will return below, I seek to intervene in the myth that the Soviet Negro project was one of unimpeded co-optation by Soviet dogma. Here, I am engaging with the line of argument presented by Andrew Wachtel in his essay on translation and Russian nationalism, in which he traces connections between a Soviet drive to make available alternative voices and a Soviet desire to adhere to the project of internationalism through Russia, and by extension, through Russian. Wachtel writes that "in a broad sense, the entire Soviet cultural project represents merely an extension of the universalizing translation project that had already been felt intuitively as Russia's mission in the 19th century."[33] Indeed, the reduction of McKay's several-pages-long speech to a few, short paragraphs that reoriented the thrust of his points would seem to support Wachtel's astute observation that Soviets yoked translation and imperialism to one another as necessarily interdependent systems. Take, for example, the headline introducing the *Pravda* version: "NEGROES INSTINCTIVELY SENSE THAT THE ROAD TO THEIR FREEDOM RUNS THROUGH MOSCOW. NEGROES [SHOULD] JOIN THE RED ARMY AND NAVY TO SYMBOLIZE THEIR UNION WITH REVOLUTIONARY RUSSIA (my translation) (6). *Pravda* herein locates Moscow as central to the fostering of socialist culture; it follows, then, as the parent language to such culture, Russian would be afforded not only preferential treatment but carte blanche in the process of integrating local dialects into the international lingua of the Comintern. Such linguistic priority directly reflected the privileged place of Soviet (read Russian) culture as the model for all future socialisms.

The idea of Russia as the promised land for blacks seemed to have purchase with Soviet bureaucrats, for a few days earlier *Pravda* had printed a poem, "Negr v Moskve" / "A Negro in Moscow" by O. Obradovich, that

2. McKay addressing the Third International in the Throne Room of the Kremlin, Moscow 1922. Yale Collection of American Literature, Beinecke Rare Book and Manuscript Library.

expressed the utility of Moscow to the future of black self-determination.[34] To be sure, *Pravda* was concerned with the importance of Soviet security against the potential encroaching forces of Western Europe (and their use of black troops), and with McKay as the Congress's representative Negro presence who could lead African peoples and peoples of African descent away from the clutches of Western militarism. But perhaps more significantly, the *Pravda* version shapes McKay's speech to emphasize the key place of Moscow in the translation of "the Negro" and his concerns into Russian. The article presents this as a transformation necessary to the establishment of internationalism.

Like its International Press rendition, McKay's speech as it appeared in *Pravda* began with the jarring sentiment that the speaker "would prefer to speak in front of a lynch mob than in front of this great gathering" (4). As an opening statement, this declaration set the tone for McKay's awareness of his audience as at once an ally against white supremacy and perilously proximate to that very regime. From this point onward, however, the two versions of the McKay speech take different roads as it were to "freedom." Skipping over McKay's lengthy exegesis about his hesitations about feeling compelled as a poet to speak in a political forum, the *Pravda* version moves directly to McKay's critical assessment of the European deployment of Negro troops to combat revolutionary movements. Both versions convey the general point that Negroes were implements for the international bourgeoisie in its fight against organized labor, and that during the recently concluded world war, England, France, and the United States alike used U.S. Negroes and black Africans to do their "dirty imperialistic work" (4). But the *Pravda* version warns that "the bourgeoisie use Negroes in their battles against revolutionary movements. . . . [T]he capitalists know that Negroes are proud of their war service, and they attempt to make use of their [the Negroes'] aptitude for fighting" (4). While the *Pravda* version stresses the natural warrior within every Negro, the English version points out how just such an attitude toward blacks has resulted in their being used as cannon fodder. Here is the corresponding line in McKay's English: "The international bourgeoisie would use the Negro race as their trump card in their fight against world revolution. . . . [T]he Northern bourgeoisie knows how well the Negro soldiers fought for their own emancipation . . . and that they also put up a very good fight for themselves on returning to America when they fought the white mobs in Chicago, St. Louis, and Washington" ("Report on the Negro Question," 16). In editing out McKay's historical examples of clashes between blacks and whites, and substituting a Negro "aptitude for fighting" in their place, *Pravda* replaces McKay's historical contingency with an invented natural capability.

Encouraging historically based assessments of racial antagonisms, McKay turns his antibourgeois directive toward the Communist movement itself. Whereas the anthologized, English version of the speech is quite explicit in its focus on racism *within* the CPUSA (citing as evidence the difficulties in organizing traditionally racist union and labor groups, the segregated factions of workers parties in the South, and the fear that such tendencies have been and are being condoned if not sponsored by the Comintern), the *Pravda* version of the speech quite openly stresses racism as a specifically *U.S.* scourge. *Pravda* distances racism from its communist shores, replacing McKay's emphasis on the damage done by U.S. communists' antiblack sentiments with the ways in which American racism fostered *anticommunist* sentiments.

While both versions condemn the illegality of integrated meetings in the South, the *Pravda* one conveniently omits both McKay's claim that the Workers Party in the United States already condoned this kind of segregation systemically as well as his injunction to U.S. Communists to overcome this "greatest difficulty" (16). Rhetorically suggestive of the links between racial and sexual suffrage that McKay would pen later in his visit in *Trial by Lynching*, these words inveigh against racial segregation as the public manifestation of social censure of miscegenation. Whereas English-speaking readers of McKay's speech might assume that Russians were aware of the degree to which the Communist movement in the United States was riddled with this kind of racism, the *Pravda* version instructs otherwise. In *Pravda*'s account, McKay indicates that racism was not a problem primary to communism but endemic to the U.S. brand of bourgeois capitalism. The idea that racism could be more difficult to combat than "capitalist" ideology per se, that legislators might also have to address issues of class, gender, and racial difference simultaneously, is lost on Russian readers. The complexities of racism's pervasive features and manifestations across the political spectrum, its asymmetrical relationships with gender and sexual difference, are not broached. The Party provided

"Not at All God's White People" | 41

just the amount of censorship or creative interpretation necessary to adjust McKay's speech so that it would sound resplendently not only pro-Communist but pro-Soviet.

And holding true to the neglect of the implications of McKay's English speech, the theses that emerged from the congress borrowed less from McKay's statements than from those of his fellow speaker Otto Huiswood. The "Theses of the Fourth Congress on the Negro Question" determined that the "Negro problem has become the urgent and decisive question for world revolution," thus establishing the Negro question as the linchpin in furthering the aims of the internationale.[35] Stressing that "the Communist International must prove to the Negro people that Negroes do not suffer alone . . . and that the Negroes' fight against imperialism is not the fight of one nation, but of all the nations of the world," the resolutions proposed international alliances between the workers of the world that pinpointed not only the toilers of Europe, the United States, and Africa but also those residing in countries under the thumb of European and U.S. imperialism.[36] Throughout, the theses display the presupposition that gender differences are subsumed under larger categorizations of "race" and "nation."

These theses thus laid the groundwork for Soviet internationalism as a movement that encouraged oppressed peoples to think not only beyond gender but beyond the parameters of nationhood—indeed, to conceive of nationhood as historically restrictive to those deemed unworthy of full citizenship and consider instead the systemic processes of disenfranchisement that connected not only the colored peoples of the Eastern and Southern Hemispheres but the global proletariat. In this sense, while promoting a heightened consciousness of racial and social inequities, the theses nowhere directly connected such consciousness to national groundedness; rather, they viewed revolutionary consciousness as by definition international, even if its genesis came about through an awareness of nationally based exclusions. These conclusions offered McKay and others an enabling ambiguity between nationalism and internationalism.

This ambiguity stemmed, in part, from Lenin's distinction between the uses of nationalism. On the one hand, there are nationalisms that flaunt themselves aggressively, with an eye to expansion and cohesion. On the other hand, there are nationalisms used in the name of self-determination. In devising two types of nationalist projects—one repressive and the other emergent—Lenin linked the oppressive policies of Euro-imperial nations with the former, and the struggle of U.S. Negroes and the disenfranchised the world over against such tyranny with the latter. But even within the definitions provided here, one can sense a tension between Lenin's implied assertion of Russian nationalism as emergent, and the practice of Soviet intervention along her southern and eastern peripheries during these same years. Rather than Lenin simply being unable to provide an adequate account of the Soviet nationalist project as either definitively emergent or repressive, though, I would argue that he attempted to parlay some of this ambiguity into support for self-determination of peoples for whom he envisioned Sovietization as the saving grace from Western domination. As such, Lenin's thinking was very much in sync with the idea of Russian universalism espoused by nineteenth-century Russian thinkers. His theorizations offered the Soviet Union as the twentieth-century space in which previous models of the nationalist project fell apart. Lenin's terms allowed for a nationalist project that could be simultaneously emergent and unifying.

As I discussed in the introduction, one of the explanations for Russia's susceptibility to Marxism was a longstanding belief in Russia as the "chosen" nation. This idea stems back to a Russian orthodox belief in the ability of Russia to integrate conflicting factions into unification through a universal motto of Russia. This idea of unity in multiplicity is taken up by Liah Greenfeld in her investigation of Russian nationalism and its links, whatever the intellectual faction, to European ressentiment. Greenfeld asserts that prior to 1917 the two leading camps of Russian nationalism—Westernizers and Slavophiles—were, in spite of their differing theorizations of Russian particularity, bound to Europe through a sense of inferiority to it. While I am largely in agreement with Greenfeld's main points, I do find it compelling that her theorization of the Russian nationalist project thus relies on this idea of ressentiment as largely a figuration of what Lenin would call an emergent nationalism. Greenfeld's contention therefore obfuscates the fact of imperial repressiveness simultaneous to feelings of national inadequacy. However full of ressentiment, Russian bureaucrats were equally endowed with the privileges of colonial suppression most often associated with the West. This is an interesting omission, signaled also by Greenfeld's choice of quotes to support her theory of tenacious ressentiment. In fact, she relies most heavily on a portion of

"Not at All God's White People" ¦ 43

Lenin's essay "On the National Pride of the Great Russians" in order to register the depths and urgency of such ressentiment. She sums up the essay as bemoaning a "we too" desire for national recognition by Europe. "Fewer explicitly nationalist arguments are more telling than these pathetically emphasized 'we *too*,' " she writes.[37] But in focusing on this passage, Greenfeld chooses not to stress Lenin's wariness of what he called "Great-Russian chauvinism"—that is, the perils of the "too" from which "we" purportedly seeks to receive approbation. Even though she includes Lenin's (pace Marx's) exhortation that "a people that oppresses other people cannot be free," (271) Greenfeld does not suggest that Lenin was aware of the difficulties of theorizing Russia without taking into account the repressive strains of empiric attitude toward its eastern and southern peripheries.

Claiming that "in his very advocacy of the sudden Russian internationalism, Lenin clarified the national sentiment behind it," Greenfeld sees nationalist ressentiment camouflaged as global goodwill as the basis of the Bolsheviks' (inter)nationalist project.[38] Greenfeld, in maintaining that the hold of such a sentiment was so blinding as to be self-destructive, allows that its impact could be only negative. So intense was the desire for recognition that Russians took up the mantle for global salvation, sacrificing themselves in the process. In this account, it was the agony of the "inadequacy which tortured them" that led to national self-destruction. But focusing on the costs to Russia of internationalism distracts from the importance of this kind of agitation for emergent nationals such as McKay.

This is not to say that Bolshevik doctrine was able on its own stream—or in conjunction with anyone else's—to theorize "the Negro" adequately. These shortcomings are particularly evident in Lenin's theory of the Negro nationalist project. Inherent to Lenin's theorization of the "Negro nation" was a determination of all blacks as ineluctably linked. Based on a contention that the "most difficult task" facing the further development of capitalism was the intensive colonization of the areas inhabited by the "black races," the theses declared that the unique history of U.S. Negroes qualified them for "a significant role in the liberation struggle of the entire African race."[39] It was in the arena of consciousness-raising that the Soviets felt black Americans could be most beneficial to the cause of communist intervention in Africa. Soviet functionaries assumed that fighting in

World War I had instilled in many black Americans who had served in the war a revolutionary consciousness:

> The longings, blood and tears of the "emancipated" Negroes helped create American capitalism, and when America, as a world power, was inextricably caught up in the world war, American Negroes received the exact same rights as whites . . . to be killed and to kill for "democracy." . . . Hardly had they returned from the bloody war when Negro soldiers came across racial persecution, lynchings, murders, inequalities, and general scorn. Persecution of Negroes became even more frequent and widespread than before the war, until Negroes once again learned to "know their place."[40]

Having experienced the hypocrisies of U.S. democracy played out so vividly, black Americans would surely be instrumental to the dissemination of raised racial consciousness. This was a sentiment that Trotsky stated even more bluntly. In a letter to McKay, Trotsky wrote that "when the hand of capitalism or even sooner the hand of militarism tears them [Negroes] mechanically from their customary environment and forces them to stake their lives for the sake of new and complicated questions and conflicts, then their spiritual conservatism gives way abruptly and revolutionary ideas find rapid access to a consciousness thrown off its balance."[41] The goal was to throw racially rooted consciousness off its nationally oriented balance and into the hands of a newly conceived Negro internationale.

The Soviet rendering of all persons of African descent as necessarily related took its lead from prominent black thinkers of the day. The idea that African Americans should serve as leaders in a Pan-Africanist movement was also propounded at the time by progressives such as Du Bois.[42] Indeed, communists in the United States were not averse to the idea of American leadership. Consider the words of William F. Dunne in an article for the *Workers Monthly:* "From American Negroes in industry must come the leadership of their race in the struggle for freedom in the colonial countries. In spite of the denial of equal opportunity to the Negro under American capitalism, his advantages are so far superior to those of the subject colonial Negroes in educational, political, and industrial fields that he alone is able to furnish the agitational and organizational ability that the situation demands."[43] Similarly, a confidential report to the Comintern states that "the American Negro, by reason of his higher education and culture, his greater capacity for leadership and because of the urgency of the issues in America, will furnish the leadership to the Negro race" (RTSKhIDNI, 495–155–17, 24). Supported by a logic that black Americans had had more exposure to and thus were more conversant in the wily ways of the modernized Western powers, the view that blacks in the United States should serve as "natural" leaders for Africans was without a doubt constraining for all blacks included under the label "Negro race." This stance mystified and essentialized the connection between black peoples, made black Americans the superior leaders, and encouraged the notion of a representative black masculinity.

Rather than reflecting policy opinions that the Comintern incorporated into its own ideological corpus, McKay's work disputed Bolshevik reductionism on both counts. In a piece titled "For a Negro Congress," written in English during the time McKay was in Moscow, he disputed the first presumption—that of black American representativeness. In a section called "A Negro International," McKay writes that "the Negro population of the world is roughly estimated to be about 200 million; but the articulate revolt against Imperialist oppression comes from that SMALL MINORITY THAT IS MORE OR LESS in close contact with the white proletariat of America and Africa, and has somewhat assimilated the culture of the exploiting race. Thus, it is the Negro population of the U.S., the Caribbean islands and West and South Africa that is active in the modern movement against imperialist exploitation" (RTSKhIDNI, 495–155–43, 56). Rather than implying that black Americans should serve as representative leaders for global radicalism, he clearly states that other black nationals are equally capable of paving the way. In fact, McKay intimates, as he observes more firmly in *Negroes in America,* that the black Americans on the cutting edge of protest against imperialism are themselves caught up in bourgeois ideology, or "the culture of the exploiting race." McKay expresses opposition to the instrumental leadership of U.S. blacks as directed by the "Theses." He maintains, "I am opposed to the American and South African parties having an altogether free hand in organizing the conference as I do not think they are familiar or class consciously enough interested in the Negro as revolutionary material. Especially in the USA the CP may antagonize the best comrades who can reach the masses. The differences existing between the American and West Indian Negro may even spoil the preliminary arrangements if they are not tactfully worked out" (RTSkhIDNI, 495–155–43, 56). Both expressing reservations about U.S. leadership and stressing the necessity of recognizing differences within the purportedly homogeneous category "Negro," McKay's essay provides an oppositional voice to attempt to construct black Americans as representative of that lump sum called "Negroes."

Echoing McKay's wariness over the exceptionalism of black Americans, Lovett Fort-Whiteman, one of the earliest black activists in the U.S. Communist movement and later head of the American Negro Labor Congress (ANLC), objected to the very term "Negro" as deployed by the Comintern.[44] In a draft of an essay titled "Some Suggestions Pertaining to the Proposed Negro World Congress to Be Held in Moscow" (1924), Fort-Whiteman writes, "In connection with the project of an international Negro Congress I consider it well to bear this in mind: that the word 'Negro' is a very indefinite term. . . . The fact that blacks imported to the New World as slaves came principally from West Africa, by no means argues that they were of the same race. . . . [T]o come to the point: the word 'Negro' has no meaning for the black man of Africa . . . for there are as many distinct black races on the African continent, each on separate territory and speaking distinctly different languages, as there are of white races in Europe" (RTSkhIDNI, 495–155–25, n.p.). Fort-Whiteman pointedly declares that the blanket term "Negro," as applied indiscriminately by Soviets to all peoples of African descent, was in essence a misnomer. Proposing that the Congress be organized under the guise of an "International Congress of African Races," he submits that the word "Negro" complicates the attempt to bring together peoples from distinct social and cultural backgrounds. Fort-Whiteman sensed that the deployment of "Negro" was only furthering the Soviets' ignorance of the specificity of racial matters as they differed from territory to territory, and deflecting attention from concrete policymaking that could intervene successfully against Western imperialism and Jim Crow.

RACISM WITHIN PARTY RANKS

As established by the emphases of the 1922 Theses, the Soviets believed that an awakened racial consciousness could emerge from exposure to international experience, whether it be literal travel across national borders or intellectual journeys alongside revolutionary rhetoric. Both alternatives, it was thought, could serve as impetuses for throwing off the mantles of slavery and imperialism. Although the Soviets may have provided a useful analytic framework for deciphering the workings of capital, a Soviet belief in the use value of black Americans to accommodate the fomenting of racial consciousness nonetheless lay in a critical misperception of race. This misperception was based on an assumption that black Americans were (in spite of the systemic exclusions of imperialism and slavery) nevertheless *ineluctably* linked to Africa. The situating of the Negro question as fundamental to Communism's future was grafted onto a continuing racial essentialism. Such an essentialism encouraged a view of internationalism that was, in practice, disconnected from the material conditions linking black Americans to the peoples of other disenfranchised nations. The Soviet perspective stopped short of interpreting what thinking transnationally (thinking about the commonalities of exclusion created by the experiences of slavery and imperialism) would do to their own cultural investments in racial difference. Promoting a nostalgic, skin-color-based logic at the onset of Soviet policy toward Negroes, the USSR expressed an inability and/or unwillingness to grasp the intricacies of racial formations, of their own implication in the international logics of white supremacy.[45]

This conservative attitude toward race on behalf of Comintern officials suggests that the theory of "nation" at work for the USSR was not emergent so much as repressive, steeped in archaic and naive misconceptions about immutable racial and ethnic difference. Lenin addressed the tendency of Russian nationals to overlook "Great-Russian chauvinism" in *The Rights of Nations to Self-Determination,* writing,

> In Russia—where no less than 57 percent, i.e., over 100,000,000 of the population, belong to oppressed nations, where those nations mainly inhabit the border provinces, where some of those nations are more cultured than the Great Russians. . . . The orgy of Great-Russian chauvinism raging in 1914–16 among the bourgeoisie and the opportunist Socialists prompts us to insist on this demand more strongly than ever and to declare that those who reject it serve, in practice, as a bulwark of Great-Russian chauvinism and tsarism."[46]

But Lenin's declarations about Russian chauvinism notwithstanding, Soviet bureaucrats continued to exercise willful displays of racial ineptitude.

3. McKay and Otto Huiswood, with unidentified companion, pose next to the Bronze Horseman in Leningrad. Yale Collection of American Literature, Beinecke Rare Book and Manuscript Library.

Documentation surrounding the reception of McKay in Russia reveals two interrelated, unofficial policies on the Negro question: a racism-obtuse schema behind the crude reading of McKay as a stand-in African; and an acquiescence to the infiltration of U.S. racism into Soviet borders. These policies were affiliated and interlocking because the documents in which they are depicted illuminate not only a deeply ingrained Russian custom of ignoring racial chauvinism and its connectedness to sexual proscriptions but also how such custom conspired with white supremacist attitudes within the cpusa—in spite of theses meant to safeguard the contrary.

When McKay arrived in Russia he was feted like a celebrity. Even he expressed awareness that his celebrity status had everything to do with the way he looked. As McKay describes it, "When the Negro delegate was invited to attend meetings and my mulatto colleague went, the people asked, 'but where is the *chorny* (the black)?'" (*ALWFH*, 177). According to McKay's account in *A Long Way from Home*, as McKay's face appeared throughout the city on placards and posters, Huiswood began to stick close to McKay. Commenting that Huiswood was received positively by the Congress only after an association with McKay had been established, McKay wrote that "Russia wanted a typical Negro at the Congress" (173) that Huiswood "was too yellow" (173) for the Russian public. In the eyes of the Soviets, McKay suggests, Huiswood was simply too *American* to be sufficiently African. He was too light skinned to afford the crucial racial distinctions between black and white that could herald the Soviet Union as the true model for global internationalism.

McKay, on the other hand, fit the conception of what it was to be representatively African in the public's mind's eye (see *ALWFH*, 173). As Wayne Cooper, McKay's biographer, notes, McKay's dark color, "his unusually high, arching brows, his bright smile and rollicking laughter made him instantly attractive" to the Soviets. McKay was marked by what Cooper terms "unmistakable Negroidness."[47] Of course, in order for the picture of "Negroidness" to appear "unmistakable," there must be some prior indication or mapping of the Negro against which McKay could be measured. Soviet attitudes toward Negroes were primarily influenced by an understanding of Africa that had developed over the course of several decades, through a long-standing czarist interest and activity in Africa. The relationships with African nations developed under the czarist regime constituted the building blocks for the field of Soviet African studies that emerged after the Bolsheviks came to power.[48] As McKay's case makes clear, however, the Comintern efforts to link Africans and black Americans were riddled with self-interest and a lack of perceptiveness about the specificities of racial and national formations, the differences between and among peoples of African nations and those descended from these peoples, and the asymmetries among race and other identity markers (such as class, gender, and sexuality) within a singular racial categorization.

Such a belief in the "family" of Africa encouraged a dichotomous logic of black/white in which "the Soviets" were ostensibly marked as white. Such "whiteness" was asserted in spite of Soviet claims of fundamental difference to the oppressive regimes of Western imperialism. The idea that Russians—white Russians—were the first among Soviet "equals" withstood the internationalist rhetoric of Soviet anti-imperialism. With links to the traditional field of Russian Africanism (that as a whole supported the merits of indigenous African populations), the Soviets could claim that the basis for McKay's reception lay in antiethnocentric, anti-Western sentiments.[49] Together, McKay's and Fort-Whiteman's descriptions of the Soviet response to Negroes in Moscow evoke what Christopher Miller, in an eloquent schematic of French imperialist racializing strategies, has termed "blank darkness, or the [European] projection of a malleable nullity onto black Africans."[50] Because McKay's physical features concurred with the commonly conceived representation (and basis for caricature) of the African as entirely other, a strategy of nullification through primitivizing (such as that described by Miller in the French context) coheres to McKay's reception. This would also explain the Soviets' rejection of Huiswood as insufficiently African. But unlike the situation of French imperialism in Africa mapped out by Miller, the Soviets could not simply term African Americans uncultured, or project their own cultural categories onto them and find them lacking. A more nuanced process of differentiation was demanded by the promulgation of McKay's image as a hero of the Revolution and his resulting celebrity.

While Miller's schema can be used as a model through which to see how Russian Africanist discourse operated under similar paradoxes as did French Africanist discourse, at the same time, it can be drawn on to demonstrate the different inflections of the relationship between blacks and Russians. Miller describes the central paradox of Africanist discourse in France: the inability to place Africa as an object in a self/other binary— that is, Africa's annulment of Europe's own binary modes of thought. "Africa" is thus an "aberrant product of the system that created it."[51] McKay's experiences reflect how Soviet discourse used similarly confounding modes, confusing "Africa's" place. Yet the confusion outlined in these modes also testifies to how the self/other terms of the French paradigm were shifted by the Russian example. While Russians were similarly disoriented by McKay as were the French by black Africans, this reaction was itself part of the larger structure of Russia's historical attempts to situate itself in relation to the West.

Just as Russia was not synonymous with Europe, Russia's "whiteness" was not synonymous with the European paradigm. In fact, Russia had for centuries been embattled over its *difference* from Europeans, in particular the French. Not only had the Russian nobility adopted the French language in an effort to be more modern in the late seventeenth century but on imperial demand they had also adopted French social customs of the court and sent their children to France for proper education. All of these efforts were undertaken in order to distinguish the nobility from the peasant classes, who in speaking and acting Russian demonstrated the cultural backwardness from which the upper classes were aspiring to escape. This kind of cultural baggage did not permit a simple appropriation of European whiteness or European ways of seeing Africa. Indeed, Russian thinkers had long seen themselves as located precariously between Western civilization and Eastern "barbarity." Consider the words of Isaiah Berlin, who, on cue from writers and philosophers before him such as Nikolay Gogol, Dostoevsky, Vissarion Belinsky, and Alexander Herzen, believed that Russians felt a combination of inferiority and superiority in comparison to Europeans: "On the one hand, intellectual respect, envy, admiration, desire to emulate and excel; on the other, emotional hostility, suspicion, and contempt, a sense of being clumsy, *de trop*, of being outsiders."[52] When compared with the predominant theme of African American self-perception as existing between two worlds, Berlin's words echo the sentiments of black Americans' striving to "satisfy two unreconciled ideals" in their relationship to white Americans.[53] Anxieties about cultural imperialism, national assimilation, and suspicions of backwardness along with general enmity that traditionally plagued some Russians also tormented racially oriented African Americans. The sharp similarities between their conscripted masculinist national filiations and cultural self-perceptions can be used to think about hegemonic structures of othering that, when brought together, present an instructive picture. Their differences should of course not be underestimated, but nonetheless, the response to McKay in Russia can be interpreted as at once an encounter with an "other" simultaneous to an encounter with Russia's own "otherness"— the "monstrousness" of the Russian as not properly European, itself a classification or attribute that was just acquiring what Paul Gilroy has aptly termed the "dislocating dazzle of whiteness."[54] What McKay's predicament shows is how a discursive construction of the Negro and Russian as necessarily dual both raises and defies the quandary of French Africanist discourse over nullification and fullness by shifting the very terms of self/other. Linking the Negro and Russian—as fundamentally other to the establishment of a burgeoning capitalist regime of a distinctly inflected and discriminating whiteness—worked as a Party line, but it also had origins in Russia's own historical relationship to the West.[55]

At the same time, of course, ascertaining difference from the Negro was never far from Party practice. Contrary to *Pravda*'s insinuation that racism was not a Party issue but an American one, the Comintern files from the period directly following the Third International indicate Soviet awareness that racism was indeed proliferating within Party ranks. The Comintern's reluctance to take action to combat this fact is well documented, both in the repeated forestalling of the promised Negro Congress and in a failure to respond with concrete intervention when the subject was raised by concerned parties.[56] McKay himself addresses this fact in "For a Negro Congress," in which he writes that a confidential report to the Comintern confirms that the CPUSA has produced "half-hearted work among Negroes [and] never has the Party lifted its voice in protest. . . . [T]he Party has no Negro organizers or officials; no Negro members on the press staff," and in general the Party "has evinced perfect indifference" to the "bitter complaint [against this Party attitude toward blacks]" (RTSKhIDNI, 495–27–43). Similarly, the acting director of the Negro Department of the CPUSA remarks candidly in a Comintern report that "white chauvinism" within the Party is starkly clear: "The attitude that Negro work does not require full-time functionaries, that it should somehow be done by communists in their spare time [pays] lip service to the Comintern decisions that Negro work be considered a major task of the American Party, but makes very little effort to provide the forces necessary for carrying out that decision." This report indicates that the oversight of Negroes by the CPUSA also effected wages, and that the "repeated instructions from the Comintern that white functionaries must share with the Negro director all funds available for wages has been repeatedly ignored. . . . [W]hite chauvinism is rampant—open and unashamed" (RTSKhIDNI, 495–28–43, n.p.). Reiterating the stumbling block that the American Party was posing to the pursuit of a racism-free CP, Fort-Whiteman wrote Zinoviev, "The American Party does nothing practically on the Negro issues nor has it made any serious or worthwhile efforts to carry Communist teaching to the great masses of American black workers" (RTSKhIDNI, 495–155–27, 42). Sen Katayama, the Japanese delegate to the Fourth Congress and a friend of McKay, echoed this sentiment, applying it to the U.S.-instigated forestalling of the plans for an international Negro conference: "The Negro conference has been postponed again by the very suggestion of the American Communist Party. With such strenuous opposition from the American Party the Negro question will have a

"Not at All God's White People" ⋮ 53

very hard future. The Comintern can hardly do much against such an opposition, because the actual work must be necessarily entrusted to the CPS concerned" (RTSKhIDNI, 495–155–17, 9).[57] These documents suggest that the Comintern was unwilling to do anything concrete to combat racism within party ranks. And in effect, by entrusting to the CPUSA the management of white chauvinism, the Comintern indirectly supported the mistreatment that McKay suffered at the hands of the CPUSA delegates to the Fourth Congress.

But a dismissal of the Soviets as oppressively essentialist in their attitude toward McKay does not nullify the pervasive infiltration of U.S. racism into Soviet borders, as evidenced by the Comintern records of the Fourth Congress. According to the Comintern records, Huiswood was a last-minute addition to the U.S. delegation. Katayama writes that Huiswood was chosen to ameliorate the agitation for some sign of action on the Negro question; while at the same time, Huiswood was chosen precisely because of his light (and less obtrusive) skin color. Ostensibly objecting to McKay's belief that the CPUSA should move out from underground, the delegates made it clear that this was not the only thing to which they objected. The U.S. delegation was angry that McKay had appeared in Moscow at the time of the Congress because McKay's presence distracted attention from their own officially appointed Negro delegate, Huiswood. For this reason, according to McKay, his own "presence was resented. The American delegation did not want [him] there," and Huiswood shunned McKay, telling him that he was "all right for propaganda," but would "never make a disciplined party member" (ALWFH, 177). The CPUSA, McKay contended, had strategically selected Huiswood as their Negro delegate because he was a light-skinned black.

The racist basis of the delegation's displeasure with McKay's presence is even more forcefully asserted in a long essay written for the Comintern by Katayama. Titled "Action for the Negro Movement Should Not Be Postponed," Katayama's essay maintains that the very inclusion of Huiswood as a member of the U.S. delegation was itself an attempt to "save face" after having "shelved willfully" the Negro question. Katayama continues,

> I say just to save the honor of the American Communist Party because the subsequent conduct of the American delegation proves so. To cite an instance. A pure or full-blooded Negro representative of the ABB

[African Blood Brotherhood], Comrade Claude McKay, was kicked out of the Hotel Lux and even was pursued or chased out from the Lux Restaurant where McKay was eating his meal with his own money. All these brutal treatments meted out to Comrade McKay by the same American delegation! Indeed, the entire delegation with the exception of Comrades Billings and Sasha were against the Negro resolution in the American section meeting. (RTSKhIDNI, 495–155–17, 9)

Unlike the celebrity treatment proffered him by the Soviets, the treatment McKay received from Americans while in Moscow only served to remind him of the radical distinction between U.S. racism and Soviet attempts to liquidate racist customs and attitudes. Moreover, the attempts by the U.S. delegates to import their own standards into the Soviet Union revealed the expropriating tendencies of U.S. white supremacy, presumption of normalcy, and imposition of domestic priority simultaneous to a disregard for the international that went hand in hand with segregationist cultural patterns. Because the record of the Congress's proceedings indicate that the "Theses on the Negro Question" passed unanimously, the resistance of the U.S. delegation to these theses has not been documented but nevertheless should not be discounted.

McKay indicated his displeasure with the U.S. delegates more directly in a "personal note" addressed to the Comintern. He writes that he found the "leader of the American delegation [Comrade Carr] very ignorant about the revolutionary trend of American Negroes. He professed absolute ignorance of the Negro organization to which I belong [the ABB], although the organization had achieved front page publicity in the big metropolitan papers" (RTSKhIDNI, 495–155–43, 157). While the Soviets may have relied on naive and stereotyping fantasies in order to imagine racial difference, they nonetheless displayed more diplomacy toward McKay than did their counterparts. Katayama observes that in spite of the "cold reception given to the Negro Comrade by the American delegation at the start, the Negro delegates Billings and McKay were received by the Congress and made a profound impression on the Congress and the Congress treated the Negro problems with a due respect and consideration" (RTSKhIDNI, 495–155–17, 9).[58] Still, "due respect and consideration" were apparently public manifestations aimed at an individual body that did not convert into Soviet policy aimed at a larger body politic.

As these passages reveal, the Comintern's willingness to let the CPUSA pave its own course in slighting race issues indicates the degree of autonomy with which the CPUSA operated. This counters the long-held assumption—propagated by policymakers and historians alike—that the CPUSA was merely a puppet of the Comintern, and is one of the discoveries to emerge from the recent opening of the Party archives.[59] But even recent forays into the newly accessible archives have attempted to reconfirm the belief in Comintern dominance. For example, *The Soviet World of American Communism* (1998), by Harvey Klehr, John Earl Hayes, and Kiril Mikhailovich Anderson, claims that the Comintern archives substantiate the financial support of U.S. Communism by the Soviets, and uses this support as evidence that the CPUSA was purely a functionary of Moscow's authority. Within these same archives, however, the files that address the Negro question indicate much greater autonomy than this study permits. Documents in the Negro file directly counter the flimsy logic that the Comintern dominated the CPUSA because "with foreign money came foreign influence."[60] A letter from Fort-Whiteman to Zinoviev dated 21 October 1924 states, "I came as a full-fledged American delegate to the Fifth [Comintern] Congress, even though the CEC [Central Executive Committee] of the Party *refused to grant anything toward my expenses.* This was done by individual Negro communists, inspired by the belief that by sending one of their group to Moscow, he might be successful in getting the Committee to take some practical steps helpful to our work among Negroes, both in America and on a world scale" (RTSKhIDNI, 495–155–27, 42). Such a statement points to the financial autonomy of black American Communists (and by *The Soviet World*'s logic, autonomy of influence) and directly counters the assumption that the power of "Moscow gold" was the single-most influential factor driving American radicals. Such assumptions overlook the specific historical conditions—such as Jim Crow—that led "individual Negro communists" to find Soviet Communism particularly "inspiring" in the 1920s.

Far from single-handedly directing orders, the Comintern deferred to what was perceived as Americans' superior grasp of racial matters. In fact, a comment such as "the Comintern can hardly do much against such an opposition" outlines the prevalent attitude that the Comintern was in effect powerless against the forces that supported racism within U.S. party ranks. Contrary to anticommunist reports that Moscow was "ordering a campaign to spread through Negro churches, schools, and settlements," the policy on the Negro question was largely directed by U.S. party leaders (RTSKhIDNI, 495–27–28, 6).[61] As indicated in a letter from the secretary of the Executive Committee of the Communist International (ECCI) to the CPUSA, the Comintern "request[ed] that your party provisionally take care of the propaganda for the development of the Negro movement, and also in general to prepare the ground for the coming Negro Congress. We ask you to notify us about the practical steps you think necessary for these purposes" (RTSKhIDNI, 495–155–16, 1). The Comintern's inaction on the Negro question thus suggests that Moscow did not rule the CPUSA with an iron fist, and in fact, the CPUSA exercised a great degree of self-government in racial matters.

This lack of action also implies, however, that the Comintern was uninterested in suppressing the trenchant racism that existed within U.S. party ranks. Such neglect expressed itself not only in response to racism within the CPUSA but also in the Soviets' own failure to take seriously the structural and institutional manifestations of racism on its own domestic front. Fort-Whiteman closes his letter to Zinoviev as follows: "Unfortunately since my coming to Russia, I have not been given the opportunity to talk with you on the American Negro social situation" (RTSKhIDNI, 495–155–27, 42). Party officials apparently felt they had more pressing concerns than educating themselves about racial matters.[62] Based on the documentation surrounding it, the bulk of McKay's visit appears as a vast enactment of the ways in which Soviet desire to be a communist haven for African Americans operated simultaneously with their wish to distinguish themselves from these same persons.

TRIAL BY LYNCHING—
OR AN EDUCATION ABOUT NEGROES IN AMERICA

While it is undeniable that the Soviet imagination was riddled with racist imagery and the Comintern provided negligible support to counter such cultural practice, it would be nonetheless far too simple to dismiss McKay's reception as evidence of a naively racist Soviet perspective. Despite the importance of these contextualizing documents, adherence to an interpretive schema that emphasizes only the dogmatism of a hierarchical party line cancels out any differential effect policy may have had on individuals. Such a depiction cannot account for the powerful reaction to this newly established role of "Negro" that McKay depicts. "You may have wine and anything extra you require, at no cost to you," McKay recalls being told (*ALWFH*, 170); "Whatever I wanted to do I did. For the first time I knew what it was to be a highly privileged personage. Didn't I enjoy it!" (*ALWFH*, 159). McKay's description of his access to private cars, luxury hotels, and banquet tables replete with numerous delicacies comes across as deliberately accentuating the ways his treatment distinguished him both from the average Soviet and the treatment he received in the United States. His exceptional status signified an acceptance into spaces heretofore reserved for whites only. In stark contrast to the delimiting experiences of U.S. racism, the open-door policy with which McKay was wined and dined while in Russia surely gave rise to an exhilarating sense of liberation. McKay articulates this feeling as one of racial parity, of acceptance, as a positive differentiation based in racial distinction, which had previously always been marked negatively. Seen in this light, McKay's interactions with Russia empowered him to pronounce the possibility of reclaiming the denigrated space of blackness within a sphere of interracial contacts, and to use these crossings as a source for a revamped notion of blackness and social change.

In spite of the fact that McKay later denounced communism and the Soviet Union, what remained unchanged in the period from 1922 to 1937 was McKay's assessment of his visit to the USSR as enabling him to rethink the cultural category of blackness as one that could be celebrated for its ability to challenge the racism of white, Western paradigms of selfhood and cultural production. McKay's and Katayama's anecdotes about the reception of Huiswood suggest that McKay was instrumental in shifting Soviet racial perspective, in prying open the Soviet imagination to include racial figures that did not easily correspond to preexisting categories of white and black. Given the overwhelming evidence of Soviet white chauvinism, it is not surprising that McKay turned to the format he knew best—writing—to further educate his Soviet comrades about the pernicious workings of white supremacy of a different national flavor. Pushing the definition boundaries of "white" and "black," McKay's writings from this period sought to educate Soviets about the topic of interracialism. In so doing, these works linked the idea of emergent (black) national-ism with the equally debated woman question. *Negroes in America* and *Trial by Lynching* instruct about the ways that blacks and women remained outside the definitional parameters of the citizen: the stories are attempts to theorize the exclusion of both from the national body politic. Although Soviet dogma held that with the dissolution of private property so, too, would the problem of patriarchy be "solved," women remained, in effect, second-class citizens in the Soviet state. In spite of legislation endorsing women's rights, commitment to sexual emancipation remained a theoret-ical pipe dream for agitators like Alexandra Kollontai and Inessa Ar-mand.[63] McKay's stories reposition the issue. Linking the idea of racial and sexual self-determination to that of self-ownership, the stories escape a consolidation of the "margin" into an explanatory apparatus that simply reinscribes the logic of the "center."

Soon after McKay arrived in Moscow in November of 1922 he was commissioned by the State Publishing House to write a book on the status of blacks in the United States.[64] The book, *Negry v Amerike*, was written during the ensuing months that McKay spent in Russia, and in 1923, was published in Moscow in a Russian edition translated by Okhrimenko. In 1925, under the Ogonek imprint, the Moscow State Publishing House put out a collection of short stories that McKay wrote alongside the collected essays. The stories appeared under the title *Sudom Lincha: Rasskazy o zhizni negrov v severnoi amerike* or *Trial by Lynching: Stories about Negro Life in North America,* also translated into Russian by Okhrimenko. It was anticipated that together the works would supply instructive tales about the lives of blacks in the United States. The combined facts that McKay's manuscripts were written in Russia, published in Russian, and subse-quently lost have had the effect of pushing them to the periphery in considerations of his work. Because of such placement, the work McKay revealed in *Negroes in America* has remained unfamiliar to most readers.[65] The issue here is not to attempt to restore an impossible authentic text, nor to insist on one, but rather to reclaim the polyglot aspect of the archive surrounding McKay. Combined with the fact of an unrecoverable original, the multilingualism of McKay's archive counters the pressure to rely on "the uncorrupted manuscript" as ineluctably more reliable than any sub-sequent translation. Written at the height of McKay's Soviet moment, *Negroes in America* and *Trial by Lynching* offer glimpses into McKay's most candid thinking about black internationalism and the ways in which it promoted interracialism while challenging notions of the properly conceived national body. As products of nonoriginary texts, these translations also expose the project of Soviet translation as a strong-arm of Soviet imperialism. The *Pravda* publication of McKay's statements would seem to support the argument that Soviets negotiated imperialism through translation. Unlike the *Pravda* version of McKay's speech to the Fourth Comintern, however, these writings suggest that within the processes of Russian translation of the local, oppositional practices could be sustained. While I am in general agreement with the position outlined by Andrew Wachtel, that the Soviet policy was to "practice translation and imperialism simultaneously," McKay's Russian work offers something of a counter to Wachtel's conclusion about the invidiousness of the Soviet approach.[66] Rather than serving as a simple reflection of Soviet ideals, these works link the questions of Negro rights to female emancipation in such a way as to challenge the Soviet stalemate on the topic. Linking women's suffrage to racial justice, this work offers a counter to the prevailing assumptions of Soviet superiority on the question of national self-determination. In brief, these works, written as they were through the imperializing pen of Moscow/Russian nonetheless were able to dispute the idea that the woman question would be solved through Leninist dogma that disengaged theories of national and female autonomies.

Coming on the heels of McKay's ten-year residence in the United States, *Negroes in America* provides a crucial picture of the author's opinions about the specific racial injustices facing black Americans, and the systemic links between his own experiences of racism and those of others similarly excluded by the constraints of national identity. *Negroes in America* sutures these issues together by placing at the center of his discussion of black internationalism the issue of social reproduction. Divided into nine parts, *Negroes in America* touches on the linguistic, historical, cultural, aesthetic, and economic permutations of reproductive politics, and how socially enforced limits and boundaries mimic underlying economic structures mandated to keep blacks and whites separate. *Trial by Lynching* offered Soviet readers one of the initial "firsthand" accounts of race relations in the United States. The three stories included in the collection—"Trial by Lynching," "The Mulatto Girl," and "A Soldier's Return"—supplied Soviet readers with an ethnographic lesson about the much-talked-about Negro question. Primarily the book is concerned with the disciplinary regimes that conspire to keep black men and women, along with white women, "in their place" under the white supremacy of the United States. The stories focus on the relationship between race, class, and sex as they intersect and diverge in three structurally interrelated narratives. McKay's efforts to reclaim histories silenced by social consensus and his insistence that readers see the various facets of reproductive politics as they inhere to internationalism stem from a similar root—that is, a concern with how one comes to understand which bodies matter.

Early on in *Negroes in America,* McKay addresses the limitations of U.S. revolutionaries who fail to see the important connectedness of sex and citizenship. Likening the Labor Party's reluctance to include the phrase "social equality" in its demands for Negro rights to the U.S. South's fear of miscegenation, McKay describes the hypocrisy inherent in civil rights rhetoric that attempts to separate "economic, political, industrial, and educational spheres" from social equality. Aware that the phrase "social equality" thinly veils its more blunt sibling "sex," and likewise a fear of racial mixing, McKay writes, "Every Negro knows the nature of the poison which his white brother puts into this little phrase, 'there can never be social equality.' And every Negro worker knows that, whatever the party, when it refuses to take a stand on social equality to that extent, it also refuses to approach the Negro question" (*NA,* 38).[67] Such a refusal was based, according to McKay, in a fundamental failure to understand the Negro question, as irreducible to class, a problem that "must be examined in all its nakedness" (*NA,* 44).

McKay used the space of three stories in *Trial by Lynching* to offer his Russian readers an opportunity to examine this Negro question, as it were, "in all its nakedness." One critic describes the stories as representative of McKay's "anguish at the barbarity of Southern ways and his deep-felt sympathy for those deprived of self-respect, justice, and life itself," and leaves his analysis at that.[68] But rather than providing a simple reflection of authorial emotion and sympathy, the stories portray a deep sensibility of the precariousness and hypocrisy of whiteness as a power regime. Together, the stories supply a sophisticated theorization of whiteness that links Marxist analysis of the "question of the working class" with the woman question. Whereas *Negroes in America* comes to support the idea of self-determination in the U.S. South, *Trial by Lynching* troubles the line between North and South just as it disrupts the logic of racial segregation. Instead of offering an exposure of naked realities, the stories display a complex and nuanced assessment of the issues at stake in the Negro question. As indicated by the descriptive half of the collection's title, "Negro Life in North America," the stories refuse strict differentiation between regions in revealing the logic of white supremacy. Linking "lynching" and "lives" across the broad terrain of the United States in this way, these stories impart lessons about the material and psychological powers of U.S. whiteness following World War I. The phrase "trial by lynching" asserts not simply the lawlessness of unchecked regimes but rather the fact of lynching as law, as a disciplinary practice of racial and sexual control that extends its power across the North/South divide.[69]

In the story for which the collection is named, "Trial by Lynching" a southern belle, Nathalia Cord, vies with her father, Andrew Cord, for the outcome of her matrimonial future. Nathalia wishes to marry a northern Jew, Michael Sanovich, whereas her father has his eyes set on the locally grown Dr. Taylor, whose father was a close friend of his. Their divergent desires are intertwined with a historical narrative of post–Civil War Reconstruction, widespread discontent, and racial uprising in the U.S. South. The story opens with white hearsay about a sermon by a local black preacher named Jo White, who advocates black collective organization. "What are the limits of their unheard of impudence?" Cord asks his daughter. Cord's question sets up its own answer, thereby providing the conditions at stake in white concerns over racial "limits." "Here we don't let them into the churches and schools, and, thank God, Middelsville won't allow Negro shops within its borders for anything."[70] Mr. Cord clearly outlines the investment of whites in an unperturbed flow of monoracial commerce. His fear about a Negro penetration of borders bespeaks his anxiety about the future of his daughter and who she will marry. His worries conjoin the material interests of the white populace—a desire to keep their churches, schools, and shops segregated—with their reproductive ones—a wish to keep their women contained. Drawing on Friedrich Engels, in the 1920s Soviet theorists of the bourgeois family such as Inessa Armand and Alexandra Kollontai were arguing that a main aim of the family was to produce children of undisputed paternity so as to ensure the smooth transfer of property from one generation of men to the next.[71]

McKay hones in on this central tenet of the woman question and ties it to the Negro question.

The story demonstrates how Cord's fear that his daughter might marry a Jewish northerner exhibits white bourgeois apprehensiveness about the legitimacy of paternity (even if it is known). Cord worries that Nathalia will disrupt this transfer, that she will surrender her "refinement and aristocratic grace" (8) to the unseemly forces of northern mercantilism. McKay explores a classic dichotomy between North and South: the North as destructive force of modernity and modernization, and the South as a once vibrant but now decaying bastion of agrarian aristocracy. The racial group that threatens to undermine this line of distinction is, according to Cord's calculations, not blacks but Jews. Jews represent for Cord "the greatest threat to the existence of American civilization." He asserts that the "cock-and-bull story about the 'yellow peril' was invented by Jewish journalists with the aim of leading patriots astray and averting their gaze from the Jewish peril which was growing every day" (*TBL*, 2). But Cord's claim about the true "evil" behind Asian immigration in the early part of the twentieth century enables the reader to see his own doublespeak. In effect, Cord has created his own "cock-and-bull story" about the "Jewish peril" so as to avert his gaze from the purported truancy of his daughter's desire to marry a Jew. To be sure, for all of his protestations about Jews, Cord preserves equally vitriolic condemnation of blacks. But Jews receive the brunt of his bile because they are seen as instigators of upheaval, "enemies of Christ" who together with Catholics, lead the "negrophile, Abolitionist school" and "led to the ruin of the Southern states in 1865" (10). In Cord's estimation, blacks are simply automatons who follow the lead of more enterprising whites. For Cord, then, if his daughter were to marry a Jew it would replicate for him the ruin of the South in 1865, the opening of southern doors to certain racial ruin, the precarious proximity between Jo "White" and Cord's "white."

It seems that Cord desires nothing so much as to return to the idyllic, agrarian days of slave-owning aristocracy prior to the Civil War. Yet paradoxically, Cord doesn't come from the southern aristocratic stock that suffered loss of property and prestige in the war. In fact, in order to become a commercial success, Cord benefited from northern intervention and military victory. His present desire to restore a bygone era is therefore actually a desire to hide his lower class roots in the guise of southern gentility. In this sense, Cord is not unlike Michael Sanovich or any other enterprising "impostor" to whiteness.[72] Cord's own rise to whiteness is precisely what makes his position as monied white man appear so precarious. It is only by asserting a new kind of Southern whiteness, a new anti-Jewish, antiblack, and antiwoman whiteness, that he can hope to preserve what he calls "American civilization." It is this civilization that supports his sense of entitlement, that enables him to experience his citizenship as a disembodied one by projecting the burdens of embodiment onto blacks and women while denying them not only self-ownership but self-determination.[73]

Cord's is not really a longing to return to the past (which would mean his own disenfranchisement) at all but rather to create a new future, a new nation of whiteness. In this, Cord's aspirations resemble those put forth by D. W. Griffith in his film *Birth of a Nation*. As we in fact learn, Cord's close friend Henry Ray "was a sponsor of the movie," a reworking of Thomas Dixon's *The Clansman,* whose author "depicted the free Negroes as people who had lost their minds from happiness, who robbed the homes of white plantation owners, who raped their wives and daughters, and who were organizing a massacre in the free states under the protection of Federal troops" (*TBL* 17). Cord's enthusiastic membership in the Ku Klux Klan (KKK), which he joined "when the threat of Bolshevism appeared like a bomb with a lighted fuse" (10), is thus made to represent the simmering zeal in the postwar U.S. South for the establishment of a new nation of whiteness. Unlike Dixon's *Clansman* trilogy, which embraced immigrants as it segregated blacks, however, Cord's Klansmen see Jews as the linchpin between black and white. "He sincerely hated the enterprising Jews who took customers away from him. He especially could not stand Mordecai Rosenthal who recently had introduced an unheard-of practice: to serve all customers on a first-come, first-serve basis instead of forcing the Negroes to wait until all the white customers had been attended to" (11). The problem with Jews, according to Cord, is that they know the market better than he does. With "unheard-of practices," they don't simply take "customers" away but have seduced his daughter—his most prized possession—away from him. Against the aspirations of Cord's nativist KKK, Jews and other European immigrants represent the new face of national whiteness—a face that not only reflects the material process of Cord's own enculturation into this brotherhood but threatens to become Nathalia's as well.

McKay's tale is in conversation with Griffith's film. Based on the narrator's description, it is unclear whether or not McKay was aware that many of his Russian readers were indeed familiar with *Birth of a Nation*. Following its U.S. release, Griffith's film was shown in Russia, although the history of its commercial release there is somewhat vague.[74] What seems certain is that members of the film community had seen it by 1920. Vsevolod Pudovkin, Sergei Eisenstein, and Sergei Gerassimov credit Griffith's influence on their school of montage.[75] In *Film Form*, Eisenstein wrote, "I wish to recall what David Wark Griffith himself represented to us, as young Soviet film-makers of the 'twenties. To say it simply and without equivocation: a revelation."[76] This sentiment was echoed by Gerassimov: "All the films of Griffith were for us revelations and models."[77] The importance of this intersection between U.S. and Soviet filmmaking to an analysis of *Trial by Lynching* is that it highlights not only the frame of reference in which McKay was working but also the burden of rerepresenting to Soviets a relationship between "black" and "white" in the United States. Although Eisenstein recognized the "repellent elements" of *Birth of a Nation* in which Griffith presented himself "as an open apologist for racism, erecting a celluloid monument to the Ku Klux Klan, and joining their attack on Negroes," as a filmmaker Griffith was nonetheless viewed as a revelation for aesthetic reasons, primarily for his use of parallel montage.[78] For the most part, Soviets separated the aesthetic form of Griffith's filmmaking from its ideological punch. But as Michael Rogin has argued, the two cannot be easily disentwined.

In the case of its Soviet reception, this point seems all the more urgent. A letter from Fort-Whiteman to the Comintern requesting an interview with Anatoly Lunacharsky documents the disregard for the dissemination of racist images in the Soviet Union of the 1920s. Writing in 1924, Fort-Whiteman comments that "in America, one of the common social evils against which we Negroes are constantly in active opposition is the practice of caricaturing Negro faces in advertisement literature. In Russia, one would not expect to find such practices. Nevertheless, at present throughout Russia, it is common to notice prints of caricatured faces of Negroes advertising cigarettes, films, pictures, etc. Though there be no anti-Negro feeling behind it, the results are the same" (RTSKhIDNI, 495–155–27, 71).

"Not at All God's White People" ┊ 65

Fort-Whiteman's dissociation of racist images of blacks from "anti-Negro feeling" is disingenuous, as is his dissociation of a U.S. attitude toward Negroes from a Russian one. As he observes, "The results are the same." In spite of Soviet policies directed toward mitigating racist attitudes, caricatures reflecting and supporting antiblack sentiments circulated with impunity throughout consumer culture. By pinpointing the use of caricatures in Russian advertising, Fort-Whiteman is making a point about how cultural consumption takes part in the psychological makeup through which others are perceived. His letter stands out as the only record of objection not directed specifically to Party policy but to the realm of cultural production in which racist images continued to thrive in spite of Party resolutions and theses. As there is no record of a reply to Fort-Whiteman's request, nor any record of Comintern attention to the dissemination of racist images within the Soviet Union, it is likely that Fort-Whiteman's concern was overlooked as immaterial.

Along with the influx of racist images proceeding from Russian consumer culture outlets, based on the reintroduction of a contained capitalism under NEP, the diagetic impact of Griffith's presentation was clearly marked. In his autobiography, *Immoral Memories,* Eisenstein wrote, "In Thomas Dixon's American novel *The Clansman,* glorifying the birth of the Ku Klux Klan, this absurd idea of an image fixed in the retina is used as material evidence to prove the guilt of a Negro accused of rape."[79] And yet the idea of a fixed image may not have been so absurd, for as Eisenstein was apparently aware, *Birth of a Nation* instructed viewers how to read U.S. racial difference. If as Jeffrey Brooks has demonstrated, the Bolsheviks were unsuccessful at their attempts to devise a sufficient popular image or idiom for the "new Soviet," then they certainly were unable to combat the popular image of "the American" disseminated in popular culture. The American image of race remained fixed in the eyes of Soviet viewers. Soviets' ways of seeing gender and race collided with the distribution of films from the United States, but the collision produced little friction. For the most part, U.S. films provided stereotypes with which Russians could identify and emulate as images corresponded to the patriarchal attitudes of their own inherited system of social and national inequalities. There is not the space to engage in a lengthy discussion of the film, which has received significant attention elsewhere, and whose distribution in Russia is murky at best.[80] For our purposes, the point to be culled from other explanations is that the film reduced identity to a deceptively uniform mark of skin color. From this vantage point it is unlikely that many Soviet viewers (if they were able to see the film), officially sympathetic though they might have been, endeavored to cross the color line to side with the rapacious Negroes as represented by Griffith. McKay's story thus serves as an important counterexample to the visual economy of *Birth of a Nation* and its use of parallel montage as a means of projecting Griffith's "dualistic picture of the world, running in two parallel lines towards some hypo-thetical 'reconciliation' where . . . the parallel lines would cross, that is, in that infinity, just as inaccessible as that 'reconciliation.'"[81] Replacing false reconciliation with a determined critique of a dualistic diagetic economy, McKay's story elicits visual elements to tell an alternative birth of a nation that begins with a trial by lynching. The Soviet audience was still captive to U.S. images of race on the silver screen and the myth of America as the land of opportunity: they didn't connect the disenfranchisement of blacks with the marginalization of women. This was the economy against which McKay was writing.

In "Trial by Lynching," the "new woman" that Nathalia threatens to become represents the encroaching effects of industrialism, the newly shaped permeability of once trenchant boundaries.[82] McKay's endorse-ment of the mutating spaces of the city is echoed in the essays in which he bristles at the idea that Negro folklore is regarded as the "distinctive con-tribution of Negroes in the artistic world of the West." As McKay writes, "But they [white critics] make a great mistake when they transform this exotic flower which grew up in abnormal, alien circumstances in the heart of the industrial development of the New World into a basis for criticizing the artistic aspirations of contemporary Negroes" (*NA*, 69). Rather than seeing Negro art, and especially Negro folklore, as itself an impure product of bastardized conditions, white critics "proceed from these false prem-ises" to approach contemporary Negro art with the presumption that a true Negro art can be tapped only in the neighborhood of dialect and folklore. Equally harmful, according to McKay, is the attempt by Negro writers to fulfill this falsely derived expectation, and in their attempt to satisfy, these writers end up "becoming imitative down to trivial details and slavishly banal" (69). This emphasis on the "folk" as a bonding, pure aesthetic root not only overlooks the increased urbanization of American Negroes (and the resulting hybrid forms of cultural production) but also conveniently "hushes over" the fact that Negro folklore is itself the product of "abnormal, alien," and crossbred conditions.[83]

When McKay writes that "of all Negro literature the only literature which merits any attention is that which has the character of national propaganda" (*NA*, 73), he implies that the national Negro "character" must be seen as itself "alien"—that is, shipped in from international shores, but at the same time capable of asserting one's entitlement to specific rights within a given national space. The national Negro character thus relies on a constant influx of the new, a turning and twisting of the constantly adapting original. Through the character of Nathalia, McKay suggests that this kind of adaptation extends the Negro question quite forcibly to the woman one. Although Nathalia is described as "languid and coquettish," standing "out sharply from the expansive and self-assured women of the Northern states," Nathalia's developing sense of herself as diverging from her father's ideal is alluded to several times (*TBL* 9). For instance, "Nathalia looked upon Northerners with unfeigned delight. She liked their enterprising spirit and their great commercial abilities. She admired the freedom of her Northern sisters and their bold candor in relations with men" (*TBL* 11). As a figure of accommodation and resistance, Nathalia stands for the potential of this kind of permeation, and Cord for the crisis of patriarchy that engendered a Western preoccupation with a nationalist, segregationist, "white" consciousness.

The mutual contingencies of the Negro and woman questions were quite vivid according to McKay. The story's elaboration of their connectedness may have been due in some part to McKay's awareness of the continued antagonism displayed by U.S. Communists toward Negroes. McKay writes,

> comrades, in fear of the American bourgeois taboo, are unwilling to meet the black comrades as social equals. At a *Liberator* magazine dance given last winter, the manager, a white member of the CP, reported to me that radicals who had bought tickets refused to enter because there was mixed dancing on the floor. (RTSKhIDNI, 495–155–43, 157)

McKay's example of American comrades' fear of attending a racially mixed dance provides revealing evidence not only of racism in the Party but of the ways in which political and social "mixing" across racial lines were intimately related. Just as the fear of mingling at a dance suggests an underlying anxiety about miscegenation, the undoing of the purity of whiteness, so too did the fear of "racial uprising" and unwillingness to work among black Americans speak to the anxiety about maintaining white supremacy across the political spectrum. U.S. leadership in Party resolutions on the Negro question, McKay indicates, would only reinforce the social taboo of interracialism, the boundaries separating white and black world comrades.[84]

To elaborate on the costs to an imagined multiracial internationale that the perpetuation of such taboos would effect, McKay depicts the struggle over Negro self-determination as intimately related to that over female self-determination. The struggle over Nathalia's status as an object focuses on the figuration of her hands—both as a metaphor for her maidenhood and site of her own labor. When a suitor who works as manager for her father's store pays a visit to Nathalia, she "met him kindly and sometimes condescended so far as to even play on the piano for him" (*TBL*, 16). This display of nonproductive labor, of her hands literally at play, encourages the manager, Jones, to imagine Nathalia as a future reflection of his potential surplus.[85] "And the deluded Jones already saw himself, in the not-too-distant future, as the partner of his patron and a claimant to Nathalia's hand" (*TBL*, 16). Exemplifying a conventional exchange of women—as a commodity represented by the idleness and objectification of her hand—between men so as to solidify their bonds as "partners," this scene also elaborates Jones's delusion in imagining such an exchange.[86] When Cord returns that evening from his ride, Nathalia has already "let the servant go home. Her mother had taught her to cook; she was proud of this, and always prepared easy dishes with her own hands for her father and his close friends. When he had returned, Nathalia set the table and put it in the corner of the room; then she closed the piano" (*TBL*, 17).

The status of Nathalia's hands as stand-ins for her selfhood has clearly shifted. Refusing the position of woman-as-surplus proffered her by Jones, she takes pride in her ability to make use of her hands to cook, to be useful conduits of labor. The fact that she let the servant go home indicates that she is aware of this usefulness and revels in her ability to serve as a stand-in for the laborer. "Do you want some coffee, Papa?" she asks, "I let Bella go and made the coffee myself" (17). It is important that Nathalia was taught by her mother to cook, for as Cord enjoys his coffee, he reminds her of her mother's shortcomings: "Your mother was a splendid woman, but a passion for politics was also her weakness. She could've become a senator if she'd been a man. But I don't know what you've taken into your head to imitate her" (19). In fact, Nathalia has disturbed her father because she has begun to "imitate" her mother too fully.

What one learns from this juxtaposition of Nathalia's resourceful deployment of her own use value and her insidious naïveté about her racial privilege is that both are connected. Nathalia's awakening is only partially shaped, and indeed her coming into her own as a woman relies on a certain blindness to the privileged status of that womanhood as white. Obviously, the fact that she was able to "let Bella go" reflects her ability to do so because she is in a position of power over her black servant. That she cannot simply stand-in for Bella suggests that McKay was attempting to deconstruct the category of "woman" in conjunction with that of "Negro."

Cord's attachment to Nathalia's position marks this differentiation between Nathalia and Bella all the more forcibly. He complains that "if you had lived in the North it would have been very harmful for you, and could've spoiled you completely. Perhaps, I say, that's the most important reason I want you to marry young Taylor and stay in the South" (20). Resonant of Cord's earlier fear about the "limits" of black impudence, Cord's desires here link his daughter as property to the rest of his material assets. Cord wants both to remain lodged within impermeable boundaries in a safe house of southern whiteness. Any penetration of these boundaries, any mobility across them, threatens to spoil the contents, and likewise, the offspring of the contents, Cord's legacy.

To emphasize that at stake in his daughter's future is for Cord the identity of national citizenship, McKay manipulates the gendered figurations of a visual dichotomy between black and white in the two scenes that close the book. While Cord and Nathalia have been enjoying their meal, another feast of sorts has been proceeding. Nathalia notices a "burning" smell and hears shots—"they are lynching someone," Cord admits, "none of us can say what will happen when Negroes begin to get out of hand" (18). Of course, Cord's words are stunningly duplicitous. Cord knows exactly what will happen when "Negroes begin to get out of hand"—his statements from the outset of the story have made this clear. Cord's willingness to play by the "unspoken" ("none of us can say") law of lynching is not, however, a reflection of lynching's unspeakability. In fact, Cord has come right out and condoned lynching as a "necessity": "They can spoil the Negroes as much as they please among themselves in the North, but we will stick to a different policy in the South" (19). Cord seeks to retain his sense of gentility by projecting the crime onto others. The "they" that are "settling accounts" with Abe Mitchell [a black man who has asserted his rights] doesn't include himself, although he is a primary "we" who negotiates the policy of the South. Cord's protestations are again revealed to be duplicitous, though.

In her pioneering work on the topic, Robyn Wiegman explains the symbolic and specular anatomies of lynching. She writes that "the myth of the black male rapist serves to compensate for this economic loss, transferring the focus from the white man's quasi-sanctioned (because economically productive) sexual activities to the bodies, quite literally, of black men. Located there, within the 'logic' of an excessive hypermasculinization, the black male's claims to citizenship—voting rights, employment, and more abstract privileges of the patronymic—are violently denied." Wiegman sheds light on the white patriarchal investments in the lynching scene, to "recognize the symbolic force of the white mob's activity as a denial of the black male's newly articulated right to citizenship. . . . In the lynch scenario, the stereotypical fascination and abhorrence for blackness is literalized as a competition for masculinity and seminal power."[87] Cord's eagerness to participate in this competition is fully elaborated. When Dr. Taylor arrives to relay the evening's activities, Cord can barely contain himself: "And how did Mitchell conduct himself? Did he squeal like a fat, black pig that is being slaughtered, or howl like a mongrel that has been beaten with a stick?" (*TBL*, 20). As a pioneering member of the region's KKK, Cord's enthusiasm threatens to eviscerate any distinction between "they"—the mob—and "we"—the policymakers. Cord's ravenous appetite for detail also reveals a voyeuristic pleasure that simmers with the sexual ante at stake in the grotesquely violent scene. "He even took a long stake with him to poke the nigger in the crotch until he lost consciousness" (20), Taylor confides to Cord.

The excess of visual detail here echoes the excessive nature of torture to which Cord's cohorts subjected Mitchell. This indulgence provides a rhetorical signal that Cord's pleasure in prurience owes its origin to a systematizing structure of subjectivity that denies blacks selfhood. This denial relies on a visual economy of white male potency that buttresses the emasculation of Mitchell through castration, hanging, and torturous death. The capes that hide the individual identities of the white knights provide a cover of disembodied citizenship. Against this specter, the black man is forced to anatomize all that citizenship is not. McKay's point, which he talks about in *Negroes in America*, adheres in a morbid fascination of whites with lynching and castration. The use of sex as a "smokescreen" for crimes of "class inequality, lynching, and exploitation of labor" has created a "Negro neurosis" that has acquired the qualities and "force of an instinct" (*NA, 82*) that makes use of the "sexual taboo" as a "form of black magic splendidly serving the aims of the master class" (*NA, 79*).[88] "Trial by Lynching" displays before the reader an emasculation of the black victim that denies citizenship by removing the penis, which returns as phallus to the white men as a sign of entitlement. As Wiegman explains, "Not only does lynching enact a grotesquely symbolic, if not literal, sexual encounter between the white mob and its victim, but the increasing use of castration as a preferred form of mutilation for African-American men demonstrates lynching's connection to the socio-symbolic realm of sexual difference."[89]

Anticipating Wiegman's linking of the gendering of blackness with the gendering of whiteness, McKay's story is not only concerned with exposing the visual economy of whiteness that forces blackness to embody disentitlement. It is also concerned with exposing the links of this spectacle to the image of white femininity. In this regard, the story again specifies McKay's contention that "the Negro question is inseparably connected with the question of woman's liberation" (*NA, 77*), that the bourgeoisie has successfully manipulated cultural anxiety over miscegenation to "artificially maintain a war between the sexes over race" (76). McKay relates the white patriarchal fear of an infiltration of the privileges of their status quo to the permutations of this fear as they get played out across the social field. As William Maxwell observes, "Black men and white women were fettered together in the manifest sexual content of the latent attack on Emancipation."[90] Similarly, "Trial by Lynching" emphasizes the link between the two productions of feminization, but it also explores the deep disparities between them. If as Michael Rogin claims, counterpoising the two hides a fear of black male and white female union, then critical attention ought to be paid to the counterpositioning of black men and white women in terms of their mutual correlation in the visual economy of whiteness, as outlined by McKay.[91] When the lurid description has finished, Nathalia utters a "half-suppressed 'Oh.' She changed her pose, and her face grew red. Her father was visibly embarrassed" (*TBL*, 21). Like his daughter, Cord is embarrassed not at the inhumanity of the mob but at his own arousal. Their mutual arousal over the figure of the lynched black male body occupies the story's last paragraphs.

Nathalia's little "oh" and the blush of her cheeks signal how the white patriarchal scripting of the black male body as a visible terrain is connected to her own self-speculation. In figuring this connection, McKay provides an antecedent to critiques of white feminism as racially biased and delineates how the economy of the visible though disenfranchised body does not simply privilege white patriarchy. Having become disarmingly hot and bothered, Nathalia speaks "excitedly" after reprobating Taylor for his involvement in the lynching. Interestingly, the line between "they" and "we" in defining proper citizenship, who should belong and to which group one should belong, seems to be the issue for Nathalia as well: "I'll never marry a man who has taken part in a lynching. . . . The aristocrats of the South shouldn't humiliate themselves by participating in such dirt" (21). Nathalia finds lynching distasteful not because of its inhumanity but because of its relation to the abject. Lynching is a commoner's activity beneath her sense of refinement, simply repugnant, but not unnatural or unethical. In feeling superior to those who lynch, Nathalia overlooks the fact that she relies on lynching because its law is also the law that enables her to trade in her value as value. Without trial by lynching, the value of white femininity would be undone. Her dismissal of Taylor as likewise an unsuitable suitor allows her to move on to other prospects, and the fact that she has taken offense enables her to take even greater pleasure in her own image. "She didn't go to bed immediately, she sat for a long time in the white, comfortable chair with the soft cushions. Then she got up, having thrown a glance at herself in the large wall mirror built into the wardrobe. She opened the door of the wardrobe slightly in order to see the contours of her back, curved and soft, and her luxuriant, silky shoulder length hair. She was thinking about her trip to the North, to Philadelphia and New York" (22).

What one learns from Nathalia's immediate transformation from breathless "horror" to self-adoration in a mirror is that to undo the logic of mutilated black male body would undo the economy on which she depends for her value. In this sense, Nathalia is not simply a victim of southern patriarchy but a beneficiary of it. The depth of detail offered here, of Nathalia's "contours," "curved and soft, and her luxuriant, silky shoulder length hair," is directly correlated to the depth of detail used to portray the lynching of Mitchell. The two scenes stand out—unmatched by others in their reciprocal content.[92] This affinity suggests much more than coincidental rhetorical affiliation or parallelism. The pleasure that Nathalia takes in hearing about a lynching suffuses the delight she takes in her own image. Her scopic investment in the lynching scene is, to borrow from Laura Mulvey, a precondition of her "to be looked at-ness." This is an image that moves from the embrace of a "white, comfortable chair" to her wardrobe— the repository of her riches—to the Northern city. This closet holds the outfits with which she will festoon her body so as to bolster her value, and thus it serves as a mirror to her "natural" endowments—hair, skin, back, and so on. Nathalia sets in motion her exchange, from the "white comfort" of her father's house to the Northern reaches of Michael Sanovich. Nathalia comes to life in this exchange at the same time that she is reduced to a sign of her value, which is the content of her self, her sexuality. On the other hand, Nathalia's enraptured self-attention also implies female awareness of the constructed hetero-normative routes through which she must travel in order to "claim" and/or activate her value.

> She smiled to herself in the mirror. Yes, she would go and live in the North; and for the pleasure she had given her father, she would receive from him a fairly large sum of money for expenses. She already imagined herself to be the most beautiful, the most cheerful, the most brilliant of the Southern trio in New York. . . . They would compete for first place with the Northern beauties. . . . Then she again threw a look at herself in the mirror and her thoughts returned to Michael Sanovich. (*TBL*, 23)

In her many self-affirming glances into the mirror, Nathalia sees an image of her marketable self. In maintaining fidelity to this image of social wealth, Nathalia believes she can own that image, can maintain a possessive relationship to her own sexuality by placing herself in circulation as both an available and rare Southern beauty. This story is thus not only one about the inescapability of the market for women but also about Nathalia's desire to participate in it. The moment that expresses her repulsion for the practice of lynching also shows her complete involvement in and reliance on it. Her refusal to marry Taylor is actually a reflection of her instrumentality to the system of white supremacy. Nathalia's sexual value, as McKay shows, is not only dependent on her exchange, the transfer of her value from Cord to Sanovich, but also always dependent on the actual and imagined denigration—the "kick in the groin"—of black masculinity. McKay's story outlines the differential yet related disenfranchisements of white women and black men in U.S. white supremacy. Her ability to speculate on herself is enabled by the disenfranchisement of blacks. This is what she doesn't see in her mirror.

McKay's story challenges the Russian myth of American success and mobility in the market. The question that remains is whether Nathalia, for all her faults, nonetheless really has the option of "self-speculation," if not self-ownership. Or is she, like her sisters in the North, so deluded to think that putting herself in circulation is a form of autonomy, of self-assertion so very different from the enterprising acts of a Mr. Cord? Nathalia believes that by marrying a Jew she can escape her father's logic. But are her dreams of Sanovich just relacing one patriarch's aspirations with another's? When Nathalia firmly shuts the piano on Jones, she tries to signal the end of her status as a mere reflection of property, but by the story's conclusion, she cannot escape consuming herself with this exact reflection. The fact that Sanovich is Jewish and lives in a city in the North suggests that McKay may have been rejecting the idea of the "folk" mythos of proletarian fiction. McKay may have been reminding his readers that the "exotic flower" of Negro culture emanated from "abnormal" conditions; that for him, the future of "American civilization" lay in interethnic couplings and the industrial messiness of the urban metropole. The story presents a message about women's role in this reconfiguration as dependent on a movement from "to be looked at-ness" to agency, but is finally unclear if white women can escape—or want to escape—the scopic regime underwritten by the market in which their power is constituted.

If this final exchange between men performed by Nathalia's "turn" in her thoughts from Daddy to Sanovich is racially coded by the necessary but absent black male body, an even more eviscerated figure is that of black femininity, which is the subject of McKay's next story. However undeveloped *Negroes in America*'s theorization of the ways collaboration between white women and black men occluded "the corporeal violence attending black women," *Trial by Lynching* answers this oversight by centering its three stories around the tale of "The Mulatto Girl."[93] "The Mulatto Girl" opens with a very different "look" than the narcissistic gaze of Nathalia at her own reflection. "The landlady looked intently—almost maliciously—at my comrade when she opened the door."[94] Whereas in the previous story the reader has been occupied by a white woman's glance at herself, in this story one is greeted by the stern gaze of a propertied black woman who looks with apprehension at a white male interloper, the "comrade." If the scene seems to have shifted, McKay lets the reader know that it indeed has: "We were in the center of the Black Belt; the very lively and busy point in Harlem where the majority of New York's Negroes live" (27). As "Mulatto" makes clear in designating Harlem as "the Black Belt," the multiple locations of racially segregated zones distends the expected designation, the seamless continuity between the U.S. South and the major habitus of black Americans. This disruption seems strategically poised to confuse Russian readers who would assume that race was primarily a regional issue. And in subverting the expected geography of the black belt, this story also departs from the idea that the U.S. South could be imagined as an autonomous black region.

But in moving from Middelsville to Harlem, a thread of critique of white supremacy and white male selfhood as mediated by property is maintained. This time, the pincers of critique are lodged not in the backbone of southern gentility but in the heart of the offspring of progressive, reconstructed whites. "My parents didn't subscribe at all to the opinion, wide-spread in the South, that every Negro girl is a slut," says the protagonist Gustaf (29). Elevating himself above those around him who disparage blacks, Gustaf, aka the "comrade," fancies himself quite advanced in race relations. To prove his reconstructed attitude toward race, Gustaf relates to his black friend the story of a young black woman he knew in college. "The Mulatto Girl," as indicated by its title, tells the tale of a young light-skinned black woman, Mathilda, as recalled by Gustaf.

What makes this story remarkable is not the fact that it replays stock stereotypes about white male youth as voraciously interested in black women—"if any student didn't have a 'niggergal,' then we looked upon him as eccentric" (29)—nor that it hints at the "eccentricity" of those who refuse to play the hetero-normative game of white male/black female interracial coupling. Rather, it is the figuration of Mathilda in respect to Nathalia that is remarkable—both are positioned as conduits of exchange to solidify bonds between men. Together, the stories outline the juxta-posed participation of each in a system of sexual valuation. "And young Coleman [the son of a rich Texas cattle dealer] was very proud of his abso-lute, unimpeded possession of Mathilda. She knew unerringly how to deck herself out beautifully in the dresses which he gave her" (30). Like Na-thalia, Mathilda is an expert in self-speculation, emphasizing her "beauti-fully built" body with clothes purchased by the interest of a primary male. But unlike Nathalia, Mathilda is circumscribed as a black woman within the confines of white female speculation. Mathilda's arguably "tragic" end arrives when "somehow rumors began to spread that half a dozen students had to go to the hospital, and that Mathilda was the cause of it. It was not known where these rumors came from; many thought that they were the work of the white ladies" (30). Although Gustaf describes this denigration as "a sacrifice to the morality of the whites of the town" (30) it is possible to see this as a key point of distinction between white and black femi-ninities. Mathilda's self-speculation is not possible in the same way as Nathalia's because the speculation of white femininity not only takes pre-cedence, it has superior value. "Very soon after that rumors about Ma-thilda began to circulate" (31). It is not actually Mathilda's sexual pro-fligacy but the propagation of rumors about her that circulate among white men and women. She is "born" through exchange as rumor, as language. If following Nancy Armstrong's lead, the female body is thought of as a grammar of subjectivity capable of regulating desire, pleasure, conduct, and so forth, then it becomes clear how Mathilda is forced to abandon her material body as female at the same time that its materiality could not be stronger in evidence as black.[95] In this sense, words constitute a material form of power, to be sure, but one that is racially scripted and endowed. It is not Mathilda but the rumors that are contagious.

Predictably Coleman, whose first name is Dick, loses interest in Ma-thilda. Her denigration threatens his sense of self because others' percep-tions of her no longer validate Mathilda as a desirable object, a worthy reflection of his, Dick's, manhood. Coleman strikes her, saying, "That'll teach you, negress, not to forget your place" (MG, 31). Gustaf, driven by outrage to hit Coleman in Mathilda's defense, recalls that "this episode had a greater effect on me than a lynching" (32). This is a curious state-ment, evoking McKay's own declaration before the Fourth Comintern Congress that he would rather speak "in front of a lynch mob" than before their "respected gathering." The comparison of the confrontation between Gustaf and Coleman to a lynching suggests that one scene's depiction of triangulated desire mirrors the other. The lynching's evisceration of the black male body is connected to the spectacle of violence against black femininity. The story, then, seems to be concerned primarily with forefronting that violence—literal and systemic—that reduces black femininity to a sign of its own negativity. Its placement as the centerpiece of a collection titled *Trial by Lynching* implies that McKay was attempting to reclaim the denigrated space of black femininity often occluded in conventional accounts of the lynching scenario and certainly overlooked by Soviet theorization on the woman question. For Soviet readers, the lesson would therefore inhere not simply in the disruption of a presumed North/South boundary but the conviction that the ideology of "knowing one's place" could not be effectively countered through self-determination in a black belt without taking into consideration the differential effects of how such dogma effected women and men.

The concluding story of *Trial by Lynching*, "The Soldier's Return," narrates the return home to Georgia of Negro soldiers following World War I. Describing the situation of raised racial consciousness caused by participation in the war, this story shows how such consciousness was perceived as "uppityness" and subsequently suppressed by attempting to strip black soldiers of their sense of experience. This story is linked to the others through the specter of lynching, and like the other stories, it asks the reader to see the hypocrisies of the color line and the disciplinary practices of racial control embodied in lynching. For example, through a rumor that stymies the protagonist, Frederick's, movements, the reader witnesses a return of female speculation and its ability to reduce black masculinity to a negative sign of blackness. "Among the white population of Great Neck the refusal of Frederick, the octoroon soldier, produced lively rumors"[96] (38). Frederick is punished for wearing his uniform and driving a buggy—for not wearing "work clothes" and exhibiting signs of leisure. The response to Frederick's refusal to assume the expected visual markers of his race and class reveals the anxiety surrounding unconventional displays of the ambiguously racial body: "We will take the uniform of a soldier of the U.S. off you and give you an outfit which is more appropriate for you" (41). The townspeople rely on constant visible markers to establish difference. And the danger presented by Frederick is not only that he looks white but that he wears clothing that signify whiteness. "There is still plenty of work for niggers in Great Neck. We won't put up with even one of them loafing without work and putting on airs, even if he was in France, and they treated him there just like a white man" (41). In returning to the confines of his home, Frederick must also be returned to home-coded visual signifiers of blackness. The story suggests that race inheres not only in skin color but cultural accoutrement; that anxiety results when blacks don't look black. As evidenced by the reception of Huiswood in Moscow, the connection between skin color and racial identity was a topic with which McKay was unduly engaged while in Russia. His deployment of it in "The Soldier's Return" may have been meant as a warning to the Soviet's own dogged belief in a purported visible difference from Negroes.

In "The Soldier's Return," the notion of white purity becomes explicitly linked to anti-internationalism. It is assumed that Frederick must be punished for thinking that French custom might penetrate the United States. Race is presented as a domestic problem; lingering affiliations between blacks, and between blacks and whites, left over from the experience of war are to be not merely contained but eviscerated. "The Soldier's Return" extends the ideas of anti-interracialism to anti-internationalism, an idea more fully elaborated in *Negroes in America*.

For McKay, as he asserts in *Negroes in America*, the opportunity of Soviet internationalism lay in its ability to foster connections across the parameters of nationhood and create productive alliances among those similarly excluded by the conventional bounds of national identity. Identifying links between the experiences of slavery, Jim Crow, and colonialism, McKay describes a black internationalism that not only accommodates but is the logical answer to the "drawing together," as a result of the systemic connections between black-skinned peoples, of Negroes from various backgrounds (*NA*, 51). As McKay writes, "For the Negro in America it is very useful to be imbued with race consciousness, but it is still more useful for him to look at the problem which disturbs him from a class point of view and to join the class struggle as an 'internationalist'" (*NA*, 4). Like the Soviet policy outlined in the theses, McKay articulates a black revolutionary consciousness as by definition international, and allows for the coming about of such consciousness through an awareness of the nation-oriented exclusions of blacks from full citizenship.

In portraying the international as the utopic contact zone for world blacks, McKay remained aware of the challenges of such cross-national mixing. In describing the American reaction to the French attitude toward Negroes, and in turn the "favorable disposition" of American Negroes toward France, he directly joins a fear of internationalism to a fear of racial hybridity: "English and American writers wittily mock the fact that in the end the French will become a hybrid [*pomes'*] race. But the American Negro is not worried about such an outcome at all. This is for him a practical step toward internationalism" (52).[97] Pinpointing hybridity as a "practical step" on the path toward internationalism, McKay outlines the anxieties at root in the American resistance to black revolutionary consciousness. According to McKay, cross-pollinization, the twining of racial and sexual suffrages, exists at the root of black internationalism. Such interracialism is likewise directly related to attempts to read McKay in the present, to reassert the polyglot linguistic interracialism to which his archive directs one. As McKay himself instructs, such hybridities challenge the notion of a "pure" source through which black internationalism should appear. If Russia provided the opportunity, a model for hybrid consciousness, what was it about McKay's Russia that enabled this to be the case?

A DIFFERENT SHADE OF WHITE

In his introduction to *Trial by Lynching,* the editor A. M. McCleod comments that McKay made "no mention of these stories in his correspondence," nor in his autobiography; that McKay eschewed the theme of *Trial by Lynching* in the work he published in the United States. He writes that this "lets us know something of his understanding of 'audience.' "[98] But what is it about McKay's understanding of his audience that this assertion reveals? To be sure, the stories fulfilled crude Marxist expectations about the evils of capitalism, but they also established bourgeois *whiteness* as a capital-derived problem related to the emancipation of women. The Soviets turned a deaf ear to these analyses, which tended toward an exposure of their own investments in patriarchy and, relatedly, white chauvinism. McKay's ability to shed light on social inequities was a reason Soviets warmed to him, yet it was also a reason they ignored key parts of his theorizations.

Some of McKay's observations about the connections between anti-internationalism and racism, then, may seem paradoxical. For example, his remarks about the French treatment of African nationals pose suggestive questions about the Russians' own investments in racial superiority, the looming specter of anti-internationalism that accompanies the rampant inattention to white chauvinism in the CP. McKay's own warnings about American Negroes liking France so much that "they are beginning to forget about the vile exploitation of Africans by the French," serves as a heady reminder of the Russians' preferential treatment of black Americans simultaneous to their own tense racial relations along their eastern and southern peripheries, to the long-standing "Jewish question," the history of Jewish pogroms, and related racial tensions within Russia proper (*NA*, 50). The stories are a counter to the then-prevailing assumption of a uniform Negro category. They are attempts to teach Soviets to see blacks in the United States not as Africans but as products of unfounded theories of racial differentiation. However unrealistic the aim, McKay's work from this period indicates that he did not believe Russians could be seamlessly inserted into the position of European.

In his 1923 essay "Soviet Russia and the Negro," McKay offers a framework for the way in which he understood Russia to bear a different shade of white from that of the Western European powers. This essay makes a distinction between whitenesses by differentiating between the reception he received from Russians, which he describes as curiosity "in a friendly, refreshing manner," and that which he found in England and Germany. He writes, "To the Russians, I was merely another type, but stranger, with which they were not yet familiar. . . . [T]heir curiosity had none of the intolerable impertinence and often downright affront that any very dark colored man, be he Negro, Indian or Arab, would experience in Germany or England."[99] The positive sense of his Russian experience was not only about racial categorization per se but intimately connected to McKay's belief that this acceptance had everything to do with his acceptance as a human. Russia not only offered an alternate route to internationalism, it offered an alternate route to imagining black subjectivity as well:

> The English people from the lowest to the highest, cannot think of a black man as being anything but an entertainer, a boxer, a Baptist preacher or a menial. The Germans are just a little worse. Any healthy looking black coon of an adventurous streak can have a wonderful time

palming himself off as another Siki or a buck dancer. When an American writer introduced me as a poet to a very cultured German, a lover of all the arts, he could not believe it, and I don't think he does yet. An American student tells his middle-class landlady that he is having a black friend to lunch: "But are you sure that he is not a cannibal?" she asks, without a flicker of a humorous smile! But in Petrograd and Moscow, I could not detect a trace of this ignorant snobbishness among the educated classes, and the attitude of the common workers, the soldiers and sailors was still more remarkable. It was so beautifully naive; for them I was only a black member of the world of humanity.[100]

McKay's articulation of a different experience of whiteness in Russia forefronts the distinction between the primitivizing tendencies of Western Europeans and universalizing ones of Soviets. This sense of himself as a member of a "world of humanity" enabled a new sense of self, an alternate racial consciousness, at once grounded and transnational, to emerge. It has been argued that the experiences of Europe by numerous African American writers and artists caused these figures to shift their "perceptions of America and racial domination."[101] Although Russia has remained tellingly absent from such formulations, it is clear that McKay's experience there not only shifted his perception but fundamentally reorganized it. McKay's belief that Russians saw him through a naive lens as a type "with which they were not familiar" provided him with a liberating and refreshing experience of his own selfhood. He describes this as dizzying, for it brought about a "loss of self-consciousness with the realization that I was welcomed thus as a symbol, as a member of the great American Negro group—kin to the unhappy black slaves of European imperialism in Africa—that the workers of Soviet Russia, rejoicing in their freedom, were greeting through me."[102] McKay's "loss of self-consciousness" facilitated a gain of collective consciousness, an awareness of himself as a symbolic representative, a transitional subject who stood for both the "great American Negro group" and "unhappy black slaves of European imperialism in Africa."

Russia provided McKay with a space within which he could reconfigure the very term Negro, to imply both a national orientation and foundational transnational mobility. That McKay represented a link to Africa for the Russians suggests that the Negro could be interpreted as a kind of transnational social position based both in national delineations and an international mobility. The loss of self-consciousness McKay notes indicates in its place a sense of commonality of those similarly disenfranchised—a simultaneous opening of the national and international that was itself the promise of Soviet internationalism. McKay writes, "Although an international Socialist . . . I believe that, for subject peoples, at least, Nationalism is the open door to Communism."[103] McKay articulated his experience of Russia as one in which a body could be linked to others not through the attainment of a higher *self*-consciousness, the "better and truer self" as mapped through culture or race, but through a collective sense of selfhood brought about by awareness of the disenfranchisement rehearsed on a daily basis against those similarly constituted as "subject" bodies. At the same time, McKay's own attentiveness to the collaborations between racial and sexual differentiation would seem to propose asymmetrical relationships to the body, and lead one to ask whether (or not) gender troubles the delineations of such subjects. Perhaps McKay's assessment of the potential of Bolshevik internationalism resonated with the nineteenth-century Russian maxim of "unity in multiplicity," but McKay's unique interpretation of this position put it at a remove from Russocentric ideologies of the nineteenth and twentieth centuries. In his stories for the Russian public, McKay tried to evince some of the awkwardness of male representativeness, traducing his readers in their attempts to glide over the specifics of gender differentiation, to follow the Soviet subordination of women's issues to those of class.

But, in having found such an affirming sense of subjectivity in Russia, he was quick to connect his sense of ease among Soviets with white American anxiety. Mocking the U.S. fear of mixing between Russians and blacks, McKay wrote that the Russians' "interracial understanding" and "demonstration of friendliness and equality for Negroes may not conduce to promote healthy relations between Soviet Russia and democratic America. . . . [T]he anthropologists of 100 per cent pure white Americanism may soon invoke Science to prove that the Russians are not at all God's white people."[104] Reiterating the point of Soviets' illegitimate whiteness in his memoir, he introduced an Englishwoman (formerly a governess under the old regime) with whom he was clearly enamored and who told him that she kept British souvenirs stashed about her house because "when Russians don't understand, they will ask. I have to have these English hints around to remind me that we are a superior people" (*ALWFH*, 218). The constellation of whiteness around which power converged continued to marginalize the Russian as non-European. And the Soviet positioning of itself as the potential synthesizing link between East and West contributed to this placement of Russians as other to the West. Although this sensed affinity may have provided the building blocks for McKay's attraction to Russia and vice versa, it was an affinity that was less productive than McKay may have hoped. Although his Russian work sought to reassert the necessity of rethinking women's relationship to the nation in the movement toward global socialism, it was a message that fell, and has continued for the most part to fall, on deaf ears.

PARTIAL CLOSINGS

McKay eventually parlayed his experiences in Russia into the bedrock of what was to become a reactionary political stance. *A Long Way from Home* became the well-known record of his renunciation of communism and the Soviet Union. But even though he changed his mind about the particular meaning of the "Negro" in Negro art, McKay's experience of the Soviet Union enabled the articulation of specific kinds of racial and revolutionary consciousness that typified his writing during the early 1920s. This consciousness reflects a pattern of black internationalism—that is, a simultaneous awareness of the specific racial injustices imparted to McKay as a black man residing in the United States as well as the general, systemic links between his own experiences of racism and those of others (from a wide variety of social and national backgrounds, and including women) excluded by the limited bounds of national identity. Later, in *A Long Way from Home,* McKay described his experience of Russia as cementing his desire to be a great artist, a spokesperson for his people. This desire proved inconsistent with McKay's earlier expression of an antiethnocentric, antiimperialist internationalism. Whereas the Negro in *Negroes in America* and *Trial by Lynching* queried censure of miscegenation, in the memoir the Negro became the repository of a fundamental blackness rooted in Africa.[105] In his later years, aspiring to be a representative black author, McKay of necessity confronted the difficulty of trying to distill from his art a specifically Negro racial essence. Eschewing the systemic production of Negroness he had so well perceived fifteen years earlier on the political front, and all but severing it from the woman question, McKay sought out depth of feeling as the realm where Negroness could best be apprehended in art. This very tactic, while liberating to be sure, was also one shaped by Western patterns of racialization, of viewing blacks as closer to feelings than thought, as more linked to emotion than rationalism, and of linking all black persons to Africa. In short, McKay's very renunciation of internationalism in the name of aesthetic interests belied an origin in Western standards of discriminating aesthetic taste that were indissolubly linked to those of political exclusion, the marginalizations of women and nonwhites.

Though it is of course difficult to determine the impact McKay had on the Russian cultural imagination of blackness, there are intriguing moments in Russian cultural production that suggest McKay's importance in Soviet thinking about race.[106] And though tracing the Soviet influence on McKay's work (and vice versa) requires a recuperation of writings by him that exist in approximations, careful reconstruction and analysis can reveal these routes of influence. What is certain is that the cultural intermixings that gave birth to McKay's theories and his stories produced the hybrid social spaces through which subsequent black American visitors to the USSR would create their own similarly conceived social offspring. Thus, in spite of McKay's eventual renunciation of the Soviet Union, the importance of investigating the interactions between McKay and the Soviets during the period of the Third International cannot be overlooked. Not only did McKay's visit establish a pattern, a prism through which one can better understand the Soviets' reactions to figures such as Robeson, Hughes, and Du Bois, it also gave shape to a tradition of black internationalism in which the Soviet Union was a key factor and component. Considering how McKay's relationship with the USSR developed from both the Soviet and McKay's perspectives enables one to examine how race operated as a symbolic structure in the formation not only of McKay's agendas but also in those of the Soviets, thereby providing a fuller picture of the transnational genealogies of black internationalism.

CHAPTER TWO

Between Harem and Harlem:

Hughes and the Ways of the Veil

Space may be the projection of the extension of the
psychical apparatus. No other derivation is probable.
—Sigmund Freud, "Findings, Ideas, Problems"

In April 1956, Hughes wrote a letter to his friend Arna Bontemps in which
he described his resumption of work on a manuscript he called "my *No. 2
Life.*" This manuscript, eventually published as *I Wonder as I Wander* in
1956, was a project Hughes had worked on periodically since the 1930s.
Hughes had been deterred from work on the book that included recollections of the year he spent in the Soviet Union, from June 1932 to June
1933—as Bontemps had said in 1939, it was the "poorest possible time to
issue anything on [the Soviet theme] to the American market."[1] Now, in
1956, Hughes wrote to Bontemps that he was pleased with his recent
reworking of the manuscript, satisfied by his editorial ability to "cut out all
the impersonal stuff, down to a running narrative with *me* in the middle
on every page. . . . [T]he kind of intense condensation that, of course,
keeps an autobiography from being entirely true, in that nobody's life is
pure essence without pulp, waste matter, and rind—which art, of course,
throws in the trash can."[2] As Hughes's correspondence of the 1950s makes
evident, there is a portion of the author's work that he excised in response
to perceived pressures to dissociate himself from the USSR. These removed materials include some of the essays he wrote about his time in the
Soviet Union, including drafts of *I Wonder as I Wander*, and a series of
essays on Uzbek women that Hughes published in the early 1930s in maga-

zines such as *Travel* and *Woman's Home Companion*. These excised pieces include the record of Hughes's fascination and identification with Uzbek femininity contained in "In an Emir's Harem," "Farewell to Mahomet," "The Soviet Theater in Central Asia," "Tamara Khanum," and "Boy Dancers of Uzbekistan."[3] His decision to purge these writings from his 1956 memoir can be seen as in part a reflection of the bitterly anticommunist climate of the 1950s in the United States. Hughes chose to rework and publish *I Wonder as I Wander* just three years after he testified before the Senate subcommittee and renounced his previous connections to the Soviet Union. When Roy Cohn asked Hughes if he " 'would say that [his] complete change in ideology came about 1950?' Hughes replied, 'I would say certainly by 1950. Yes.' "[4] Remarking on this testimony, Hughes's biographer, Arnold Rampersad, says, "As in the case of his sexuality, he had allowed the expression of his radical political zeal to wither, to atrophy, to evaporate."[5]

As Rampersad's comments indicate, the political pressures of anti-communism must be seen in tandem with the social pressures of sexual conformity. During this era of frank homophobia, government sponsored "witch hunts" correlated foreign influence with domestic depravity, so-called deviant political impulses with sexual ones.[6] Although Rampersad's linking of desire and politics in Hughes's work from the 1930s is thus an important connection, his terminology and the absences it highlights comment on the inability of scholars to adequately address the linkages between desire and politics in Hughes's work from this period. For instance, Rampersad leaves unexamined the complex dyad of Cohn interrogating Hughes. In spite of his own sexual tendencies (or because of them), Cohn throughout his life maintained a hostile, state-empowered public stance against homosexuality and was, in fact, instrumental in efforts by the government to route out homosexuals from its employ.[7] The year the Senate passed a directive meant to guard against the "Employment of Homosexuals and Other Sex Perverts in the U.S. Government," 1950, may well have served as a coded means for Cohn to harass Hughes into submitting to public realignment of his past proclivities.[8] In his testimony before the Senate subcommittee, Hughes continued his dissociation from previous alliances by averring that "a complete reorientation of my thinking and emotional feelings occurred roughly four or five years ago."[9] This statement not only dates Hughes's "reorientation" to "roughly" the

1950 moment of intense government surveillance of and aggressive antagonism toward homosexuality but also suggests the proximate relationship between the language Hughes used to describe his political and personal allegiances.

Thus, it was less Hughes's will than the unspeakability of Hughes's earlier identifications that likely helped to underwrite Hughes's reorientation of this portion of his memoir. Not only do the discarded writings make manifest Hughes's enthusiasm in the 1930s for the experience of racial equity to which the Soviet experience in Central Asia exposed him, they also provide a means of tracking the instrumentality of feminine identification to this experience. As elaborations of Hughes's substantial engagement with Soviet intervention in the lives of Muslim Central Asian women, the essays stand on their own as important pieces of the Hughes oeuvre that have been overlooked. At the same time, these works provided themes and patterns on which the anthologized work drew liberally, and therefore these writings help one to better understand those works from this period that have been passed down as the official record. Only by reclaiming these rejected portions of Hughes's oeuvre can the fuller picture be grasped of the more familiar Hughes texts that emerged from his trip to Russia. "Cora Unashamed," "Slave on the Block," and "Poor Little Black Fellow" were composed while Hughes was in Moscow in 1933, just following his return from several months of study and travel in Central Asia. First published individually and later included in the collection *The Ways of White Folks*, the stories written in Moscow draw on a vocabulary of unveiling and boundary crossing with which Hughes's Uzbek essays are imbued. Although women play key roles in the positing of racial transfiguration in *The Ways of White Folks*, Hughes's use of the feminine in the stories has not been linked to the fascination with the women of Soviet Central Asia that his essays display. Read together Hughes's prose pieces, unlike his poetry from this period (which as James Smethurst has eloquently argued, follows a more conventional occlusion of femininity from a redemptive rhetoric of black masculinity), enable one to read nuanced and subtle portraits wherein the zeal of Hughes's political longings work in tandem with the arc of desire that accompanied them.[10]

Dismayed by the persistence of race-based injustices in the United States, especially in the southern states, in the 1930s, Hughes had turned to the Soviet south as an example of the new Russia's efforts to formulate a society free not only of class hierarchies but racial ones as well. Traveling through the republics of what had recently been a predominantly Muslim region colonized by Russia, Hughes was particularly impressed by what he perceived as Soviet advances over the socially mandated inequities of Islam and Russian colonialism. As early as the 1920s, Soviet Russia's ideological alliance with decolonization movements—concretized in the 1924–1945 transformation of the racially segregated Russian protectorates of Bukhara, Khiva, and Kokand into the racially integrated Central Asian republics of Uzbekistan, Kazakhstan, Turkmenistan, Tadjikistan, and Kirgizistan—appealed to those, like Hughes, who supported global liberation.[11] In his essays he demonstrates a preoccupation with the Soviet program of compulsory unveiling as symbolic of these advances. Because Hughes's essays correlate the gender segregation of the harem with the racial segregation of a czarist colonial practice, they offer parallels between the dismantling of the harem—encapsulated for Hughes in the abolishment of the veil—with that of the color line. Thus he came to associate the specific practice of female unveiling with racial emancipation in general. For Hughes, unveiling became the representative means of establishing the extent to which the new Soviet freedom contrasted with the inequities of the color line back in the United States.

Galvanized by the project of unveiling, Hughes's interest in the Soviet project extended some of the ideas of black internationalism pursued in the previous chapter into the juncture between culture and interiority. By the 1930s, Hughes was persuaded that some sort of socialism promised relief for the masses and latched onto the cultural work of communism as a means of combating the material inequities of racism in the United States. His interest in mapping both the psychic manifestations of racism and potential for new modes of consciousness drew him to use the unveiling of Uzbek women as a model. Whereas McKay outlined interest in the boundary-challenging formations of black internationalism, Hughes introduced specific uses of the feminine to these formations—both in concrete terms of actual women and the more ambiguous terms that the "feminine" came to represent for him.

The equation between the Soviet and U.S. Souths was not only enabling for Hughes's renegotiation of the Jim Crow boundaries in which he operated at home, it also offered him a new vocabulary for meditating on an interrelated blurring of normative routings of sexual desire. Since, drawing on the work of Du Bois, he associated Negro consciousness with a "life of the veil," the Soviet program of unveiling seemed to offer an alternate mode of self-consciousness, of selfhood. Unlike the double consciousness thematized by Du Bois, this myth of selfhood established itself by crossing previously proscriptive boundaries among which the separation between "black" and "white," reinforced by compulsory heterosexual desire, remained most trenchant. Rather than relying on recognition as the key to self-consciousness, Hughes rewrote Du Bois's Hegelian-inspired trope through a renegotiation of desire and a nondialectical position of betweenness. His work established a way of being "colored" without being veiled, a way of being unveiled without being "white," and hence a means of rejecting the heterosexual economy of desire on which Du Bois's formulation was based. As such, Hughes's interpretation of Uzbek unveiling took on vastly symbolic proportions—"unveiling" became the act that best represented transgression, the permeability of so-called natural boundaries, of all previously delimiting delineations as a route to a racialized sexual emancipation. Using the figure of the Uzbek woman in this way, Hughes's experience of the Soviet Union in the 1930s enabled an open engagement not only with a new political framework but also with new routes of identification. Repeatedly, it is Hughes's narrative identification with the figures of the Uzbek woman that engages, extends, and complicates his 1930s' political message of racial emancipation.

Hughes elaborates on the stakes of his identification with Uzbek women most fully in an essay that, at first glance, seems not to address women at all. "The Boy Dancers of Uzbekistan" is a piece that was published in *Travel* magazine in 1934, just following Hughes's return from the Soviet Union. It discusses the traditional boy dancers, or *bacha*, of Uzbekistan who performed throughout the land, intermittently selling themselves to rich beys or teahouse proprietors, and making names for themselves through the superiority of their girlish beauty and delicacy of their gestural dances. While the subject matter seems to be confined to the phenomena of a strictly masculine culture, the essay reveals how such subjects can be deceiving. In fact, Hughes's essay provides a layered vocabulary that reveals how he used the Uzbek context to broach the expected gender gap between men and women. Anticipating the potential disapproval his readership might extend to boys who dressed like girls for the entertainment of men, Hughes presents a portrait of the tradition of boy dancers "who danced as women [and] put on wigs and dresses and cultivated the delicate gestures of rhythmic pantomime" that purports to place these cross-gender performances firmly in the past. "All this was yesterday—fifteen years ago, twenty, thirty . . . far back into the past as long as man can remember."[12] Hughes approaches with caution, aware of how the fact of a boy-loving-male culture might strike a U.S. readership, and confides that "none of the younger members of the present theater would talk with me about this particular phase of old native life. . . . [T]hey knew it was something visitors from the West might not approve of, or understand" (BD, 36). And yet, like the non-Western attitude with which his words imply sympathy here, Hughes's prose clearly delights in this age-old tradition of boy dancers "who were known and loved by the men" who lavished public attention on them (ibid.). The widely enforced unspeakability of the old practice is undermined by Hughes's artful depiction of it. "Uzbek dances," he writes in a related essay, "are delicately patterned, graceful body-rhythms, often weaving a subtle story in plastics that the uninitiated would not understand."[13] Drawing on the accepted tradition of boys' feminine-identified dance, Hughes offers a vocabulary for reading his own "delicately patterned" and "subtle" stories, the significance of which might elude those inattentive to detail, those searching for literal or empirical evidence about Hughes's disavowed sexuality. This reading is not an attempt to recuperate a clear-cut definition of Hughes's own sexual orientation, or to identify him as a "gay" writer who produced "gay" texts. Rather, it is important to see how his texts from the 1930s engaged Soviet cultural intervention in Central Asia so as to gesture toward the collaboration of racial, sexual, and national boundaries in the American imagination.[14]

Identifying with the initiated, Hughes's words pose an appeal to the "uninitiated" to pay close attention to the coded messages within his prose. He repeats this disidentification with a "Western" perspective on the dance, commenting that "to Western eyes nothing would have seemed unduly strange—except that the dancers with their long curls, smiling and beckoning with their eyes, were boys, not girls" (BD, 37). Hughes incorporates Western homosocial anxiety into his account, cautioning that "about these dances there was nothing vulgar or uncouth" (36).[15] If one can detect a note of defensiveness in Hughes's tone, it arrives couched within a pursuit of avenues with which to convey the so-called improvement on past Uzbek custom: the practice of female unveiling. In part, Hughes's piece attempts to recuperate its nostalgia for a lost male culture by insisting that Soviet intervention *has* improved on (as his readers would expect) the exclusion of women from the public sphere: "What could have happened to change the customs of a thousand years—to start women pouring out of harems, tearing off their veils? The Revolution!" (BD, 49). Past indulgence has been channeled into "healthier, if less traditional amusements" (49), the posturing of boys "in girlish curls" (36) has succumbed to the public regimenting of female bodies, unveiled for public consumption. The "beautiful traditional movement," "the delicate turnings of the head and wrists" (37), are now performed by women who have abandoned their veils and quite literally stepped into the boys' dancing shoes.

In this sense, Hughes's prose coheres to a standard narrative technique in tales of transvestism in which straying from expectation—Rabelaisian crossings of societal norms—is permitted so long as an established social order is somehow recuperated. As Marjorie Garber elaborates in her work on the topic, "this tendency to erase the third term, to appropriate the cross-dresser 'as' one of the two sexes, is emblematic of a fairly consistent critical desire to look away from the transvestite as transvestite, not to see cross-dressing except as male or female manqué, whether motivated by social, cultural, or aesthetic designs."[16] Inasmuch as Hughes's words may seek to distance his writerly position from that of the typically "Western," his prose also reveals the difficulties of any spontaneous casting off of the social and symbolic condensations of racial and gender identity, particularly across national boundaries. Hughes's writings expose the problematics of attempting to bypass his own indebtedness to Western constructions of identity, presumptions about gender as binary, and notions of cultural "backwardness." At the same time, however, although Hughes commends the outing of women from their harem secludedness, he abstains from endorsing with anything other than halfhearted enthusiasm the corrective treatment assigned boys who purge memories of pantomime and "full of the present" dance the Komsomol. He resists the tendency described by Garber, the "desire to look away from the transvestite," and instead infuses his vision of unveiled Uzbek women with the image of gender-blurring boys.

Hughes walks these lines between readerly expectation and other proclivities by offering connections between the cross-gender performances of the past and the emergence of women into public life in the present. For example, most famous among the new women of Uzbekistan who have defied the veil is Tamara Khanum, the first Uzbek woman to dance publicly, who Hughes introduces as "neither male nor female. . . . [H]ad Gertrude Stein been there, surely a bell would have rung" (TK, 830).[17] Because Khanum has taken over the dance from the boys, Hughes's investment in Khanum enables his enchantment with the boy dancers to proceed into updated, modernized, seemingly "heterosexualized" channels. By portraying Khanum as embodying a defiantly nongendered public spectacle of "feminine" performance, though, Hughes's meditations on unveiling retain some of the gender ambiguity that so intrigued him in the tradition of boy dancers. Each time he discusses unveiling, he is also conjuring a space of cross-gender identification, harkening back to the cross-dressing boy dancers, and moving forward into the boundary-defying transgression of oppressive male culture with which he identifies racial segregation as well as the suppression of "vulgar and uncouth" displays of the colored body. Hughes notes in two different essays that Khanum's most famous dance is part of the Uzbek native opera *Farhar Va Shirin,* based on the folktale of a prince who "looked into a forbidden mirror and saw the face of a girl so beautiful that he knew he could not live without her" (TK, 830). This tale is, of course, a twist on the traditional allegory of Narcissus besotted by his own image, but when placed in the context of Hughes's own fascination with Uzbek women, it allows the reader to conjecture about differently channeled conduits of desire and identification at work in Hughes's writings from this period. Seeking an idealized yet unattainable female reflection of himself, Hughes's retelling of Shirin's predicament poses the problematic of male desire that operates through feminine identification, not male identification that operates through desire to possess a woman sexually. Bypassing conventional routings of heterosexual desire as based in difference, Hughes troubles the line between male and female by suggesting what it could mean to be like women without submitting to the societal expectation to like them amorously.[18] Similarly, the adornment of the boys' bodies in girls' clothing offers a conceptual link to Hughes's own identification with the Uzbek women around him, which gets thematized as a desire to accumulate and/or wear femininity without impropriety, uncouthness, or shame. In her ungendered dynamism, Khanum comes to embody both this lack of shame and the ideal unveiled being—a subject disencumbered from the accoutrement of an expected social role. Khanum will resonate strongly with the female characters that catalyze Hughes's stories—Cora in "Cora Unashamed" and the dancer Claudina Lawrence in "Poor Little Black Fellow."

This chapter reintegrates into Hughes's oeuvre the record of his encounter with Soviet Central Asia in general and Uzbek women in particular to demonstrate the ways in which the Soviet Union enabled Hughes to renegotiate the potentials of internationalism for his own uses. For Hughes, the promise of a Soviet-inspired internationalism lay not only in its ability to disrupt conventional national boundaries, but in its ability to remap culture and in so doing reconfigure subjectivity. Through an extended engagement with the concept of unveiling, Hughes's work from this period explored the possibility of thematizing the disruptive potential of internationalism in general through figures of femininity and sexual difference, and of using a vocabulary of internationalism to broach a more marginalized thematic of sexuality in the United States. As a conceptual apparatus, unveiling fostered a rethinking of in-betweenness, a comfort with gender dislocation, and a corresponding critique of conventional mappings of "home" and masculine selfhood.[19] Drawing on the tradition of boy dancers, Hughes locates in Khanum not only an opportunity to explore his own intense cross-gender identification across national borders but a way of linking this identification to his own artistic practice. Khanum exhibits an "ability to create new patterns of her own and produce art that is also social force, that changes life, that makes it better" (TK, 835). Hughes's Soviet work highlights the costs of aborted desires—of the writing out of unspeakable crossings, "waste matter, and rind" that art properly conceived in a 1950s' context may disparage. This work serves as a reminder that one may have access to its new patterns only by peering into Hughes's "forbidden mirror," and seeing not a revelation but a blurred image of femininity without which the messages of his stories cannot survive. Hughes's Soviet work constitutes a social force that enriches and "makes better" an understanding of his practice, offering an ambiguous site that both registers and seeks to disavow a renarration of African American masculinity.

BACKGROUND IN THE USSR

In the 1920s and 1930s, the Soviets pursued a program for the reconstitution of identity beneath the mantle of the so-called novy Sovetsky chelovek or "new Soviet person/man."[20] This new figure was made known in the United States by popular films and journalistic coverage, and many Left-leaning Americans were drawn to the Soviet Union to explore a reconstruction of identity across purportedly classless, raceless, and genderless lines. Films such as Eisenstein's *Battleship Potemkin* (1925), Pudovkin's *End of St. Petersburg* (1927), Dziga Vertov's *Man with a Movie Camera* (1928), and Nikolai Ekk's *Road to Life* (1931) were shown to audiences intrigued by the aesthetic innovation of the editing technique known as montage, which through the juxtaposition and crosscutting of images, offered a new way of seeing film and thinking about vision. Journalists such as Dorothy Thompson, Eugene Lyons, Louis Fischer, and Walter Duranty sent dispatches from Moscow and Leningrad outlining the rapid industrialization under way. And beginning in the mid-1920s, writers such as Theodore Dreiser, Waldo Frank, Ella Winter, Anna Louise Strong, Maurice Hindus, Joshua Kunitz, and Erskine Caldwell made journeys to see the revolution at work, and each produced significant published records of their experiences of the Soviet experiment. Lincoln Steffens, married to Winter at the time, became reknowned for his pronouncement, "I have seen the future, and it works"—a proclamation of support for the Soviet project (*SUC*, 84).

Hughes put his own spin on the sentiment that the future was happening in the present: "New times demand new people. In the Soviet Union, new people are coming into being."[21] Hughes's alternative texts take seriously the plausibility of new people under a rubric of "red": "Come together, fellow workers / Black and white can all be red," he wrote, thereby articulating an irreverence for proper lines of racial demarcation.[22] Echoing a rescripting of "No Mo', No Mo'" that was published in the *Liberator* in 1931, in which the chorus proclaims, "Negroes ain' black— but RED!" Hughes inferred that a life without borders could be colored, it could be "red."[23] This insight would prove to be fundamental to Hughes's perception of the new structures of subjectivity being wrought in Soviet Central Asia.

Initially part of a group of twenty-two African Americans invited by the Meschrabpom Film Company to partake in a movie to be titled *Black and White*, Hughes spent a total of twelve months touring the Soviet republics in 1932–1933. James Ford, the black CPUSA member who later in the year ran for vice president on the CP ticket, secured the invitation during his winter trip to Moscow in 1932. But although Ford may have initiated the scheme, its execution was the result of Louise Thompson's organizational savvy. Already the host of gatherings of the Friendship Society with the Soviet Union, Thompson sought and received support for the trip from among her connections in broad business, artistic, and intellectual circles of the day. She instituted the Cooperating Committee for the Production of a Soviet Film on Negro Life, recruiting W. A. Domingo, a former follower of Marcus Garvey, as chair and herself as secretary. Other prominent names among the list of committee members included the actress Rose McClendon, William H. Davis (owner and publisher of the *Amsterdam News*), Bessye Bearden (mother of the artist Romare), Malcolm Cowley, Floyd Dell, and Waldo Frank. Support for the film was possible, Thompson writes, "partly because the depiction of Negroes in Hollywood was so abominable."[24] A desire to counter this abysmal representation did not necessarily coincide with pro-Soviet views, however. As Thompson continues, "The people who joined the Cooperating Committee supported the film project while representing a broad range of views regarding socialism"—a diversity of views that attested to Thompson's organizational ability and her ability to see beyond political factionalism to foment alliances for the betterment of peoples' lives (LTP 2, 3). With support in place, Thompson quickly set about locating trip participants. Working under a deadline to find at least fifteen "actors" willing to undertake the Soviet adventure, Thompson contacted everyone she knew. Hughes's inclusion in the group of twenty-two that boarded the Europa en route to the Soviet republics on 12 June 1932 was due to Thompson's tenacity, and her sense that Hughes's writerly and political leanings would be newly ignited by a Soviet trip.[25]

The group of Americans who traveled to the Soviet Union with Hughes

4. Louise Thompson and Langston Hughes on board the
Europa in June 1932. Yale Collection of American Literature,
Beinecke Rare Book and Manuscript Library. Reprinted by
permission of Harold Ober Associates Incorporated.

were not primarily interested in financial gain. A motley bunch of students, journalists, social workers, and artists, they had been promised round-trip passage (to be reimbursed at the project's end), and "guaranteed expenses and salary."[26] Although certainly a plus in the job-scarce days of the depression, the guaranteed sum of two to three hundred dollars for the four or five month's duration of the project was one impetus among others. The group was as enthusiastic about what might greet them in the USSR as they were dejected about the "inability of our social system to resolve the problems of poverty, hunger and unemployment" revealed during the early 1930s (LTP 2, 9). Contributing to the appeal of Soviet Communism were frustrations with the intractability of the color line, national poverty, and government scandal, and the apparent beneficence of the Soviets toward black Americans. Thompson observes,

> In a sense, many of us were leaving America in search of an alternative social system. We had heard that there was no unemployment in the Soviet Union and that the socialist system was committed to feeding, clothing and sheltering every worker and peasant. We had also been told that the Soviet Union was free of racism. The Czarist Empire that had oppressed the peoples and nations south and east of Russia had reportedly been replaced by a system that respected non-European cultures. Even though most of the Meschrabpom Film project was not particularly political, we were leaving a country that was sharply polarized over Depression-era social policies and that was engaged in a bitter propaganda battle with the USSR. It was inevitable that some would look toward the Soviet Union with the hope of finding new and better models of social development. (LTP 2, 10)

While these twenty-two embarked on a unique adventure to explore the Soviet model of social development, hundreds of African Americans were encouraged by this idea of an alternative, racism-free society to forsake the barriers of the color line by transgressing the borderline of "East" and "West."

Although only one of the twenty-two was an official member of the CP (Alan McKenzie), as the trip went on, many of those involved in the film project became increasingly interested in communism. A self-described leftist before she left for Russia, Thompson wrote with excitement that having been exposed to the Soviet system, previously apolitical group members were becoming more politically inclined. Thompson outlined this in a letter to her mother: "It is interesting to notice how many members of our group who came to Russia without a single idea in their heads have been stimulated to read and to question and desire to know more about Russia and communism" (LTP 1, 60–61). Their interest did little to help complete the film, which finally was postponed some two months after their arrival and before a single frame had been shot. If the film had come to fruition, it would have been a strange document. The director was a German who spoke little English, and the screenplay displayed what

Hughes called "a pathetic hodgepodge of good intentions and faulty facts."[27] Thompson, later dubbed "Madame Moscow," reiterates that "the Russians in charge of the film understood Negro life only its barest outlines and their propaganda aims were crudely apparent" (LTP 2, 21).

Thompson's summary of the film projected the challenges of the script. Her comments confirm that the script was unworkable. It "began in Africa and featured wailing villagers, Arab slave traders in fezes, a naive missionary and the greedy, cruel captain of a slave ship. The scene shifted to an auction block in the U.S. South where a family was being torn asunder and then to a Civil War battle scene. . . . [T]he main action of the script revolved around a labor dispute in a factory. . . . [O]ne version of the script had the Red Army arriving to assist the anti-lynching forces" (LTP 2, 20–21). The Soviets' admission of limited knowledge and a desire to know more about racial configurations in the United States had come earlier, when they requested that the *Black and White* troupe bring "outfits to be worn in [the] picture and certain historical and sociological books on the Negro in America" as well as "several different kinds of phonograph records."[28] Nonetheless, the trip to Russia afforded Hughes a chance to investigate colored life under a different domain and share his own perceptions of the U.S. color line with a vastly curious Soviet peoples.

After the dissolution of their film project, the acting troupe was invited by the Soviet government to tour an area of their choice in the Soviet Union.[29] While several members of the group chose to leave Russia for Europe, eleven others selected Soviet Central Asia as their destination. In spite of the fact that the territory was at the time officially closed to tourists, they were able to secure the necessary documents to make their wish a reality. The group's choice of Soviet Central Asia, despite their eventual exhaustion from the pomp and circumstance of Soviet southern hospitality, testified to an interest in the Soviet south. And as expressed by Thompson, in terms of racial liberation, the region lived up to their expectations. Optimistic that Soviet intervention in Central Asia provided a source of hope for improved race relations in the United States, Thompson concluded, "What I had witnessed, especially in Central Asia, convinced me that only a new social order could remedy the American racial injustices I knew so well. I went to the Soviet Union with leftist leanings; I returned home a committed revolutionary" (LTP 2, 47).

Thompson's articulation of the impact of the Soviet trip on her ex-

5. The *Black and White* troupe pose beneath a Leninist banner in Central Asia, 1932. Yale Collection of American Literature, Beinecke Rare Book and Manuscript Library. Reprinted by permission of Harold Ober Associates Incorporated.

emplifies the vibrancy that the Soviet project brought to black Americans beleaguered by the persistence of racial oppressions in the United States. Another member of the group, Matt Crawford, reiterated Thompson's comparison between race-based persecution of Uzbeks under the czarist regime and Jim Crow in the United States. Crawford wrote that "there is an exact parallel between the condition that these people were under during the czarist regime and the position of Negroes in the States now."[30] For all, the elimination of segregation—along both racial and gender lines—the introduction of compulsory education, and industrialization stood as hallmarks of a new era, new way of living, and "new people." As Thompson noted, the Soviet experience not only awakened a sense of political consciousness but did so because it juxtaposed sharply with the experience of segregation and racial persecution back home. She wrote to her mother that "wherever we go [we] are surrounded by workers, greeted and cheered, and led to feel that there is no difference. Often when we have no one to translate for us workers will by gesture and sign tell us that we are all brothers as long as we are all on the same side, working for the emancipation of the international proletariat. It is a grand thing, I tell you. One of our common jokes among ourselves starts out like this, 'now, when I return to oblivion in the U.S.'" (LTP 1, 62). For the troupe of Americans, the contrasts between the United States and USSR could not have been starker. Not only were the Soviets championing the cause of the downtrodden, they were also building alliances between previously factionalized groups into which many of these peoples had been divided.

Positive messages about the inclusory emancipatory policies of the Soviet Union reached friends and family members back in the United States, igniting an already existing curiosity about the Soviet south among some African Americans.[31] Accordingly, the would-be actors were not the only African Americans who expressed interest in and traveled to the region during this period. During the early 1930s, in fact, the Soviets established an unofficial policy of recruiting African Americans to work in the Soviet south.[32] The Soviets hoped to use African American expertise in industry and agriculture, in particular cotton farming to boost the production of what the Soviets reverently called "white gold." One such American, Oliver Golden, was instrumental in organizing a group of "Negro specialists" to emigrate to Tashkent, and he engaged the help of George Washington Carver, then president of Tuskegee, who put him in touch with two dozen such specialists. Like Golden, these experts signed work contracts with the Soviet Union because the opportunities in Uzbekistan outshone those in the States. As Golden's granddaughter, Yelena Khanga, has written, "For several of the men . . . the Soviet offer meant their first, and only, chance to work as professionals rather than waiters."[33] When Hughes reached the township where Golden and others had settled, Yangiyul, he was surprised to find a veritable colony of African Americans in this remote area, two hours distance from Tashkent.[34] For their part, the Americans were thrilled to host the famous poet, and Hughes spent Christmas of 1932 with the Golden family. When the remaining members of his *Black and White* troupe went on to Baku, Hughes continued on to Ashkhabad alone and eventually spent an additional eight months touring the region.[35]

The idea that a comparison between Uzbek slavery under czardom and the present predicament of race relations in the U.S. South could be drawn with seeming ease sparked Hughes's interest. As did others, Hughes voiced his admiration at the Soviet's ability to abolish Jim Crow–like laws of racial segregation that had been implemented in Central Asia during the czarist regime. But breaking away from the group to remain in Soviet Central Asia for several months on assignment for *Izvestiia*, the Soviet newspaper, Hughes remained captivated by the enforced unveiling of Uzbek women. Even though, as Thompson put it, "the campaign for women's freedom quickly became identified with removing the paranja [Uzbek Muslim veil]" for Hughes this Soviet policy took on proportions that while not excluding also exceeded women's freedom.[36] "Unveiling" encapsulated the emancipation of a colored, southern people, previously oppressed by segregation and slavery. The veil symbolized to Hughes not only the backwardness of gender segregation under Islam but also his own understanding of a predominant paradigm for racial consciousness in the United States as elaborated by Du Bois's *The Souls of Black Folk*.

REVAMPING DU BOIS'S VEIL

Hughes's stated interest in the Soviet south revolved around the elimination of segregation and the equitable treatment of colored people under the new Soviet regime. At the same time, Hughes's writerly interest was consistently caught and remained focused on how this new regime altered the condition of women. The unveiling of Muslim women resonated not only with Hughes's general desire for an end to segregation on all fronts but with a more specific longing to escape from a "life beneath the veil," which in Du Bois's work is coded as a specific type of masculine racial consciousness. Enshrouded beneath two distinct yet related discourses of the veil, Hughes's essays about Uzbek women seek out new territory in which to negotiate the racial consciousness he associated with the veil. He at once embraces and refuses the "feminine" aspects of the Muslim veil, at times reasserting a proper distance from cross-gender identification, and at others, leaving traces that challenge the dominant paradigms of the masculinist, heterosexual Euro-imperial gaze thematized in *The Souls of Black Folk*.

With the publication of Du Bois's *The Souls of Black Folk* in 1903, a rhetoric of the veil had established itself in black American consciousness as *the* phenomenology of black masculinity.[37] Exemplifying the foundational status of *Souls*, Hughes described the book as comprising, along with the Bible, his "earliest memories of written words."[38] In *Souls*, a young girl's refusal to exchange visiting cards with the adolescent Du Bois provokes his revelation of the veil. Du Bois remarks that it suddenly dawned on him that he was "different from the others, or like, mayhap, in heart and life and longing, but shut out from their world by a vast veil. . . . The Negro is a sort of seventh son, born with a veil," with no true self-consciousness, who sees "himself through the revelation of the other world." Just as he likens slavery to the era of the Old Testament (Isa. 25:7), Du Bois loosely compares post-Reconstruction to a rereading of the book of Corinthians II. In this rescripting a "new vision" was discovered, only to bring disappointment to the youth who in his striving "saw himself,— darkly as through a veil."[39] Adjusting the "mirror" to a "veil," the distance between enlightened self-knowledge and the distorted image of self re-fracted from without defines, for Du Bois, the gap between liberty and oppression, freedom and confinement. Du Bois's use of the veil would appear to conform to a metaphysical discourse of truth, wherein white-ness is clarity and blackness opacity. Du Bois's words thus produce a bias against the superficiality of the veil behind which purportedly lurks a true self-consciousness. As others have indicated, Du Bois's indebtedness to G. W. F. Hegel emerges pointedly here—the presentation of the Negro as a "seventh son" is an attempt to append African Americans onto Hegel's list of world historical peoples.[40] The occlusion of Africa from Hegel's account is one Du Bois tries to reconcile by positing a forward march of freedom, thereby selectively rewriting Hegel's Eurocentrism. At the same time, Du Bois's reliance on Hegelian recognition as the register in which conscious-ness could be achieved bespeaks a longing for a gaze that would, like the colonialist one, order and administer all bodies, black and white, into freedom by diffusing the gap through the symbolic act of unveiling.

Du Bois's alienation gives rise to the "veil"—a term, as Robert Young has helpfully elucidated, already imbricated within an ideology of race based in both the enforcement and policing of differences between whites and blacks as well as a fascination with the products of miscegenation.[41] Du Bois finds the veil both repulsive and protective—both a reminder of and shield from the pain of his denied access to whiteness. The veil arrives as a reminder of the necessity that a border remain intact. The black man must always be reminded of his physicality from which stems his limitations as an outsider within the national polity. As Robyn Wiegman explains, "It was the repression of specific racial and gender markers of privileged identity—of whiteness and maleness—that characterized the figure 'American citizen' and inaugurated its rhetorical definition as an inclusive social body. In this constitution of the citizen as a disembodied entity, bound not to physical delineations but to national ones, the white male was (and continues to be) 'freed' from the corporeality that might otherwise impede his insertion into the larger body of national identity."[42] But for the black male, it was his excessive bodiliness that distanced him from full citizenship, and the "veil" portrayed by Du Bois served as a constant reminder of this very embodied and embodying difference.

By using the figure of white femininity as the definition of imagined difference between whiteness and blackness, however, Du Bois codes racial difference in terms of masculine access to female sexual exchange. Du Bois states, "The exchange was merry, till one girl, a tall newcomer, refused my card—refused it peremptorily, with a glance."[43] Coded through the forbidden coupling with white femininity that is signaled by a wordless but all-knowing look, Du Bois's use of the veil both reinscribes and recodes its Euro-imperial web: Du Bois resists the standard notion of blackness as total difference from whiteness ("or like . . . in heart and life and longing") by positing the veil as an immobilizing obfuscation of his sameness—a sameness not exterior to but contoured by sentiment or desire. The veil becomes a reminder of sexual access to the figure of white femininity, across the body of which lies the "difference" between black and white masculinities.[44] While establishing racial difference as based on an economy of sexual exchange that trades in white femininity (and as McKay explored in *Trial by Lynching,* peripheralizes black femininities), this configuration at the same time posits desire as unequivocally, compulsorily heterosexual. One's desire to belong to a community (in which disembodiment is a privilege and unlimited access to white women defines one as properly self-knowing) can be read as an index of one's acceptability, and vice versa: the links between a proper black masculine consciousness, the privileges of disembodiment as a prerogative of full citizenship, and heterosexual desire remain firm.[45]

Unlike Hughes, who welcomed the challenge that unveiling would pose, Du Bois remained uncertain about the rewards of its removal. Du Bois posits a key ambivalence toward lifting the veil, reading it in terms of sexual entitlement and empowerment—the lifting of the curtain or skirts of a denied femininity that would grant equality to the "white man"—and in terms of a necessarily appropriative and disempowering gesture of exposure that could reveal that there was nothing exterior to be seen. A complete rending of the veil would mean, for Du Bois, the loss of difference—a difference on which his sense of self relies. "I had thereafter no desire to tear down that veil, to creep through," Du Bois writes of his stunned youthful self. Yet at the end of *Souls,* Du Bois makes an appeal to "sweep the veil away"; "America shall rend the veil and the prisoned shall go free."[46] These two sides speak to Du Bois's attachment to both the notion that integrated self-knowledge exists as "whiteness" and "difference" (as something incommensurable with whiteness). In both cases, Du Bois's articulation of the veil is removed from Hughes's, for even Du Bois's demand to "sweep the veil away" retains the remnants of a symbolic that would posit integrated selfhood as the proper goal of all subjects. The woman, in either scenario, remains an object of exchange between men.

Du Bois's sampling of the dominant paradigms through which economic and political trafficking of colonialism were conceived left an indelible imprint on Hughes's pieces on Soviet Central Asia both in relation to their fascination with the veil and "black life in America." Just as Hughes's pieces read parallels between the Soviet and U.S. Souths, Jim Crow and the harem, they also suggest parallels between Du Bois's "veil that unites black men" and the "veil" of colonialist discourse. The space that emerges in this convergence is a polyvalent one—one that cannot be read unilaterally as it opens contestation between what a liberated African American selfhood might look like, what kind of woman emerges beneath the mantle of Sovietization, and what shapes of the "feminine" Hughes leaves behind, both in the United States and Central Asia.[47] Nonetheless, Hughes's veil differs from Du Bois's, for it (in its absence) posits a countersymbolic not based in an insider/outsider framework but one that negotiates through a position of in-betweenness where the other threatens properties of definition. Unlike Du Bois's Hegelian-derived insistence on recognition as the liberating hinge between self and other, Hughes's recoding of the veil proposes a nondialectical position of betweenness in which a refusal of whiteness (and the cross-gender desire with which he associated it) rephrases the emancipatory potential of unveiling.

Advocating a radical revision of "the veil" as articulated in Du Bois's *The Souls of Black Folks* in which the veil represents U.S. racial difference, Hughes's discussion of the Uzbek veil also illustrates the ways in which such a reconfiguration is embedded in anterior postulations of the veil in Western philosophy—postulations that underlay the gendering, exoticization, and denigration of colonial space as "feminine." Throughout Hughes's essays, links between psychic and social spaces proceed both to decompose and refurbish a traditional iconography of the veil as intimately related to sexual difference.[48] Because of such intimacy, the topic of the veil has created a burgeoning arena of debate in feminist scholarship in recent years. In her study *Transfigurations of the Maghreb,* Winifred Woodhull provides a useful overview of differing viewpoints produced by this feminist work. Woodhull outlines, on the one hand, the ways in which Western scholarship has tended toward reductive representations of "the Muslim woman" and "the veil" as if together they represented one, cohesive symbolic unit of women's oppression under Islam. "The veil has been seen in the West as the sign of women's oppression in Muslim societies," Woodhull writes, "as if all women were equally and identically oppressed in those societies, as if their oppression stemmed uniquely from the power of Islam (rather than the power of Western imperialism), and as if Islam and 'Muslim society' themselves were monolithic entities impervious to historical change." Woodhull is attentive to the critiques lodged against such Western misapprehensions. Citing the work of Chandra Talpade Mohanty, Woodhull elaborates how criticisms of Western-biased feminism have connected the reductive approach to veiling to the more general reduction of all women within "the third world" to a composite "third world woman."[49] This paring down of the heterogeneity of women across a huge range of political, national, and cultural allegiances simultaneously produces "the Western woman" as all that her third world other is not: progressive, modern, educated, rational, autonomous, and so on. As Mohanty asserts, "The one enables and sustains the other."[50] Thus, while historically some Western critics have been quick to contend that veiling is inherently antifeminist and only reinforces the purported patriarchy of Muslim society, others have claimed that the act of unveiling is inherently

Euro-imperial and question the very foundation on which such Western feminist views are based. From varied viewpoints, the latter position has been eloquently articulated by a range of scholars. Malek Alloula, Lila Abu-Lughod, Fatima Mernissi, Leila Ahmed, Assia Djebar, and Inderpal Grewal have each written compellingly about the material and discursive complexities involved in the practice of veiling among Muslim women in regions as distinct as North Africa, India, and the Middle East.[51]

Although I position my work within the arguments presented by Woodhull, Mohanty, and others (and their reluctance to talk in general terms about the veil), I also draw on the insights of Gayatri Spivak in order to think about the structuring devices enacted by systems of veiling. Specifically, and without denying the importance of different contexts and locations in which the Muslim veil historically appears, I am thinking about the way in which the veil can be understood both as a metaphor for the harem and, in this guise, a mechanism for exploring linkages between its deployment in geographically distinct realms. In this manner, the veil and harem can be examined to elaborate, as Grewal (borrowing from Spivak and James Clifford) writes, "transnational complicities" between "first" and "third" world accounts and theories.[52] Identifying the cultural flow of the veil between the United States and Soviet Central Asia enables one to scrutinize the complex and asymmetrical routes of identification through which Hughes appropriates and resists both a notion of subjectivity that is new to him and the discourses in which he is interpolated as a subject in the United States. To this end, Spivak has provided the phrase "regulative psychobiography" to understand the process by which harem-ification works within a given society. Spivak's term helps reveal how the harem can be used as a cipher through which to read the ways in which societies used a gendered discourse to imagine their own proscriptive boundaries, exterior and interior, public and private, male and female. As a reminder of the harem, the veil symbolized an establishment of proper social boundaries.[53]

Thinking about the harem and veil in this way enables one to then contextualize the Uzbek veil with which Hughes came into contact in the 1930s, and think more specifically about the ways in which this particular site of the harem and (un)veiling provided Hughes with a means of exploring societal and social boundaries in the United States. Richly suggestive for Hughes's own internalization of the modes of segregation, contemporary feminist views that challenge the ethnocentric assumptions of requisite unveiling have little in common with Hughes's desire to rend the veil. In fact, Hughes's celebration of Uzbek unveiling would appear to speak more to feminist views that see veiling as vastly destructive to women's freedom. Hughes's linking of unveiling with freedom, however, was not primarily based in a familiarity with debates surrounding its Euro-imperial deployment as a metaphor for the harem but rather with a lexicon of the veil ingrained in African American literary tradition through the work of Du Bois. By crossing the Uzbek boundary and championing unveiling, Hughes complicated any simple decoding of the discourse of the veil. His essays challenge both contemporary feminist scholarship and African American literary studies by bringing them together at the site of the veil. Read in this way, Hughes's work offers three important challenges to existing scholarship in these areas: it disputes not only the masculine but the hetero-normative bias of the black veil as engaged by critical discourse on the topic; it offers a point of entry to rethink the exclusively female focus of postcolonial discussions of the veil; and it confronts the othering of the discourse of the Muslim veil as external to the disciplining of non-Muslim U.S. bodies in the 1930s.

ORBITS HITHERTO RESERVED

When Hughes arrived in Central Asia, he was not only willing to renounce an African American exceptionalism, he was eager to do so. Having just completed an extensive book tour of the western United States, Hughes found in the USSR an opportunity to escape from the old cultural baggage of U.S. racial policies into new transnational alliances that seemed to reconfigure "race" from the ground up. Thus, he focused his attention on the new modes of subjectivity that the Soviet model appeared to offer—new myths of consciousness that seemed to circumvent the perpetual outsiderness of the Du Boisian schema.[54]

Because travel was an ordering principle of Hughes's life—as a sailor, lecturer, and journalist—it figures prominently in his psychic and social apprehensions of race. And his expressions of color consciousness are often caught up in the question of mobility. As he wrote in his notebook,

"On the Tashkent express I thought how in the thirty years of my life I had seldom gotten on a train in America without being conscious of my color."[55] Compelled by the equitable treatment of dark-skinned peoples in the Soviet Central Asian republics, Hughes compares his own experiences of "going South" in the United States with those of "going South" in the Soviet Union, and finds the former newly repugnant: "To an American Negro living in the northern part of the United States the word South has an unpleasant sound, an overtone of horror and fear. . . . [I]t is in the Southern states that the color line is hard and fast, Jim Crow rules, and I am treated like a dog."[56] Hughes's inability to move freely in the States contrasts with the absence of segregation in Central Asia, which is marked by its traces—a partition on the train, signs on public parks implemented under British and Russian colonization. His travels south in Soviet Central Asia provided him with an opportunity to rethink racial topographies in terms familiar to him. Hughes comments that "people who less than thirty years ago had to travel under Jim Crow conditions, now travel as freely as anyone else."[57] Contrasting confinement and openness, Hughes poses the unhindered crossing of previously demarcated spaces as an ideal, a representation of the "liberation of Central Asia . . . truly a land of the Before and After," and his imagining of racial equity in the United States. Central Asia's "after" state corresponds in Hughes's eyes to its entry into the "anticolonial" era of Sovietization (GSIR, 77). While this may sound paradoxical in light of the Soviet practices of unveiling and de-Islamicization that more befit European projects of colonization than postindependence decolonization, Hughes remains emphatic that with the aid of Russia, Soviet Central Asia was moving forward into the "modern world" of "big plants, electric stations, textile mills," and trains, and that this forward movement was unequivocally one of progress (GSIR, 78).

Leaving to our speculative assumptions just what a United States "after" desegregation might look like, Hughes subsumes the complex contours of Soviet colonization in the positive, forward-moving machine of industrialization. He remarks that he "once heard a foreigner object to what he termed the possible Russification of Central Asia. Very quickly the answer came back to him, 'not Russification, but modernization.' "[58] Hughes's recollection marks his own awareness of the links between the two terms, "Russification" and "modernization." At the same time, however, his descriptions of the changes Soviets brought to Central Asia betray an allegiance to the replacement of the former with the latter; a belief that, indeed, questions surrounding the Russification of a non-Russian region could be bracketed by the more immediate advances wrought by a modernization unhinged from its Soviet derivation. Exemplary of such advances, just two years earlier the Moscow-Tashkent rail line had been finished. As Anna Louise Strong—an American reporter who spent many years in the Soviet Union—commented, thirty journalists from the United States, Germany, England, and Italy arrived, aware "that this railway changed the history of Asia."[59] To this end, Hughes's attitude toward progress in the Soviet south bespeaks his filiation to and alignment with his Western colleagues. A belief that new roads and railways paved over the isolation and stagnation of "backward" countries, thereby preparing them for social evolution, revolution, and hence historical relevance, registers throughout Hughes's at times critically inflected essays.

His commentary on Central Asia illustrates crucial aspects of the complexities involved in establishing progress while resisting Western assimilation. Not only does Hughes's linking of travel and progress betray an allegiance to Western colonial notions of modernity indebted equally to Marx and Hegel but also the perception of self he begins to articulate reveals itself to be that of a subject necessarily interpellated through American racialist discourse. As part of an educated elite of American writers and intellectuals, Hughes is indebted to European notions of the self, which evolved in part from a tradition of Orientalist narratives connected to commerce and the amassing of Western wealth under capitalism.[60] But in reflecting a certain ease with the very terms and conditions that enabled hegemonic systems of whiteness to prevail, Hughes identifies with the racial persecution perpetrated by such institutions and social customs. As a member of a disenfranchised racial group—of the same American black belt region that Stalin had recently declared a colonized "nation"—Hughes also incorporates an image of himself as a substitute for that very Orientalized or othered self on which much of post-Enlightenment thinking is based. According to Thompson's memoir, Hughes's identification with the people of Central Asia was intense. She writes, "In my photographs of Langston in Central Asia he looks as though he is among his own people" (LTP 2, 40).

Hughes's exchanges with his sometimes traveling partner, Arthur

6. Hughes in a Beluchi turban on a collective farm near Merv, Turkmenistan, 1932. Yale Collection of American Literature, Beinecke Rare Book and Manuscript Library. Reprinted by permission of Harold Ober Associates Incorporated.

Koestler, a member of the German Communist Party who was covering the trials of suspected anticommunists in the region, shed light not only on this tension but also on Hughes's sensitivity to it. In his memoir, Hughes stages a scene of homosocial rivalry over the interpretation of race between Koestler and himself. Aware of the purported discontinuity between "Western" self and "Eastern" other, and the way in which Soviet Central Asia—a theoretically anticolonial site of intervention—had specifically thrown the shadow of this disjunction into relief, Hughes remarked to Koestler that he could "hardly believe" that "colored people" were being introduced to industry "from the ground up." "I was trying to make him

7. Hughes, unidentified comrade, and Arthur Koestler in Soviet Central Asia. Yale Collection of American Literature, Beinecke Rare Book and Manuscript Library. Reprinted by permission of Harold Ober Associates Incorporated.

understand," Hughes stated, "why I observed the changes in Soviet Asia with Negro eyes. To Koestler, Turkmenistan was simply a *primitive* land moving into twentieth-century civilization. To me it was a *colored* land moving into orbits hitherto reserved for whites."[61] Hughes is even more explicit in his manuscript notes about his feelings toward Koestler: "Koestler (is a) this white man (he) doesn't understand Tadjikistan."[62] Identifying with the colored peoples of the Soviet south, Hughes conjoins his stance toward progress with the question of perspective. One tactic he uses to achieve this end is to adjust the gesture of cultural superiority. Hughes avoids the pitfalls of primitivization to which Koestler is prey. Establishing distance from the view of his white colleague, Hughes preserves difference through mechanisms of perspective and sight along with the interpolation of self within these visions. He intimates, without renouncing his allegiance to and imbrication in Western modes of seeing per se, that there is a difference in perspective enabled by his own identification with the Uzbeks, particularly with Uzbek women. At stake is a preservation of difference in the face of a hetero-normativity associated with whiteness and an opportunity for alternate modes of masculinity with which he associated this difference.

Whereas "double consciousness" has come to be understood as this duality in which the body is a constant reminder of one's outsider status, Hughes's exchange with Koestler provides a scene in which Koestler, and not Hughes, is the outsider. Surrounded by people who look not unlike him, Hughes is afforded a moment of disembodiment; a momentary escape from the burden of masculine physicality that, in the United States, is a continual reminder of his secondary status as "colored." In Central Asia, Koestler is forced to bear the mark of physical difference. The two are talking about race relations in the United States at the time, a topic of conversation that presumably would remind Hughes of his peripheral status in a U.S. context. But his experience in Central Asia provides a means of being outside the States, and dislocating Hughes's rote associations with being "colored" and "male." The usually repressed markers of citizenship—white and male—are foregrounded and pronounced against a colored background. They emerge in sync with the reshaping of an international citizen as an inclusive body not delimited by physical attributes. Looking back at the United States from the vantage point of Central Asia, Hughes is able not only to sharpen his perspective on race relations at home but also to imagine what it might feel like to escape a life of the veil. For Hughes, this is an unambiguous moment of freedom that challenges the Enlightenment equation of freedom with a specific kind of vision: the injunction to "see" and "be seen." He imagines the sensation of disencumbering himself from that enforced embodiment of otherness, of unveiling himself not to an integrated self-consciousness associated with "whiteness" but to an ease with a sense of displacement from the "proper," hetero-normative self. Hughes comes to this understanding of internationalism's potential through moments such as these in which the female-inspired model of unveiling serves as a means of repositioning both masculine subjecthood and citizenship.

Keen on maintaining a sense of distance from Koestler while aware of his own discontinuity with Central Asians, Hughes latches onto a rhetoric of displacement as a means of keeping this tension alive. This discussion of displacement is related to mobility, and the crossing of previously demarcated spaces represented by unveiling, and yet finds its fullest expression in Hughes's preoccupation with Koestler's distaste for dirt. Denouncing the propriety associated with cleanliness becomes not only a point of pride for Hughes but also a key way in which he reinforces his distinction from Koestler. Several times in his memoir, Hughes notes how his own comfort with dirt and disorder distinguishes him from his traveling partner. Describing Koestler's reaction to Central Asia, Hughes writes that he "had a German sense of sanitation, and neither Russians nor Turkomans were very hygienic. In fact, Koestler complained that Russian and Asiatic dirt together made a pretty thick layer. And every time he came back to our hotel he would wash. I had not known him long before I heard him say what I was often to hear him repeat, 'If the Revolution had only occurred in Germany, at least it would have been a clean one.'"[63]

In the first volume of his work on *Male Fantasies,* Klaus Theweleit argues that in Weimar culture a connection between homosocial culture and misogyny was rooted in a fear of dirt. This observation, while addressing an earlier period, nonetheless has resonances with the scene portrayed by Hughes.[64] In particular, the correlation between dirt and other bodily fluids, and Koestler's anxious attempt to stem their flow, is suggestive of a struggle against a misogynistic purity that Hughes's prose seems to wage. Resisting the temptation to editorialize, Hughes continues to relate how Koestler found especially disturbing the convention of sharing tea bowls that was customary in Central Asia: " 'Slobbering in each other's bowls,' said Koestler, '[is] a bloody disgusting filthy habit!' " Hughes is quick to note, however, that unlike Koestler, he "simply went ahead and drank and re-drank with the others, and forgot about it."[65] For Hughes, the dirt of Central Asia offers yet another comparison to the U.S. South. Regarding a hotel that Koestler called a "filthy hole—it will take more than a revolution to clean up this dive," Hughes asserts, "The whole ugly barren room reminded me of cheap Negro hotels in the South where such hotels are the only ones in which colored travelers can stay. Here I was not segregated, but it was certainly dirty."[66]

Hughes's relationship to dirt is not a preference for filth over cleanliness. He writes, "Just as the dirt in Central Asia upset Koestler, so it upset me. Dirt without Jim Crow was bad—but dirt with Jim Crow, for me, would have been infinitely worse."[67] Rather, embracing dirt becomes a means of de-systematizing European strategies of knowing, and establishing order and distance. Hughes encourages one to see through Koestler's mockery of Asiatic and Russian dirt, to see his disdain as an example of the way in which "whiteness" presumes itself to be transparent, normal, natural, the measure by which all else should be judged. At the same time, Hughes's attitude reflects a consciousness of the hypocrisies based on skin color. Unfounded bases of separation, markers of the culturally taboo are signified through this engagement of emphatic trespassing. His relationship to dirt becomes a means through which Hughes signals difference from Koestler—as a prototype for the white, hetero-, Western male. Hughes's internationalism, his forging of alliances in the name of anti-racism and anti-imperialism, becomes a critique of the proper, of the cultural and intellectual vestments of European propriety bound up in a homosocial fear of the feminine/dirt.

Hughes, unlike Koestler, is not attempting to feel "at home" in this distant locale. Rejecting the move of subject/object that grounds Koestler's rejection of the filth of "Asiatic" custom, Hughes refuses to reduce the Uzbek to a reflection of his own alienation. He preserves the otherness of the other through an acceptance of and participation in local custom, while also opening himself to contagion. Carrying with him his memory of otherness back in the United States, he immerses himself in the "threat" of the other. Hughes embraces the possibility that the other could be housed within him by creating a new category of otherness. Koestler, the communist, disparages the habits of communal tea drinking. Hughes partakes in communal sharing, interpreting it as intimately connected to the removal of physical barriers between white and nonwhite, male and female—for which unveiling came to serve as the crowning symbol, and to which he ascribed a new internationalism. For although veiling was not a Western practice per se, as Du Bois's appropriation of the term implies, it was as surely as Jim Crow invested in establishing boundaries of the proper and improper. Hughes evokes a racial and gendered heterogeneity within the vast arena of colonization, seeing progress as intertwined with mobility, and mobility with the webbed networks from which internationalism might emerge.

In what was to be the opening passage of his book, Hughes provides a means of understanding his interpretation of unveiling as a rewriting of the category of otherness. Hughes wrote, "During my months in Central Asia, I often wondered how did I, a poor American Negro, get way down yonder in the southern part of the USSR. . . . I sat in the courtyard of Tamerlane's tomb and wondered, 'Am I dreaming?' I looked at the long camel caravans starting out into the Kizil Kum, saying to myself, 'Is this me, way over here in Asia?' "[68] In this short passage, Hughes adopts the modern terms of fantasy and enchantment common in Western writings about the Orient. In conventional Orientalist narratives, the fantastic quality of the foreign territory "refers both to its image in the Western mind and to a state of consciousness"—for example, Hegel's "dreaming Indian" who comes to represent the ontological instability of the Orient.[69] Hughes reinterprets this paradigm by inserting himself as subject—"a poor American Negro"—into the space of the object of disorientation—"Is this me?" Uncertainty underwrites this introduction of self into object, however, so that in place of a totalizing absorption of the object of otherness resides a question mark. This rhetorical gesture denotes an unanswerable, and inassimilable, alterity, as if to ask, "What's the difference?"[70] This unsettling experience of disorientation—neither here nor there; "Am I dreaming?"—disturbs easy absorption of the other into the self, fusing instead a recognition of difference within the self. Hughes's placement of selfhood at a crossroads of reconciliation and fragmentation displays a subject who cannot correlate his experience of himself with any idealized image. As in Hughes's differentiation of himself from Koestler through an established distance from insistence on the homelike qualities of "propriety," Hughes's articulation here is not a reiteration of Du Boisian double consciousness because "proper self-consciousness," an integrated selfhood, is not the goal.

Hughes clarifies the possibilities for living in difference in an interview he gave when back in the United States. On his return from Soviet Central Asia, Hughes's assessment of the possibilities for a liberated African American selfhood provided an aesthetic model that defied the then-current frameworks for black art. In February 1933, Hughes stated in an interview with the Baltimore *Afro-American*, "We need now an art and a literature which will arouse us to our fate. Already we have had too much literature in the vein of the spirituals, lamenting our fate and bemoaning our condition, but suggesting no remedy except humbleness and docility."[71] Hughes's refusal to link black art with lamentation was a radical move away from the aesthetic contours dictated by efforts to locate the specificity of a Negro art in the sorrow songs of rural African Americans. Indeed, Du Bois's *Souls* provided a pronounced instance of this connection between lamentation and art—mourning and melancholia thematize the use of the sorrow songs as structuring devices. Hughes's "antibourgeois" intervention radically countered Du Bois's depiction of the veil as an instrument of anguish in *Souls,* and may have been Hughes's most "radical" moment. Resisting the veil as a basis for a theory of black aesthetics that would enable an untrammeled continuity between bodies and languages, Hughes applied his own methodology for establishing the contours of an oppositional American art. As Hughes portrays it, rejecting the veil and thereby opening oneself to disorientation, an opening of previously demarcated spaces, relinquishes the fantasy of the proper self. Departing from the notion of solidarity in suffering, Hughes reconfigures the "abject" self for his own resources. He invites a feeling of internal oddness as the mark of membership in a community.[72] Casting a solidified mythos of racial suffering as ontological privilege, and a site for communal solidarity, was specifically what Hughes refused at this moment in order to maintain the idea of antivictimization, anticapitalism, and anti-Depression—as the shifting foundation of a liberating artistic practice.[73]

As ethnographic pieces, Hughes's essays trace the ways in which, in the words of Mary Douglas, "where there is dirt, there is system."[74] What is abject, then, is a reminder of the provisionality of boundaries, the ways that barriers are constructed in order to ward off the uncertainty aroused by betweenness. As a mark of separation between the sexes and segregation between races, the veil marks just such a site of provisionality—it, like dirt, is an indicator of "system." But through its association with an excess of bodiliness (female and black male), the veil in both its predominant discourses is also representative of the dirt with which such excess is associated. Restoring order, the veil replaces dirt. Thus, Hughes's comfort with the shared dirt that Koestler finds so distasteful provides him not only with a means of establishing difference from his partner, it also enables him to bolster his sense that in abolishing the veil, one crosses into the messy, dangerous, and impure territories that the founding of a new subjectivity demands. In conjunction with a rejection of the veil, his essays suggest reclaiming an otherness heretofore obliterated by the enforced separation between self and other, subject and object, black and white, male and female. Rather than retaining this otherness as a mark of total difference—a means of consolidating whiteness or maleness as the exemplary, coherent subjectivity—such a move offers the possibility of using the abject as a reminder of otherness within. Like the previously rejected, inassimilable part of Hughes's manuscript, the abject returns—in the shape of the Uzbek woman—to configure Hughes's essays and articulate an idea of being in otherness that rejects both the narcissistic self identified with whiteness through the figure of Koestler and the seeming goal of a proper self-consciousness identified by Du Bois. Hughes's fantasized liberation thereby allows for a reconfiguration of the self that is continually open to the peregrinations, the challenges of the Uzbek other. Such openness remains the hallmark of Hughes's internationalism in which he repositioned both selfhood and citizenship by stressing the emancipatory potential of illicit and licit boundary crossings.

IN HUGHES'S HAREM

For all his attempts to shake the grip of Western attitudes toward the other, Hughes was never entirely removed from the Euro-imperial trappings of his discourse—after all, unveiling is a Western notion consummately concerned with the desire to know, and the epistemic regimenting of the female body based on Western notions of propriety and desire. The very same orbits that release Hughes from conventional historical notions of progress also bear cultural baggage. Importing his "raciality" is at the same time importing his Americanness, and it is the mark of this Americanness that affects his view of Uzbek women. In describing the rote associations with women's veils, Thompson underlines an American perspective: "The 'jah' or 'paranja' was a monstrous veil imposed on the women. Many of us in the West had thought of women in veils as romantic and exotic—the images that we saw in Hollywood movies—cute little veils over their faces revealing only coquettish eyes. But when I saw the kind of paraphernalia that women had to wear, I was astounded" (LTP 1, 52–53). Championing the unveiling of women as the definitive act of progressive reform, Hughes engages with some of the more orthodox American presumptions of heterosexual formations of romance and the exotic as well. In uniformly applauding the aggressive tactics of Soviet reform, Hughes implicitly condones not only the cultural evisceration of the regions but the link between women and territory, believing that national conformity to the new dictates of the Union would follow compulsory unveiling. While vastly liberating to Hughes's sense of what racial emancipation in the United States could look like, Hughes's comparison of the Jim Crow laws in the States and czarist Central Asia also reveals his indebtedness to American forms of cultural identity when observing the changes wrought by Soviet intervention. His linking of the regions provides an example of how striving to move beyond the nation can solicit the subject's indebtedness to national forms of consciousness, too—even those that he would ascribe to the oppressors. Hughes's essays on the region make manifest the ways in which Hughes was imbricated in modern understandings of history and selfhood in which Islam as well as Muslim and Uzbek practices were seen as backward and less evolved. At one point, Hughes describes a display at a women's club in Uzbekistan of "frightening things out of the past on exhibit: charms, dangerous herbs, fake medicines, and feather shakers used on sick children by the witch doctors."[75] Hughes's essays illuminate the ways in which a Soviet reconceptualization of identity posed promising myths of liberation for a consciousness of the intersectionality of race, gender, and nation, and how this very consciousness was at the same time bound in somewhat delimiting notions of what that promised future should reveal.

The notion of orbits "hitherto reserved for whites" not only implies unquestioned privilege but, more to the point, the sanctioned use of colonial territories as "feminine" spaces.[76] By focusing on women as what Gregory J. Massell has termed "a surrogate proletariat," the Soviets participated in a long-standing European colonial tradition of gendering territory as feminine. Massell contends that "one of the main stimuli for turning to Central Asian women as a potential revolutionary stratum undoubtedly was the growing Soviet awareness of the difficulties involved in applying conventional criteria of 'class struggle' in the Moslem traditional milieu."[77] But in singling out women as the social conglomerate on which to bestow the fruits of revolutionary reform, the Soviets overlooked the heterogeneity of Muslim women in the region. Much as in non-Muslim regions of the Union the Soviets created a proletariat from a diverse strata of peasants, workers, and intellectuals, in Central Asia they created "the Muslim woman" as the prototype on which to focus revolutionary zeal. This woman was seen as both a unifying force and the potential source for disruption. Hence, the lives of actual women were disposed of in the interest of an ideal, symbolic woman whose body became the territory on which to map the success or failure of the new Soviet system. The symbol of the revolutionized—unveiled—woman became a means of neglecting the contradictory, multiple, and at times overlapping positions of women in the Sovietized region of Central Asia.[78] The fabrication of this woman was of a piece with the fabrication and reterritorialization of the entire region. Shirin Akiner articulates the ways in which far from a unilateral release from the imperial oppression of czarist days, the influx of Soviet reform into Central Asia was experienced as a massively disruptive and disorienting imposition. Prior to Soviet intervention the region had existed as an entirety of Russian protectorates. "Nothing in any way prepared the ground [for this intervention]," Akiner writes. "Far from being a response to a popular, indigenous demand, the Delimitation [of the region into republics] was an administrative decision imposed on the region" from Moscow.[79] At the same time that the Soviets broke up the territories into national units, attempting to create cohesive national cultures that could be distinct from one another, they used Muslim women as a unifying mechanism through which to ensure the "modernization" of each of the newly formed republics. In both cases, the Soviets interceded in ways that forcibly ignored regional interpretations of history, heritage, and culture, as well as self-interpolations within these frameworks. In bringing together Hughes's American consciousness and the specific context of women in Soviet Central Asia, then, the question that is foremost is whether, in dislodging conventional paradigms—that is, in crossing previously untrammeled boundaries—Hughes nonetheless accommodates other similarly disabling ones. Is femininity expendable, or is it the enabling basis for a new identification? Can it be both? Does Hughes's sense of subjectivity that emerges across the figure of a Muslim woman disarticulate established social vectors that would otherwise conspire to suppress this inscrutable feminine other?

In a long piece titled "In an Emir's Harem," published in *Woman's Home Companion* in 1934, Hughes grafts colonial imagination onto Soviet liberation.[80] Unlike his other essays on a similar theme, this piece begins as a tale in which the narrator is not identified. "Bring them to the pool," the piece opens, "[and] let me behold them."[81] The reader is thus drawn into a narrative in which an omnipotent Emir summons his many wives from their locked ward to a secluded pool, where they are instructed to undress and bathe under his gaze: "No one else dared look as his lovely houris went down into the water. . . . [T]he Emir sat in his great soft chair and looked at this luxury" (EH, 12). This portion of the tale forefronts how masculine control exerts itself through vision and visibility, and female powerlessness is a result of being unable to escape the penetrating gaze of a desiring male. The women are literally trapped within the high walls of the Emir's panoptic gaze. Even when they are veiled, they are subject to the ever present production of his look.

Caught up in this earthy portrait of lascivious harem life, it is a surprise to the reader when Hughes's tale stops abruptly in the midst of its descriptive excess to assert, "That was a dozen years ago." Countering the narrative authority of his earlier vision, Hughes states that "only in my mind's eye could I see the lovely houris bathing—for the pool is empty even of water today" (91). Hughes's prose not only attempts to bring the reader (addressed as "you") into alignment with Hughes's vision but demonstrates that it has set up the Emir's gaze so that it can be preempted in favor of Hughes's own. Because of the narrative break, the reader is reminded that Hughes's imagination is the site of the harem. "In an Emir's Harem" signifies "in Hughes's harem" for it is in the author's "mind's eye" that this scenario is visible. The phrase "I saw" is repeated liberally leading up to the penultimate assertion, "I saw the royal harem" (91). By emphasizing what can be seen, and implicitly separating it from that which cannot, Hughes reorders the vision of the past. He moves between "before" and "after" as the shifting consciousness that can trespass culturally taboo spaces. Women, he writes, "can never, by any power, be brought back to the old male-dominated, harem-enclosed patterns of the past" (92). And yet Hughes's transgression of the veil solidifies the masculine prerogatives of his vision. It is his prose that conjures the "old male-dominated, harem-enclosed patterns of the past."[82] In rewriting the memory of confinement, Hughes recuperates the power differential he attempts to undermine by reasserting the romance of visionary control and discourse of "modern" liberation—all within a familiar rhetoric of racial liberation and freedom.

8. Hughes observes gender integration at a Central Asia teahouse. Yale Collection of American Literature, Beinecke Rare Book and Manuscript Library. Reprinted by permission of Harold Ober Associates Incorporated.

In championing the new world for a southern, primarily dark-skinned people, Hughes slights the notion that a new way of living could subject women to new coercive norms in which novel forms of discipline and control supplanted those under challenge.

Hughes's play with the correlative effects that Soviet "liberation" brought to women suggests the subtleties of his renarration of their emancipation. Narrative ruptures could be read as attempts to establish discontinuity with the past and its masculine oppressions. Hughes's conjuring of the harem space allows him to trade in masculine privilege for a more ambiguous mechanism of identification. Bringing readers into his vision, Hughes quickly disposes of interest in men, focusing instead on exchanges between himself and the women who dared to unveil. "Farewell to Mahomet" elaborates on the displacement of men, cast as antagonists against unveiling, describing "irate males of Tashkent" who "rose in opposition. What! Women gathering in a public tea house unveiled, drinking tea! NO! It should never happen."[83] In both pieces, the enthusiasm of his prose for unveiling soars while disdain for the dictates of a conservative male culture rings clear, providing a space wherein he can grant himself rights denied by Jim Crow culture—that is, black American selfhood—and trespass the veil. Hughes is no longer burdened by an other side in these essays. Like his emancipated women, he is "quite without a veil today, free, and self-reliant" (EH, 91). So intense is the newfound experience of freedom that even the unveiled women "have almost forgotten" what the harem was like (EH, 91).

If memories dull as time progresses, however, it is Hughes's task to reenter the harem, to depict, chart, and reembody what he saw. His liberating gaze reorders the space of the past and enables him vicariously to experience the lifted veil, to identify with the resulting sense of being "free, and self-reliant." "No one else dared look," he writes (EH, 12). An identification with the process of unveiling as at once a woman's activity and his own allows him to write forcefully about the resulting effects: he describes unveiling as a "brave," "heroic," "daring," and "defiant" casting off of the "long hideous *paranja*—a heavy black horse-hair veil from head to foot, through which their faces could not be seen."[84] Focusing on the paranja as the literalization of the harem, Hughes outlines the ways in which the harem operated as a kind of hegemony, reinforcing the "common sense" of sexual difference through a requisite separation of the sexes. The lifting of the veil would then challenge the hegemony of the harem while exposing the collaborative illogic of racial delineations, thereby energizing that "static world" in such a way as to have "enormous personal effect" (FM, 31).

But while articulating links between two discourses of the veil, Hughes's work also establishes its own differences from them. If in Du Bois the veil represents a forbidden though nonetheless necessary (denied) commerce with women, then Hughes's enthusiastic appeal to abolish the "hideous veil" may speak to a discomfort with the very promise of heterosexual plenty, a promise implied in Du Bois and in traditional Orientalist narratives. In fact, Hughes calls harem life monotonous; "they had nothing to do," "they were not happy," "there was nobody to amuse them . . . and there were not even enough contacts with the outside world to supply gossip . . . there was nothing to do but be bored. Sometimes in sheer desperation they would wash their hair" (EH, 91). In renouncing the amusements of the Oriental tale, textual ruse for sexual entitlement, Hughes undercuts the traditional narrative of the Eastern woman by foreclosing expectation. He routes racial emancipation through ambivalence toward the very terms that would assert conventionalities of hetero-, cross-racial desire as adequate measures for ascertaining acceptability and belonging. Yet in challenging the hetero-normativity of the Du Boisian dyad, Hughes also forecloses the possibility of women creating alliances and bonds—erotic and otherwise—within the female community known as the harem. A disjunction between Hughes and the harem remains. As a westerner, Hughes can know the forbidden mystery of the veil by recasting it in suggestive narratives. In order to enter the public sphere, however, these women must do so through the approved avenues of mediation: the "language" of modernity and its epistemic regimenting, its rehareming, its reveiling, of the female body.

Recoding the veil, Hughes performs a double motion of defrocking and redressing; his essays bear the mark of modernity's ordering regimes as they reterritorialize the harem and the story of its undoing. Yet informed by his own racial configurations and Du Bois's discursive veil, Hughes also strays from the path of hegemonic Western discourse about the Muslim world by resisting the narrative of pure exoticism and reconfiguring Soviet dogma to his own ends. Whereas Du Bois's ambivalence toward the veil could be seen in his desire to maintain a protective shield against the horrors of white supremacy, Hughes's attitude appears less ambivalent, denigrating veiling's predominant discourses. Even though the veil may appear to be an arbitrary marker, it wreaks specific race and gender encoded experiences by imposing its historically specific discourses of otherness. This oversight on Hughes's part reflects his own racial and gendered interpolation in the United States. It reflects the ways in which Hughes's own subjectivity is inescapably routed through the confines of gender segregation back in the States. Reverberations of his transgression of the veil can therefore be detected both locally, in Hughes's Uzbek encounter, and on the home front, where the readers for whom Hughes is writing bear historically specific expectations of their own.

If Hughes's thoughts about racial aesthetics at this time were somewhat contentious, in recasting them into articles for the popular press he reentered a discursive space more familiar, and more reassuring, to his readers. By portraying the harem in the titillating terms of murder, tyranny, and unbridled sensuality, Hughes's essays consoled his readers that the very promise of their U.S. citizenship was the guarantee of home as an anti-harem. In this projection of harem life into the past, he both reminds his curious, Western readers of *Woman's Home Companion* what confinement was like and assures them that it exists no longer. This gesture serves to distance the home's companion, the woman, from imagery of her own domestic confinement, encapsulated as it is in the magazine's very title.[85] If for Hughes the paranja literalized the life of the veil described by Du Bois, thereby proving the arbitrariness of modernity's adherence to skin color as the revelatory mark of identity, his readers likely came away from Hughes's harem with quite a different lesson. "In an Emir's Harem" and "Farewell to Mahomet" conjure the "primitive" aspects of life in the harem as entirely other worldly. As in "Boy Dancers of Uzbekistan," the harem is the promise of all that is outside the genericized white, middle-class community. Even while calling attention to their own layeredness, to the multiple crossings and translations necessary to make the journey from Hughes's experience to American living rooms, these essays give the appearance of immediate access to this other world. They provide a means of prioritizing visibility as the inviolable regulatory regime that ensures that difference *will* be seen even if the veil has been lifted.[86]

Hughes's tales, then, participated in imposing a distance between "fantasy" and "reality." His essays confirmed that travel could indeed *be* the woman's best home companion. Escorting her from a world of domestic drudgery to a land of sheiks and harems, these tales would always reinforce that she was better off at home. The proximity of the "new" and "old" orders in Central Asia highlighted the tenuousness of the revolution that had "rumbled its slow way" across Asia. Readers might believe that Uzbek women were always on the verge of slipping back into the stifling confines of harem life—a life that existed there and not within the bounds of American domesticity. But do Hughes's crossings point unilaterally to a reinscription of colonial power differentials? Should his tales of Oriental intrigue be discounted as simply another instance of crippling, ethnocentric fantasy? Might a counterdiscourse be detected emerging at the very moment when the Du Boisian veil disengages from that of Muslim Uzbek faith? Is there a way to see Hughes at once deploying the feminine as a means of relinquishing the fantasy of a proper self?

THE TURN HOME: THE WAYS OF WHITE FOLKS

Against the notion of a pure African American consciousness, Hughes drew on his experiences in Central Asia to rethink the uses of Soviet internationalism and what the rhetoric of transnational alliances, the re-formulation of citizenship and belonging, had to offer African Americans on a local level. Refusing the "white male" delineation of citizenship with which he associated the exclusions of U.S. national identity, Hughes em-braced internationalism as a means of preserving national dislocatedness to combat white hegemony. At the same time, he revealed an indebtedness to the Soviet-sponsored ambiguity over the relationship between the mul-tinational federation it idealized and its promotion of national units such as the so-called black belt. With ambiguity intact, Hughes extended this idea of internationalism to posit the emancipatory potential of between-ness, openness to a feminine other, on a subjective level that refused to renounce identity per se. This double-layered negotiation of, on the one hand, a new internationalism and, on the other hand, a new liberated subjectivity had at its center the apparatus of unveiling as the conceptual arena in which the crossing of national, cultural, social, and subjective boundaries fused for Hughes. With the promise of new opportunities foremost in his mind, however, in migrating from Central Asia to write about the United States, Hughes seemed to ask himself: Can one really choose to ignore the constraints of nation even if the nation in question has forcibly ignored oneself? The asymmetrical routes of identification through which Hughes appropriated and resisted existing discourses of the veil leads one to see how Hughes's experiences in Russia both enabled him to realize new affinities with the USSR and renegotiate older ones with the United States.

The influence of Hughes's experiences in Soviet Central Asia shape not only the unanthologized pieces of his work but also some of his better-known, canonized writings. Indeed, it was in the three stories composed in Moscow and later published in *The Ways of White Folks* that one finds the influence of Hughes's Uzbek encounters clearly charted onto the U.S. social topography.[87] Inspired in part by D. H. Lawrence's collection of stories *The Lovely Lady* (1930), which he read after returning from Uzbek-istan, Hughes reoriented his vision from Central Asia to the United States and quickly composed "Cora Unashamed," "Slave on the Block," and "Poor Little Black Fellow."[88] The proscriptive delineation of the color line as mediated through double consciousness and a life of the veil, the woman's role in racial liberation, the ways in which otherness becomes denigrated as feminine, and the generative potential of disruptive boundary crossings associated with a summoning of matter out of place, are all ideas that carry over from Central Asia to figure prominently in the stories about U.S. society.

As well, because Hughes's encounter with Lawrence's *The Lovely Lady* had such a marked effect on him when he returned to Moscow from Central Asia, Lawrence's stories can be seen as a bridge between his recorded experiences in Uzbekistan and his writing about race relations in the United States. On reading Lawrence's "The Lovely Lady"—a story about the fascinating but terrifying power of a wealthy white woman over her thirty-year-old son—Hughes was riveted: "I could not put the book down, although it brought cold sweat and goose-pimples to my body."[89] Arnold Rampersad conjectures that Hughes, who before he left for Moscow had dissolved his arrangement of patronage with Charlotte Osgood Mason, was reminded by "The Lovely Lady" of his own thwarted and complex relationship with Mason. To be sure, the interrelated ideas of female power and racial liberation were at the forefront of Hughes's writings, and Lawrence's stories provided something of a model that Hughes refashioned for his own devices.[90] Bringing together the "shame" associated with a lack of heterosexual desire and the driving force of a "strange female power," Lawrence's stories in *The Lovely Lady* open the possibility for a critique of whiteness—as practiced and produced by women of wealth—through the prism of sexuality. Women throughout the collection are depicted as possessing "a strange muscular energy" that annihilates men.[91] And yet, rather than suggesting that women embody a natural power, what these stories outline is the relationality between disenfranchisements of various types, and how sexuality figures into discourses of race and gender. To this end, Hughes's stories borrow the idea of female power from Lawrence and bifurcate it. He investigates both the suffocating aspects of white femininity as it intersects with and lays bare its subjects, and the more redemptive power of a racially enlightened feminine sexuality. If Hughes's stories are thought of as in part a rereading of Lawrence's, then one can begin to see how Hughes's portrayals work to demystify U.S., wealthy, white femininity and expose the limits of the racial ideology in which it is inscribed. Hughes, unlike Lawrence, also offers the unashamed expression of conventionally uncouth, feminine desire as an antidote to the confining manacles posed by characters such as Lawrence's Pauline Attenbourough and Hughes's Mrs. Art Studevant.

By introducing an Armenian into the plot of "Mother and Daughter," Lawrence's story sets the stage for Hughes's transposition to a racially charged template. This story brings together an awe-inspiring power of wealthy white femininity and the stay that racial difference places on this power. By elaborating with excruciating precision just how completely an Armenian man undoes the "magnetic connection" of the "double Circe" mother and daughter team, Lawrence remarks on, among other things, a British inability to fathom racial difference (LL, 103). Although the British colonial context is specific to the racial commentary that Lawrence engages, a relevance to Hughes's experiences can be ascertained in at least two areas: first, in contemplating the power structures inherent to racial and cultural difference; and second, in summoning the issues of the harem with which Hughes had recently been occupied in Uzbekistan. The delimitations of a privileged, white, Anglo femininity are revealed in terms of a virulent racism, as if such racism were ultimately the price paid for the curious female energy that Lawrence, like Hughes, found so fascinating. But in implying that either female power and racism necessarily go hand in hand, or that female capitulation to the patriarchal, tribal order that "harem" (in Lawrence's terms) suggests is the cost for being nonracist, Lawrence doesn't leave any alternative (LL, 127).

While Hughes's intertextuality with Lawrence is marked, his stories are equally engaged with his encounter with female empowerment in Central Asia. Hughes's visceral reaction to Lawrence's stories, and his related urge to whip off a series of stories in reply, surely had some relation to his recent experiences in Central Asia. Feminine identification in *The Ways of White Folks* crosses over differently gendered bodies in the same way it does in "Boy Dancers of Uzbekistan" and Hughes's descriptions of Tamara Khanum. Hughes, unlike Lawrence, wants to reconfigure the relationship between the feminine and race, to show how the establishment of racial and sexual taboos are collaborative projects, and recalling McKay's work in *Trial by Lynching*, how sexual emancipation might be related to racial liberation. He wants to transfer the female power Lawrence outlines into a positive, proleptic force for an internationally awakened racial emancipation. And it is this idealization that leads him from Uzbekistan to the United States.

Even though the stories in *The Ways of White Folks* foreground the female-coded international element of Hughes's rescriptings of racial identity, Hughes scholarship that has discussed the collection has not addressed this connection sufficiently. Ignoring the geographic routing of ideas—from the United States to Central Asia and back again—readings of the stories have primarily focused on the national boundedness of Hughes's pieces.[92] For example, Joyce Ann Joyce describes the stories as providing a "comprehensive glimpse of the various manifestations of race relations throughout the United States."[93] While such readings are certainly instructive, in delimiting Hughes's vision to a "comprehensively" U.S. focus, they not only supply simply a partial account of the stories' genealogy but in so doing replicate a standard mode of isolating U.S. racial discourse from its international ties. In overlooking the background of Hughes's experiences in the Soviet Union, and in particular Central Asia, critical accounts have been unable to offer a fuller picture of how the transnational flow of Hughes's meditations on otherness serves as a basis for divulging "the ways of white folks." The essays on Uzbekistan provide a vocabulary of boundary tampering that registers the way racial and national boundaries collaborate with the formation and enforcement of sexual difference. To read *The Ways of White Folks* without Hughes's vision of Uzbek boy dancers, or Khanum's ungendered dynamism, is to miss the subtle power of Hughes's reconfiguration of black subjectivity.

Having traced colored life in the Soviet south, Hughes turned his ethnographic eye to the unveiled of America—that is, white folks. What the Uzbek pieces show is that a recoding of the veil in *The Ways of White Folks* transpires into a reframing of colored life as a way of being unveiled without being white. In *The Ways of White Folks,* this idea is encapsulated in Hughes's very project: reading whiteness as the official face of U.S. national identity through a juxtaposition of the corresponding "illegitimate" face of blackness. As others have pointed out, in order to write about white folks, Hughes used blacks as his primary characters. He revealed that the ways of whiteness depended on blackness in order to assert and differentiate themselves. But the stories in this collection demonstrate not only how the racial categories of black and white are interdependent (that is, one needs nonwhite in order to establish that which is white), and how the presumed dichotomy between the two relies on a false binary logic. They also chart how such interdependence has historically created the need for the fictive other. The longing for identity traced in these stories, far from being a call for assimilation into whiteness, latches onto disruption and discontinuity as a means through which a self can be known and selfhood established without resorting to oppositional affirmation. In the midst of querying the boundaries of racial categories, and outlining their fictitiousness, the stories show how a desire to adhere to blackness as an identity worth living creates a compelling counternarrative: that one needn't be white in order to be. Taking as their point of departure the presumption that racial categories are themselves the product of a confluence of social and material conditions whose logic of othering relies on a series of fictions and thus proves arbitrary, the stories associate being colored not with skin tone per se but a comfort with disorientation and the challenging of proscriptive boundaries. This productive dislocation emerged through cross-gender identification, the renunciation of hetero-normative desire—the routing of Hughes's racial consciousness through Central Asia back to the United States underwritten by the promise of Soviet internationalism.

In order to better situate Hughes's stories in their critical milieu, it is necessary to step back and attend to the ways in which his work was imbricated in the terminology and streams of thought of the 1920s and 1930s. Like his essays on Uzbekistan, Hughes's stories are very much engaged with the ethnographic discourses and debates of those two decades. The project of *The Ways of White Folks* as a collection not only "signifies" on Du Bois's *Souls* (and to a lesser extent on his 1920 "The Souls of White Folk") but also is an ironic reinterpretation of the "salvage" idea current in anthropology at the time. George W. Stocking Jr. highlights the sense of urgency that characterized the ethnographic endeavor, "and the consequent commitment to the importance of 'salvaging' the (presumed) pristine human variety facing obliteration by the march of European civilization."[94] Hughes's friendship with Zora Neale Hurston in the 1920s along with his key role in that decade's proliferation of black cultural production exposed him to the debates that Franz Boas's work raised around the issues of primitivism and black modernism. Like Du Bois's *Souls*, Boas's work took seriously the cultural wealth of African American productivity in the arts, both conventional and unconventional, as a means of countering pseudoscientific determinations of the inferiority of blacks.[95] Boas countered social Darwinism with an antievolutionism that prized cultural specificity, and Boas and his students, including Hurston, were particularly invested in the "folk" contributions to black culture.[96] The "ways" of Hughes's title, then, is clearly a wink at anthropological terminology of the day, and his coupling of "white" and "folk" an extension of this ironic gesture. Certainly, the notion of studying whites as a race under threat of erasure by the "march of European civilization" was meant as satire, but satire with an edge that at the same time was quite serious about the necessity of viewing whites as a race and whiteness as a racial culture. Far from a "docile and humble" approach to art, Hughes's stories used a modified notion of the folk to incorporate a new primacy of the international. Like McKay's relocation of the black belt to Harlem, Hughes's folk is self-consciously fabricated, moving easily between rural outpost and urbane metropolis.

This shifting of terrain echoes the shifting between nationalism and internationalism encouraged by Soviet understanding of black culture in the 1930s. Following the 1928 Comintern decision to advocate the U.S. South as comprising a black belt, Soviet support of black nationalism was an exception to policy that denounced national factionalism in favor of an international proletarianism. But as Robin Kelley has discussed, while Soviet support of black self-determination in the U.S. South seemed to be in conflict with communist ideology, it also "opened up space for creative expressions of black nationalism and race pride" that heretofore were unprecedented.[97] This new sense of cultural freedom stemmed from a Soviet interest in "Negro" art as "folk" art. As I discuss in chapter 4, Soviet enthusiasm for all things folk was itself an invention based on the need to establish a common Soviet culture in which all citizens could partake. Believing that black folk art forms contained an inherently revolutionary strain, Soviet ideologues and communists in the United States enthusiastically supported Negro art as unified by an authentic expression of proletarian consciousness. Kelley maintains, however, that the enthusiasm with which communists and black nationalists alike embraced black culture was wrought "on the terrain of gender" in which these otherwise antagonistic groups "found common ground—a ground which rendered women invisible or ancillary."[98] Unlike the typical narratives of black communism, in which a dichotomy between communist politics and literary culture often took the shape of a masculinist project, though, Hughes's tales put women at the heart of an emancipatory politics.[99] As elucidated in his essays on Uzbek women and as borne out in his stories about white folks, Hughes undid the masculine imagery in which revolutionary propaganda was conventionally cast and made women central to the struggle for liberation.

The connective fibers between the Uzbek essays and U.S. stories include Hughes's explicit rendering of an international perspective enabling African Americans to see U.S. racial politics more clearly. But they are also linked by the pervasive figure of the feminine as routed through this international perspective, and thus the touchstone for an invigorating liberation. Of the three stories that Hughes wrote while in Moscow, "Cora Unashamed," the first piece in the collection, portrays these concerns most vividly. In "Cora Unashamed," the protagonist comes to denounce the proprieties dictated by the upper-middle-class strictures of her white employers, the Studevants, after she takes on a white lover, Joe, and bears his child. Joe is described as "an I.W.W. but Cora didn't care. . . . This white boy, Joe, he always smelt like the horses. He was some kind of foreigner" (*WWF*, 6). As a member of the most radical of the unionists, the Wobblies, Joe figures the political influx of socialism, with all its foreign associations, into Melton, the town where the Studevants reside. Joe represents the international, political realm of white leftism that is mutated and realigned by Cora. Cora transforms the foreign link or impulse embodied by Joe, shaping it into a counterdiscourse against the stifling bonds of the white Studevants. Her counterdiscourse emerges through a focus on threshold moments in which the culturally taboo threatens to emerge and disturb the systematic flow of white American upper-class life, and Cora not only encourages but nurtures such disruptions, such unveilings.

In narrating the tale of a poor, middle-aged black woman named Cora Jenkins who works slavishly for an ungrateful family, Hughes repeatedly engages a crossing of borders that evokes the preoccupations his Uzbek essays associate with unveiling. He uses Cora as the conduit who undoes previously intact spaces around which whiteness has congealed. In this way, the unveiling with which Cora is engaged is an unveiling of the purportedly already unveiled—the white folks. As in his essays on Uzbekistan, this is again a rescripting of the Du Boisian configuration in which the putative goal of ruptured "colored" consciousness is the integrated selfhood associated with whiteness. But in Cora's tale the tables are turned, so that the ease with which Cora challenges boundaries—an indication that she, like the idealized Uzbek woman, refuses to adhere to the veil—reads as an index of the struggles she faces in attempting to unveil the whites with whom she lives.

In demonstrating how whites, too, exist within the parameters and structures of the veil, how whites, too, could be awakened to an internal otherness obliterated by enforced difference, Hughes plays fast and loose with the logic of the Du Boisian veil. His implication recalls a description from "In an Emir's Harem," in which he marks his fascination by focusing on the various skin tones hidden beneath the Uzbek veil. He depicts the members of the harem in color-specific strokes: "The young bodies of some of the girls were milk-white and fair but most of them were a little golden like the grapes in the arbor, or like peaches in the fall. Others were brown as russet pears and one or two were dark as chocolate" (EH, 91). Hughes suggests that the juxtaposition of the physical veil with an intuited one reveals how race as an assignation adheres to skin color without any supportable basis for a determinate distinction between shades. The life of the veil is lived by both ivory- and chestnut-hued women. Stressing that most harem members fell somewhere in between these fruitful extremes, Hughes points to the arbitrary nature of the race consciousness portrayed by Du Bois. He teaches one that double consciousness, a life of the veil, pursues both light- and dark-skinned others.

Thus, it is to the "milk-white" veiled women that Hughes turns in "Cora Unashamed." He centers Cora's tale around her denigration of boundaries and the related scenes of white disclosure that ensue. Cora's interruptive powers are positioned as a reminder of her foreign link, as if the very notion of a purely domestic African American consciousness were itself a fiction, and Cora's encounter with Joe tapped into a political unconscious in the sense of a newfound proclivity toward illicit crossings and boundary tampering. The international impulse behind a reoriented understanding of race relations in the United States, in turn, links back to the way in which Hughes wrote about his own encounter with the Soviet Union.

Among Cora's messages is the warning that the cost of reproducing normative whiteness is life itself. And her prediction holds true when, after divulging to Mrs. Studevant that her daughter, Jessie Studevant, is pregnant by a Greek local, the Studevants force Jessie to have an abortion she does not want, and Jessie dies from complications related to the procedure. In her final scene of unveiling, Cora attends Jessie's funeral and there denounces the Studevants for killing their daughter. Cora's denunciation is reminiscent of a different funeral scene that Hughes depicts in his essay "The Soviet Theater in Central Asia" (1934). Hughes writes that the funeral of a young actress, Nurhan, who was put to death in 1930 by her parents for appearing unveiled on the stage, "was made the occasion for a stirring appeal to all women to take off their veils, to refuse to remain in harems or to submit to the slavelike customs of the past."[100] Hughes's correlation between youthful femininity trespassing societal boundaries and dying at the hand of parental authority for the transgression is unmistakable.[101] In the case of Soviet Central Asia, women like Nurhan and Khanum paved the way for "freeing others from the chains of the old life," and in Cora's tale one can likewise hear Hughes's appeal to break from old patterns of suppression and silence, to challenge custom in spite of the risks. In both contexts silence offers only shame (ST, 591).

Hughes uses the Uzbek example to expand on the sacrifices endured to ensure the reproduction of whiteness to include quite specifically the costs of aborted desire. During the funeral outing of Melton society, Cora gestures toward the related "campaigns of purity" the Studevants have launched in order to rid Melton of undesirables. Jessie's improper sexuality, reminiscent of Cora's own, is translated into an improper orality: when asked to explain why Jessie is sick, Mrs. Studevant says that Jessie had "an awful attack of indigestion. . . . Jessie had eaten the wrong thing" (*WWF*, 14). The "wrong thing" is directly linked to Greek contamination, and indeed Mrs. Studevant spreads a rumor that the Greek boy's father was "selling tainted ice cream" (15). The female speculation of racial impurity recalls McKay's depiction of Mathilda's downfall. In both cases, rumors sponsored by white women circulate to eradicate the agency of the "othered" bodies in question, thus showcasing the abilities of these white women to be self-speculative. Her plan is to "rid the town of objectionable tradespeople and questionable characters. Greeks were bound to be one or the other" (15). Connected to a fear of foreign contamination, Mrs. Studevant's worry is that the tradespeople/foreigners will come to know the market better than the whites, that they will become more effectively speculative and displace white hegemony. Fear of ingesting "bad" ice cream becomes a way of denouncing deviant desires, a way of articulating horror at the thought of domestic contamination by the foreign, and a refusal to admit the interdependence of the two.

Thus, Cora is a reminder that politics and desire can intertwine and operate simultaneously. Cora certainly does not become politically active in any conventional sense through the contact with Joe but rather her political gestures take place in a different register. She becomes a conduit of betweenness, her comfort with impropriety recalling Hughes's assertion of his difference from Koestler in Central Asia, and like Hughes she exposes previously intact spaces around which whiteness has solidified. In this way, Hughes suggests how an international political impulse—loosely disguised as the IWW—supplies the charge that disrupts the smooth flow of national racial inequities, and how this charge can register on a personal level, in the shape of desire not commonly thought of as political. Cora is reminiscent of Khanum, unashamed, "a living symbol of that new freedom . . . brave and creative, breaking down old taboos," but the lack of institutional support for her challenges to the status quo leaves her unable to effect the kind of social change that Hughes idealizes, that Khanum ignites by "helping others to break them [taboos] down . . . to throw their veils forever into the fire, in spite of conservative and dangerous men-folk about the house" (TK, 835). As elsewhere Hughes distances himself from the proverbial "men-folk," allowing identification instead with these defiant, "self-reliant" women. The critique of white society that Hughes routes through the character of Cora is an indictment of the "economic trap" that keeps black, working-class women in subservient roles. As Angela Davis has argued, "The hypostatized notion that woman, as contrasted with man, is only a creature of nature, is blatantly false and a camouflage for the social subjugation women experience daily. But even in its falsity, there is also a hidden truth: the real oppression of women is inextricably bound up with the capitalist mode of appropriating and mastering nature."[102] Divulging how the Studevants attempt to control "nature" by forcing Jessie to abort her child, Hughes links this kind of meddling directly to the economic interests of the family. But whereas the fact that the economy of social reproduction puts whites in positions of power may come as no surprise, the ways in which Hughes writes about Cora's internalization of these institutionalized subjugations offers a novel way of linking material realities with a politics of black subjectivity. Again, what

Hughes reveals in his suggestive alignment of Cora with Khanum are the stakes of aborted desires and the imperative of unveiling in spite of extreme danger.

When placed in the context of Khanum's death-defying acts of social transgression, Hughes's romanticization of Cora's naturalness reveals how Hughes adapted accepted rhetoric about women to serve his own ends. Hughes describes Khanum "in a land where men still believed in veils and harems in spite of Soviet decrees, her participation was extremely dangerous. But she stuck" (TK, 834). Similarly, Cora is depicted "like a tree— once rooted, she stood, in spite of storms and strife, wind, and rocks, in the earth."[103] In Cora's case, Hughes makes use of conventional descriptive tools of comparing women to nature, of positioning the nonurban female as a repository of folksy authenticity to imply something quite different than a female acquiescence to active male norms and examples. Infused with the knowledge of what it costs to go "against the will of the family," Cora recognizes the boundaries of the Studevants' ambitions, the family recipe for acceptable desires. Hence, Cora's tale is not simply a story of class hardship and the resulting racial tensions that come out of economic traps. It is also a tale of identity and why, given the deprecations of life as a poor African American woman in the 1930s one would want to maintain that racialized experience as a way of life preferable to whiteness. And yet neither is this a plea to reify black experience as a direct reflection of a superseding reality. Hughes is at the same time positioning himself against the temptation to insist that there is one, definable, "proper" way of being black. As Joan Scott has cautioned, "Experience is at once always already an interpretation and is in need of interpretation."[104] Hughes's presentation is an assertion of black experience as of necessity an expression of the systemic, historically contingent patterns of oppression and the ways in which some blacks internalized these patterns to create subjectivities. Cora's story illustrates an awareness of the need to thwart an assumed transparency of subjects, and instead demonstrate the ways in which subjectivities are produced and agency made possible within the given coordinates of those experiences. Cora "on the edge of Melton" with the other "Jenkins niggers, Pa and Ma and Cora, somehow manage to get along" (*WWF*, 18). Cora's life is perhaps a destitute one, but nonetheless a life worth living precisely because of the ways in which this life has provided an alternate site for a working-class woman's consciousness at a far remove from the tyranny of the proper. Hughes transmits this alternate consciousness through Cora's story so that his exposure of whiteness is hers: the black woman plays the key role in the unveiling not only of herself but of whiteness as well.

Hughes was well aware of the risks that an overromanticization of black folk posed, and he addresses these risks directly in the next story in the collection, "Slave on the Block." Also written in Moscow, this tale elaborates on the critique of modernity suggested in "Cora" and takes to task the primitivist longing of 1920s Harlem, with its anthropological underpinnings. In brief, this story is linked to "Cora" in at least three ways. First, Hughes moves from rural to city setting in order to show the racial complexities of the folk encountering the urban center and how the very idea of the folk is itself a construct filtered through an extremely urban perspective. Second, Hughes satirizes the notion of a black folksiness celebrated unconditionally for its simplicity and vitality, in this way underlining Cora's exposure of the tainted strands of otherness and selfhood that bring together the domestic and international. And finally, "Slave on the Block" again poses and unveils the problem of white femininity. This problematic is, in this case, read through the central figure of Luther, the young "slave on the block." This story reveals how cross-racial desire exposes both the subordinancy of the white female and black male to white masculinity, and at the same time divulges the relational power white women hold over black men, in spite of a shared lack of agency vis-à-vis white men. In this story, Anne's desire for Luther, while naive and blatantly racist, is also a reflection of her own suffocation under the stultifying tentacles of whiteness. The point of this story is both to pose a rereading of the primitivist urge underlying the consumption of black cultural production in the Harlem of the 1920s, and show how differentially, across the gender spectrum, blacks and whites suffered from the structure of patronage in the arts during that period. In making this point, the story taunts the vapidity of whiteness, uncovers the dullness of life without the veil—if one wrongly equates being unveiled with whiteness—and demonstrates how processes of racialization both link and distend the structural relationship between white women and black men.

If the international element seems to have fallen out of "Slave on the

Block" thematically, it is never fully absent. Hughes's working contention throughout the collection is that the processes of racialization link the domestic and international. In the two stories that follow, "Home" and "Poor Little Black Fellow," the international is front and center. As in "Cora," its impulse is linked to unveiling. In the ironically titled "Home," a young violinist named Roy Williams, sensing that he is fatally ill, travels home from abroad to visit his family. The story opens with a telling description of Roy's luggage, which along with his violin case is covered with "bright stickers and tags in strange languages" and "the marks of customs stations at far-away borders." These foreign letters and incongruous marks "made white people on the train wonder about the brown-skinned young man to whom the bag belonged" (*WWF*, 33). Back for the first time in several years, Roy takes but a moment to acclimate himself. In the station he hears someone mutter "Nigger" and "for the first time in half a dozen years he felt his color. He was home" (37). Roy's feeling of color constraint and the ensuing deprecations associated with the derogatory label "Nigger" are synonymous with "home." This feeling, however, is presented as a refresher course in the meaning of belonging. The "wonder" that white people display about Roy due to the "strange marks" on his belongings is a reflection of the provincial attitudes of U.S. whites who think in bounded, domestic terms about the place of race. It takes them no time to put Roy "in his place," inasmuch as his place is, within a U.S. conception of difference, beneath whites. Nonetheless, Roy's strangeness stands out—it is coded as his internationalism, a foreign element garnered from travel abroad, an "unreadableness" posited in languages that whites cannot decipher. It is this alien marking that is associated with him materially, it is his "belonging." Thus, it is the anxiety created by the inability of the whites around Roy to locate him to their satisfaction, and an adamant refusal to accept a black representative from an outside community, an international one—whose symbols do not cohere with the national fantasy shared by whites of what it means to belong—that together spark the animosity and hatred that ensues. At once a parable about the refusal of internationalism between the wars and the related vitriol toward artistic black males who present as "strange," as odd, who refuse to conform to expected white standards of black masculinity, "Home" is a devastating tale that ends with Roy's violent expulsion from the community.

In each of these stories the reader is shown how African Americans transform political rhetoric to create personal meaning, and the role of women in this transformation is highlighted. Hughes's use of Europe and Paris as background is not simply a reiteration of the importance of European travel to the emerging race consciousness of black Americans. Europe is used as a launching site from which Hughes's characters move on to realize a more radical understanding of the limits of U.S. citizenship. As with the insertion of leftist characters who represent the impulse toward socialism in the 1930s, the revelation of internationalism to which Arnie comes at the end of "Poor Little Black Fellow" is meant to reposition the tale of European awakening.

In "Poor Little Black Fellow," the notion of home (and the revelation of home as the site and source of stultifying color constraint) that plays itself out in terms of fantasies and fears of miscegenation, happens in reverse for Arnie, the protagonist. It is when Arnie is abroad in Paris that he realizes "here it didn't matter—color," as if providing the background for what Roy must have himself felt when he traveled through Europe as a musician. By providing a glimpse into the story of what may have happened "over there," though, "Poor Little Black Fellow" is more pointed about the transformative potential of internationalism, as conceived of by Hughes (and perhaps less pointed about the costs of ignoring and destroying it). Hughes makes this observation by structuring the first part of the tale around a single moment of intervention: the introduction of a dancer perhaps modeled on Josephine Baker, but equally reminiscent of Khanum, named Claudina Lawrence.[105] Following Claudina's appearance, Hughes underscores her importance to the story. Without Claudina, "everything would have gone on perfectly, surely; and there would have been no story" (*WWF*, 143). The story is only a story because of an international black character: as Hughes writes just following her momentous introduction, eleven pages into the story, "here the tale begins" (144). Hughes's tactics here recall those used in "In an Emir's Harem" in which calling attention to a rupture in narrative provides a means of reassessment, of challenging the course of the tale that has preceded it, and of dissociating the narrator from the structure of male omnipotence in which the earlier portion appeared invested. Demonstrating both that the international impulse interrupts the tranquil flow of U.S. domestic narratives of racial piety supported by Christian charity and "niceness," and that a woman is key to this interruption, Hughes deconstructs the first half of his story. By beginning the story in its middle, he emphasizes the instrumentality of an international impulse for transgressing conventional narrative and political expectations. The tale starts with a digression, a break, a rupture, an unexpected crossing conceived of by a female that sets the stage for the enlightenment of a black male. "Why, Lord, oh why?" asks Arnie's white matron, Grace Pemberton, and then in repeating her question, answers it, "for the sake of Arnie, why?" (144). When the Pembertons decide out of their seemingly unending supply of niceness to take Arnie on a European tour, they don't predict the tour's outcome. That Paris would awaken a racial consciousness in Arnie is least of what they expect. The interpretive intervention performed by a black woman thus works not only to awaken Arnie but to expose the limits of the racial ideology in which the Pembertons circulate. As in the previous stories, Arnie's unveiling is linked to an unveiling of whiteness in the sense that in Europe, Arnie sees whiteness in a new light. The connection between the two unveilings supplies the basis for the rewriting of conventional mappings of Europe in the formation of black American subjectivities.

By setting his tale in Paris, Hughes is playing on a theme familiar to black American tales of European awakening. This idea of European instrumentality in triggering a reconstructed sense of U.S. raciality has received attention from both historians of black culture such as David Levering Lewis and cultural critics such as Paul Gilroy.[106] But Hughes's intervention here differs from the black Atlantic paradigm and brings unfamiliar territory into the geographic schematic mapped out by Gilroy. As I discussed in the introduction, Gilroy's elision of the Soviet Union in his charting of the links between modernity and double consciousness is significant. In Arnie's story this significance becomes pointed, for although Arnie's racial awakening occurs in Paris, the means by which Arnie is awoken challenge the dominant patterns through which African American experiences of Europe in general and Paris more specifically have come to be understood.

Gilroy has extended readings of the instrumentality of Europe to African American racial consciousness by connecting this transnational development to black modernism. As Gilroy reiterates, African American intellectuals changed their perceptions of the United States and racial domination by traveling abroad, and their peregrinations lead Gilroy to stress the importance of thinking in terms of "routes" in place of "roots" when considering black cultural production. Gilroy's model of the black Atlantic provides a way of thinking about transnationalism that derivates, in Gilroy's words, in "a desire to transcend both the structures of the nation state and the constraints of ethnicity and national particularity that go along with it." At the same time, the black Atlantic is for Gilroy a "modern political and cultural formation" that "frames the doorway of double-consciousness."[107] As useful as this formulation is, it doesn't offer one a means of explicating how desire and double consciousness can work in asymmetric ways in the formation of black internationalism. Hughes's work does enable one to do so, and it does this by querying the moment constitutive of Du Boisian double consciousness, the moment in which the veil appears, which is, as discussed above, a moment routed through and rooted in cross-racial, heterosexual desire. Thus, although Gilroy does not provide any specific mapping of desire as it relates to either the black Atlantic or double consciousness, Hughes's stories rethink Du Boisian desire and in so doing offer a new way of thinking about Hughes's black internationalism.[108]

Having witnessed the cohabitation of two discourses of the veil in the Uzbek pieces, Hughes returns conceptually to the United States with a more pointed framework in which to rethink the Du Boisian paradigm. Unlike writers such as Du Bois and James Weldon Johnson who preceded him in writing about the African American experience of Europe, Hughes underlines the interplay between race consciousness and sexual desire in the story that most explicitly draws on his written experiences of Uzbekistan. While those essays gave Hughes an opportunity to begin to rethink the lessons of the veil, it is in his writings about the black veil in the United States that his reformulations of Du Bois and the Du Boisian veil become most clear. Hughes's revision of Du Bois consists in his portrayal of the ways in which Du Bois's configuration ignores alternate agencies and erases the black female. In attempting to construct a racial imaginary in which the allure of the white woman would not necessarily be linked to the black man's demise, Hughes shows how a feminine sexual agency disrupts the heterosexual compulsion undergirding Du Bois's white female/black male dyad.

The focus on female agency in the undoing of embedded cultural patterns of exclusion and delimitation is the resonant connection that links Hughes's Uzbekistan to his Arnie. Wresting away from men the upper hand in the economics of agency to instead assert female will, Hughes proclaims a feminine desire integral to the racial liberation he associates with unveiling. Hughes's Paris, for example, is splayed out in a rhetorical gesture that sensualizes the city landscape into a female form, caressed by a necklace of lights and proffering lips that kiss "without fear." Replacing proscription with permissive sexuality, Hughes rereads Du Bois's proverbial moment of masculine veiling to show a woman fearlessly expressing desire. Recuperating female agency, Hughes demonstrates how the very definition of racial liberation rests on the emancipation of denigrated drives and desires, among which female sexuality emerges as one of the most vital.[109] Hughes's work thereby suggests the failings of a masculinist ideology, such as that of Du Bois's *Souls,* that is so deeply invested in the redemptive power of a heterosexual black male body.

In providing this counternarrative to Du Bois, Hughes's tale offers three suggestive rescriptions: the unveiling that defines Hughes's internationalism is not limited to blacks alone; the emancipation of female sexuality is key to racial liberation; and the isolation of these issues has contributed to a notion of citizenship as exclusively the domain of whites. Outlining the first reformulation, Hughes reiterates the simultaneity and interdependence of black and white unveiling. The Pembertons' whiteness is depicted in a full regalia of rigidity, dullness, and conformity to effete norms. Hughes demonstrates how Arnie can only really see what the Pembertons represent—can only really see the confines of their whiteness—against the backdrop of Paris. At the same time, this international perspective plays with expected geographic routings by engaging the Romanian character of Vivi, the woman for whom Arnie forsakes the Pembertons. Thus, Paris is destabilized as a specific center of internationalism—internationalism itself crosses national boundaries, enabling a newfound sense of racial autonomy that emerges from and is fused with female agency and desire.

Rather than establishing a simple dichotomy between black and white, however, Hughes chooses instead to propose that the international defines "colored" life, and that the internationalism he proposes is by definition colored not by skin tone per se but by forging heretofore unchallenged boundaries. As evident from his portrayal of the Carraways in "Slave on the Block," what Hughes refuses, or more precisely what he parodies, is the primitivistic longing displayed by a white embracing of black culture as unmediated by material conditions. By contrast, what Hughes embraces is a colored culture infused with the material. Just as black culture is for Hughes by definition fabricated, conceived out of historical conditions, and likewise international, it is the refusal of the international by whites to whom a false universality is ascribed that he chastises. In other words, it is the notion of American exceptionalism that he takes to task through his portrayal of the Pemberton family and their notions of Christian duty and niceness. When the Pembertons travel in Europe, they tote with them their notions of racial entitlement as whites. Their "program of cultural Paris" and the sights they plan to see—Versailles, the Louvre, the Eiffel Tower, and the Café de la Paix—reconfirm this sense of deserved entitlement. Bolstered by a sense of national citizenship and belonging that adheres to them even in Paris, the Pembertons strive to keep domestic and foreign boundaries intact, even while traveling abroad.

Differently, Arnie's desire to explore the Parisian nightlife of smoky jazz clubs and trendy cabarets signals his discovery of blackness not only as a beginning, an initiation into sexual agency and the fantasies of belonging that ensue, but as international in genesis. Arnie tells the Pembertons that he "didn't care about going to the Odeon" and his eyes glaze over in the Luxembourg gallery: "He was thinking about Claudina and the friends he might meet . . . the Paris they could show him, the girls they would be sure to know" (*WWF*, 146). Arnie's "thinking about Claudina" quickly flows into "the girls" he might meet with her. His race consciousness is linked to the problematic of citizenship in which sexual desire circulates. As seen in Du Bois's work, sexual desire has been used to regulate proper and improper citizenships through the social prohibition of miscegenation. By anthropomorphizing Paris, Hughes connects the emancipatory racial consciousness that emerges in this international setting with emancipated desire. Although it is clear that female agency is key to this configuration, the gendered contours of an unfettered sexual awakening obviously extend to Arnie as well. Hughes suggests, however, that racial liberation does not simply rely on an assertion of masculine agency vis-à-vis the veil but rather (as in Uzbek unveiling) depends equally on a reassessment and valuation of feminine desire. Hughes's Uzbek essays are instructive here because they imply that Hughes does not restrict "feminine" to women. The best example of the variegated contours of Hughes's international arrives during Arnie's first night out in Paris where "he'd met dozens of nice girls: white girls and brown girls, and yellow girls" (149). Recalling the women of various hues who once wore the veil in Uzbekistan, the presence of these women and Arnie's ability to associate freely with them signals that the veil is also an intuited boundary to which both racial and gender segregation can be likened. The veil, as Hughes reconfigures it, is neither race nor gender specific. Seeing life unveiled is thus for Hughes a way of refusing whiteness, a means of espousing an internationalism that preserves national dislocatedness as a means of combating white hegemony. And Hughes reads sexual emancipation as fundamental to such combat.

Hughes's critique of the Pembertons is not simply a programmatic, Marxist-based analysis of the inequities of class. Arnie's identity is layered within the intersections of racial disenfranchisement and class privilege. Although he has suffered from the ignorance of white gentility, he has also been steeped in and identified with its more pervasive ideologies. Hughes proves this to be the case when, having been refused admission by the local Boy Scout camp, Arnie is sent to a Boston charity camp. Arnie's reaction to the camp is unequivocal: "[He] hated it" (138). His shock and surprise to find "black kids from the slums of Boston who cussed and fought" causes such distress that he quickly leaves. Arnie's alienation from the other children who make "fun of him because he didn't know how to play the dozens" signals his outsider status not as a "poor little black fellow" but a "rich little black fellow." In other words, Arnie's alienation is a result of his "whiteness," the fact that he has been raised to be a "nice" black fellow. Pinpointing this discrepancy, Hughes writes, "So Arnie, to whom Negroes were a new nation, even if he was black, was amazed and bewildered and came home" (139). Arnie is unable to locate himself within this "new nation" of blackness. Presented with an epistemological crisis, he can identify neither with the oral culture signified by the playing of the dozens nor the class-inflected demeanor of kids from the slums. Faced with his own embodiment of an incompatible blackness once again, it takes Arnie's exposure to an international setting to soothe his bewilderment over this new nation, to enable him to connect his own sense of racial identity to a less circumscribed sphere. Clearly, the affluence of Claudina and her friends smoothes over the "amazement" that colored his reaction to the charity camp. His newfound comfort with blackness and subsequent embracing of black culture are a result of a class mobility not evident in the "nation" he encountered in Boston.

If Claudina interrupts the even keel of whiteness in which Arnie has been immersed, Vivi disturbs the smooth flow of blackness he has come to know and embrace in Paris. Vivi is the character that derails the familiar reading of Paris as a haven for black American expatriates. Her depiction enables Hughes to suggest that his use of the feminine is not simply an advocation of the female as the source for a resistance associated with the culturally taboo but imbricated in and articulated as an internationale. Arnie confides in Vivi "how white people had raised him, and how hard it was to be black in America," but Vivi is almost impatient in her response. Color is not the issue in Paris or Romania, she replies, "Here it's only hard to be poor." In reply, Arnie concedes that "he wouldn't mind being poor in a land where it didn't matter what color you were" (153). Arnie's sheltered upbringing—he has never been poor, and when he was surrounded by poor blacks, he fled—is again reflected when he asks, "What Revolution? . . . Where we live it's quiet. . . . My folks come from Massachusetts" (153). His class privilege and racial disenfranchisement collide. He is certain how he "fits" in with Claudina's cosmopolitan set, but unclear how this sense of belonging rests in class privilege. Although "even the Pembertons had heard of Claudina Lawrence in the quiet and sedate village of Mapleton" (144), the Russian Revolution is at such a distance from their concerns as to not disrupt their quiet life there. The awakening that Claudina prompts is likewise only partial. It is Vivi to whom Arnie is indebted for exposing the ways in which his own raciality has heretofore contributed to (rather than diminished) racist thinking.[110]

Arnie's real awakening is therefore finally a revelation about national belonging. His protracted journey toward belonging is cast as an unattainable fantasy in which Vivi plays a crucial part. Excited by the thought of showing the Pembertons that "there actually was a young white girl in the world who didn't care about color," Arnie imagines that he finally has the key that will unlock the door to acceptance, which has throughout his life been denied him. Whereas Arnie is convinced that by bringing Vivi to dinner as "his" girl he will be granted access to the family and accepted as a true member, the Pembertons "couldn't imagine that so lovely a white girl would go out with a strange Negro unless she were a prostitute" (*WWF*, 155). In both cases, white femininity serves as the symbol around which both Arnie and the Pembertons stake their claim. For Arnie, she represents a fantasy of belonging; for the Pembertons, she is the paragon of national dismemberment. Not only is she imagined as impure but as doubly so: she doesn't simply represent the threat of miscegenation but the mere fact of her association with Arnie is so unspeakable to the Pembertons that they can only envision her as always already tainted, as immoral, "a scarlet woman," her whiteness colored beyond recognition (*WWF*, 155). The Pembertons' description of Vivi as "scarlet" provides a critical moment of misrecognition. In mistaking one "red" for another, the Pembertons misread Vivi's political profligacy for a sexual one. Inserting one interpretation of potential defilement over another, the Pembertons supply the means of demonstrating the inherent link, or slippage, between the sexual and political to which Hughes has been gesturing throughout the story. Vivi's potential defilement of whiteness harkens back to Claudina, Cora, and the unveiled Uzbek woman. What these women have in common is the way in which they suspend easy interpretation, and in generating this gap, offer a means of rethinking the connection between feminine sexual agency and racial liberation. Of course for Arnie, that Vivi is coded as colored is less clear: she represents for him the fulfillment of a longing that has been denied. At the same time, this desire is presented as so programmatic as to be compulsory. Arnie seems to be following a code imposed on him, just as he has followed all the other "leads" the Pembertons placed before him when he was a youth.

Arnie also distinguishes himself and the lessons of Vivi when, realizing that fulfillment will not be forthcoming, he separates himself from the Pembertons. In turn, his parents exclaim, "But your father died for America." "I guess he was a fool," Arnie replies, revealing that he has finally realized the depth of black American disenfranchisement and hence the limitations of a national identity to which whiteness is ascribed as universal (157). Harkening back to Cora's unabashed defilement of white propriety, Arnie scorns that which he knows the Pembertons hold dearest—an imperturbable sense of national belonging, and the even more dogged belief that death in the service of patriotism equals unspeakable honor. In patriotism's place, he opts for the uncertain future that Vivi's internationalism offers him.

Although it would be a stretch to say that Cora and Arnie are presented as unambiguous heroes, it is fair to say that they represent the partial triumphs associated with challenging a system in which they are, and know they are, mercilessly inscribed. Perhaps Arnie's ultimate ambivalence about Vivi's ability to ensure that he will live "happily ever after" is meant to register a sign that Hughes may be tinkering with the idea that heterosexual denouement is by definition sufficient to solve Arnie's yearning to fit in. Because Cora remains jobless in the "nowhere" town of Melton, because Arnie will likely be jarred by the reality of poverty and joblessness once the Pembertons cut off his allowance, their stories are nonetheless ones that explore an emancipation that leads at its basis back to Uzbekistan and the boundary crossing Hughes associated with unveiling. While the stories extend and move unveiling into varied arenas—including female sexuality, agency, motherhood, miscegenation, and national belonging—all of the themes can be related back to those Hughes recounted in his tales about the Central Asian woman and her unveiling. These tales reflect the infusion of political notions into private lives, the theoretical forgings of black internationalism with the experiential trajectories of African Americans. If a sense of shared exclusions wrought by systems of disenfranchisement the world over was what Lenin's internationalism had to offer diasporic blacks, Hughes was determined to show how this could be so: how African Americans could make use of these ideas—transform them and be transformed—in their day-to-day lives. Thus, in designating the pieces of Soviet Asia part of his *"No. 2 Life,"* part of the "pulp, waste matter, and rind" that he would edit out of his autobiography in 1956, Hughes himself provides the terms for understanding the significance of this writing. What Hughes's work attests to is that "waste matter," that which has been cast aside and rejected, can house productive and generative material for rethinking that which has been deemed proper.

As Bontemps correctly predicted, Hughes's Soviet work was rejected forcefully by his publisher Blanche Knopf in 1933 as insufficiently fresh.[111] Similarly, Hughes's friend and literary mentor/colleague Carl Van Vechten termed Hughes's "political" work "very, very weak."[112] And largely in accordance with this verdict, the instructiveness of Hughes's essays as envisioning the possibility for an African American interiority alternative to the one offered by Du Bois has been heretofore discounted as of secondary status. Although not without its own ideological snares, Hughes's musings nonetheless negotiated across proscriptive boundaries to try and imagine what that self between here and there might feel like. As Du Bois would point out in the 1950s, and as Hughes's own rewriting of his memoir confirmed, such negotiations were strongly countered by U.S. attempts to strap a continuous color belt around the globe during the post–World War II era. In order not to reify this belt retrospectively, reconsidering liminal areas that have been passed over may disrupt patterns to which one has grown accustomed and generate new ways of thinking about junctures between race, gender, and internationalism. The shades of Hughes's becoming other are visible through his articulations of the territories of the veil, castaway sites his work entreats us to contemplate in its dispersal of a subject that is constantly crossing from home to harem and in so doing receding before our very eyes.

CHAPTER THREE

Du Bois, Russia, and the "Refusal to Be 'White'"

At the turning point in historical events that is indicated, if not
constituted, by the fact of "Soviet Russia," the question at issue is not
which reality is better, or which has greater potential. It is only: which
reality is inwardly convergent with truth? Which truth is inwardly
preparing itself to converge with the real? Only he who clearly answers
these questions is "objective." Not towards his contemporaries (which
is unimportant) but toward events (which is decisive). Only he who,
by decision, has made his dialectical peace with the world can grasp
the concrete. But someone who wishes to decide "on the basis of
facts" will find no basis in the facts.—Walter Benjamin, *Reflections*

I stand in astonishment and wonder at the revelation of Russia that
has come to me. I may be partially deceived and half-informed, but if
what I have seen with my eyes and heard with my ears in Russia is
Bolshevism, I am a Bolshevik.—W. E. B. Du Bois, *Russia and America*

In rescripting internationalism by asserting a desire to open identity to
reconfiguration, Hughes rewrites one of the most cited and anthologized
passages from Du Bois's best-known text, *The Souls of Black Folks*. By
lending a position of prominence to Du Bois's *Souls* in this way Hughes,
like many African American writers to follow him, marks the importance
of this book to American literature. Du Bois's notions of the veil and
double consciousness have provided so enduring a model for black masculinity that this model has become, in the words of Gwen Bergner, "standard shorthand to describe African American subjectivity."[1] Given the
pervasiveness of this sentiment, however, it is somewhat surprising that its

terms have not been more fully interrogated. As Hughes's work demonstrates, other black subjectivities can interrupt this paradigm for black masculinity, putting pressure on a presumed synonymity between masculinity and subjectivity. Similarly, the work of the last quarter century of Du Bois's career, from 1940 to 1963, resituates this central paradigm for reading African American subjectivity. Nonetheless, an incessant focus on *The Souls of Black Folks* as the representative Du Bois text and double consciousness as his representative textual statement has deflected attention from Du Bois's later work.

In this work, Du Bois reveals a shift in his thinking, a political realignment from liberalism to socialism, and later from socialism to communism. Yet Du Bois's interest in the Soviet Union predated his political conversion to communism by several years. In 1922, he described Russia as the "most amazing and most hopeful phenomenon of the postwar period" and commissioned McKay to write up his 1922 trip for the *Crisis,* of which Du Bois was at the time editor.[2] Impressed with McKay's portrait, Du Bois was "determined if ever the chance came to visit Russia and see for myself" (*RA* 15).[3] And indeed three years later, in 1926, Du Bois made his first of four journeys (1926, 1936, 1949, and 1958) to the USSR. Du Bois later described his early visits to the Soviet Union as instrumental to the evolution of his political thought:

> I think it was the Russian Revolution which first illuminated and made clear this change in my basic thought. . . . [I]t made the assumption, long disputed, that out of the downtrodden mass of people, ability and character sufficient to do this task effectively could and would be found. I believed this dictum passionately. It was, in fact, the foundation stone of my fight for black folk; It explained me. . . . Since that trip [to the Soviet Union] my mental outlook and the aspect of the world will never be the same."[4]

As Du Bois explains in this passage, in his thinking about the philosophical impetus behind the Russian Revolution—Marxism—and the Soviet Union there was a degree of overlap. It was not only travel to the Soviet Union per se but a combination of Marxist analysis and Du Bois's impressions of the Soviet Union that led him to depict the USSR as "the most hopeful nation in the world." In Du Bois's records, his trips stand as unparalleled challenges to U.S. policies of government-sanctioned racism

9. Du Bois and Khrushchev at the Kremlin, January 1959. Special Collections and
Archives, W. E. B. Du Bois Library, University of Massachusetts, Amherst.

and likewise unparalleled moments of self-reconfiguration. Unlike McKay
and Robeson, however, Du Bois did not experience the phenomenon of
being an "icon" when in Russia. He was, however, warmly received by the
Soviets, celebrated by Khrushchev, and later awarded the Lenin Peace
Prize. Du Bois's attraction to the Soviet Union was somewhat more like
Hughes's—based in an idealized vision of racial emancipation. Soviet
funding of his trips, translations of his work into Russian, publication of
his articles in prominent Soviet periodicals, the founding of the Africa
Institute at his suggestion, and support for his *Encyclopedia Africana* project did not, of course, deter his enthusiasm. But unlike Hughes and
McKay, who also received financial backing from the Soviets, Du Bois's
positive vision was fully vested in the intellectual analytics of Marx and
Lenin. His enthusiasm for the Soviet Union emerged from an enthusiasm
for the potential racial emancipation that could emerge from a Marxist
restructuring of the flows of capital and an enlivened sense of the potential
for revolutionary consciousness that evolved not from a belief in race as

The "Refusal to Be 'White'" ¦ 151

essential but in a return to racial identity as a linking, experiential relationship to the world.

A focus on the early Du Bois thus loses sight of his output during the sixty years of his life following the publication of *Souls* in 1903. In particular, it is Du Bois's move beyond double consciousness and his post–World War II refiguring of the color line—both of which correspond to his move toward communism and a personal alliance with the Soviet Union—that historically have been overlooked.[5] In more recent scholarship, Gerald Horne, Cedric Robinson, Manning Marable, Adolph Reed, Arnold Rampersad, William E. Cain, and Eric Sundquist have offered sophisticated renderings of Du Bois's later career.[6] In differing ways, each of these authors have sought to come to terms with Du Bois's stated affiliations as a Communist and his earlier investments in liberal individualism.[7] Despite their various stances on the significance of Du Bois's turn to communism, however, none of these readers has focused on Du Bois's sustained engagement with the Soviet Union. Critical stress on certain Du Bois texts to the exclusion of others has resulted not only in the marginalization of his Soviet work but also a general ignorance about the breadth of Du Bois's engagement with the Soviet Union. In order to fully appreciate the importance of the Soviet Union in Du Bois's career, both well- and lesser-known portions of his late work must be retrieved from the Du Bois archive.

Du Bois outlined the significance of the evolution of his thinking in his autobiographies, of which, following *The Souls of Black Folk* and *Darkwater, or Voices from behind the Veil* (1926), there were two substantial reformulations. They are *Dusk of Dawn: An Essay Towards an Autobiography of a Race Concept* (1940) and *The Autobiography of W. E. B. Du Bois: A Soliloquy on Viewing My Life from the Last Decade of Its First Century* (1968). In addition to these volumes, in 1952 Du Bois published a lesser-known text, *In Battle for Peace: The Story of My Eighty-third Birthday*, which employs the same self-narrative style found in the other autobiographies. Although scholars have generally agreed that the subject of this latter book traces the climax of Du Bois's intellectual life—his indictment as a suspected foreign agent for the Soviet Union—*In Battle for Peace* has received surprisingly little attention. Similarly, Du Bois's most thorough examination of the Soviet Union—a three-hundred-page unpublished manuscript titled *Russia and America: An Interpretation*, written in 1950—has been virtually ignored by critics.[8] A completed manuscript that

Du Bois sought to publish to no avail, *Russia and America* offers insight into the complexities of his relationship to the USSR during the last fifteen years of his life.

In order to interpret this relationship, it is necessary to look beyond frameworks that would view this alliance as one wrought from a model of perfectly defined choices between good and evil. The late Du Bois can neither be dismissed nor can his turn to the Soviet Union be explained through an uncritical celebration of his logical disillusionment with the United States. In the post-Soviet era, Du Bois's commitment to the Soviet Union must be seen as linked to a philosophy of history and an investment in the legacy of intellectual countertraditions. As Du Bois makes clear in *Russia and America*, he believed in the fallibility and unpredictability of any attempt to narrate the past, and emphasized the inevitability of misrepresentation, the failure of a grand master plan, which was in his mind ultimately linked to how his work would be interpreted in the future. Du Bois's work, then, poses a challenge: to tread the fine line between over-identifying Du Bois with the ruin of the Soviet empire—and hence assigning to his idealism a necessarily "tragic" fate—and underidentifying or not fully appreciating the ways in which Du Bois allied himself with the Soviet Union through a consciousness of outsider status and thus as a counter to what he insisted were the monolithic goals of a post–World War II Americanization. Given the innumerable accounts of the past tyrannies, bloodshed, and corruption of the Soviet system that continue to pour out of the ex-Soviet state, this is a difficult though necessary task. In resisting an easy triumphalism, a space must be carved out wherein the commitment of Du Bois to the Soviet Union can be acknowledged without condemning his vision. The affective sweep and inspirational power of the explanatory framework offered him by Marxism and the Soviet model needs to be appreciated as one that appealed to both the unquestionable depth of his intellectual prowess and correlated to his unflagging commitment to global liberation, decolonization, and peace movements, as well as to his opposition to militarism, corporate tyranny, social inequality, and racial segregation. As Du Bois himself comments in *Russia and America*, "Whether or not Russian Communism is a success is beside the point; the point is, are the ideals of human uplift as conceived by Marx and Lenin ideals which ought to be realized? . . . even if Communism as tried in Russia had completely failed, it was a splendid effort, a magnificent vision"

(*RA*, 247). The depth of the impression the USSR had on Du Bois must be seen within the framework of the options available in the 1940s—conceived of in part as an antidote to the lingering effects of the depression of the 1930s, the persistence of legal Jim Crow laws, the monopolies of corporate capitalism, the court-ordered suppression of civil liberties, and the vilification of all things "un-American."

As Du Bois averred, his racial politics, from 1930 onward, owed much to Marxist analytics along with the Soviet interpretation and implementation of these concepts. He writes,

> What amazed and uplifted me in 1926 was to see a nation stoutly facing a problem which most other modern nations did not dare even to admit was real. Taking inspiration directly out of the mouths and dreams of the world's savants and prophets . . . this new Russia led by Lenin and inspired by Marx proposed to build a socialist state with production for use and not for private profit; with ownership of land and capital goods by the state and state control of public services including education and health. It was enough for me to see this mighty attempt. It might fail, I knew; but the effort in itself was social progress and neither foolishness nor crime. (48)

The key question in approaching the complexity of Du Bois and the USSR is: Can Du Bois and his allegiance to the dictum of the Russian Revolution be read as anything other than a necessary breakdown, a personal tragedy, a replication of the "hard, domineering consciousness" of Stalinism?[9] Because the Soviet Union did not achieve its promise of global democracy, must Du Bois's commitment to the aspirations of the Soviet promise also be read as an ultimate indicator of the failure of one of the twentieth century's most influential thinkers?

In *Russia and America*, Du Bois begins to plot out the framework for an answer, albeit incomplete, to these questions. Written in the first person, *Russia and America* lays out the concrete steps that led Du Bois to embrace Marxism as a superior explanatory framework for decoding both the social and psychic renderings of racial life in the United States. Fundamental to Du Bois's adherence to the Soviet Union was the outlawing of racism mandated by Stalin's constitutional amendments of 1936: "Neither language nor color of skin . . . can justify national and race inequality."[10] Presenting the most dynamic challenge to the inequities of U.S. racism and social inequality, the Soviet Union in the 1930s, 1940s, and 1950s increasingly appealed to Du Bois on the basis of a reformulated community that would arise theoretically from such a premise. Determined to unhinge the prevailing misconception that communism was an antidemocratic conspiracy posturing as a peace movement, Du Bois composed *Russia and America* with a fixity of purpose. Following World War II, he was firm in his belief that more than any Western nation, the Soviet Union promised a democratic as well as egalitarian society and not an abandonment of civil liberties to the collective forces of evil. To Du Bois's thinking, the Soviet Union had proven as much in its heroic stance against fascism during the war, and continued to concretize its goals in the shape of active support for decolonization and global liberation.

The pattern of Soviet influence that Du Bois expounds in his later autobiographical works thus has a history that can be traced to *Dusk of Dawn* and *Russia and America*. Although *Dusk of Dawn* concludes with an explicit rejection of communism (one he would later change his mind about), the book introduces the significance of the Soviet Union to Du Bois's thinking. *Russia and America* revises this stance, allying Du Bois with the Soviet project. The importance of Soviet Russia to Du Bois continues in his *Autobiography* where it is elaborated in conjunction with Du Bois's stubborn avowal of a communist stance. In spite of their differences, particularly the conclusions of *Dusk of Dawn* and the *Autobiography*, these books are interrelated, and a discussion of one necessitates an involvement with the others. This chapter attends to the significance of the Soviet Union to Du Bois's thinking, from 1940 onward, while acknowledging how the discourse of communism, so enabling to Du Bois from the late 1930s onward, was also fraught with imperfections.

In spite of these imperfections, however, one cannot simply dismiss the powerful ways in which Du Bois's interactions with Soviet communism aided him in constructing a counter to what he felt was the incendiary nuclearism, proimperialism, and racism of a post–World War II United States. Attempting to resist assignations of "positive" or "negative" assessments of Du Bois's political alignment, this chapter examines connections between what Michael Denning has delineated as "cultural politics" and "aesthetic ideologies." Cultural politics denote an author's expressed political affiliations and allegiances (which the author understands as a choice), and aesthetic ideologies a necessary imbrication in a politics of form.[11] I invoke these terms in order to look at the ways in which an investigation of the impulses involved in Du Bois's turn toward the Soviet Union may facilitate a better understanding of the formal record, in both its published and unpublished faces, of this involvement. A reassessment of the importance of the Soviet Union to Du Bois offers a counter both to the deflection from politics and the overdetermination by politics seen in attempts to read the late Du Bois. This corollary to my argument is therefore less about the specific bounds of genre than it is the way in which autobiography in particular has been used as the touchstone through which to judge the author's worthiness as a subject—either as appropriately representational or not representational enough—with these assessments turning on Du Bois's stated political affiliations.

THE TEXTUAL AND THE POLITICAL

In Du Bois's case, politics and form are always interrelated. His textuality is highly political. As Eric Sundquist eloquently puts it, "What is notable about Du Bois is the fundamental mutability of his conception of the represented life itself."[12] The same attention to mutability and openness to form must be held in regard to Du Bois's changing politics. Keenly aware in his later work that future interpretive assessments of his life went hand in hand with his present engagement with self-narration, Du Bois repeatedly reminds his readers that one can never predict the future, that a totalizing appraisal of the past is necessarily beyond one's reach. At the same time, he stresses the importance of acknowledging hope, aspiration, and the utopian impulse toward new modes of being. As Du Bois makes clear in *Russia and America,* he constantly refined his views because he believed that the link to the future was necessarily embedded in interpretations of the past. This openness to fallibility marks Du Bois's narrative of his own life as an assessment that was implicitly and at times explicitly engaged with contemporary reception. Although they differ from one another in their conclusions, *Dusk of Dawn, Russia and America, In Battle for Peace,* and the *Autobiography* use materialist frames to exert pressure on the past and situate the problematic of history in the ideological forces of "the present."

Paul Gilroy has described Du Bois's type of writing as coming out of an ambivalence toward the prevailing modes of modernity, thereby supplementing "recognisably sociological writing with personal and public history, fiction, autobiography, ethnography and poetry."[13] Du Bois's patchworking of diverse genres and disciplines can be connected to his search for a vocabulary with which to understand the workings of modernity. Just as autobiography serves as an insufficient term to capture his late work, so too do the categories of "race," "class," or "nation" appear unsatisfactory for charting a history of political subservience and potential revolt. Du Bois's refusal to be satisfied with one mode of historicizing corresponds to his dissatisfaction with autobiography as a genre. Nonetheless, the Soviet Union provided Du Bois with a new political framework, and this manifested itself in what I am calling, for lack of a better term, a reconfigured socioautobiographical model. First formulated in *Dusk of Dawn*, and then reapplied in *Russia and America*, this model was spawned by travel and catalyzed through Du Bois's experiences in the United States and USSR, and between the two as they vied for global preeminence in the late 1940s and 1950s. Because Du Bois links his understanding of the "race concept" with his own story, racial politics and autobiography are for him intimately intertwined.[14] As he writes in *Dusk of Dawn*, the concept of race "lacks something in personal interest, but personal interest in my case has always depended primarily upon this race concept. . . . [M]y autobiography is a digressive illustration and exemplification of what race has meant in the world in the nineteenth and twentieth centuries. . . . [M]y living gains its importance from the problems and not the problems from me" (*DD*, 97, 221). While he maintained that race was a social construction, and composed much of *Dusk of Dawn* as a lengthy exegesis on the topic, Du Bois's intellectual life was activated by his identification as a black American. Du Bois realized that the experiential could not be excluded; that race, in spite of its paradoxically illogical underpinnings, was nevertheless lived through all its contradictory vectors, impulses, and libidinal investments as real. His linking of personal and general continues as a shaping frame in *Russia and America*. It becomes part of the fabric of his quasi-sociological praxis, in which concern for objectivity and support through social data is coupled with personal account, anecdote, and the repeated situating of the narrator, Du Bois.

According to Du Bois, his experience of the Soviet experiment would always affect the way in which he composed his life story, and his life story would always affect the way in which he viewed Russia. His late work exhibits not only a turn toward communism but a concurrent interest in the internalization of the cultural determinations wrought by structural and institutional inequities. He explains, "I can interpret the Soviet Union today through my experience with ten million American Negroes in the last half of the nineteenth century. . . . The tangled complex of our feeling of inferiority before arrogance and power tore the finer fabric from our inner soul and left us too often naked to ridicule and rebuttal" (*RA*, 296). Du Bois's engagement with Soviet Russia enabled him to understand the processes of racial and cultural differentiation as *trans*nationally oriented, and thus Du Bois sought to align leftist and black activism through the key insight that experience did not mandate specific epistemological certainties about essential racial difference.[15] His move in the *Autobiography* away from race as the defining category of his critical assessments, then, marks less a divergence from his prior theorization than a continuity established as early as the 1940s. Du Bois's focus on the systemic violences of industrial capitalism encouraged him to seek crucial links between disenfranchised peoples around the globe. In turn, he encouraged others to see white supremacy as economically based yet experientially deployed—an insight at odds with attempts to establish the other as ontologically different. From the Alien and Sedition Acts of 1798 to the 1949 Foley Square Smith Act (under which Robeson and others with Communist affiliations were pursued, and Du Bois indicted), the notion that a necessary relationship pertained between so-called outsiders and radical thought was promoted in the United States. It was into this vortex of otherness and outsider status that Du Bois felt he was continually and increasingly thrust from the 1940s onward.

Seeking an alternative structure of community in which he could place his aspirations for a more democratic future, Du Bois based his interpretive acumen regarding the USSR on his "experience with ten million American Negroes." This declaration not only emphasized how experience was for him always a site of theorization but also established within this site a seeming parallel between African Americans and Soviets. Marked as nonhistoric peoples by Western philosophies of identity, Russians—like African Americans—were marginalized, excluded from the Hegelian *geist* of historical progress. Du Bois was keenly aware of these historical resonances between "Slavs" and "Africans," and found in Russia a nonoppositional counter to Western European constructs of selfhood.[16] Elaborating on the details of historical connections between the abolition of serfdom and emancipation in the nineteenth century, Du Bois moves on from historical data to assert the structure of feelings wrought by a "tangled complex of our feeling of inferiority before arrogance and power" (*RA* 296). This complex became all the more vivid for Du Bois when, in 1951, he was arrested, indicted, and tried as a suspected foreign agent. The primary narrative related in *In Battle for Peace* is the tale of Du Bois's 1951 trial, during which he experienced marginalization in a new way. This ordeal not only prompted linkages between himself and the Soviet Union; it altered his view of the color line. On the heels of his trial, in a series of articles, Du Bois exposed the attempt in the United States to reformulate the color line following World War II in response to what he termed the Soviet Union's refusal to "be 'white.'" In this Du Bois presaged what Richard Wright, in his 1956 report on the Bandung Conference, coined *The Color Curtain,* a rephrasing of Winston Churchill's "iron curtain" that brought together the social and symbolic valences of the East/West divide. In the 1950s, Du Bois directly related a move toward what he saw as superficial racial solidarity in the United States to the terms of the East/West barrier. With the "white" on the West and the "nonwhite" on the East, the true "other" to be feared became all things and beings pertaining to Communism. Aware of an antioutsider mentality being propounded, Du Bois maintained that domestic racial issues were being increasingly separated from international issues.

The near invisibility in racial discourse today of Du Bois's 1950s' political analyses and autobiography mirrors the success of this reshaping: the dislodging of the domestic from the international, the situating of East/West barriers, what Du Bois termed a "partial breaking of the color line," a hesitancy to see how U.S. racial histories are interpreted as connected to the legacy of Cold War mentalities. An overemphasis on Du Bois's early career exemplifies a tendency in American literary studies to be suspicious of links between U.S. history and that of the Soviet Union, particularly when it comes to the subject of African Americans. In the years since the decomposition of the Soviet Union, past communist interests of minority groups (who no longer seen as a threat, pose no risk of exposing U.S. racism to U.S. political enemies) have been more or less glossed over. In the 1950s and 1960s, antiracism was intimately connected to the barometer of a communist threat—the United States lost international esteem as

Soviet media pounced on visuals from 1957 Little Rock and distributed depictions of race rioting across the USSR's fifteen republics as well as in strategic points of interest in Africa and Asia. Without endorsing Soviet antiracism as a political or social accomplishment (or implying that Du Bois could somehow have foreseen, for example, the debacle in Prague in 1968), one can read contemporary anticommunist remarks as situated within a climate of desensitization to the threat of communist insurgency, of the Soviet menace as a thing of the past.[17]

The exclusion of Du Bois's later volumes of his autobiography speaks not only to the tensions surrounding Du Bois's oeuvre but more generally, to the politically fraught space of African American autobiography. A genre that has always troubled formal delineations, autobiography has historically provided a relatively continuous forum in which African Americans could proclaim their humanity through literacy.[18] For this reason, autobiography has a particular attachment to black American cultural production. But as a preferred form in which African American writers established (often in the act of dissimulation) the legitimacy of an undeniable subjecthood, autobiography is no innocent bystander in the racial hostilities with which aesthetic debates have long been laden. As Henry Louis Gates Jr. points out, "It is the birthright of the black writer that his experiences, however personal, are also automatically historical."[19] In spite of attempts to write against the grain of this tradition, the notion of African American autobiography as the standard-bearer for racial consciousness has held fast.[20] The exemption of an author's autobiographical work on the basis of a failure to blend into a preordained, overarching narrative thus resonates with the convention of white editorship that so frequently accompanied the slave narrative—as explanatory scaffolding to legitimate (or not) the proceeding narrative as properly representative. African American autobiography has by definition been bound by its historical conditions, within parameters where what could be said was always attenuated by the less lenient powers of what would be believed.

Du Bois's engagement with autobiography as the genre most embedded in African American experience is an attempt to negotiate a materiality of life as lived, with the color line, as discursively constructed and historically contingent. Recognizing the epistemological dilemmas inherent in adopting autobiography against type, Du Bois's involvement with its terms remains wary of an isolationist, monolithic approach to the complexities of translating experience into text. Without rejecting the fact that language plays a crucial role in the kinds of experience one "has," Du Bois poses an engagement with capital through its own abstract manifestations, recognizing how "the income-bearing value of race prejudice was the cause and not the result of theories of race inferiority" (*DD*, 129). Race prejudice is an accretion of value; it bears the burden of the accumulation of capital. Racism is "income-bearing."

Russia and America and *In Battle for Peace* exemplify both the influence of the Soviet Union on Du Bois's thought and the reworking of self-narration. These books offer a framework for understanding why Du Bois felt that the civil rights advances of the 1950s had to be seen in light of the international exposure of U.S. racist policies. In this sense, these books outline the international dimension of U.S. racial politics in the 1950s. Determining that the governing forces after World War II had recuperated the terms of resistance to bias on the basis of skin color, Du Bois reformulated the terms of the color line he set out in *Souls of Black Folk*. Like *Dusk of Dawn* and *Autobiography*, both *Russia and America* and *In Battle for Peace* forward the importance of travel to Du Bois's emerging sense of racial subjectivity, but the specificity of the Soviet Union to this sense is reiterated here by an enforced alliance of Du Bois and peoples of the Soviet Union in the U.S. public eye as others. Through his trial, Du Bois came to realize the slipperiness between the designated categories and to believe more firmly in the promise of the Soviet project. Describing his feeling that the USSR was more successful than other nations at combating racism, Du Bois wrote, "Russia seems to me the only modern country where people are not more or less taught and encouraged to despise and look down on some group or race" (*RA*, 27). This sentiment, based on Du Bois's sense of racial parity when in the USSR, paved the way for his aggrievement with the United States during his trial, and his subsequent statements in 1953 and 1956 that specifically reformulated the color line so as to include the Soviets as nonwhite.

MOSCOW ALLER RETOUR

As Paul Gilroy describes in *The Black Atlantic*, Du Bois frequently commented on the importance of travel to his political commitments. Gilroy reads Du Bois's numerous journeys as spaces wherein "what was initially felt to be a curse—the curse of homelessness or the curse of enforced exile—gets repossessed. It becomes affirmed and is reconstructed as the basis of a privileged standpoint from which certain useful and critical perceptions about the modern world become more likely." Gilroy's readings have been instrumental to my own formation of ideas about the significance of and complexity inherent to Du Bois's relationships to, as Gilroy puts it, his "lack of roots and the proliferation of routes in his long nomadic life." Further, Gilroy observes that even "temporary experiences of exile, relocation and displacement" can raise crucial questions "about the content and character of black culture and art."[21] Gilroy emphasizes Du Bois's links to Europe, and in so doing posits a triangulation between the United States/Europe/Africa. It is here that my reading strays from his. In drawing attention to the USSR, I question the efficacy of any geographically bound configuration that prioritizes national spaces and formations to the exclusion of others in the positing of a black modernism. The delimiting vectors of "the transatlantic black subject" presuppose the exemption of positions not contiguous to the Atlantic.[22] In order to think through the circuits of transnational capital, the category of "black" must be opened up to include antiessentialist challenges set in motion by a lingering essentialism of the black Atlantic paradigm. As Du Bois was well aware, travel was not a neutral category. Its availability to some belied its unavailability to others. The echoes and discontinuities in travel reflect on transnational connectedness: when he moves between borders, Du Bois imports his own imbrication in American national identity so that travel becomes the other of expansionism. This said, my focus remains on the distinct relationship between Du Bois and the Soviet Union. Although Gilroy provides sophisticated and compelling readings of Du Bois's incorporation of and ambivalence toward the logics of modernity and cultural momentum of the black diaspora, he overlooks the strategic place that the Soviet Union occupied in Du Bois's writing: how it was that the USSR specifically influenced and affected Du Bois's understanding of racial identity, and the heterogeneous ways in which Du Bois came to express an alliance with Russia.

In *Dusk of Dawn*, Du Bois marks the importance travel plays in his renegotiation of the conventional polarities between knowledge and its objects. His attempts to grasp race through scientific theories were first stymied when he traveled to Europe: "All this theory, however, was disturbed by certain facts in America, and by my European experience" (*DD*, 101). As he traveled through and beyond Europe, Du Bois found that travel enabled him to renegotiate the individual self through social coordinates. Travel—as a crossing of previously *imagined* and real boundaries—restructures Du Bois's understanding not only of himself but of his own emplottedness in the tale of global economic restructuring following World War I. But rather than supplying a simple mirror in which to reflect the ills of U.S. society or giving Du Bois a privileged vantage point outside the grasp of capitalist restructuring, Du Bois's travels yielded links between the disenfranchised abroad and the disenfranchised at home. "I made my first visit to Africa in 1923. . . . I became vividly aware of a Negro problem far greater than I had envisaged in America, and my mind leaped further; more or less clearly I found myself asking: is the problem of color and race simply and mainly a matter of difference in appearance and cultural variation, or has it something in common with the industrial organization of the world? With Poverty, Ignorance and Disease? Has Revolution in Russia something fundamental for the Negro Problem in the United States and the Colonial Problem in Africa?" (*RA*, 12). Du Bois links his interest in the Russian Revolution to U.S. racial inequities along with the ways in which industry and the structure of capital proved these domestic issues to be of international dimension.

Du Bois privileges travel in order to concretize the significance of the Soviet Union to his intellectual evolution. In the *Autobiography* and *In Battle for Peace*, "travel" and "character" are used interchangeably, signaling not only a link between the two but also the representative features of Du Bois as a role-player, as a character he both impersonates and scripts. Thus, Du Bois's interest in travel does not limit itself to a concern for the reckless crossing of boundaries but rather welcomes the theorization that accompanies specific movement across specific national borders as internationalist counters to Americanization. Chapter 1 of the *Autobiography* opens with a characteristic Du Boisian move: a departure.

This departure of 8 August 1958 is of particular importance to Du Bois as it signifies the return of his passport, which had been denied in 1951, and the beginning of a journey that would lead him to spend several months in the Soviet Union.[23] To open the *Autobiography* with both departure and

10. Du Bois relaxes in Lenin's apartment at the National
Hotel, Moscow, 1958. Special Collections and Archives, W. E. B.
Du Bois Library, University of Massachusetts Amherst.

return emphasizes the importance of mobility in a climate of imposed
monolithic political and social goals. One of this climate's most constrict-
ing elements, as Du Bois and his fellow passportless knew well, was the
suppression of voices that directly challenged the ways in which the discourses of containment were rife with powerful expansionist ideology.[24]
Du Bois had been refused a passport "on the excuse that it was not considered 'to the best interests of the United States'" that he travel.[25] As was the
case with Paul Robeson, the purported danger of Du Bois traveling was
linked to the threat of Soviet insurgency and a desire to subdue disruptive
energies not only within domestic boundaries but beyond. Du Bois's August 1958 departure thus receives special, featured attention because

it was one of the most important trips that I had ever taken, and had wide influence on my thought. To explain this influence, my Soliloquy becomes an autobiography. Autobiographies do not form indisputable authorities. They are always incomplete, and often unreliable. Eager as I am to put down the truth, there are difficulties; memory fails especially in small details, so that it becomes finally but a theory of my life, with much forgotten and misconceived, with valuable testimony but often less than absolutely true, despite my intention to be frank and fair. . . . What I think of myself, now and in the past, furnishes no certain document proving what I really am. Mostly my life today is a mass of memories which are forgotten accidentally or by deep design. (*A*, 12)

In place of an "indisputable authority," Du Bois offers "but a theory of [his] life," one spawned by a failure of memory. Hence, not only does theory reflect a necessary site of disintegration but autobiography—as the recuperation of this site—"theorizes" through this failure. The theory of autobiography offered here can nonetheless serve as a valuable testimony not because of its truth-bearing accuracy but rather through bearing witness to a "mass of memories" that may open up a new relationship to the past. Du Bois offers socioautobiography as a political theory, advising that occlusions of "truth" create histories. Such challenges to predominant modes of historicizing are foregrounded in *Russia and America*, in which the rescripting of travel into personal narrative becomes a crucial means of dissent.

So, while a shared sense of consciousness with the Soviet Union effected Du Bois's amendment of the terms of the color line, the effect of this shift in his thinking can be gauged by his use of autobiographical formations. Louis A. Renza has called such formations "digressive illustrations" that manipulate "the autobiographer's split from his persona [that] not only creates the possibility—for the writer, not the reader—of an alternative text to which the written version is but an oblique 'prelude' or 'failure,' it also denominates the autobiographical act as such to the writing self."[26] If offering this kind of split autobiography by definition generates failure, this is hardly reason to foreclose on autobiography's potential to engage politically. Du Bois orchestrates the splitting between self and character to designate autobiography as a political act that from its inception engages various ideological dilemmas of "failure." At the heart of an analysis of failure's far reach is a condemnation of the language of opposition (good versus evil, East versus West, individual versus collective, slavery versus freedom, coercion versus consent, containment versus expansion, and so forth) through which much cold war discourse was tendered. Du Bois's desire to create a new autobiography was connected to a need to shape new models of citizenship and community. He was certain of one thing: that Western European nineteenth-century models were outdated, insufficient, that they had failed. Read in conjunction with one another, Du Bois's later autobiographies offer themselves as a theory that uses the alleged failure of the old, of the particular, as a means of moving toward the possibility of an alternative text, a collective future. Russia becomes the site of this Du Boisian transformation from "soliloquy" to "autobiography."

THE FATE OF *RUSSIA AND AMERICA:*
BETTER DEAD THAN READ?

The very fact that Du Bois wrote at least five autobiographies attests to his resistance to the teleology implied by an autobiography's final say, the definitive *word* through which readers can filter retrospectively the relative worth or depravity of a given life. In these renditions, Du Bois advances portions of a life that spanned nearly a century, from 1868 to 1963. And yet one result of attempts to focus on Du Bois's early work has been the suppression of the versions of his life that Du Bois offered during his last twenty years, when he shifted his ideas about race to reflect a fastidious attachment to communism, in favor of those he wrote in his first forty.[27] In a letter dated 3 November 1952 to Arna Bontemps (then head librarian at Fisk University) about the possibility of archiving Du Bois's papers, Du Bois humorously alluded to this "custom" by pointing out the fact that most studies of him ignored his work after *Souls.* He wrote, "My career did not end with Booker T. Washington, and if, therefore, you are still working on those comparative biographies I hope you will not either over-stress that earlier part of my career or forget that latter part. There seem to be a considerable number of persons who think that I died when Washington did, which is an exaggeration."[28] Du Bois's dismay over the unbalanced attention given to the breadth of his written work speaks directly to the interpretive oversights I am addressing. Not only was Du Bois frustrated by a desire to move beyond his association with Washington—who died in 1915—and their differences over what Du Bois termed the "Tuskegee Machine" but also by his desire to be credited for the work in which he was at the time engaged. As is by now clear, the work refused acknowledgment in the 1950s, some fifty years after his critique of the Tuskegee establishment (and Du Bois might argue, his rightful ascension to the position of black leadership following Washington's demise), is the work Du Bois wrote in alliance with the Soviet Union.

Russia and America was summarily rejected by his publisher, Robert Giroux. Given this, Du Bois may not have been surprised at the oversight of his contemporary work in the 1950s. In a letter to Du Bois, Giroux deemed the book "an uncritical apologia for Soviet Russia and an excessive condemnation of the United States."[29] And yet, part of the purpose of *Russia and America* was to anticipate and detonate assaults such as this. Well aware of the anti-Soviet sentiment in the United States, Du Bois composed *Russia and America* as a summation of the reasoning behind the misinterpretation of Russia in popular U.S. imagination. Seeking to remedy misinterpretation by uncovering repressed stories as a point of critical departure, Du Bois's sense was that misinterpretation on behalf of the United States had everything to do with exclusions of citizenship and historical censorship. Both had their basis in the defense of what Du Bois termed a "Way of Life," one that championed the ideal of "individual freedom." For Du Bois, a direct corollary to this notion of autonomy was a belief in the nonhumanity of blacks. He remarks, "Both individual freedom and exploitation of labor developed side by side in America and were confused in world thought, as differing aspects of the same expanding culture. This was possible because Negroes came to be regarded as not human in the same sense as whites, and as thus presenting no challenge to humanity or religion" (*RA*, 158). In order to combat "humanity's" mean delimitations, the early Du Bois sought to prove the humanity of Negroes—a task that seemed tantamount to claiming deserved access to freedom. Du Bois, however, relates that his encounter with Marxism helped him to rethink this strategy; he inveighs against the exclusion of Marxism from his formal education and the censorship of reliable accounts of the Russian Revolution as responsible, in part, for his misplaced energies to that end. He observes, "In my early years then the problems of property, work and poverty were to me but manifestations of the basic problem of color. . . . Race problems, therefore, to my mind became the main cause of poverty. . . . Nothing in my college courses at Harvard led me yet to question the essential justice of the industrial system of the nation. . . . But still there came no word of Karl Marx" (3–4). Direct access to Moscow was key to the reformulation of his opinions: arriving in Moscow in August 1926, Du Bois was amazed to read in the *New York Times* a story that directly countered an event he witnessed firsthand, an experience that led him to conclude that "we tend to learn our history backwards" (47). To safeguard his book's status as a counter to what he felt was a continuum of misinformation about the USSR, he highlighted the various ways in his own life access to facts about Russia and Marxism had been limited, to demonstrate how he, too, had learned his "history backwards."

In much the same way that McKay envisioned *Negroes in America, Russia and America* was meant to be an antidote to such backward knowledge. Like McKay, Du Bois received ongoing institutional support from the Soviet Union—his trips were organized and financed by the All-Union Society for Overseas Cultural Links (VOKS), and his visits were covered enthusiastically by the state press. *Russia and America* interprets the interrelatedness between the two nations and the importance of this relationship to the future of the globe's darker races. Of the book's eight chapters, the first four are devoted to a meandering explanation of the Russian Revolution, punctuated by the high points of Du Bois's first two trips to the USSR in 1926 and 1936. In the last four chapters, he suggests that the specter of the Soviet Union was never far behind him in the postwar years. The last of the book's chapters, titled "World Peace," details Du Bois's 1949 trip to Moscow, where he attended the World Peace Congress (also attended by Robeson). The middle chapters attempt to dissuade the reader from summarily rejecting Du Bois's intellectual turn to the Soviet Union. Titled "The Witch Hunt" and "The Union of Soviet Socialist Republics, 1950," these chapters link anti-communism to a historical fear of and enmity toward Bolshevism and abolitionism, and provide a point-by-point counter to what Du Bois supposed were the most common critiques launched at the Soviet system. His interest in the Soviet Union was thus directly related to his sense that the future of antiracism had everything to do with the international dimensions of communism. For Du Bois, it was not a question of if the Soviet Union and communism would play a part in the futures of Negro peoples but what part. Against a retrogressive return to the exclusions wrought by "nineteenth-century methods," Du Bois posed the challenge of Soviet reform—reform that not only affected the fabric of national community within the Union but stressed its international import. In making this claim, Du Bois drew on a sense of shared consciousness fostered by a historical parallel: in Russia, "the darker peoples were serfs without land control" whose history "paralleled that of American freedmen" (86). Du Bois's contention was not that all blacks were the same throughout the world but rather that they shared positions of social marginality. Like McKay, he believed that structural similarities were wrought from shared experiences of exclusion. And similar to McKay in 1922, Du Bois felt that the Soviet inclusion of national customs and rituals within the Union promised a flourishing of nationalism within the larger internationale. Du Bois writes that

> this did not remain mere declamation. . . . [I]n 1936 over the whole area between the Arctic Ocean and the Black Sea and the Asian mountains, with vastly differing races and nationalities, men and women, irrespective of physical traits or color of skin, even including occasional African Negroes, could associate freely; travel in the same public vehicles and go to the same restaurants and hotels; sit next to each other in the same colleges and places of amusement; marry wherever there is mutual liking; engage in any craft or profession for which they are qualified; join the same societies; pay the same taxes and be elected to any office without exception. No other nation on earth can boast of such a situation. Nor did the Soviets forget the oppressed peoples of the earth. (122)

Like McKay and Hughes before him, Du Bois latched onto a freedom of mobility, association, and implicitly, miscegenation as deserved entitlements denied them in the United States, and which registered deeply in their experiences of the Soviet Union. Du Bois's description of the 1949 Peace Congress in Moscow echoes Hughes's portrait of the Soviets as a "new people." Illustrating the range of peoples represented by delegates from the Union's fifteen republics, Du Bois commented that the "crowd was a sight to make one bend forward and stare. Not that it was bizarre or especially strange, but it represented a nation, a new nation, a new world."[30]

And similar to McKay and Hughes, Du Bois's interest in countering U.S. accounts of history was caught up in his interest in the new and boundary-challenging aesthetic forms put forth by the promise of the new Soviet world as by definition integrationist and internationalist. To fashion his own opinion of what was taking place in the Soviet Union, Du Bois felt that travel there was necessary. He structures his record of his trips as a counter to what he considered mangled facts: "I read the books of other visitors. Then I said, I must write a book" (*RA*, n.p.). The way in which he processes his experiences as correctives to misinformation creates a narrative style comparable to that of his autobiographies. Reported speech, informal interviews, and anecdotes are linked to statistical data and reports, with first-person assessment creating the connecting fibers. His efforts to write an account of the Soviet Union are driven by an awareness of the fragility of the historical legacy at stake, by how his present would be viewed and interpreted in the future: "In coming years, we will look back on 1950 with astonishment, explaining laboriously to our grandchildren why sane people acted as they did and yet wanted right and justice to prevail" (203).

In spite of his positive projections onto the Soviet project, however, Du Bois refrained from unanimous approval. He notes that he "expected no miracles" in Russia, nor did he find them. Repeatedly, Du Bois stresses that "this is no Utopia, no fairy land of joy and plenty," and cautions his reader throughout that his "reasoning may be strained" (105, 156). Still, because he sensed an eagerness on behalf of much of the reading public to find fault with everything Soviet, Du Bois emphasized the aspects of Russia that to him seemed most promising. While attempting to open up these alternate analyses of the past, Du Bois necessarily confronted some of the topics of enforced collectivization and liquidation of the kulaks by Stalin. This section is far and away the most lamentable of passages to be found in the book, but at the same time it offers a perspective on Du Bois's attempts to read the Soviet process through a world historical prism. It is tempting to read this section as an oversimplified rationalization for Stalinism, and thus a place where Du Bois's reasoning is more than strained. He writes, "The kulaks had the mentality of capitalists, enforced by ignorance and custom. The opportunity to cheat and coerce the poor peasant was broad and continuous. Stalin knew the kulak; his fathers had been their slaves for generations. He did not hesitate. He broke their power by savage attack.

This revolution was more radical than in 1917 and Stalin knew it" (76).[31] This section seems to confirm the wisdom of Giroux's rejection of the manuscript. Yet to simply dismiss Du Bois's book because of its doggedly indifferent vindication of genocide is perhaps too easy. It is impossible to deny that Du Bois tries to rationalize the slaughter and enforced dislocation of the kulaks. Commenting on Du Bois's silence about Stalin's crimes, David Levering Lewis explains, "Du Bois adjusted the Russian casualty tables in light of the Atlantic slave trade, the scramble for Africa, the needless First World War, Nazi death camps, and the color-coded poverty and wage-slavery raging within and beyond North America. To Du Bois, the degradation of the communist ideal in Soviet Russia was philosophically irrelevant to the expiation of the sins of American democracy, whose very possibility he now deeply doubted."[32] Thus, while one need not agree with Du Bois's rationalization of the necessary costs of the Russian Revolution, his interpretations must be read as part of a larger effort to understand development in terms of global inequities, tragedies, and genocides, driven by international greed and corresponding flows of capital. "If the cost of revolution was excessive and revolting, the fault is not to rest on Russia alone" he writes (RA, 78). The analytical efforts behind the scope of Du Bois's perspective can be appreciated without drawing the same conclusion. The question is not whether Du Bois should be condemned for perhaps attempting to countenance one evil over another, but if one is willing to take responsibility for keeping open the archive in which these difficult issues are addressed.

Because Du Bois always sought to turn the lens of his critical gaze back onto his readers, it is important to remember that Du Bois's trips to Russia not only led him to praise what he saw as the "world's greatest experiment in organized life" but to rethink social relations in the United States (104). Returning to the States from Russia, Du Bois writes, "Now after this first glimpse of Russia I traveled home. I had made a great pilgrimage; the sort of journey of which one dreams. . . . I came back to re-interpret to myself my native land" (53–54). He connects his sense of the decay of Western society, fortified by his time in Greece and Rome, with the sense of uplift and hope he projected onto the Soviet Union as the most promising site for a reincarnation of all that he valued in Western culture combined with the communalism with which he associated ancient Africa and the kinship structures of the East. Russia is the zone in which all elsewhere gets imagined; it provides the impetus for a reconfiguration of race relations because "there is hope here, vast hope" (151). His circuitous route home enabled him to poise himself as the link between East and West, and this is nowhere more evident than in the title of the chapter that describes his journey home: "I Gird the Globe." While establishing Du Bois as the global link par excellence, the verb "to gird" suggests both a constraint and mobility that runs in course with Du Bois's traversing of the world. With the globe below his belt, he becomes an exemplar of black internationalism.

COLD WAR TOPOGRAPHIES I

The second half of *Russia and America* depicts the developments surrounding World War II and the U.S. role in European reconstruction, and how these events bring one, as a reader, to the seeming standoff between communism and capitalism that characterized the 1950s. At this moment, Du Bois expressed that the Soviet Union was providing the only safety against the United States as the new post–World War II, standard-bearer of capital. Against the dollar-driven formulation of a world market, Du Bois poses a correlation between the Soviet and African American—a correlation that he locates in the philosophical designation by German idealist philosophy of these peoples as historically marginal and that materializes in the relationship of the nineteenth-century Russian peasant farmer to the black sharecropper. It is this theoretical parallelism and the importance of agricultural restructuring, the "Western technique" of profit-motivated industry at the turn of the twentieth century, that eventually leads Du Bois to reconfigure the color line into one of the proletariat.

In so doing, though, he repeatedly stresses the psychological component that goes hand in hand with economic restructuring. He juxtaposes the Soviet workers' psychology that emerged from a legacy of ever sensing his twoness between Europe and the East with his own experiential correlative, and uses this juxtaposition to discuss how a refurbished, nonoppositional Soviet notion of community could realign the drives and impulses that bind a community of whiteness in the United States. Describing his filiation to the United States as a bond not of "affection, but grim duty," Du Bois gestures to an incommensurability between "Negro" and U.S. citizen" (*RA*, 154). Du Bois elaborates this sense that the Negro exists as a legalized fiction and yet remains outside the purview of the law's protection when he portrays his affective connection to "Negroes less fortunate than" himself. As he puts it, he "searched for and read details of every lynching and died horribly with the victim. I vividly imagined what I did not see or even hear of" (154).[33] Du Bois's self-described identification with the mutilated bodies of lynched men and women creates a deeper shame for the moral hypocrisy at the root of a nation with which he identifies but that, paradoxically, identifies itself in opposition to him. Still, Du Bois refused to give up on the enforced paradox of his identity as "un-American," resolving, "I shall never live elsewhere" (*RA*, 154). Fluidly stressing the point of the historical moral advantage of the Negro in the United States, Du Bois nonetheless presses on to connect the depth of his sense of exclusion in the States with that of his acceptance in the USSR. He states, "My reasoning may be strained; but whether the reader agrees or not, I am sure he can understand the impact which Russia had on me in 1926. I was not naive enough to think I had visited Utopia. On the contrary I knew quite well that I had had but a brief glance at a small part of a vast land and of a desperately complicated problem" (156).

Du Bois's rhetorical connection of the bodily and psychic damage wrought by the largely condoned practice of lynching in the United States to his descriptions of movement without constraint in the USSR, attempts to align the reader with Du Bois's experiential truth—"whether the reader agrees or not." As he says, "My emotional sympathy with a depressed class of human beings will doubtless exaggerate its influence, and for this margin of error the reader must make allowance" (157). Circling back to the affective connection between himself and the imagined victims he portrayed lines earlier, Du Bois suggests the limits of the bonds of affect, the attendant "margin for error" that such a link might—or might not—foster. This is a surprising gesture for someone who argues for the importance of "common experience" as the crucial link in the formation of community. The margin for error Du Bois depicts is precisely the limitations of affect produced by common experience and the reification of community through common suffering. Contrary to Du Bois's protestations, his explanations of a lack of complete objectivity, it is exactly Du Bois's racial life and commitment elsewhere to commonality of experience that motivates his analysis of it. Intellectual activity becomes a correlative of racial identity that enables him to think beyond the constraints of "black" and "white." In this sense, Du Bois's turn toward the Soviet Union can be interpreted as a key part of his racial politics, even if this turn was impelled by thinking beyond the color line. At the same time, Du Bois reminds readers of his own limits: his comparison of lynching to the czarist pogroms and not to the liquidation of the kulaks, his "emotional sympathy" for the downtrodden workers of the world and not for the millions displaced by Stalin. As Du Bois himself would later contend, the causality for consciousness—revolutionary or otherwise—is not entirely predictable but located somewhere within that "tangled complex of inferiority" that itself could generate the most bitter of animosities between so-called inferior consciousnesses. Du Bois's identifications are both racial and racializing as well as selectively deracinating. In spite of the potential stopgaps between the Soviet and Negro as conjoined in anything more than a highly ephemeral sense of spirit, the Soviet Union offered an alternative to the discourse of "outsider and continuous visitor" status that Du Bois identified with his life in the United States.[34]

Then, too, Du Bois includes himself among the "us" designated by the "we" in which "we" designates the United States. A playing with the nuances, the imperfections, the ill-defined options and confusions between "us" and "them" becomes characteristic of the late Du Bois. Underlining the connection between common experience and common sense as potential corollaries to one another, he believed that from the common experience of multiformity united by a shared goal could emerge a "strong common sense of the nation." By refusing the oppositional transmutations of dichotomous couplings such as good/evil, East/West, and so on, popular in postwar U.S. political rhetoric, the common experience of a shared community could translate into the common sense of its members. Again, this is not an excuse for the lack of freedoms in the USSR but an idealization of community as a site in which nonoppositional thinking would be fostered, in which a "vitality" of "multiformity" promoted by the ideals of the Soviet state would create a hegemony in which the end would justify the means.

It was in reflecting on his trip to Russia in 1949 that Du Bois formulated more fully his filiation to Russia. On invitation from voks, founded in 1925, the state sponsor of intellectuals, art exhibits, film screenings, and concert tours, Du Bois traveled to Moscow to attend the August Peace Conference.[35] This conference was planned as a follow-up both to the New York and Paris congresses at which Robeson, as Du Bois notes, announced that African Americans would not enter into war against the Soviets (*RA*, 308). For Du Bois, this trip was important for it concretized his thoughts about Russia: "I spent ten days in Moscow and sensed the substance and reality of what we call the Soviet Republics beginning to take definite form. I do not yet know this land in any scientific sense of the word. But in the three visits in 23 years I have a sort of spectroscopic roundness of conception and sense of time which replaces figures" (254). In this last description of his conception of Russia, Du Bois pinpoints his methodology, what I have been calling socioautobiography. Painfully aware of the imperfection of his own viewpoint, the dissolution of his access to scientific facts, he replaces reliance on "figures" with what he labels a "spectroscopic roundness of conception and sense of time." Du Bois relies on unpredictability as the root of possibility, honing in on what he calls the "paradox of human deed," whose unanticipated results leave to "a more instructed age and much fuller knowledge the possible explanation" (87). In questioning causality, and acknowledging that "scientific hypothesis" must recognize that "miraculous freedom of action which is the Uncaused Cause of a certain human deed and of development of human life," Du Bois marks his refusal to be deterred by the horrors of Stalinism (87). He crafts a window of opportunity in place of retrenchment, a space wherein he again admits a margin for error. Yet Du Bois, in finally turning to the question of whether or not Russia has eradicated racism, remains vigilantly attached to the significance, no matter how "overemphasized," of the lack of segregation and racial discrimination in the USSR. He writes, "I, who am supersensitive in matters of discrimination, could see none in the Union of Soviets. . . . There was no shadow of segregation nor discrimination" (284). In an unpublished essay titled simply "Russia," Du Bois notes that the Soviets are "unconscious of race—unparalleled in the world."[36] At this point, such a statement should come as no surprise. Du Bois, however, does not rationalize a lack of discrimination through "superior ethics." Rather, he says that the reason for Russia's attitude is not superior ethics, but her early consciousness of the danger of racial and cultural discrimination" (*RA*, 284). Du Bois again ascribes to Russia a potentially transformative consciousness, one that clearly stems back to his articulation of a "tangled complex of inferiority," the legacy of generations of subordination to the West and Western philosophies of identity, in which he placed the hope that a superior society would indeed

The "Refusal to Be 'White' " | 175

come to pass. In this vein, Du Bois's pronouncements seem to echo that of his nineteenth-century Russian predecessors, philosophers such as Dosto-evsky and Grigor'ev, who believed that the enduring momentum of a populist messianism would launch Russians beyond their European coun-terparts on the path of historical progress.

Always forward-looking, Du Bois's insistence that the past can never be fully grasped conjoins with his assertion about the "Uncaused Cause" of actions and development—an assessment of which he leaves "to a more instructed age." Du Bois, in part, places responsibility for interpretation onto his readers, as "more instructed" readers of the events surrounding the 1950s. In this sense, he remained keenly aware of the potential over-sight of his later work, estimating that future readers would at some point come to appreciate if not his accuracy, then at least his effort in trying. Du Bois's feeling that in his readers' "fuller knowledge," they would permit these later words to share equal ground with his 1903 pronouncements about the color line, that they would be better able to assess his words, was perhaps his greatest oversight of all.

COLD WAR TOPOGRAPHIES II

By the early 1940s, Du Bois's interests had shifted from concern for the liberation of black Americans to an alignment with the decolonizing agenda and anti-imperialism of the Pan-Africanist movement. Interested in the linkages between the fates of the peoples of Western European colonies and future of African Americans, Du Bois had turned to the Soviet Union as an alternative political model.[37] As Gerald Horne points out, in the years following World War II, Du Bois increasingly allied himself with Moscow "because he felt that most major initiatives on peace and disarmament came from their foreign ministry and that this created favorable conditions for social progress."[38] More concretely, as surely as avenues were shut down to Du Bois in the United States, they opened to him in the USSR. In the late 1950s, numerous articles about and by Du Bois began to appear in the Soviet press, and translations of his major works were solicited and published, often before they appeared in English in the West. In a letter to the Russian translator of Du Bois's *Mansart* trilogy, Vasily Kuznetsov, Shirley Graham summed up the situation: "For nearly a year we have been trying to get this novel [*The Ordeal of Mansart*] published . . . [B]ecause he is a victim of suppression regular commercial channels are closed to him. His publications are greatly curtailed and distribution of his writings difficult."[39]

Convinced that the United States had done everything within its power to destroy the Soviet project, Du Bois's alliance with the Soviet Union echoed the Soviet desire for a collective solidarity against the emerging front of Americanism during the decade following the end of World War II.[40] Du Bois discerned that the war had transformed the socioeconomic and political conditions of the West so deeply that the intractability of the color line no longer provided a sufficient means of maintaining the balance of wealth. In 1953, Du Bois summed up the restructuring of capital along East/West lines: "There is but one aspect of this deepening world rift along the Color Line which saves it from being complete, and that is the peoples of the Soviet Union and her sister group of states. . . . For this fact, Britain, France, and the U.S. ought to be thankful to Russia and her refusal to be 'white.' "[41] Soviet Russia's refusal to "be 'white' " not only exposed a rift in social theories that used skin color as a determinant of race but fueled a demand that "race" be reconfigured to better encompass political ideology. Du Bois reiterated this point in a piece written for the Soviet periodical *New Times,* published in English. Contending that the "dominant exploiting countries may today be willing to yield more to the demands of the peoples who are striving for independence than they were in the past," he reasoned that "yielding takes the form of becoming fellow capitalists with the white exploiters."[42] In 1956, Du Bois once again alleged that race was being used as a field on which to engage the political ire of both the United States and Soviet Union: "The partial breaking of the color line was used to answer the stand of the Soviet Union against color discrimination."[43] If indeed Soviet Russia had forced a wrenching open of the color barrier so that the twentieth century's "problem" inclined toward internationally oriented labor rather than nationally bounded color, then the United States responded by attempts to redress class issues in shades of race, international implications in terms of singularly domestic ones. The near invisibility in racial discourse today of Du Bois's 1950s' political analyses mirrors the success of this reshaping. In shifting attention back fifty years to Du Bois's contemplative double consciousness as the pinnacle of his aesthetic output, judgments of his literary merit carry with them a deeply rooted political fiat, and vice versa. And in contemporary debates over American national identity, an interpretation of domestic racial difference as unrelated to international political arenas again reaffirms how Du Bois's work has been misappropriated, with double consciousness serving as a bedrock for a singularly African *American* experience.[44]

Du Bois's admonition that the United States should consider itself indebted to Russia implies at once the success and failure of race rhetoric in the States during the postwar period. In response to lingering suspicions of national self-doubt, race became a focus of unheralded attention following World War II. By pouring the bulk of social concern about U.S. autonomous relations into the problems of "race" as inherently (that is to say, superficially, given standard understandings of race as based on skin color) solvable, other less visible factors (such as class) could be eclipsed. The promise of a resolution of racial strife could thus serve not only as a triumph for U.S. integrity but a screen for manifest social inequities. Distracting attention from both the economic underpinnings of racial inequities and U.S. imperial interests in the emerging "third world," the perceived racial problem could be elicited, made visible, and addressed without really doing anything to alter its derivations. As long as the public perception of racial difference was that it could conceptually be solved by the goal of assimilation—a simplistic rendering based on the visible—the status quo that produced and benefited from systems of persistent, effectual segregation could remain intact while giving lip service to the social injustice of racism.[45]

And while a fortuitous deployment of race as the central concern of national identity served as an enabling scrim for the perpetuation of other class antagonisms, Soviet Russia's refusal to be white allowed for an unctuous rhetoric of racial equality—bound together against the Soviet enemy—as the rallying point for patriotism and national citizenship. As Soviet bureaucrats bought political leverage against the United States by calling their race bluff, with satiric depictions of U.S. racial strife appearing throughout Soviet media, this reformed way of talking about race took shape back in the States: Blacks and whites in solidarity against the Soviets—with the Soviet "other" created through available terms heretofore reserved for persons of color. Of course, the convenient slippage between "black," nonwhite, and "red" permitted an easy and familiar fixation on "the Red" as an identity category of its own.[46]

Although one would not want to make the argument that Soviet Russia

11. This image, drawn by Boris Leo, is called "Education American-Style," and its caption states, "So, you want to go to school? Well, we're prepared to teach you a lesson!"

had overcome her own issues surrounding racial conflict, nor that the Communist powers comprehended the specificities of the complex workings of race in the United States, it is not absurd to posit that Soviet thinkers had reason to believe that "race" could be exploited as a potential weakness in the structure of the U.S. economy. Through a keen understanding of Marxist-Leninist apprehensions of capitalism, such thinkers could see a vulnerability in the U.S. economic imbalance, which was increasingly dependent on the exploitation of colonized peoples.[47] In the vein of Lenin, Du Bois suggests that Russia's refusal to be white actually provided a slap in the face of this very same U.S. whiteness, and exposed it as an ideology dependent on race as *the* shaping lexicon of identity. In proposing "thanks" as the appropriate response to Russian "generosity," Du Bois articulated the limitations and necessary failure of any formulation of "identity" as exclusively race based. Race and the issues it made evident—paranoia about social injustice, the misrepresentation of free relations, and a lack of true democratic process—therefore provided a potential structural fault or crack in the ideological scaffolding of capitalist industrialism. If U.S. citizens believed that the integrity of their social system relied on a fulfillment of these claims, then inasmuch as a condoned, institutionalized racial discrimination—which segregation obviated—persisted, the United States could never be true to herself. National "identity" would always be necessarily misplaced.

By thus exposing the failure of an attempt to strap a continuous color belt around the world, Du Bois at the same time designated how this supple bond could be used to shed light on the hypocrisies of mainstream liberal race rhetoric. Certainly this was a bond that the Soviets capitalized on as well, going to great lengths to reconfigure so-called U.S. failure into the grounds for an alleged Soviet success. In denoting the vulnerability of the United States on the racial front, the Soviets played on U.S. paranoia and efforts to repair the injustices of race relations. It was around the issue of race that Soviet Russia garnered so many international brownie points, and after World War II, when Russia became the prominent threat to U.S. global imperialism, race became a strategic pawn. As Du Bois wrote in a letter to Dorothy Sterling dated 19 December 1949, "In general big business in the United States has recently become desperately afraid that Negroes in the United States would turn to the left and consequently it has been taking many steps to appease them."[48] One way that U.S. policy maneuvered this pawn, Du Bois contended, was by promoting a rift in the color line by entertaining the notion of racial similarity in order to reassert essential racial difference, the supremacy of U.S. whiteness. For this, according to Du Bois, the United States should be eternally grateful.

"LIONS HAVE NO HISTORIANS":
DUSK OF DAWN AND THE SHAPING OF COMMON EXPERIENCE

Du Bois's reconfiguration of the color line on a global scale reaches back to assessment of the personal genealogy he describes in *Dusk of Dawn*. By the mid-1930s, Du Bois had declared his allegiance to the ideals of Marxist philosophy, but in *Dusk of Dawn* the abstract political commitment becomes grounded in personal context. It is here that he formulates some of his strongest, most dogmatic statements about the importance of the Soviet Union to him and his "race concept." *Dusk of Dawn* addresses Du Bois's burgeoning apprehension of the complexities of race in the post–World War I era and the periodic shifts in his assessments of the color line. In *Dusk of Dawn,* he toys with a color line reconfigured, displaying the inadequacies, hypocrisies, and inevitable failure of the hierarchized racial status quo. *Dusk of Dawn* was published in 1940, before the United States had entered World War II and allied itself, however superficially and temporarily, with the Soviet Union. And although Du Bois by no means could predict the outcome of the war, by 1940 he understood the growing strength of the United States as a world power and the need to consolidate a sense of national identity commensurate with such fortitude. Du Bois sensed the growing expanse of a ruthless and monolithic Americanization as a phenomenon that was being meted out through racial consciousness. If one towed the line of whiteness, one could be accepted into the fold. Dissension from the majority opinion would not be tolerated. Not surprisingly, Du Bois, who was by this time a committed socialist, turned elsewhere for inspiration.

Dusk of Dawn outlines both the reordination of Du Bois's understanding of race prejudice and his "new and comprehensive plan" for the reconfiguration of black life in the United States. Broadly speaking, the book describes how Du Bois's dissatisfaction with the idea that racism was based on "ignorance and deliberate ill-will" led him to pursue other explanations. Marxism provided an analytic framework that helped explain the "stronger and more threatening forces" that "form[ed] the founding stones of race antagonisms" (*DD,* 283). The conclusion that Du Bois draws at the end of *Dusk of Dawn*—that Negroes should pursue independent means of commerce—results in part from his reconfigured Marxism and was buttressed by Stalinist support for the black belt thesis with which McKay was earlier engaged. The long-debated notion of southern blacks in the United States comprising a nation within a nation was finally endorsed at the Fourth International in Moscow in 1928.[49] Du Bois explicitly connects his contention that "Negroes must proceed constructively in new and comprehensive plans of their own" to the significance of the Russian Revolution, stating that it was "the Russian Revolution which first illuminated and made clear this change in my thought" (*DD,* 284). In championing the efforts of Bolshevik Russia to implement Marxism, though, Du Bois does not portray Russia as a utopia. Rather, he emphasizes the difficulties, failures, and future tenses involved in the Soviet attempt to "eventually" put the power of the state in the hands of its workers. Seeing the limitations of an unrefined Soviet Communism apportioned onto the

The "Refusal to Be 'White'" ⋮ 181

United States, Du Bois tempers his enthusiasm with several caveats. Not only does he stand by his 1932 decision to condemn the Soviet backing of the Scottsboro boys but he explicitly declares, "I was not and am not a communist" (302). Du Bois explains his dissension from "the Communist philosophy" specifically because of its inability to account for or comprehend the racial politics of the United States. Du Bois believed that Communist Party's abolition of the color bar was its downfall, since in obliterating the color bar, the CPUSA "absolutely blocked any chance they might have had to attract any considerable number of white workers to their ranks" (205). In fact, it was precisely in the notion that "racial thought must go," which Du Bois thought was endemic to "imported Russian Communism," that he located the seed of a revised Marxism that became his plan and outline for black Americans. This plan was based on the role of the consumer in a segregated Negro community that harkened back to African communal societies, and in which Negroes would "work for ourselves, exchanging services, producing an increasing proportion of the goods which we consume and being rewarded by a living wage and by work under civilized conditions" (214–15).

Thus, in 1940, Du Bois was reluctant to embrace communism although he saw in its analytic strategies much that he admired. His intellectual attachment to Marx as "one of the greatest men of modern times" was confirmed by his visits to Russia in 1926 and 1936 (303). In the concluding section to the book, titled "Revolution," he describes these trips as solidifying the intellectual aspect of the appeal of Marxism. Du Bois writes, "Never in my life have I been so stirred as by what I saw during two months in Russia. I visited Leningrad and Moscow, Nijni Novgorod and Kiev and came home by way of Odessa and Constantinople. . . . But this was physical. Mentally I came to know Karl Marx and Lenin, their critics and defenders. Since that trip my mental outlook and the aspect of the world will never be the same" (287). Du Bois identifies a dialectic of "physical" and "mental" arousal associated with Russia.

The prioritization of mental challenges, testing of wits, and intellectual agility are nowhere more in evidence than in the long section titled "The White World." "The White World" paves the way for Du Bois's later reformulation of the color line by staging an elaborate dialogue with an imaginary white rival, Roger Van Dieman. In this battle of wits, Du Bois exposes the fictitiousness of race as a biological fact, undermines the intractability of the color line, and reveals the inherent dynamism at the basis of racial differentiation. Both of these sections not only exhibit Du Bois's indebtedness to Marxist thinking to reveal race prejudice as an agent in the accumulation of capital but also illuminate a limit to the analytic powers offered by Marxism. In particular, the malleability of the color line exhibited in "The White World" nonetheless attests to the so-called fact of race as an experiential reality: "a racial folk-lore grounded on centuries of instinct, habit and thought and implemented by the conditioned reflex of visible color" (205). Du Bois's point is that white supremacy may be economically based, but it is still experientially deployed. While the racial "difference" between Du Bois and his alter ego Van Dieman proves to be nonexistent, the fact remains that difference is enforced through institutional, systemic forces that operate in such a way that their structures are internalized. Having shown without a doubt that Dieman and Du Bois are both "white" inasmuch as they are "black," Du Bois notes that they nevertheless are racially differentiated because "the black man is a person who must ride 'JC' [Jim Crow] in Georgia" (153).

Again, Du Bois anticipated that the ways in which one thinks about his meditations on race and difference would relate to the question of historical knowledge. To Dieman's charge that he has never heard of achievements by "black and yellow men" commensurate with those of whites, Du Bois replies, "Lions have no historians" (149). Not only does Du Bois argue that racial difference is experienced as real but he suggests that its reality is often preemptively removed from the historical record. It was the oversight of the experiential realm in which race is perpetrated for which Du Bois criticized Soviet Communism and the U.S. practice of communism found in the CPUSA. At the same time, it was the danger of a failure to account for alternate experiences of the status quo and the occlusion of alternative records of experience against which Du Bois cautioned.

In denoting the paradox of race as both an impossibility and a fact, Du Bois outlines the malleability of racial identity and the potential for Negroes to be incorporated into the system of Americanization that he came to equate with whiteness. In the years that followed World War II, this sensitivity to the workings of the color line would prove proleptic. Du Bois's statements about Russia's refusal to be white replay the dialogue between Du Bois and Dieman. *Dusk of Dawn* anticipates a crisis of the color line that following World War II, became articulable as its reformulation into geographic camps that placed a wall between what were seen as the East and West, and recruited preexisting racial stereotypes to demonize the difference therein. By denoting motion at the root of subordination and the conscripting of women into these battlements, *Dusk of Dawn* prefaced Du Bois's post–World War II reconfiguration of the color line, articulated as a recognition of motion as both a site for potential displacement and the opportunity for hegemony to usurp counterforces and corral them into convention.

UNITED WE FALL: BODIES IN BATTLE

Du Bois opens *Dusk of Dawn* with an "Apology": "If the first two books [*The Souls of Black Folk* and *Darkwater*] were written in tears and blood, this is set down no less determinedly but yet with wider hope in some more benign fluid" (xxx). By beginning his autobiography in this manner, Du Bois establishes the lens through which one is expected to read what follows: this is not "mere autobiography." Nonetheless, although Du Bois has foresworn the "tears and blood" of an individual body for the "more benign fluid" of a disembodied intellect, he is still elucidating "the significance of the race problem by explaining it in terms of the one human life that I know best," his own (xxx). This movement from epistemological certainties guaranteed by one's experience of a specific body to epistemological certainties vouchsafed by intellectual prowess is a movement that I analyze in this section. As Du Bois came to terms with his increasing age, his mind remained the plane on which infirmities were refused. At the same time, if by 1940 Du Bois was able to reimagine the national community as one in which a collective could replace the reification of the individual, in the process of so doing he displaced contradictions about the effects such evisceration would have on women. As *In Battle for Peace* makes prominently manifest, Du Bois's forfeiting of the individual body relied on the persistence of the masculine mind, and this male privilege left marginal space for women—real and imagined.

In Battle for Peace: The Story of My Eighty-third Birthday narrates the tale of Du Bois's trial for failing to register as a foreign agent during his tenure at the Peace Information Center (PIC), from 3 April to 12 October 1951. Indicted under the Smith Act, Du Bois and his five colleagues at the PIC were charged with publishing and disseminating the "Stockholm

Peace Appeal," a document that denounced the proliferation of nuclear weapons and advocated global peace. Although critics, whatever their stated views on Du Bois's later life, generally agree that the trial was the climax of his intellectual life, for the most part they have ignored the significance of *In Battle for Peace* as an autobiographical text.[50] This book exemplifies how his trial functioned as a pivotal motivating force for Du Bois's ensuing political thought. Du Bois not only demonstrates in this book how his engagement with the peace struggle countered the white supremacy with which he equated U.S. containment and expansionist cultural as well as political policies. He also rejects the Talented Tenth idea (the belief that an intellectual elite of African Americans could lead and instruct the black masses) as too narrowly conceived and in its place proposes community, based neither in national nor racial filiation, but in political allegiance to the "downtrodden" of the world and global peace— in other words, to the common experience he outlined in *Russia and America*. In highlighting the international links necessary to combat U.S. capitalism, Du Bois's reappraisal of his Talented Tenth theory paved the way for the reformulation of the color line he articulated in 1953 and 1956—a reformulation that established class and not race as the twentieth century's most pressing issue. And although *Russia and America* credits the Soviet Union with momentous leaps forward in women's emancipation in the pursuit of this new class-based egalitarianism, *In Battle for Peace* offers a unique opportunity to put some of this rhetoric to the test. Unlike any of Du Bois's other works, *In Battle for Peace* was authored in part by his second wife, Shirley Graham. Graham wrote extended closing commentaries for four of the book's fourteen chapters.

In spite of its stated affiliation with the attempts to instill gender equity in the new Soviet state, *In Battle for Peace* nevertheless portrays how Du Bois's political reorientation retained some of its prior assumptions about gender roles. Du Bois's turn was, after all, toward an analytic in which gender, like race, was subordinated to the dictates of class. As in his earlier texts, Du Bois uses his own birthday as a moment of reflection, a way to expound on his awareness of himself as one of the century's most influential thinkers and attend to the ways in which his story could be used as an exemplar, a collective marker. Like McKay and Hughes, Du Bois grounds his political theories in an American paradigm—himself. Using his own body as a site of social negotiation, his language presumes a seamless continuity between masculinity and subjecthood. While locating race within a historically sedimented accretion of differences in social and cultural power, Du Bois slights attention to the ways in which these same formations are inflected by gender. *In Battle for Peace* not only demonstrates the connectedness of narrative and political authority by exemplifying the ways that history lives with us, is constantly reproduced and carried forward, but also enacts the ways questions of gender often get reduced and overlooked in communistic endeavors.

It was during the trial period that Du Bois rejected his previous Talented Tenth idea of racial uplift and replaced it with the terms of black struggle as primarily class based. More than any other prior event in his life, his trial sent him into a frenzy—he railed against the hypocrisies of freedom anew. Yet while shocked over his treatment at the hands of the judicial system, Du Bois was even more stunned at the way he was neglected by those he considered his natural allies: black intellectuals. Where were his racial brethren in his time of need? He harbored deep resentment over this experience and sought refuge in a sense of intellectual superiority to all those around him as well as in the lessons of his friend Robeson, who eschewed personal attention. Du Bois drew on his own thinking in *Russia and America*, and replaced his earlier notion of racial community with a community based in an intuited otherness that de-emphasized the particularity of skin color as necessarily determinant of a psychic bond. In becoming "American," Du Bois suggests that these "Negroes of intelligence" had taken on the parameters he identified as "whiteness."[51] Their nonaction on his behalf caused him to realize that the "future of the Negro race in America and the world lies far more among its workers than among its college graduates."[52] Du Bois's stated dependence on workers and not college graduates is a huge reversal for the man who previously preached racial uplift of the lowly masses by an educated elite. Still, Du Bois's words don't completely abandon the hope for leadership by someone who will "rise" above his peers. As surely as he sees his previous colleagues deploying the weapons of wealth with which he has come to identify whiteness, Du Bois reformulates black struggle in terms of class—without forsaking his rightful position of leadership. As evidenced from Du Bois's acerbic ranting against his foes, his refashioned community relies on the guidance of a superior masculine intellect.

The migration of Du Bois's allegiance from a belief in the reliability of the individual Negro body to the intellectualized connections between racialized experiences as not necessarily identitarian based is thus somewhat confounded by his own tale of how he arrived at this new location. Du Bois is both interested in the common experience of hardship and shocked by his own, individual experience of being treated like a commoner. Guilty according to the U.S. white commercial press, Du Bois was handcuffed like a "common criminal," and stuck in the seats "often occupied by murderers, forgers and thieves" (*IBP*, 119). It was a devastating blow to a man who had prided himself on being an intellectual leader and part of an educated elite. Du Bois stresses the humiliation with which he associated the affronts dealt him, including an arraignment one week prior to his eighty-third birthday, the refusal of several lawyers he approached to defend him, a highly contentious racial showdown during jury selection (in which all eligible Negroes were also conveniently government employees), the blatant intimidation of witnesses, the deployment of federal agents to illegally subpoena defendants, intimations of "unanswerable" evidence, and the betrayal of his former friend, John Rogge, who surfaced as the chief witness for the prosecution. Moreover, the trial took place in segregated Washington, D.C., so that Du Bois could not socialize comfortably, nor stay at a hotel, with his codefendants. Ultimately the case was dismissed. The government had such a weak case against Du Bois that it could not even prove that the PIC was a front organization for another suspected front, the Peace Defense Council. All of these degradations registered as assaults on Du Bois's sense of himself; he still imagined himself as representative, his trial and eventual acquittal serving as intellectual stomping grounds through which he reentered the plight of the working class. And yet, Du Bois strove to assert how the individual was overrated, how the shared experience of the collective would be the basis for an improved future.

The epistemological double motion evident in Du Bois's own theorization of his experience is mirrored in the enforced attention to Du Bois by the government and the judicial system. During the trial, Du Bois was singled out to represent the dangers of "collective thought." On the one hand the group was tried together, indicating that the defendants could be known as a group and persecuted on that basis. On the other hand, by focusing on Du Bois as if he were an individual on trial, the message seemed to be that one could escape the clutches of the group if one acted as an individual. One could be accepted into the fold—the correct group—as a singular entity; one stood to gain through legal redress based on individual concerns. According to Du Bois, the press did everything they could to make it into a personal case by censoring "all the news about the white defendants [with whom he had been indicted] and any general aspects of the case" (83). At the same time, the singling out of Du Bois was clearly an effort to contain the most potentially toxic member of the group. The focus on Du Bois during this trial likewise indicated to Du Bois that although blacks were persecuted and segregated as a group, they were forced to seek legal redress (and potential reconstruction) individually. Du Bois understood this enforced singling out to be an inherently depoliticizing gesture, a divide-and-conquer tactic. And thus, the "real object" of the case, in Du Bois's view, "was to prevent an American citizen of any sort from daring to think or talk against the determination of Big Business to reduce Asia to colonial subservience to American industry; to reweld the chains of Africa; to consolidate U.S. control of the Caribbean and South America; and above all to crush socialism in the Soviet Union and China" (120). While this may sound like one man's exaggerated sense of self-importance, it is also Du Bois's attempt to point out that "containment" as an official national policy to counter Soviet expansion was deeply embedded in expansionist interests of its own.

So, Du Bois seems to ask, was it the individual or collective that was to be feared? Uncovering the hypocrisy of oppositional thinking that posits freedom versus enslavement, individual versus collective, Du Bois declares that "it is ridiculous today for any nation to call itself 'free'" (164). Against the narrative backdrop of liberty, equality, and freedom of choice propounded by political discourse and popular culture, Du Bois exposes the ruse of an "option" to choose full autonomy over one's life versus the international concession of one's civil rights to a centralized, foreign power. In this framework, black masculinity was hardly an option, nor had this "choice" ever included true autonomy. Du Bois notes how within the dominant discourse of nation, black masculinity has instead occupied a position of disenfranchisement, of dependency made to feel at times like freedom.[53] Noting that he would have "gone to jail by default" if he had not been able to raise money through friends, lectures, and fund-raisers, Du Bois counts himself lucky as a part of a "sensational" case that caused enough of an uproar to dislodge even the determination of governmental "power and money" in collaboration with one another (*IBP,* 150).

Ultimately able to prove himself sensational instead of invisible, Du Bois notes the slipperiness of the slope between the two, with his own body acting as the slide. Du Bois's observation of the usefulness of his body, however, does not emphasize its uniqueness. To the contrary, it is precisely because of its lack of specialness, its manipulability through experience disseminated as racially based truth, that Du Bois's body is open to misuse. Realizing that he could easily have been one of the thousands of the "poor, friendless, and black," whereas the ideal citizen for whom the nation stood was wealthy, connected, and white, Du Bois remarks that there are certain privileges accorded invisibility, but only when one has achieved the status of citizen and does not have to prove oneself an equal. At the same time, he reserves an intellectual space for superiority, for thinking through the dilemmas of material processes that endow experience with technologies of truth. *In Battle for Peace* reads as something of a struggle between these visions, between Du Bois's understanding of experience as highly mediated—the conviction that minds must struggle with their enforced orchestration—and the implication that a masculine mind could nonetheless serve as representative of the good fight.[54]

GENDER IN BATTLE

In attending to the important insights of Du Bois's political acumen, I would like also to recall the shape of autobiographical praxis here. For although Du Bois's primary narrative challenges, as Alan Nadel puts it, that gap "between events and history," it is executed through strategies that recall some of that history's chief paradigms—namely, the framing of community through a dialectic of male dominance and female subservience.[55] Du Bois's tale repeatedly stages his superiority to the men around him while offering odd positions of peripheral significance to women. While Du Bois presents reformulated versions of his life under the guise of a redrafted, Marxist politics, assumptions about gender and sexual difference that he honed under the rubric of the Talented Tenth remain largely intact. He articulates a positive reconstruction of community in his later autobiography, yet the prototypical member of this community is an ideological holdover from his earlier formulation of an exemplary black masculinity as outlined in *Souls of Black Folk*.[56] Du Bois's redrafted political commitments also clearly ally him with the interests of a materialist feminist politics. Again, his stated affiliations to women's rights need to be simultaneously acknowledged along with his adherence to a trope of privileged black masculinity within these political commitments to women. Even as Du Bois launches critiques of U.S. white supremacy and patriarchal discourse, the language with which he does so creates tensions between Du Bois's racial politics and his purported class and gender representativeness.

In Battle for Peace is the only published book of Du Bois's in which he consciously shares authored space with a woman. Although the title page positions Du Bois as the author, Shirley Graham is mentioned as the authorized commentator. The book thus positions Graham as an authority on Du Bois's text, and in so doing poses larger questions about Graham's place in Du Bois's late work: To what degree does Graham fulfill Du Bois's idealization of self-sacrifice and the subordination of the individual to the higher cause of the community? Is it significant that it is a woman who achieves the purported goal of self-abnegation? To what degree does the dissolution of the female body in the interests of a collective cause replicate the problematics Hughes encountered in his reliance on the Uzbek woman as the model for an emancipated subjectivity? How might these marginalizations of female bodies correspond to the Soviet project of a new "gender-free" subjectivity that far from disintegrating the bonds of gender, reinscribed them with a newfound forcefulness?

In spite of their shared space of authorship, Du Bois and Graham offer quite different perspectives on their own function as author. At no point in his text does Du Bois express awareness of his wife's presence beside him as a commentator or an intellectual equal. Rather, her presence is always beside him as a loving support, confidant, and nurturing supplicant. While *In Battle for Peace* asserts that Graham was the motivating force behind Du Bois's defense, her work to this end is couched in terms that complement her remarkable capacity for self-forfeiture. Differently, Graham's sometimes lengthy commentary repeatedly focuses on the masterful clarity of Du Bois's intellect. She writes, "God forbid that I should take upon myself the presumption of adding anything to W. E. B. Du Bois's facts or style. His is a grand simplicity that needs no clarification" (*IBP*, 11). Graham states that the purpose of her commentary is to "share related confidences with the reader" (10). Likewise, the superficial effect of her commentary is to largely compound the marginalization of women to anecdotal asides. The commonplace association of women's place on the confidential sidelines of social discourse becomes confirmed in marginalia that far from undermining the main text, focuses on de-emphasizing its own import.

On the other hand, Graham directs readers to interpret her interpretive forays as defined by the French word *comment,* or "how come?"[57] To what degree of dissimulation should readers attribute her protestations of "God forbid"? If there were truly no need for her commentary, then why is it here at all? It is particularly difficult to read Graham's purpose here, and impossible to decide whether her self-sacrifice reads as another of Du Bois's triumphs of ego over those around him or if her selfless devotion to Du Bois was part of her own larger goal. Both readings seem tenable. Perhaps Graham is using the means necessary to stage a savvy critique of attempts to remove women completely from historical relevance. Even as her words do little to unseat Du Bois's presumption of masculine representativeness, she establishes herself as the bedrock behind the exemplar. When word of Du Bois's indictment came through, she determined, "I must be in a position to stand at his side—I felt this was essential" (*IBP,* 59). In order to attain this position, Graham sped up their marriage plans because "with him in jail, only a wife could carry his case to the people. . . . I had a program worked out" (59). Indeed, Graham was largely responsible for the money raised for his defense. And her rendition of Du Bois in *In Battle* also appears to be part of presenting him as a "case" whose representative function was crucial to the future of African Americans.[58] Graham's efforts on Du Bois's behalf both attempt to instill in the reader a sense of the significance of Du Bois's contributions to racial liberation (even if he himself doubted it at the time) and stake a case for the appalling injustice of his indictment.

Given the importance of Graham to his cause, and likewise to his manuscript, it is surprising that in Du Bois's text there is no expressed awareness of it. Rather, readers receive the following depiction of Du Bois's union with Graham: Du Bois explains that "there was a young woman, a minister's daughter, to whom I had been a sort of father confessor in literary affairs and difficulties of life for many years, especially after her father's death fifteen years ago. I knew her hardships and I had rejoiced in her successes. Shirley Graham, with her beautiful martyr complex, finally persuaded herself that I needed her help and companionship, as I certainly did; so we decided to get married a few days after my next birthday" (*IBP*, 62). Without pursuing the actual intimacies of this relationship, readers can investigate the language with which the couple is portrayed by one of its key members. As Hazel Carby has shown, even the best of intentions can be hampered by language that reproduces conventional gender power inequities, and such inequities not only inhabit the discourse of private matters but often exist in a dialectical relation to their public counterparts.[59] The pattern of the relationship Du Bois describes is self-consciously presented in terms of a father-daughter bond, with Graham the "beautiful martyr" to Du Bois's aged neediness. This concession could be read as an admission of Du Bois's own infirmity, a dwindling physicality that he hoped would be at least sustained, if not revived by Graham's comparative youth. Overcoming the body, however, is also posited as a privilege more accessible to men than women, as women's bodies function as property that cements the heterosexual contract between men. As Du Bois grows older and more disembodied in his thinking, replacing physical virility with psychic prowess, he overlooks the ways in which women are forced to occupy bodiliness, even if in denial or sacrifice of it. And yet, the "persuasion" of which he speaks gives one pause. Labeling their marriage a result of Graham "finally persuad[ing] herself" sounds like an odd reformulation of persuasion as exclusively an internal, unmediated process. Persuasion in this case is made to appear at a remove from coercion, at last transforming into consent. But why the "finally"? What were the forces holding her back? And why does her decision emerge only in the context of self-sacrifice? Would it not be possible to see Graham's choice as a decision not to be a martyr but to seek a particular kind of "help" and "companionship" that her relationship with Du Bois would provide so that she could effect action in accordance with her own political consciousness, even if that consciousness at times circled back to aiding Du Bois?

It would be easy to see Du Bois's attitude toward women as one that reflects an inability to fathom them in any way except such matronly martyrdom as his portrait of Graham conveys. This attitude coheres with the withering away not of Du Bois's masculinity but the contestations over gender inequities evoked by his socialist vision. His description of the defense committee secretary, Alice Citron, follows suit: Citron "threw herself into the work with unfaltering sacrifice," "she hung on even when shunted to the cold and inaccessible attic" (*IBP*, 94). Although it is clear from the events depicted that Graham was largely responsible for energizing and organizing the committee for Du Bois's defense, arranging a lecture tour of the West, and assuring information reached abroad, the passages that address her are those primarily concerned with the wedding, Du Bois's birthday, and domestic matters. The chapter "The Pilgrimages for Defense" that obviously relied on Graham as the bedrock of stability is not sufficiently addressed to Graham's political work. Yet in spite of claims to displace experience as the most reliable mode of epistemology, to grapple with the systemic forces that claim experience as privilege, Du Bois's "living" is perpetually meted out across the figures of women. In this sense, while positing a critique of a national ideology that encourages Americans to participate as individuals (a depoliticizing effort), and instead proposing a group-based sense of (trans)national identity and belonging, Du Bois maintains in his reformulation a gender status quo.

At the same time, it is not known how much of Du Bois's inattention to Graham was a result of her own wishes to forward her causes through less visible avenues.[60] It is known that as Du Bois became older, Graham traveled in his place and delivered his speeches. Her participation in the All-African Conference at Accra, Ghana, in 1961 was significant, both because she was the only non-African permitted to attend the gathering and because of the words she delivered—words that Du Bois cites in his *Autobiography*. Reiterating a point that came out of *Russia and America*, Graham stated, "Your bond is no mere color of skin but the deeper experience of wage slavery and contempt. So too, your bond with the white world is closest to those like the Union of Soviet Socialist Republics" (*A*, 404). This kind of substitution of one physical body for another should not go unnoticed, and yet, Graham for the most part remains left on the sidelines of Du Bois criticism, the eviscerated figure in the margins, the better example of a forfeited individualism. Perhaps Du Bois was trying in his own way to come to terms with this by including Graham's commentaries in his text. Nonetheless, he devotes most of the book's second half to his triumphs over male counterparts.

In contrast to his inattention to Graham, Du Bois dedicates an entire chapter to his bête noire, the witness John Rogge on whose testimony the prosecution largely based its case. The chapter "Oh! John Rogge" establishes, in Du Bois's words, "Rogge the Rat" (*IBP*, 188). Here and elsewhere Du Bois plays up male rivalry, stressing his intellectual superiority to former colleagues. He describes Rogge as "an ambitious man, not too stable in his intellectual outlook" (115).[61] He applies this depiction equally to Henry Wallace, another former ally turned foe, writing that Wallace suffers from an "uncertainty of intellectual orientation" (*IBP*, 46). But in Wallace's case Du Bois goes even further. "In a sense Wallace lacked guts and had [a] small stomach for martyrdom," writes Du Bois, and when Du Bois "tried gingerly to strengthen his faith" by explaining the historical linkages between popular dissent from abolitionism and communism, he "received no reply" (46). Whether or not Du Bois assigns blame justly, what interests me is the language with which he dismisses a masculinity that is not martyr enough to be delicately guided by Du Bois. Because Du Bois clearly places such value on the self-sacrificing qualities of women, it appears that rather than providing an elevated vision of women as political agents, Du Bois prefers people who can be directed by his own intellectual might. Du Bois thereby establishes his own subject position as leader of the faith to whom those around him should "gingerly" submit. The idea is that gender should no longer matter in a socialist community—that all regardless of sex should subordinate themselves to a higher calling—but in championing this rationalization for self-sacrifice, Du Bois retains some of his presumptions about the gendered contours of this higher calling. He laments the fact that "in a 'Time for Greatness,' the great are dead or dumb" (174). Just where such a pronouncement places Du Bois becomes imminently clear as he continues in this mode, asserting that "the country is led by Harry Truman, a man with no education in economics or social development and too much training in 'practical politics' " (174). This is a strange statement for someone who has just declared that the great leaders will more likely come from "practical" folk than college graduates.[62] Plainly juxtaposing himself with the "great" who are "dead or dumb," of which he is evidently neither, Du Bois makes it quite apparent that he is still looking for a leader for whom the prototype may be none other than himself.

While emphasizing Du Bois's political acuity, it should be pointed out that his positive reaction to the Soviet stance against U.S. imperialism was also influenced by the treatment he received, and sensed that others like him received, in the Soviet Union. As I discussed in chapter 1, Soviet interest in McKay as a "stand-in" African was largely based on Lenin's belief that racism and imperialism were inextricably linked, and that like individualism, they were components of bourgeois capitalism that would contribute to its self-implosion, particularly once colonized peoples were introduced to Communism and the promise of a class-based elective federation. Prior to and just following the Russian Revolution, Lenin's faith in the ideological supremacy of world Communism enabled him to endorse, for the time being, the inherent right of all colonized peoples to national self-determination, including secession. Ironically, under Lenin, Soviet Russia's own colonial policy (*korenizatsiia,* the term for "nation building," literally meaning fortification of the roots) actually laid the foundation for emergent national types based on so-called racial difference. And although Lenin's policies were revoked under Stalin, this national self-consciousness, newly rooted in territorial claims, continued to flourish even amid the compulsory Soviet patriotism modeled on the Great Russian people, informed by the danger of "capitalist encroachment," that Stalin mandated following World War II. Yet for all the attraction of this kind of nation building, imagined as it was as a kind of unity in difference, neither Lenin nor Stalin were interested in the patriarchal confines of *narodnost',* the Russian term for nationality.

In fact, following the war Soviet patriotism—which had largely relied on women and women's morale boosting during the war—was rerouted through its more conventional domains. New marriage laws were passed, including revamped divorce procedures, abortion laws were tightened, and natal and maternal health care received increased government support. In addition, the mother became instituted as an exalted public servant—with attendant awards for mother heroines titled the "Order of Mothers Glory" and "Medal of Motherhood." All of these reforms were aimed at reconsolidating the Soviet citizen, whose figural and literal image had been fractured during the war, and as during the war, it was up to women to lead the way, to show how patriotic duty should triumph over personal discomfort, patriarchal interests over women's political agency.[63]

Part of the appeal of Soviet communism was the unjustified belief that, in effect, the woman problem had been solved. As were other U.S. citizens who had traveled to the Soviet Union, Du Bois was impressed with what he believed to be the eradication of gender segregation there. During her 1932 visit, Louise Thompson Patterson noted that "women do everything here. Work on building construction, on the streets, in factories of course, and everywhere."[64] During his 1949 visit to the Moscow Peace Conference, Du Bois observed that the women delegates prided themselves on statements such as "women share in every activity of the Soviets," and "women have become a great and creative force in the Soviets."[65] With women fully integrated into the Soviet system, "race" and "class" could serve as politically viable categories free of the trappings of gender constraints. Du Bois was clearly interested in the issue of liberation, and the Soviet advances in this realm were important to him. It is impossible to deny, though, that in spite of these advances, there still existed an implicit masculinism in both Soviet rhetoric and Du Bois's emulation of it.[66]

Numerous articles about Du Bois began appearing in the Soviet Union in the early 1950s, and the steady flow of articles written both by and about Du Bois continued until his death in 1963. Whereas in the United States, as Graham so succinctly put it, "his publications are greatly curtailed and distribution of his writings difficult," Du Bois's work was widely distributed in Russia. Books translated into Russian by 1960 included *Black Reconstruction, The Souls of Black Folk, In Quest of the Silver Fleece,* the *Mansart* trilogy, and *Color and Democracy.* His articles appeared in such periodicals as *Innostranaia Literatura, Literaturnaia Gazeta, Izvestiia,* and *Pravda.*[67] The eighteenth chapter of his *Autobiography* appeared in *Sovetskaia Antropologiia (Soviet Anthropology)* in 1960, a placement that contrasted greatly with Du Bois's thwarted attempts to publish his *Autobiography* in the States.[68]

Less famous than Robeson in the Soviet Union, Du Bois did not receive the same amount of coverage as his compatriot. But although lacking the mass appeal of a Robeson, Du Bois maintained a certain degree of celebrity based on his reputation as an esteemed scholar and academician. When Du Bois received the 1958 International Lenin Prize for the promotion of peace between nations, his snapshot accompanied that of the four

12. Shirley Graham looks on as Du Bois receives the 1958 Lenin Peace Prize from Mikhail N. Smirnovsky (Soviet chargé d'affaires) at the Soviet Embassy in Washington, D.C. Special Collections and Archives, W. E. B. Du Bois Library. University of Massachusetts Amherst.

honorees, all men, alongside a feature article in *Ogonek*, the leading and most popular human interest magazine.[69] An article in *Literaturnaia Gazeta* which included excerpts from Du Bois's speech to the Peace Congress in Moscow in August 1949, quoted Du Bois as stating, "Today of all the countries on the earth only the USA desires war, prepares for war and encourages other countries to fight"—a quote that was picked up in both *Voprosy Istorii* and *Sovetskaia Etnografiia*.[70] This kind of indictment enabled the Soviets to portray themselves as the singular purveyors of peace; and it was this sense of *"mir v mir"* ("peace in the world") with which most Soviets understood their national mission. Against U.S. involvement in wars in the Philippines and Korea, the Soviet Union juxtaposed its peace conferences and support for the peace movements of colonial nations. And on the face of it, in its prominent journals and periodicals, the Soviet Union was presenting a show of unity in difference.[71] With the ill-defined choice between "peace" and "freedom," Du Bois chose the former.

The "Refusal to Be 'White'" ¦ 197

In Russia, publications like *Pravda, Izvestiia, Trud,* and *Ogonek* rallied to his side, and prominent scholars (nineteen men and two women) penned a letter to the editor of *Voprosy Istorii* (*Questions of History*) in protest of Du Bois's arrest.[72] But the Soviet Union, with all its commendations and public shows of support, could do little to lessen the assault on Du Bois's self-esteem.

MISSING THE END

In Du Bois's later years, he came increasingly to rely on the Soviet Union for institutional and intellectual aid. As Gerald Horne has pointed out, Du Bois "was a friend of the Soviet Union because he saw it alone among the big powers as rendering concrete aid, military and otherwise, to the colonized and semicolonized world."[73] Du Bois's friendship with the Soviet Union also progressed because of his increasing interest in Africa and instrumental role in the founding of the Soviet Africa Institute, which Du Bois conceived in tandem with his final project, *Encyclopedia Africana.* In January 1959, he submitted a formal proposal to the Soviet Academy of Sciences in which he suggested that the academy "establish a course of cooperative international and interracial study" working across a panoply of disciplinary fields that would together aim "at the promotion of scientific research into all the activities, past and present of the peoples of Africa, in their cultural, political and economic organizations; together with a simultaneous study of their physical, psychological and biological environment; their work in literature and art and in all human accomplishment."[74] The *Encyclopedia Africana,* a project that Du Bois left incomplete, began in correlation with the Soviet Africa Institute, founded in October 1959. In composing his proposal, Du Bois imagined that the institute could be used as a base from which the research for the *Encyclopedia* could be conducted. He wrote that "while this enterprise should start in the Soviet Union and center there," it should be international in focus, seeking first of all the "cooperation of Africans." This was a point Du Bois had made in an article he published earlier that year in *Sovremennyi Vostok* (*The Contemporary East*), titled "Lenin and Africa."[75] Based on their familiarity with Du Bois's scholarship, Soviet scholars responded positively to his ideas. Like Du Bois, Ivan Z. Potekhin, the director of the Africa Institute, was interested in compiling an encyclopedia of Africa, and he turned to Du Bois to "inform us . . . of the main steps taken to carry forward the preparation of the Encyclopedia." Writing to Du Bois in May 1960, Potekhin asserts that "the Encyclopedia should become an enterprise of international scale, and the center of the whole work should be in Africa, preferably in Ghana, and the control and coordination of the efforts should be placed in the hands of Africans."[76] At a time when Du Bois could not find institutional backing in the United States, when policy toward Africa was aimed at taking control out of the hands of Africans, the Soviet response to Du Bois was increasingly positive, and it continually sought to concretize its approval through the establishment of, in addition to the Africa Institute, international conferences and associations that focused attention on the participation of African scholars and activists.[77] As mentioned earlier, Du Bois was awarded the Lenin Peace Prize, for which he received numerous commendations and an outpouring of support in the Soviet press. From 1950 to 1958, Du Bois was, like Robeson, denied his passport by U.S. bureaucrats and effectively put under house arrest. Simply put, whereas U.S. publishers and policymakers denounced Du Bois and saw him as a threat, the Soviet Union championed him and his Pan-African interests. So far as Du Bois was concerned, when the Soviet Union advocated a free Du Bois, they advocated a free Africa, and vice versa.

As one for whom the personal life story was always about the larger contextual narrative of that man he called the "Negro," the blending of support for both also affected the autobiography of each. At ninety, Du Bois was well aware of how he would be read in perpetuity, of his significance to American literature. In rewriting the conventional autobiography, not once but four times, he disrupted expectations for originality and newness, often lifting large sections of text from previously published materials. In so doing he manipulated sites of overlap, contradiction, and/or emptiness. Deploying imperfect repetition as a kind of ideological displacement, the autobiographies provide a way of reading Du Bois's reworking not only of an ideal community but also autobiography as political praxis continually in process.

In his *Autobiography*, the final of Du Bois's analyses of his life, he describes his response to his earlier representations of his life as "conclusions which now disappear or return as quite strange" (13). But rather than discounting these texts, Du Bois proposes that each of his autobiographies has been in its own way a failure, and he cautions that "one must then see these varying views as contradictions to truth, and not as final and complete authority" (13). Thus, while admitting that *Autobiography* is composed of "what he would like others to believe," Du Bois explicitly refuses the authority conventionally appointed the author, and in its place, demonstrates how a disarticulation of continuity—that is, a breakdown in signification; a failure—presents a condition of possibility. Refusing the expected singularity of an autobiography, Du Bois gestures toward a space that refutes not only authority but also finality. Placing the Soviet Union in a prominent position, linking his autobiographical project directly with his political one, Du Bois's autobiography reiterates what was to be forgotten—his "later years"—and thereby challenges miscalculations of his life by opening up the status of "the present." Demonstrating how time gets determined by what can be said, Du Bois invokes autobiographical representation as a challenge to those who would prefer to forget, to superimpose his early life over his latter. As such, the way in which one reads Du Bois has everything to do with the responsibility one is willing to take for one's own participation in the prolongation (or evisceration) of the writing life.[78]

Recalling the past involves constantly refining and changing representations and framing devices; as Du Bois wrote, "No idea is perfect and forever valid. Always to be living and timely, it must be adapted to changing facts" (*DD*, 303). If Du Bois sounds a bit proleptic here, it is precisely because the history of democratic process in the United States—the very condition of possibility for liberal individualism—will always be connected to the history of slavery on which it was founded. And this link does not exist by way of some essence-loving hocus-pocus nor through a nominal "social constructionism." Rather, liberation and bondage interface in the day-to-day mechanics of monopoly capitalism. "What is Africa to Me?" Du Bois asks himself in *Dusk of Dawn*, and replies, "The real essence of this kinship is its social heritage of discrimination and insult, and this heritage binds together not simply the children of Africa, but extends through yellow Asia and into the South Seas. It is this unity that draws me to Africa" (117). Du Bois's story has taken on vaster proportions than that of one life: at issue is the present of a past that has been largely occluded from history. At the end of his *Autobiography*, Du Bois says, "You are not and yet you are: your thoughts, your deeds, above all your dreams still live. So too, your deeds and what you forgot—these lived as your bodies died. With these we also live and die, realize and kill" (422). In the closing pages of his *Autobiography*, he seems to suggest that individuals are haunted less by specific bodies than by processes and institutions that create bodies, and that continue to make the living, in effect, dead. An occlusion of counters to conventional modes of evaluating the past risks repeating the same stultifying processes of decomposition. Du Bois's insistence that "the dead do live on" implores one to attend to what appears dead, but is nonetheless undeniably alive. If nothing else, Du Bois's late autobiography is concerned with survival, with living on. One could read this as the ego-driven impulse of an elderly man confronting inevitable mortality, but I believe this is unfair. In reconfiguring his life for public record numerous times, Du Bois believes he has successfully negotiated the pratfalls of "mere autobiography," restored the asymmetry and differentiation within "black" experience, and hit on some of the similarities found in *all* cultures of social and economic disenfranchisement. The concept of "one long memory," the "unity" of which Du Bois speaks, attests both to the fact that far from subordinating race in his final years, Du Bois remained convinced of the ways in which race is reinvented daily. His invocation could be seen as one directed less toward messianism than to the force of social relations in which the wealth of an American democratic tradition continues to transform the living into the dead. The inclination to pass judgment on Du Bois's late political and aesthetic output as on a course with the breakup of the Soviet Union thus participates in yet another level of the social amnesia in which U.S. democracy insists on trading.

CHAPTER FOUR

Black Shadows across the Iron Curtain:

Robeson's Stance between Cold War Cultures

[Paul Robeson] is not to be understood unless seen in the context of
the most profound historical movements of our century. And, at the
same time, the most profound historical movements of the twentieth
century cannot be understood without taking into consideration
Paul Robeson.—C. L. R. James, "Paul Robeson: Black Star"

By the winter of January 1955, the road show of Ira Gershwin and Dubose
Heyward's *Porgy and Bess* was an international hit. Since 1952, it had
played in Berlin, Antwerp, Marseille, Genoa, Mexico City, Rio de Janeiro,
Caracas, and São Paulo. The U.S. State Department applauded the tour,
seeing it as excellent public relations, and over the years had contributed
more than $700,000 for production and travel costs to keep the show
going. Based on the overwhelming popularity of the show, *Life* magazine
called the musical "possibly the most successful cultural promotion ever
sponsored by the State Department."[1] President Dwight Eisenhower himself described the cast as "in a real sense, ambassadors of the arts."[2] Swept
up by his company's success, *Porgy*'s manager Robert Breen approached
the State Department with the proposal of extending the tour to the Soviet
Union. The Soviets had expressed a definitive interest in *Porgy,* and given
the troupe's success elsewhere, it seemed a promising venture. Breen's
appeal was met with mixed response. The State Department agreed to
grant the visas, but it refused to lend any financial assistance. Breen looked
elsewhere, and the Soviet Ministry of Culture agreed to front the estimated

$150,000 that it would cost to transport eighty-five cast and crew members, and to cover rehearsal and performance costs.

If *Porgy and Bess* had been such a success elsewhere in the world, then why would the State Department be hesitant to support its trip to Russia? Why would it agree to issue visas, but refuse to underwrite the bill? Breen speculated that there was a worry that the play would confirm the Soviet contention that the United States suppressed civil rights and extend negative press regarding racial strife in the States by exposing the "squalid living conditions of the opera's characters."[3] But in granting the visas, the State Department accepted this risk, and seemed willing to gamble, as it had elsewhere, that *Porgy and Bess* would strike a resounding chord for U.S. cultural unity and acceptance of racial difference. As soon as the train carrying the crew pulled into the station in Leningrad, it became clear that whatever the message *Porgy and Bess* delivered in Russia, it would have a large audience. As the first U.S. theater group ever to perform in the USSR, the cast was hailed with enthusiasm and applause. *Time* magazine reported that "traffic was blocked for a mile when 1000 Russians surrounded Earl Jackson [who alternated with Lorenzo Fuller in the role of Sportin' Life] and Helen Thigpen [who played Serena]," two cast members who caused a further sensation by getting engaged on the trip.[4] In spite of the hefty price of tickets (sixty rubles, or about fifteen dollars), the shows in Leningrad and Moscow were sold out. *Life* magazine called the show a "whacking cultural and personal success for the U.S."[5] The *New York Times* was even more explicit about the contours of such "success" when it reported that "*Porgy and Bess* is regarded as one of the most effective instruments for meeting the Russians on their favored terrain—that of waging the East-West struggle on the cultural front."[6]

As echoed in the language used by Eisenhower and the *Times*—describing the cast as "instruments" or "ambassadors"—the State Department did not pretend that culture and politics could not fraternize. Such terminology underlined the fact that these were cultural emissaries bearing a political fiat. These ambassadors earned their stripes by fronting a show with a particular kind of politics, one that did not proclaim peace, denounce Western imperialism, or accuse the United States of racial genocide. The message clearly not intended by *Porgy and Bess*'s champions in Washington was that American culture equaled the dehumanizing process of racial differentiation as depicted in the play itself. (According to James Hicks, who wrote for the Baltimore *Afro-American* in 1952, *Porgy* was "the most insulting, the most libelous, the most degrading act that could possibly be perpetrated against colored Americans of modern times.")[7] Further, advertising the success of the *Porgy* trip as one that met the Soviets "on their favored terrain," media accounts were careful to sidestep the personage who obviously was on most Russians' minds: Paul Robeson. Yet according to Truman Capote, who accompanied the cast on assignment for the *New Yorker,* the Russians frequently asked, "Why is Paul Robeson not in with the players? . . . It is because you . . . do not permit him his passport."[8]

In 1951, Robeson's passport had indeed been rescinded, and he remained stateside in 1955—one of America's greatest cultural producers kept from the frontlines of artistic expression. Unlike the cast members of *Porgy and Bess,* Robeson had chosen the "wrong" kind of culture—he explicitly conjoined politics and performance, expanding his repertoire beyond show tunes and spirituals to include an international array of working people's songs, and transforming his stage into a platform for political dissent. Unable to travel to the Soviet Union since 1949, Robeson was left behind in the United States while his *Porgy and Bess* compatriots traveled under the wing of the U.S. Information Agency. Not lost on the Soviets was the irony of the State Department taking credit for one group of African American performers while limiting the performances of another. And Robeson worked to counter the impression that the events portrayed in *Porgy and Bess* were entirely unrelated to the present—"set in the past," as Breen had been instructed to print in the opera's program, and therefore "no more reflect[ing] the present than if it were about Czarist Russia."[9] The state paper *Pravda* published a New Year's greeting from Robeson to the *Porgy and Bess* cast members in which Robeson wrote, "I know that they [the cast members] are proud of the heroic struggle of their people who fight for equality and human dignity in Mississippi and in South Carolina, where the events performed in their play unfold."[10] As Robeson underlined, the antagonisms portrayed in the opera were fully relevant to the contemporary struggles of African Americans for racial emancipation because in Mississippi and South Carolina, as in other southern states, white supremacy continued to benefit from the strong-arm of empowered consent.

13. Du Bois and Robeson shake hands at the Paris Peace Conference, 1949. The original UPI caption described this as a "red-sponsored world 'Peace' conference," and denounced Robeson for lashing out at the land of his birth and then singing "Ol' Man River" and a Russian army song. © Bettman/Corbis.

The State Department engaged in political strategizing by deploying cultural emissaries such as the *Porgy* crew and yet bounded the space of what constituted appropriate "culture," placing limits on political affiliations. The logic by which Robeson's cultural activities were curtailed by his political interests was evident in a 1949 *New York Times* editorial about Robeson that called him "politically misguided and misled." This declaration was in response to Robeson's comments at the Paris World Peace Conference (where he stated that it was "unthinkable that American Negroes would go to war [against the Soviet Union] on behalf of those who have oppressed us for generations"). Instead of pursuing political engagements, the *Times* proposed that Robeson should stick to his "great gifts. . . . We want him to sing, and to go on being Paul Robeson."[11] Robeson's refusal to "go on being Paul Robeson" in the sense the *Times* implied resulted in an effective silencing of him—one that lasted for decades.[12] As a 1998 article documenting more recent attempts to revive the memory of Robeson put it, "Robeson's story, well known to people over 50, vaguely familiar to people in their 40s and 30s, [is] all but unknown to most of those younger." The same writer, Peter Applebome, suggests that only with the end of the Cold War, can Robeson's name be uttered without a "sting."[13] Indeed, the hundredth anniversary of his birth arrived in 1998, and was commemorated by more than one hundred festivals, lectures, and exhibits in the United States and abroad. His 1958 autobiography, *Here I Stand*, was reissued; a major exhibit titled "Paul Robeson: Artist and Citizen" toured in several cities; he received a posthumous Grammy award; several of his musical recordings were rereleased; he was the focus of a PBS special; many cities sponsored film festivals; and countless newspapers featured stories. As Martin Duberman worried publicly, however, "[Robeson's] story is likely to be smoothed out and polished up for mainstream consumption. The breadth and tenacity of his challenge to the status quo . . . will likely be blanketed in a surfeit of hollow hallelujahs."[14]

The question of how Robeson's work will be remembered is a critical one not only because the reception of his work was so politically fraught but because political exclusions affected and continue to affect the relationship of his work to the mechanisms underwriting cultural production. In 1998, the texts that were called on to reinstate Robeson as "the quintessential genius of American history" were drawn largely from his earlier work—his films and musical recordings, and photographs of him from the 1920s—many of which were made before Robeson became politically aligned with the Soviet Union.[15] The effect is that in the bulk of the 1998 celebrations, Robeson the artist becomes detached from Robeson the activist in the creation of a new *American* "genius," and Robeson's commitment to internationalism gets left behind. The bulk of restorative considerations of Robeson that have taken place since 1991 have largely turned away from the specifics of Robeson's relationship with what C. L. R. James would certainly agree to have been one of the most "profound" shapers of the twentieth century—that is, the Soviet Union. This oversight is related to an occlusion of the international in Cold War histories that divided the world into international and domestic spheres, carefully locating questions of racial and cultural difference in the domestic. Thus, while efforts have been made to reclaim Robeson as one of the most celebrated of artists of the "American century," this has largely been done at the expense of Robeson's internationalist political stance.

In order to understand his internationalism, it is necessary to juxtapose not only the U.S. demonization of Robeson as "un-American" and Robeson's purportedly un-American activities but also Robeson's experience of the USSR, the popular perception of Robeson in the USSR, and the conditions of his acceptance there—the assumptions of identification that enabled his warm reception and the ways in which his representation produced a symbolic reality. The Russian side is, of course, lesser known in the United States, yet it is crucial to achieving a fuller picture of Robeson's artistic and social commitments. It is only by looking at both the United States and Soviet perspectives on Robeson that one can begin to understand how it was that he came to feel, in his own words, "for the first time like a full human being" when he visited Russia.[16] And while it was Robeson's articulation of being at home in the USSR that crosscut U.S. efforts to be the exemplary state of racial harmony, the fissures he created can best be attended to by sifting not only through U.S. investments in a postwar global and cultural security but also the Soviet mythos of "Robson."

In this sense, this chapter follows those that have preceded it by conjuring the work of scholars such as Mark Naison and Robin D. G. Kelley who have provided rich interpretive historical models with which to rethink the relationship between black radicalism and political agency in the twentieth century. But in shifting the focus to Robeson's post–World War II alliances with the Soviet Union, and integrating the Soviet picture, this chapter moves beyond these discussions to open the question of black/red relationships up to a new set of concerns. Although Naison and Kelley have persuasively argued for the comparative autonomy of black radicals in devising their own political programs through and with communism, for the most part the Soviet side has been left unexplored. Looking at the Soviet context (which to be sure, enabled new kinds of identifications for the cause of black internationalism) permits one to see the complexity of the picture at hand. As elaborated in chapter 1, as a historically "marginalized" nation, the USSR supplied a rich site for these cultural crossings, while at the same time this very richness contained ideological shortcomings and contradictions within the conceptualization of "race"—ambivalences that related back to a thwarted relationship to the very idea of "nation" and "national identity."

In contributing to a dialogue initiated by the new historicism of Naison and Kelley's pre–World War II studies, I am also engaging with cultural and literary histories that have elucidated narratives of U.S. Cold War culture. Such works as those by Alan Wald, Elaine Tyler May, and Alan Nadel have offered nuanced understandings of the ways in which these narratives impacted gendered, racial, and class antagonisms domestically.[17] But left out of this picture are the interrelations of these antagonisms and similar ones abroad. In the context of the global imaginary propounded by anticommunist U.S. foreign policies, what was the idealized place of black masculinity? Little or no attention has been given to the ways in which Robeson attempted to counter U.S. anticommunism by deploying an international imaginary that challenged expected boundaries around an acceptable identification with, embodiment of, and presentation of black selfhood. Such an imaginary found inspiration in a particular kind of Soviet national self-understanding, and it is this connection—between Robeson's championing of "the folk" and a Soviet fostering of *narodnost'* (again, roughly translated as a folk-based nationality)—that has been overlooked. Investigating Robeson's political agenda alongside Soviet manipulation of Robeson's image offers a framework with which to understand how the Soviet model provided a mobilizing discourse not only for Robeson's internationalism, embodied in his musical performance of folk ballads, but also for U.S. and Soviet doublespeak in the midst of racializing agendas.

ROBESON SPEAKS OUT

From the 1920s through the early 1940s, Robeson was regarded in the United States, in Martin Duberman's words, as "the symbolic Negro, as proof that the system worked, as proof that there was no significant [racial] prejudice in this country."[18] The factors driving Robeson's fame were numerous: Robeson introduced spirituals to Carnegie Hall; performed Shakespeare on Broadway; starred in eleven feature films; was a model for modernist artists such as Nicholas Murray and Eugene O'Neill; and created the show-stopping rendition of *Showboat*'s "Ol' Man River." But by the early 1940s, Robeson had taken a decidedly international, collectivist turn. He had, as Hazel Carby notes, "assertively wrenched his body away from performative associations with modernist strategies of inwardness, and acted in defiance of all cultural aesthetics that denied or disguised their political implications."[19] Rejecting his previous location as the representative American Negro, he embraced an openly political aesthetics.

For such political realignment he suffered.[20] Not only was Robeson's passport denied for eight years (1950–1958) and his name rubbed out from the roster of college All-Americans but he was effectively barred from pursuing his acting and singing career. His income plummeted, he was publicly defamed, he was hounded by the FBI and CIA, and his friends were arrested and indicted, some convicted and imprisoned. Robeson attracted the ire of many Americans for looking to the Soviet Union as an alternative political model that linked the fates of the peoples of Western European colonies to that of African Americans.

In pursuing the Soviet promise of a society free of racism, Robeson was not alone. Yet as we have seen, while the Soviet opportunity posed an attractive option to many black Americans for a variety of reasons, for Robeson the lure was quite specific. Describing the overwhelmingly positive reaction he experienced during his stays in Russia, Robeson wrote that he believed that the Soviet Union provided a truly inclusive society that involved "Soviet workers of all nationalities and shades of color. . . . [There are] no empty promises such as colored folk continuously hear in the U.S., but deeds."[21] His wife, Eslanda Robeson, put it similarly when she reportedly said, "The Soviet Union has a great variety of people and they have done the opposite of Americans for Russia helps people to retain and develop their individuality and the people become 100% citizens and are routed in their own background and are absorbed into the Soviet people."[22] Lacking in the United States, both Robesons felt, were on the one hand the basic entitlements of equal citizenship, which were reserved for the most part for whites only, and on the other hand, a substantial concern for the transnational connections between poor Americans and other disenfranchised peoples. Dismayed by the limited fulfillment of national promise, Paul Robeson promoted an "international" outlook, a dynamic mix of democratic, socialist, anti-imperialist, and antiracist ideals.

Following very much in the footsteps of McKay's path toward the internationale in the early 1920s, Robeson's idea of internationalism sprung from the Leninist doctrine of the early 1920s that encouraged indigenous nationalist movements to the extent that these movements could be used to further Communist objectives—namely, the downfall of capitalism and the undermining of imperial and neoimperial states. What Leninism offered Robeson was a means of promoting simultaneously both the drive toward self-determination and internationalism. In the years 1917–1921, Lenin had clarified this policy in the Soviet "Appeal to All the Toiling Muslims of Russia and the Far East." As discussed in chapter 1, this appeal contained two pivotal purposes for black internationalists. First, it assured "key minorities within the Soviet Union that the Bolsheviks were proponents of the free development of all nationality groups," and second, it demonstrated the intention to extend the revolution worldwide so as to thwart the imperialist powers.[23] As Michelle Stephens has argued, the merging of the themes of national self-determination and internationalism enabled black nationalists to believe that a revolutionary identity could thus be based not singularly in a circumscribed national identity but in extended cross-national alliances, thereby facilitating new conceptions of citizenship and national community.[24]

At the same time, as scholars of black internationalism have been reluctant to point out, this reasoning was not without its ideological oversights. Revisions of Lenin's internationalism that took place at the Sixth Comintern challenged the very practicality of such new conceptions coming into being because these reforms commandeered focus on domestic issues, largely to the exclusion of the international. Moreover, policy changes made in 1928 had specific ramifications for black internationalists. The resolution of the Executive Committee of the Communist International at the Sixth Comintern stated that "Negro Communists must clearly dissociate themselves from all bourgeois currents in the Negro movement . . . in order to guarantee the hegemony of the Negro proletariat in the national liberation movement of the Negro population, and to coordinate wide masses of the Negro peasantry in a steady fighting alliance with the proletariat."[25] In addition to averring that bourgeois-led nationalist movements would eventually enable imperial powers, these changes also asserted that the "national question" for nonwhites was subordinate to class issues. Both of these decisions disabled attempts to theorize nationalism and race in site-specific ways that could have furthered Soviet understanding of the ways in which race, class, and gender oppressions are integrally conjoined. These decisions also made it less likely that the dream of "international racial formations" would materialize, with Soviet support, into any kind of reality in the near future. In addition to the reversal of Soviet policy on the national question in 1928, other facts supported the unlikelihood of Lenin's internationale. During World War II, the Soviets all but abandoned an internationalist focus in order to combat German and Japanese fascism. An emphasis on domestic policy continued into the postwar period. And by the late 1950s, Soviet bureaucrats were only beginning to rethink the importance of nationalism.[26]

Nonetheless, the ideals articulated by Leninist internationalism stood firm in Robeson's mind. For this reason, the utopian aspirations inspired by early Bolshevik policy cannot be dismissed out of hand.[27] As Ronald Grigor Suny has maintained, in spite of later attempts to curb internal, minority nationalist impulses, these earlier policies laid the groundwork for a flourishing of national culture that was not stopped by the repeal of central support.[28] Indeed, it was transnational formations of a Leninist tradition that Robeson strove to foster in his performance of national folk songs. In Robeson's case, it is difficult and perhaps unnecessary to draw a definitive line between his interests in Soviet internationalism (as focused on creating bonds between nations) and the transnational theorizations of a reconstituted nation that this internationalism inspired.[29]

Of all the accounts of communism's ability to entice, perhaps the most compelling is the one composed by Richard Wright. Prior to his public renunciation of communism, Wright located its appeal in a "sense of similarity of the experiences of workers in other lands, by the possibility of uniting scattered but kindred peoples into a whole. . . . My life as a Negro in America had led me to feel . . . that the problem of human unity was more important than bread, more important than physical living itself; for I felt that without a common bond uniting men, without a continuous current of shared thought and feeling circulating through the social system . . . there could be no living worthy of being called human."[30] Robeson echoed this sentiment when he wrote that an understanding of connections between the toiling classes of the globe—"bound by the web of history and human suffering"—made real for him the concept of international solidarity (*HIS*, 54). In communism, according to Wright, the Negro could find "a home, a functioning value and role" outside the parameters heretofore defined by whiteness.[31]

Such an aperture on the rigid outline of an emerging post–World War II whiteness was just what the scholar and activist Du Bois identified when he described the "thankfulness" U.S. and European powers should feel toward Russia for her "refusal to 'be white,'" as discussed in the previous chapter. Like Robeson, his friend and colleague, Du Bois discerned that segregation would have to be dismantled in order to answer the challenge of the Soviets on the race question. Exposing the hypocrisies of a land that preached the text of equality and freedom for all, but that remained rife with institutionalized racisms, the Soviet Union ridiculed U.S. social policy, and people listened. In refusing to be white, the Soviets supplied more fuel for the good versus bad, West versus East, freedom versus repression dichotomies that were the bread and butter of anticommunism. In refusing to be white—that is, Euroamerican—the USSR not only set itself in distinction to the Western powers but at the same time provided the necessary components of otherness—that is to say, not whiteness—against which the United States set out to define itself. As the Soviet other was depicted through available terms heretofore reserved for women, homosexuals, and persons of color, a new rhetoric of racial equality—framed as us versus them—became a rallying point for patriotism and national citizenship. To better encompass the political message of anticommunism, this call for a revamped understanding of national identity as white and yet also capable of including the right nonwhites—a kind of collective whiteness—required a reconfiguration of the community imagined to constitute the national polity. And this imagining of who was understood to belong—in contrast to who wasn't—became the literal and figural stage on which Robeson played a starring role. In a period in which "many inter-racial organizations and most liberal organizations" were "branded as 'Communist front'" at one time or another, Robeson became an enemy magnet for racists and anticommunists alike.[32]

In addition to alienating himself from conservative and liberal white groups, Robeson also suffered from unpopularity among black liberals. Alienation from white groups occurred for any number of reasons: because Robeson refused to play the pliant representative Negro, because he supported communism, because he was black. Alienation from black liberalism occurred because Robeson refused to prioritize a patronage that not only placed national solidarity between black and white America above and beyond the interests of global liberation but imposed such solidarity as an obligation of citizenship as well.[33] As Penny Von Eschen maintains, Robeson's unflagging concern for the connections between Jim Crow culture and the encroachment of U.S. racial policies into Africa and Asia can be seen as "eclipsed by the emphasis of African American leaders, intellectuals and journalists on differences between African Americans and Africans, rather than on the bonds that had been so forcefully articulated during WWII."[34] At the Bandung Conference in 1955, Adam Clayton Powell Jr. rebuked Robeson and "dismiss[ed] as 'Communist propaganda' that no progress was being made in the United States toward equality for its black citizens."[35] To denounce Robeson became tantamount to proving one's patriotism.

Showcasing how differently from Robeson one might be included in the U.S. community, anticommunist propaganda promoted a rhetoric of promised inclusion. Movies like *The Red Menace* (1949) and *Big Jim McLain* (1952), in which John Wayne starred as a House Un-American Activities Committee (HUAC) investigator, invariably contained the conversion narrative of a previously misguided black or person of color who rejects Communism to partake in the privileges of a newly wrought American identity, this collective whiteness. But as Robeson recognized, the very requirement of banding together against the enemy "Red" contained a proviso that contradicted the so-called singular emphasis in the United States on the domestic sphere. Bolstering ties against the USSR also demanded the participation (willing or unwilling) of the supposedly free nations of the world, for which the United States stood as exemplar and leader. In this sense, in spite of conventional readings of anticommunism as primarily concerned with strategies of national containment—that is to say, with containing the impulses and energies of potentially subversive actions on the home front—anticommunism, as Robeson was well aware, also contained powerfully expansionist ideals. The notion that the United States was ascending to its rightful place as leader of the free world demanded not only that the United States serve on its own as an exemplary state of racial harmony but that it disseminate this picture of inclusiveness to the outside world.[36]

While recognizing the persistence of racial inequality in spite of the civil rights acts of the 1950s, it is important not to slight the entitlements offered by desegregation and the sheer rhetorical power of a reformulated American identity as inclusive. Such concessions caused black membership in leftist organizations to dwindle, and as others have argued, even black liberalism became a bastion of anticommunism.[37] The fear of being branded a communist was equaled perhaps only by the satisfaction of being considered a true American for articulating such fear and renouncing explicitly the international. But the price paid for such exclusionary thinking has been the oversight of the message of figures like Robeson. These figures demanded that the granting of civil rights entitlements in the 1950s be seen in the broader context of international pressures, not simply as the benevolence of a nation that finally acknowledged its founding principles of equal rights and extended these rights to nonwhites. In an interview with the magazine *V Zashchitu Mira*, Robeson notes this context, stating that the "Warren decision against racial segregation was carried out namely under the pressure of world opinion."[38] For just as *Brown v. Board of Education* was being decided, HUAC was heating up, the State Department was denying passport privileges to suspected communists, including Robeson and Du Bois, and the Smith and McCarran Acts were being invoked to detain and persecute those suspected of having foreign, communist ties. Maintaining that domestic civil liberties were inescapably linked to international issues, that repression at home was a direct consequence of a pathological fear of the Soviet Union, Robeson was aware that in the midst of *Brown v. Board*, the principle of equal rights was being violated everywhere a putative un-American looked. Against the notion of gradual change advocated by some liberals, Robeson contended that "the viewpoint that progress must be slow is rooted in the idea that democratic rights, as far as Negroes are concerned, are not inalienable and self-evident as they are for white Americans" (*HIS*, 76). Robeson identified in the idea of collective whiteness an inclusion of others that remained shallow, provided social band-aid concessions to "difference," and ignored the international connections and ramifications of institutionalized racisms.

THE FOLK CONNECTION

Against the denunciation of folk culture, Robeson throughout his career asserted the legitimacy of folk-based art as a distinctively American art form. In the late 1930s, however, Robeson began to use a folk aesthetic to cement the appeal of his performances across national boundaries. In aspiring to represent an international working class, Robeson deployed a folk-based performative praxis—a praxis that itself had traditionally been viewed with suspicion precisely because of its populist origins. Intermixing the particularist and internationalist, Robeson adhered to what Sandra L. Richards has termed a "central principle" of a folk aesthetic, the juxtaposition of "radical differences that generate deep emotional responses from those assembled, challenging them to imagine some interpretive resolution."[39] For Robeson, the "radical differences" took the shape of multinational folk ballads. These songs were sung for racially mixed, progressive audiences who together created a space for community understood as both hetero- and homogeneous, "in some sense solidified by sharing a particular performance event, yet segmented by its production of a variety of meanings."[40] Shifting focus from the performer to the context, Robeson's concerts worked with an appeal that was both from and to collective, not singular or individual, purposes.

This desire to adhere the individual to the collective was underlined by Robeson's chosen repertoire of music that represented several cultures, each song of which he sang in its original language. Fluent in several of these languages, Robeson believed that folk music contained a "common undertone" through which peoples of different nations articulated their marginalizations from majority discourses, and through which such peripheralized peoples could be reached and politicized. This common undertone bespoke a marginalized subjectivity, an outsider status, for which music offered a kind of antidote. This antidote can be understood in terms put forth by David Lloyd and Abdul JanMohamed as a type of "minority discourse."[41] Such a discourse distinguishes itself from so-called majority discourse by relaying a sense of otherness into previously denied territories of identity and selfhood. As Lloyd and JanMohamed describe, "Coerced into a negative, generic subject position, the oppressed individual responds by transforming that position into a positive, collective one. Therein lies the basis of a broad minority coalition."[42] The art of transforming enforced negativity into a positive may skim over questions about the presupposed uniformity of any discourse that presents itself as majority, the usefulness of dividing discourses into majority and minority, as well as the coercive aspects of any resulting positive. Nonetheless, the concept of minority discourse is helpful in thinking through the simultaneous expression and sublimation of oppression housed in marginalized cultural formations. These formations foreground responses to self and group denigration in order to stake a claim on selfhood, preserve that fragile claim, and challenge the existing status quo to which minority positionality is indebted. Robeson's performances capitalized on this sensed collectivity, and its call to critique the status quo, and Robeson used "internationalism" as a kind of minority discourse to delineate as points of commonality the political exclusions created by slavery, segregation, and imperialism.[43]

But Robeson's deployment of internationalism did more than simply turn the tables on white supremacy by asserting a counterclaim to nonidentity based on an equally valid assertion of identicalness, of integrated selfhood. Robeson used the stage to affirm his conviction that the right of artists to voice grievances abroad "has been of great value to the struggle for Negro rights in America. . . . [F]rom the very beginning of Negro history in our land, Negroes have asserted their right to freedom of movement" (*HIS*, 66). For the Negro artist, Robeson continued, "the right to travel has been a virtual necessity" (71). This affirmation of a "right to travel" and voice grievances abroad establishes Robeson's internationalism as a type of minority discourse that cannot be reduced to an oppositional consciousness pitting outsider against insider, East against West. Rather, his claims suggest the importance of nonoppositional coalitions between multiple outsiderness and enforced nonidentities as a basis for the positive transformation of the oppressive effects of Western philosophies of identity. Understood in this way, Robeson's work was not simply about establishing a simulacrum of the same but an effort to locate within histories of excludedness a practice—the expression of grievances abroad as a way of safeguarding selfhood—that challenged presumptions of national identity as exclusively nation bound.

Robeson's stance seems to anticipate what Paul Gilroy has eloquently described as a black Atlanticism, a structure that draws on Du Bois's notion of double consciousness to extrapolate a structure of subjectivity that in spite of its indebtedness to modernity, cannot be reduced to the official, master narrative of modernity based as it was in practices of exclusion and normalization. This double consciousness, in Gilroy's terms, "emerges from the unhappy symbiosis between three modes of thinking, being, and seeing. The first is racially particularistic, the second nationalistic in that it derives from the nation state in which the ex-slaves but not-yet-citizens find themselves rather than from their aspiration towards a nation state of their own. The third is diasporic or hemispheric, sometimes global and occasionally universalist."[44] Robeson's interest in linking strains of music prefigures the transnationalist thrust of the counterdiscourse Gilroy maps in black Atlantic expressive cultures. But as did McKay's, Hughes's, and Du Bois's writings, Robeson's work also extends the geographic confines of Gilroy's mapping, moving it beyond Anglophone limits and challenging the restrictions of a Europe-Africa-U.S. triangulation. Locating an international link in pentatonic scales that span from Beijing to Bakersfield, Robeson formalizes solidarity against exclusive practices by conjuring class (and not singularly racial) consciousness. Whereas Gilroy uses black Atlanticism to rethink modernity, Robeson, relying on Marxism, opts to focus on the worlding of capitalism. In the words of Neil Lazarus, who challenges Gilroy's occlusion of "countervailing or alternative theories of transnationalism or globalization"—namely, Marxism—"the only form of politics capable of presenting a decisive challenge to the globalism of actually existing capitalism is an internationalist socialism."[45] It was Robeson's nascent internationalist socialism and his ability to traverse the specifically racialized axis of modernity (to understand social formations from a perspective that criticized capitalism's determining role in shaping modernity) along with his ability to rouse in his audiences identifications across this divide that caused the State Department to admit that they supported suppressing Robeson because "his activity in behalf of independence for the colonial peoples of Africa was potentially a 'diplomatic embarrassment,'" and that Robeson's interest in "colonial liberation abroad and equality for blacks at home constituted the basis for the animus against him."[46] In 1955, a federal district attorney representing the State Department went so far as to declare Robeson "one of the most dangerous men in the world," pronouncing that Robeson represented a "direct threat to the security of the U.S."[47]

Despite such restrictions, the attempts to make Robeson imminently containable did not fully succeed. Robeson had to some degree circumvented these limitations by arranging international recordings in place of personal appearances, in order to take his political stance virtually. At first glance, this disembodied version of Robeson's voice clearly went against the grain of his staunch politics of embodiment. For it was precisely the body's capacity to exert its usefulness as an irrefutable reminder of physical, human presence that had led Robeson to choose the musical/political project that he did. It would seem, then, that a dependence on the body's usefulness as a tool breaks down when its voice becomes dislodged and the body absent.

Or does it? In fact, one could argue that the strategy Robeson deployed in performing his songs actually refused to bend to the project of disembodiment. One Soviet writer explained, "You can arrest the singer, but you can't arrest his song."[48] As affirmed by the reactions to Robeson's voice Soviets and others around the world described even after Robeson's house arrest—what the Soviets called his "continental incarceration" ("*kontinental'nyi zakliuchenie*")—Robeson's vocal performances, whether live or taped, continued to profess a located, embodied political message that could not be fully deterred by the denial of his physical presence.[49] The recorded voice defied containment, soared over airwaves, permeated and permutated to find homes on unlikely shores. Switching emphasis from the identity of Robeson to the iterability of his words—that is, to the way in which by singing Robeson was doing—his performances opened up a space whose radical heterogeneity depended on contestability, partiality, and dissent. Inasmuch as reaction could not be thoroughly predetermined, these performances operated under the logic that justice is linked to that which is incalculable in advance, to that which is not predestined but open-ended. As attested to by the national grounding of his body by the state, Robeson's ability to arouse and inspire feelings beyond the nation itself was perceived as toxic to the United States precisely because such potential arousal was neither preordained nor part of the national recipe for citizenship.

Instead, Robeson's performative strategy created a space in which Robeson can be likened to what Antonio Gramsci has called an "organic intellectual," albeit one with internationalist, transnational goals. Contra Lenin, Gramsci argued for an organic fusion of elite and popular elements of political struggle, and saw the revolutionary process as a "national-popular" phenomenon. To this end, the organic intellectual would mediate between the intellectual sphere and popular consciousness. Such mediation is necessary because

> the popular element "feels" but does not always know or understand; the intellectual element "knows" but does not always understand and in particular does not always feel. The intellectual's error consists in

believing that one can know without understanding and even more without feeling and being impassioned: in other words that the intellectual can be an intellectual if distinct and separate from the people-nation, i.e. without feeling the elementary passions of the people. . . . One cannot make politics-history without this passion, without this sentimental connection between intellectuals and people-nation.[50]

In likening Robeson to Gramsci's organic intellectual, however, it is essential to point out that unlike attempts by literary critics to incorporate the folk as a kind of raw material from which intellectuals can weave a fine quilt of cultural tradition, Robeson's performances clearly established him as both producer and craftsperson, laborer and artisan. Both representing and seeking out this "popular element," what he termed the "consciousness of an inner spirit" housed in folk culture, Robeson (unlike Gramsci, who might have queried the theatricality of folk performance for international ends) advocated political action that was ignited by the pathos of national membership and extended transnationally. In this sense, Robeson's tactics are more in sympathy with what Neal Lazarus has labeled "nationalist internationalism," an idiom he uses in a different context to elaborate how the nation is the terrain on which "an articulation between secular intellectualism and popular consciousness can be forged."[51]

Yet the ignited passions of an audience can create incalculable emotions that can cut both ways, can simultaneously arouse both liberating and not-so-liberating energies. As Andrew Parker and Eve Kosofsky Sedgwick have noted, "A performative utterance is one, as it were, that always may get sick."[52] Herein lies the dilemma of Robeson's organic intellectualism, his political/performative praxis of performing multinational folk ballads. Planning his repertoire as he did, Robeson presumed that transnational thinking would overwhelm nationalism's sometimes quite mean limitations. A reliance on invoking a shared sense of identity as oppressed, as nonidentity, as excluded, and so on, by definition claims the culturally constructed elements of oppression as if they were without mediation and, more important, difference. An emphasis on a politics of apprehension as necessarily innate assumes that each song could tap a natural consciousness outside bourgeois categories, values, and gender inequities.[53]

These inconsistencies can be related back to Robeson's invocation of the folk as an organic cultural stem that conjoined Russian and black culture through a "kinship" relation based in his thinking in "the common element of serfdom."[54] As Martin Duberman has noted, Robeson felt that "the American Negro could use Russian culture 'to advantage' . . . because 'the history of the Russian peasant closely parallels that of [the] Negro peasant in America.' "[55] In promoting what he called the "superior wisdom of the folk" that emerged from this common element, Robeson differentiated between what he described as Western culture's abstractness—"from the outside looking in" as well as Negro and Eastern culture's "pure apprehension."[56] In deontologizing the connection between serfs and slaves, he nonetheless strove to conjoin it with a particularized aesthetics of cultural production based in marginalizations from Western philosophies of identity and housed within the expressive cultures of the folk. Venturing to move away from the abstract, inward-looking aesthetic of Western culture and instead migrate toward the irrefutability of the body's presence as a political contender, Robeson at the same time aspired to an incarnation of the soul, the singularity of what he called "the human stem."[57]

For Robeson, the binding root of all folk was grounded in the counteraesthetics of the pentatonic scale. Robeson's turn to music as the great aesthetic and political leveler suggested at once a non-Hegelian perception of history (thereby linking those such as the Russians, Africans, and others seen as culturally backward) and a belief in the ontological rather than functional qualities of folk music. One need only look at appendix C of *Here I Stand*, titled "A Universal Body of Folk Music—A Technical Argument by the Author," to see how Robeson's formalist approach to music theory belies a highly subjective reading based on the author's self-termed "pentatonic ears." These ears do not hear the relations between notes as products, or functions, of a set of relations between the musical "text" and its contexts and those of its listeners who have been trained to receive the signal being broadcast. Instead, these ears hear "inherent properties" of the particular piece and folk music in general. What is special about folk music is taken to be what is essential about it: a self-evident essence that is perpetually contemporary. For Robeson, folk songs were "the music of basic realities, the spontaneous, expression by the people for the people of elemental emotions."[58] Folk music was, in this way, an aesthetic building block that pronounced the authenticating roots of mass culture.

Such a definition of mass culture was precisely what drew Robeson to the Soviet scene, and what, in turn, drew Soviets to him. In his introduction for the album *Favorite Songs of the Red Army and Navy*, Robeson observed, "In many lands, the Arts, especially Music, have been cut off from the general life of the nation. They have become the source of enjoyment for a comparatively few so-called elite—who feel that culture should be somewhat unapproachable. . . . [W]hat a revelation when first I went to the Soviet Union, to see that all forms of culture—the pictorial and plastic arts, the art of the theater, poetry, music belonged to the highest sense to the people." Robeson defines the people's culture as representing "folk material (always the real foundation of any great music)."[59] This sentiment is repeated for Russian readers in an article in *Sovetskaia musika* in which Robeson writes that "in the USSR as nowhere else in the world there is a respect for and appreciation of every artistic manifestation of the folk soul, every authentic national art."[60] Promoting a mass culture rooted in national folk expressions, Robeson strove to unite different peoples under a rubric of "soul" that was inclusive, regardless of race, class, nationality, or gender. Advocating music as one of the "quickest" ways to mutual understanding across national borders, he felt that such understanding could come about "most of all through the idiom of folk song, like the common expression of a people that is so immediate in its communication to all others."[61]

This return to the "immediate" roots that bind all humanity is replete with its own fiction of universality. In the predominant musical scales of native/folk music from around the world, one finds that some rely on the pentatonic while others do not. Underscoring a folk connection between oppressed peoples conflates a Herderian romanticization of the *volk* and one's ability to "hear" appropriately based on a previous experience of alienation. In addition to overlooking the growing urbanness of the underclass, the mutation of folk traditions in an urban populace, and the distancing from folk roots that resulted from these migrations, an aesthetics of apprehension occludes how experience lays its claim, how consciousness gets conferred by the state. If suffering provides a necessary root of aesthetics, then experience seamlessly slides into epistemology, forging a privileged site of knowledge. This knowledge can be exchanged, but will not automatically be used to encourage social and political transformation. The assumption that particular groups bear a singular revolutionary consciousness ignores a series of mediating factors, including the variations among the folk within classes, genders, and races, as well as from country to country—the way in which the folk was understood to be constituted in different cultural contexts. In other words, how were the excluded determined to not belong, and didn't such exclusionary practices belie Robeson's intention of mass inclusion regardless of one's socio-historical background?

For clearly exclusion was not Robeson's intention. In fact, most of his repertoire consisted of Western working-class songs. Robeson's allegiance to and own aesthetic rootedness in Western cultural forms makes tricky any attempt to wean away a pure, folk-based "culture of apprehension." For it was precisely Robeson's awareness of a *dual* sense of allegiance—both Western and non-Western—that forged what he articulated as parallel bases of "Negro" and "Russian" subjectivities. Indeed, Robeson's apprehensions of black folk traditions and the musicological approach to the pentatonic scale were themselves part of a Western way of reading cultural patterns. The idea of summoning folk consciousness as a root of cultural authenticity is itself a Western notion, reflecting a Herderian concept in which the major cultural values of a nation are defined by the lowest strata of the culture. Robeson's agenda, then, can be read as traditionally romanticist, relying on a kind of *volksgeist* or inward essence to bring about social change. In explaining his apprehension of his power to unite audiences, Robeson likens himself to Whitman's bard: "When I stand up before an audience I know that somehow a power is given me to convince—as Walt Whitman says: By my presence."[62] Robeson drew on Whitman's notion that the agent for social change is the bard who is one with the people, and that the vehicle for change is language infused with the vitality of spontaneous folk feeling.

And yet, to stop at the fact of physicality, to stop before the performance, is to deflect from the staging and performance of the bard's message, to igore what these moments of intervention involved. In spite of the purported irresistibility of the power of his presence, particularly when combined with the cathartic tug of the pentatonic scale, Robeson chose his songs carefully, with attention to both the words and score.[63] Prior to singing Robeson set the stage for each of his audiences, providing a translation, if necessary, of the song's message. For example, in performing "Joe Hill" in Moscow in 1949, Robeson introduced this song to his audience as "a very important song for the American working class. There was a brave man named Joe Hill. He died in a fight for the working class. He was murdered. And the words of the song go: "I dreamed I saw Joe Hill last night and I said, 'Joe, but you're 10 years dead.' Joe replied, 'No, I never died.' "[64] In this case, before the song has even been sung, nearly a minute of hearty applause responds to Robeson's Russian. This song embodies the perpetuity of the idea of the folk tradition translated into the working person's cause. So long as there is a fight worth fighting, Joe Hill is alive and kicking. With organic language such as "ain't" and "I says," Robeson's rendition focuses spiritual truths by using uncouth diction to achieve exalted expression.[65]

Robeson sought to turn the democratic principle embodied in his presence toward global, as well as national, diversity. This emphasis on diversity again raises questions not only about the role of universalism in Robeson's platform but also about universalism's basis in a *musical* scale. The latter comprises a challenge to music's foundational status that Robeson himself puts forth in an interview with *V Zashchitu Mira*. Here, he describes the ability of music to create links between different nations, but then goes on to say that "kinship between all countries emerges not only in songs, but also in poetic masterpieces, legends and oral tales, in the wealth of folklore. . . . I would even go so far to say that artistic reading is more important than singing; for me personally singing is a continuation of speech. In connection with this, let me tell you that more than once after a concert audience members have approached me and said that of all the pieces on the program the thing they enjoyed the most was the way I recited Shakespeare."[66]

Not only is Robeson's postulation about the unifying nature of the pentatonic connection somewhat undercut by an affirmation of the text but the chosen text—Shakespeare—would surely fall into the category portrayed by Robeson as Western, and therefore "inward looking," the product of a "desiccated rationalism," and so forth.[67] And the fact that some Soviet audience members apparently agreed with Robeson about the power of and preference for the spoken word also complicates an insistence on the universality of music as an underlying, connecting code.[68] These inconsistencies are not mentioned so as to discredit Robeson's project. Rather, they are described in order to highlight the difficulties of trying to establish new aesthetic modes thoroughly free of outside, "colonizing" contamination. Folk music is, after all, part of a cultural mélange, conditioned by invented traditions. The example of "Joe Hill" (written in the 1920s) shows that far from asserting timelessness, folk music actually attests to the historical and social contingencies that come to be expressed in popular resistance to cultural and governmental hegemony. Robeson's use of folk music, therefore, can be seen as the promotion of an invented tradition of collective resistance; the basis in dubious authenticating modes of popular appeal becomes secondary to the political goal of organized group action. Open to the partiality inherent to performance as an inconclusively drawn act, Robeson's concerts exhibit a counter to his championing of the alleged purity of folk consciousness. While Robeson did not publicly address the roots of invention inherent to his project, and instead appealed to its authentic basis, his conspiring to bring together the national and international itself belies any such appeal to a genuine aesthetic model for collective action. In sticking to the idea of a commonality based in folk feeling, Robeson perhaps overlooked the fact that the connection between serfs and slaves was based in both cases on servitude against the wills of those indentured. Commonality such as Robeson espoused would be not only disputed but also heterogeneous and likewise unpredictable. His performative praxis should thus be considered with an eye toward the complexities involved in attempting to de-emphasize the specificities of racial and/or national difference while in the act of performing cultural particularity.

Far from resolving this conflict, the Soviet Union was long caught up in struggles over its own self-definition in terms of its proximity to the East and West. As discussed in chapter 1, Russian self-understanding has been beset by its own uncertain and anxious relation to the "modernity" of the West and "barbarism" of the East.[69] In spite of such insecurities, the USSR offered Robeson its own version of cultural particularism through which dreams of internationalism emerged. Rather than the more obvious "national'nost'," the Russian term for nationality is narodnost'. Sentimentalizing not the nation per se but the peoples of the Soviet empire, narodnost' was a term chosen in the eighteenth century and for its likeness to the French term *populaire,* or "the people," and was a concept used to mean both nation and the many peoples living within Soviet bounds.[70]

The Russian interest in contesting assimilation into European modes of national self-understanding has a history eloquently elaborated by Dale Peterson in his book *Up from Bondage: The Literatures of Russian and*

African American Soul. Peterson demonstrates how a perceived exclusion from European cognitive traditions sparked in nineteenth-century Russian philosophers and writers a counterclaim based in an equally valid and yet different sense of self articulated through "soul." He connects the alienation of Russians by German idealist philosophy to the marginalization of African Americans, and reveals parallels between these groups rejected by the West's social order. As I discuss in chapter 1 Peterson's narrative does not explore how nationalist parallels between Russian and black American cultural patterns interacted. During the years following the Revolution, a Marxist rescripting of soul rhetoric into a folk-based workers' culture appealed to African American intellectuals and writers who sought to distinguish the particularity of African American cultural patterns, and in some cases, to use the expressive cultures of the folk as a fount of authenticating black culture.[71] In spite of initial Marxist, principled resistance to the term, on cue from late-nineteenth-century socialist populism, the *narod* became the toiling class that was appealed to during the revolution. In this way, following the forced collectivization of the 1930s, a workers' culture was created from the rudiments of a folk one. During the year of Robeson's first visit to the Soviet Union, in 1934, at the First Congress of the Union of Writers, Maxim Gorky contributed to a workers' rehabilitation of folklore, stating that "many major works of world literature had been influenced by oral folklore," and praising "the value of folk literature as an expression of the values of ordinary working people."[72] As Lynne Attwood and Catriona Kelly explain, "Subsequently the publication of folklore and its definition expanded to include not only traditional genres but also oral history, the biographical narratives of workers, including their experiences of war, Revolution, and the construction of socialism. An 'industrial folklore' was created in the form of collective worker memoirs of the history of a factory or enterprise," and in the postwar period, folk art became a formal member of expositions of Soviet socialist realism.[73] Clearly, the tradition wrought from these years of toil was to a large degree a fabricated one. Soviet workers' culture had at its supposedly authentic root a succession of invented rituals meant to replace the previously binding Russian Orthodox religious practices that had brought the folk together. In place of such religious markers, the Soviets created new holidays and events: a holiday to celebrate the border guards, awards devoted to exemplary mothers, and all-city cleaning days.

Through repetition and the required collective participation of the Soviet people, these rituals came to be cemented into the reality of a new cultural practice called Soviet narodnost'. As the editors of *Russian Cultural Studies* point out, "Soviet notions of culture, far from being based on a vulgar Marxist conception of the cultural sphere as little more than a reflection of the economic base of society, emphasized the centrality of the cultural sphere in shaping and facilitating economic development."[74] The connections between culture and narodnost' reflected attempts to foster a Soviet patriotism that promoted an appreciation for the national traditions of all the Soviet peoples, and that would contribute to and support economic flourishing. And yet, Soviet propaganda "always perceived the Russian people as 'first among equals'" so that representations of non-Russians and women were always framed in ways that highlighted their peripheral status.[75]

Curiously, in a conservative return to the Russian canon that emphasized the nationalist strains of artists' work, a taste for nineteenth-century classicism returned in the 1930s. This resuscitation of decidedly bourgeois figures from Russia's czarist past was fortuitous for African Americans, as among the men selected most prominent was Pushkin, so important to McKay, Hughes, and others.[76] Pushkin received an exclusive rendering as the "father of Russian literature." Robeson described his filiation to Pushkin in an interview with the Soviet magazine *Ogonek:* "I read Pushkin long ago, as if tasting for the first time the lifestaff of your country. And even though I grew up in America and was raised on English culture, I sometimes responded to Russian poetry and literature more strongly than I did to English. Maybe this is because . . . Russian literature more deeply expresses the feelings and suffering of the oppressed."[77] Echoing his belief that a Russian folk connection was transmitted directly through Pushkin, in a New Year's greeting to the Soviet people published in *Pravda,* Robeson maintained, "It is difficult to define where Pushkin ends and where the folk begins."[78] For Robeson, his link to the folk moved smoothly through the filter of Pushkin as avatar of both the suffering Russian peasant and descendant of French-educated African royalty. Again, his stated reliance on "suffering" as fundamental to a certain kind of knowledge that would make Robeson *more* privy to Russian than to (presumably white) U.S. experience exhibits a limited view of the complex ways experience stakes itself out. And yet, even in his limitations Robeson is never consistent. Just as he heralded Shakespeare as the most representative of bards, he meshes Pushkin and the folk, providing another instance of his unwillingness to cordon off East from West, high culture from mass culture, and black from white.

Uncomfortable with the limitations imposed on the exclusions of nationality in the United States, Robeson felt at home in the romanticism of a venerated, narodnost'-based folk culture. It was the implicit expansiveness of the term, and perhaps even its implicit inventedness, that fueled Robeson's internationalist goals. He exposed the exclusiveness of Western cultural practices in the name of humanity by invoking narodnost'. In place of this, Robeson interposed the world's minorities as the deserving gauge for "humanism's" success. But rather than moving from the folk connection to renegotiate racialism as a visible identity based in necessary difference, Robeson challenged the reduction to skin color being imparted by U.S. attempts to keep blacks in their place, proposing instead a depth of consciousness within all bodies. He was interested in the collective and coordinated power of bodies acting in concert. The way Robeson tapped into this collective consciousness was through his vocal performances, by establishing a simultaneous emerging of the national and international, and likewise taking a stand.

TRANSLATING ROBESON

As expressed repeatedly throughout his interviews and statements to the Soviet and U.S. press, Robeson felt a keen sense of kinship with the Russian people—a kinship fostered by the visits he made to the Soviet Union in 1934, 1949, 1958, and 1961. All reports indicate that his reception in Russia, like that of McKay, Hughes, and Du Bois before him, was exceedingly positive.[79] The Soviet press was fond of repeating Robeson's statement that he felt for the first time like a full human being when he visited the Soviet Union.[80] But however self-inflating the Soviet dissemination of his comments, Robeson was continually able to trespass cultural boundaries in his public performances. In so doing, he created devoted followers from otherwise skeptical Russians. Such devotion is evidenced in the Soviet reaction to Robeson throughout the years. An article in *Sovetskaia Muzika* describes the response to one of Robeson's concerts in the following way: "How deeply the noble image of the artist-citizen entered the consciousness of millions of Soviet people . . . how strongly Moscovites and Stalingraders fell in love with him, welcoming Robeson in their concert halls." The article goes on to say that "we didn't understand that a foreign artist could so enamor an entire Soviet-filled auditorium, could become so akin and close to us, as did Paul Robeson."[81] The effect of Robeson on Soviets was of course aided by media accounts of his greatness, which often hinted at the greatness of the Soviet Union, so that by taking part in the phenomenon of Robeson one was also taking part in the larger Soviet project of superiority to the West. An article in *Teatr* goes so far as to quote Robeson as saying that when he left Russia after his 1949 visit, "I left the USSR with heartfelt enthusiasm; in a sense I had sprouted wings that drew me toward a new, even more determined battle for peace. I carried with me from Moscow new ideas and new feelings, and I want to express to all of you in parting: I was, am, and will always be the most devoted and true friend of the Soviet Union."[82] The sentiments enabled by such rhetoric—of Robeson's seeming to exist outside of time and the transformative experience of Russia—are echoed throughout Soviet media coverage.

Indeed, oddly skewed translations of Robeson's English statements were the rule and not the exception. When the Soviet press translated Robeson's English writings for Russian publication, the discrepancies are likewise notable, suggesting that these citations must be approached carefully, with attention to context and detail. The most substantial of these gaps occurs in the 1958 translation of Robeson's autobiographical *Here I Stand* (*Na Tom Ia Stoiu*) in which portions of the original text are excised, sometimes with an ellipsis indicating the cut, but more often without any such editorial clue. Completely excised from the Russian version of the text is chapter 5, "The Power of Negro Action," as well as the appendixes in which Robeson explains in theoretical terms why he uses the performance of folk songs as the basis of his political praxis. *Here I Stand*'s remaining chapters appear substantially altered in structure. The multivoiced basis of Robeson's text achieved in the original through his inclusion of extended quotes from numerous sources and voices (including newspaper articles and editorials, speeches, legal rulings, letters, and so forth) is all but absent in the Russian text.

Whatever the intention of such cuts, these alterations and omissions modify Robeson's message. The excision of "The Power of Negro Action" indicates that Russian readers did not have access to Robeson's plan for organized resistance and what he calls "Negro power in motion," the character of leadership to direct mass action. Such reluctance to portray the specificities of the mobilizing strategies of a black American is related to another set of important omissions—the removal of several paragraphs following Robeson's assertion that the Negro's right to travel is historically connected to black American freedom and the deletion of long sections about racist U.S. immigration policies. What is cut, therefore, is Robeson's emphasis on the necessity of mobility, and the ability to organize openly and agitate in "righteous anger to demand that militant actions be started" (*HIS*, 106), components of civic life sorely lacking in the Soviet Union in the 1950s. De-emphasizing coordinated action, the linkages between mobility and freedom, and the many voices Robeson summons to stress his points, the Russian text reads as an individualized, monologic attack on U.S. cultural and political racial inequities. *Na Tom Ia Stoiu* deprives *Here I Stand* of its collective call to organized action as well as some of its key historical foundations. Fostering his image in a way familiar to the Stalinesque strategies of creating a "cult of personality," the effect is one of emphasizing Robeson as a representative black at a remove from the urgent call for revolutionary action based in the day-to-day struggles of and for black American life. At the end of Robeson's discussion of the Bandung Conference, in which he outlines the ten principles of Bandung, Robeson writes, "These principles I wholeheartedly support. On this platform I take my stand" (47). In the Russian, however, Robeson is in effect never permitted to take such a stand, as the ten principles have been deleted and likewise Robeson's assertion of the specific platform on which he stands.

In place of the omissions, there are also additions—changes that suggest the preferred interpretive direction to be taken by the Russian reader. These embellishments occur most frequently when the Soviet Union is the topic under discussion. For example, after citing a report by William Reed on the lack of racial discrimination in the USSR (a citation excised from the Russian text), Robeson comments, "That's how it is. I can't imagine that any Negro would not be pleased to see it, and I certainly was. So I thought it would be a good thing to send my boy to school in the Soviet Union" (36). Having excised the longish quote from Reed, the Russian slips in an extra line between these two last sentences, so that the section reads, "I don't think that this couldn't attract any Negro. In any case, all of this was made clear to me in my soul. And I decided that it would be a good thing to send my son to study in the Soviet Union."[83] Appealing to the soul as a source of fundamental, authenticating knowledge was a common strategy in the dissemination of a certain type of Russian nationalism. This focus at once intimated antiethnocentrism as well as anti-Western notions of a national collective. At the same time, though, it highlighted the Soviets' brandishing of a soul-based universalism in place of a serious questioning of their own institutionalized practices of racism and gender inequities. But if one notes the reinscription of Robeson's text, one must also note that it was just this type of universalist language that attracted Robeson to the USSR. However mistaken Robeson may have been in believing Soviet policy to be implemented as a reality, he nonetheless benefited from the Soviet promotion of folk culture and an implied internationalism. What the series of mistranslations happening across the Robeson/Soviet threshold reveals is how these very layers of misapprehension served as enabling fictions for the agendas of all involved. Rather than an indication of blind ignorance, these misreadings point to a pliancy in Soviet policy that purposefully created slippages in interpretation. Such slippages were used by both the Soviet press and Robeson as welcome footholds from which to maneuver: for the Soviets, the staging of Robeson as Soviet hero; and for Robeson, the staging of his internationalist mission.

Preferring to emphasize the valorized patina of a USSR as star attraction for the oppressed peoples of the world rather than an actual, lived-in space of highly complex negotiations around national and cultural issues, *Na Tom Ia Stoiu* continues to vary from *Here I Stand*. For instance, Robeson writes that the experiences of the many peoples and races of the Soviet Union "would be of great value for other peoples of the East in catching up with the modern world" (*HIS*, 37). In the Russian version, he says that the Soviet Union "can be of great value for the peoples of the East; it [the USSR] can help them create a new society ("ochen' tsenen dlia liudei drugikh natsional'nostei na Vostoke; on pomozhet im postroit' novoe obshchestvo") (*NTIS*, 29). Again, the focus is on the remarkable, transformative powers of the Soviet Union as a multiethnic "experience" that can be ineluctably translated into the utopian advantage of oppressed peoples around the world. Following an assertion that the charge of "communist propaganda" insults the "intelligence and sensibilities" of the world's democratically minded "people of all races and creeds," Robeson continues in the English text to state that "of course, the Communists of the world denounce racism: that's nothing new and it seems rather silly to charge that this is some kind of newfangled weapon of the 'cold war'" (*HIS*, 82). Tellingly, this claim does not appear in the Russian text. Instead, the Russian readers of *Here I Stand* hear about the "free peoples of the family of colored nations" who are our "close friends" (*NTIS*, 53), whereas English readers learn that "the peoples of the free colored nations are our natural friends" (*HIS*, 87). The distancing of "colored peoples" into a family separate from that of the white Russian one belies an admission that while the communists of the world may denounce racism, they retain subtle ways of restraining impulses and actions to that end. Not the least of these actions was a Soviet reassertion of the superiority of a Russian family of whiteness over the homogeneity of its related Euro-imperial fraternal order and the "family of colored nationals" including those housed within the USSR.

During the period leading up to the Russian release of *Here I Stand*, the years when Robeson's passport was denied (1951–1958), Robeson became an especially revered figure in Soviet eyes. The Soviet press disseminated a picture of Robeson as a much-maligned American Negro who existed in the hearts of the Soviet people as "a man of great soul and pure heart" who they in a tellingly erroneous fashion referred to as the "voice for all Negroes" ("golos vsekh negrov").[84] It was during this period that the image of Robeson as cultural hero really took root. Not only was a mountain peak named for him (and a bronze bust of the singer placed at the summit).[85] As well, numerous poems were written in his honor, portraits were painted, sculptures sculpted, articles written—all of which testified to the glory of Robeson as a great fighter for peace and a cultural spokesperson.[86] In 1952, Robeson was awarded the Stalin Peace Prize, a distinction that earned him front-and-center coverage in *Pravda* and a lengthy article detailing his specific accomplishments.[87] In 1955, Robeson was invited by the Soviet director Sergei Yutkevich to star in a Mosfilm version of *Othello*, and in 1958, *Here I Stand* was published in an abridged format in *Biblioteka Ogonek* by the Pravda Publishing House.[88]

During this period, Robeson corresponded regularly with the Union of Soviet Writers, Chairman Alexander Fadeev, and its Secretary Boris

Polevoi.[89] An influential journalist for *Pravda* and the author of several popular books, Polevoi was one of Robeson's biggest Russian supporters and produced the most writing of any single Russian author on the subject of Robeson. Among their shared moments, Polevoi counted as most precious his visits to Robeson's Harlem home during the 1950s. The first of these visits provided the material for a fictionalized account of an evening with Robeson, titled "Joe Hill Resurrected," and became the subject of a chapter of Polevoi's book *American Diaries*, which I will discuss later in the chapter. This collection details Polevoi's visit with a group of Soviet journalists to the States in 1955.

Because of Polevoi's close feeling of friendship for Robeson, his familiarity with both the United States and, of course, the Soviet Union, his letters offer a rich source in which to investigate the Russian myth of Robeson. One letter in particular provides a glimpse into the magnitude of Robeson in Russian eyes. Describing the scene of the Second Congress of Soviet Writers (to which Robeson had been invited, but was unable to attend because of his passport difficulties),[90] Polevoi writes that the minute it was announced that the congress would open with a recorded message from Robeson,

> people applauded and somehow did not want to leave the hall. . . . [T]he very announcement was met with stormy applause which did not quiet down for a long time. . . . [L]ong before the start of the session, the entire Hall of Columns was packed to the rafters. People stood in the aisles, packed the wings. . . . [W]hen the chair introduced you, a deathly quiet came over the hall, and once more we heard the hearty sound of your unique bass, enunciating the simple introductory words; a new wave of enthusiasm shook the hall, everyone jumped up and gave you a long standing ovation, greeting in your person both yourself, a courageous fighter for peace and friend of Soviet literature, whose voice, having flown across the ocean, had reached that hall; as well as all the men and women of America to whom peace is dear. . . . Dear friend, it is perhaps even difficult for you to understand and imagine what a real response your simple and courageous words found in our hearts. But in the reaction of the hall there was more than a reaction just to those words. We felt that no frontier cordons, no laws, no lying by the masters of the cold war, however refined and grandiose

it might be, can raise a barrier between cultures, between people of good will. In those moments we, the Soviet writers, saw among us as it were, a great American, representing his glorious people with honor at our meeting. (PRC, reel 1, frames 426–27)

First, I'd like to focus on the alchemic powers of Robeson's voice to transmit to Russians not only "words" but an actual "appearance" in which Robeson became a touchstone for not only African Americans but "all the men and women of America to whom peace is dear." The ability of Robeson's voice to evoke for Russians not only black America but the United States more generally conceived indicates that although such representativeness was contested in the States, it was not the case in Russia that Robeson's evocative powers of presence were restrained to only African Americans. Indeed, Polevoi remained one of Robeson's closest Soviet friends, and in his private letters to Robeson, he conveys an awareness not only of the transformative powers of Robeson's voice but also the burden of such talent. In a letter from the spring of 1955, Polevoi describes again the remarkable experience of hearing Robeson's voice, how it "seemed as if you were standing somewhere near to us . . . and our entire family thronged around the radio like flies around a cube of sugar, and listening, were frozen in thoughtful reverie." But he qualifies his perception of Robeson's ability to "sing, not as a single person, but as all Your people" by remarking that "it's not great being a symbol, but what are you going to do?—that's how it is ("ne ochen' priiatno byt' simbolom, no chto zhe delat'—eto tak").[91]

Recognizing his limitations as an outsider to Robeson's social milieu, Polevoi elsewhere realizes the qualifying factors around his ability to read comprehensively the "symbol" of Robeson. Writing that he has sent Robeson a copy of his *American Diaries*, Polevoi concedes that he did so with some trepidation: "It's difficult, very difficult, for a foreigner, who comes briefly to your grand and distinctive country to describe America in such a way as to make it seem alive and interesting and not simply a bunch of 'traveler's tales,' as we say."[92] Recognizing the difficulty of translating one country into another's dialect without sacrificing what makes it "alive," Polevoi implicitly recognizes the difficulty Robeson faces in trying to translate himself to a foreign audience without sacrificing the interest of his message and his vitality as a black American.[93]

Still, Polevoi's perceptiveness to celebrity's burdens did not make him immune to its evocative powers. He describes how his wife suggested that "it's necessary to close one's eyes" when listening to Robeson, so as to better see him and what he sings about, and Polevoi confirms, "I tried it, and it worked. I saw You, and then it seemed as if I were at Your concert, grasping your large hand and chatting with You."[94] In effect, Robeson's voice conveys a connection that Polevoi typifies as "real." And it was just this kind of reality—one beyond words—that Robeson strived to foster in his performative choices and that fueled his mythological status. Polevoi's letter continues:

> I want to tell you of a curious episode that occurred this morning in my family when I told them what happened during your "appearance" yesterday. My daughter Helen, who is going on nine, having heard me through, asked me doubtfully:—You really mean Robeson is living now and didn't live long long ago?—For her you are already a legendary figure; it is hard for her to even believe that you are our contemporary.[95]

Although this is the reaction of a nine year old, the sentiment expressed—of Robeson's seeming to exist outside of time, of his legendary, nearly transcendent being—is one echoed by Russians of greater years. In an article printed in the women's magazine *Sovetskaia Zhenshchina*, the author writes that in hearing Robeson's voice at the Second World Congress for Defenders of Peace, "we again and again felt the strength of this unique peace advocate, for whom neither barriers nor distance exist. We knew that Paul Robeson was not at the Congress but in place of this he was with us, among us, friend, comrade, fighter."[96] And again, in an article in *Izvestiia*, I. Martynov reminisces about such taped Robeson performances: "True, it was only a recording, but it nonetheless transmitted the sincere feelings of his soul" ("Pravda, eto byli lish' magnitofonnye zapisi, no i oni peredavali blagorodnye chuvstva ego dushi").[97] In addition to the uncanny ability of his voice to elicit emotional responses in his Russian listeners, Robeson's physical absence from Russia provided an opportunity to spark popular interest in Robeson through the avenues of media that were hungrily devoured by Soviet cultural consumers. The ground on which Robeson and the USSR met was one that relied on uncertainty, the slipperiness of innuendo, all of which created the enabling tools of the trade of cross-cultural exchange. Even though Robeson insisted on learning Russian so as to lessen the gap between himself and Russians, and even though many of Robeson's Russian friends spoke English, they all preferred a shared discourse of oversight, invention, and hyperbole.

LOCATING ROBESON

During the 1950s, Robeson became the focus of a keen media struggle between the United States and USSR. Typifying the Soviet image of Robeson are two cartoons that appeared in subsequent issues of the popular humor magazine *Krokodil.* Since they make manifest so many of the Soviet attitudes about Robeson expressed by Polevoi and others, I would like to take the time to discuss them. (The first I examine here; the second later in this chapter.) Founded by the writer and critic Kornei Chukovsky and published by *Pravda, Krokodil* enjoyed a wide audience of readers throughout the 1950s. Primarily a compilation of folio-sized cartoons, *Krokodil* offered satiric social commentary and often expressed views in vivid colors on the topics of the *kholodnaia voina* and *zheleznyi zanaves* ("Cold War" and "iron curtain"). By the time of these cartoons' publication, media on both sides of the iron curtain were swarming with Cold War cannon fodder. In Russia, numerous articles appeared about U.S. racial inequities in general and Robeson in particular.[98] In the United States, meanwhile, media moguls were celebrating a heyday of anticommunism. In June, the *Daily Worker* had published a full transcript of Khrushchev's famous "secret speech"—detailing atrocities during Stalin's reign—and U.S. party membership had quickly fallen off. The first cartoon can be read as a counterassault of sorts, and it shows Robeson gesticulating before HUAC, below which the caption reads, "Paul Robeson: This is the only place where I can still appear." In the upper left-hand corner an explanatory text notes, "The members of the U.S. HUAC subject Paul Robeson to a humiliating interrogation. They forbid the famous singer to make appearances outside [U.S.] borders." By 1956, of course, the State Department's refusal of Robeson's passport was news to no one. In July of that year, Robeson had been called on to testify before HUAC (which was investigating "passport irregularities by Communist sympathizers"). This appearance, in addition to Robeson's run-in with hecklers at a National Council of American-Soviet Friendship peace rally, had brought Robeson's troubles again to world attention. For this reason, the exact wording of the caption merits a closer look.

Поль Робсон:—Это—единственное место, где я ещё могу выступать.

14. Robeson: "This is the only place where I can still appear."

Robeson's assertion of "place" is significant, for as early as 1937 he stated the need for artists to choose a place, a side to stand on. He argued, "Every artist, every scientist, must decide *now* where he stands. . . . [T]he battlefront is everywhere" (*HIS*, 52). This refrain, which would become the title of his 1958 book *Here I Stand*, rings with a certain irony in the *Krokodil* image, as the place in which Robeson has been forced to stand is before the House Committee, before U.S. law. Decked out in concert regalia, Robeson is not merely standing. As the Russian verb *vystupat'* suggests, he is stepping out, appearing on stage, performing. The correlation of "standing" and "performing" is key to Robeson's politics, and key to the humor of this cartoon. In front of HUAC, Robeson testified that "I stand here struggling for the rights of my people to be full citizens in this country. . . . [Y]ou want to shut up every colored person who wants to fight for the rights of his people" (41–42). HUAC interpreted Robeson as a threat because his political stand was embedded in his artistic practice. Because he would not simply "perform" by adhering to the inward aesthetics of a previous generation, Robeson was stuck standing on the HUAC stage.

But with an actor's appreciation for the transformative potential of the performative, Robeson deployed a savvy perception not only of the inherent political sinews of all performance but also of the power of the performative to create chaos within the interlocutory space. He used every stage, in particular the HUAC one, to his best advantage. When performing concerts, he asserted the importance of folk-based performance as a political act, thereby recuperating for mass consumption a traditionally slighted mode of aesthetic/political engagement. And on the HUAC stage, Robeson's refusal to participate in the incorporation of African Americans as consensual witnesses to the Red-baiting "dares" of the State Department asserted the importance of the effectively prohibited mode of black dissent. Robeson's testimony before HUAC highlighted the structural similarity between the suspicion of populist performance and the suspicion of Robeson. In effect, when Robeson took the HUAC stage, he reiterated the liminality of performance in general and the black performer in particular. Against such attempts to peripheralize him, to make him expendable, Robeson asserted the power of a negative performative. The power of the negative performative is that it rubs against the tacit collusion expected of participants and auditors when such a threat as "are you or have you ever been" or the "request" to name names is proffered by those who by making the challenge, exhibit their grasp on power, however tentative. To such requests—attempts to reign African Americans into this kind of staid support for U.S. superiority to the so-called Red menace—Robeson responded with a resounding "count me out," an "I stand elsewhere."[99]

In return, the message received was that as a black body before the law, Robeson would not be recognized, would not be deemed a full citizen with due rights, unless he donned the garb of the performer, the minstrel, the entertainer, and parroted the consent Uncle Sam wanted to hear. This is reflected in the *Krokodil* cartoon where Representative Gordon Scherer's designation of the book on the table suggests at once that within lies the Constitution (and thereby the justification for Robeson's supposed infraction) and also a fake book, a gathering of popular tunes from which he is commanding Robeson to perform. Of course, the unconstitutionality of Robeson's appearance before the court, of the withholding of his passport, and of the general refusal of equal rights for blacks and women is equally implied by the denomination of Scherer's index finger.[100]

Robeson's earlier announcement that he "would put aside [his] concert career" and "enter the day-to-day struggles of my people and the working masses," performing only for unions and college groups, affronted the supply-and-demand-driven machinations of the market he rejected. The cartoon satirizes this market by skirting the committee's table with a cloth embroidered with dollar signs. These dollar signs also imply a critique of the hypocrisy of U.S. anti-internationalism: on the one hand, U.S. capital flowed into restructuring international, "needy" markets; on the other hand, collaborative forces detained Robeson behind U.S. borders precisely because he might bring attention to these areas in a way the State Department deemed "against the best interests of the U.S."[101] As stated in the brief released by the Court of Appeals in Robeson's passport case, "The diplomatic embarrassment that could arise from the presence abroad of such a political meddler, traveling under the protection of an American passport, is easily imaginable."[102] The efforts to keep all racial issues domestically containable, unrelated to the international trails of racist, capital-accruing policies and institutions, is a fact literally skirted by a U.S. emphasis on its exemplary integrity as the model nation-state.

ORGANIZING RESISTANCE

Robeson eschewed the previous manipulation of his image in the 1920s and 1930s by replacing the visual focus on his body (in movies, theater, and photography) with a focus on the aural possibilities of his voice from within a politically and aesthetically controlled context. This move away from the visual toward the aural presented a wealth of opportunities for Robeson to direct, to some extent, the framework of his political message. The modulation by definition entailed a specific reworking of the collective forces behind the scenes. Unlike Robeson's involvement in films (which had largely disappointed him because of editorial shaping and cutting that occurred without his consent), his concert performances were handled with a keen sense of the political message to be maintained from organizational start to performative finish.[103] What such a reworking enabled was an active acceptance of the inherent dynamism of the performative stage—that is, an understanding of performance as a collective process through which a political message of collaborative embodiment to thwart the nullifying tug of state authority could best be disseminated.[104]

In order to get a full picture of the range and registers of Robeson's celebrity in Russia as well as the United States, it is necessary to consider how Robeson's domestic tours during the 1951–1958 period resisted the depoliticizing gesture of the State Department's denial of his passport. While Jeffrey C. Stewart has argued that "after his passport was returned in 1958, Robeson again used the stage with the same style and flair as before," it is, to the contary, quite clear that Robeson's body was put to use in a particularly politicized and emphatic manner during the key years of his "virtual incarceration."[105] By emphasizing Robeson's overwhelming, singular subjectivity, an awareness of the careful construction of that presence has been lost. To understand fully the resistant politics of Robeson's message during this period and the deployment of his body to this end, a look at the management and packaging of Robeson as well as the specific details of the thoroughly contrived program reveal the structure on which he stood.[106]

Memos put together by Robeson's secretary at *Freedom,* John Gray, regarding Robeson's 1953 and 1954 tours shed useful light on the collaborative efforts that went into creating the stage on which the Robeson image was projected. These memos indicate that while Robeson's musical talents and presence were certainly forceful components, his concerts relied on a kind of "reflexive performativity," what anthropologist Victor Turner has described as a "condition" in which the primary actor or actors "turn, bend or reflect back upon themselves, upon the relations, actions, symbols, meanings, codes, roles, statuses, social structures, ethical and legal rules, and other sociocultural components which make up their public 'selves.'" In this sense, performative reflexivity is "not a mere reflex . . . [but] highly contrived, artificial . . . a deliberate and voluntary work of art."[107] It is precisely the contrived, self-conscious aspects of Robeson's performances that have fallen out of attempts to articulate their power; just as Robeson's cause was never individual or singular, so too were his concerts collective affairs.[108]

For example, in designing the character and objectives of Robeson's 1953 tour, Robeson's team decided to emphasize his involvement with the Negro community. Of the two types of concerts to be undertaken—outdoor cultural festivals and church concerts—both were to be organized with the "dominant trends and movements in the Negro community" in mind (PRC, reel 4, frame 572). This focus on Robeson "as a concert artist in the center of Negro life" directly connects to the stated political objectives of the tour, which are described as involving Robeson with small groups of "key people in the community" to discuss African independence and the struggle for peace; representative equality for blacks on a local, state, and national level; and the struggles of Negro workers to find, maintain, and upgrade jobs. The point of involving Robeson with key members of the Negro community was not only to branch out from his popular image as a poster child for the Left but more specifically, to "enable those in charge of local arrangements to open new doors through his great prestige and influence" (PRC, reel 4, frame 573).

The efforts to connect Robeson to the Negro community reflected a desire to highlight the issues raised by the denial of Robeson's passport—namely, the historical connections between travel and freedom for African Americans. At the same time, the concerts strove to make apparent what could be done on the local level to educate audiences about how these issues connected African Americans to colonial peoples and workers around the world. Both of these aspects speak to the ways in which performance can be used as a "redressive ceremony" in order to intervene where legal redress has failed.[109] Robeson's concerts were based on this kind of collective ceremony, an attempt to give shape to the historical absence and denial of legal rights to the politically, socially, and/or racially disenfranchised, and to turn this absence into an irrefutable presence through group participation. In other words, the idea was to construct a space for the articulation of legally unsanctioned, "unthinkable" bodies, such as the one Robeson had come to emblematize.[110] This idea of ritualized participation as an affirmative project that could alter the "very terms that constitute the 'necessary' domain of bodies" was drawn from his experiences growing up as a member of his father's congregation.[111] Robeson describes his belief in the "oneness of humankind" as extending from a belief that "the simple, beautiful songs of my childhood, heard every Sunday in church and every day at home and in the community—the great poetic song-sermons of the Negro preacher and the congregation . . . [were] in the tradition of the world's great folk music" (HIS, 57). In combining folk songs from different nations, and audiences from different sociocultural backgrounds, Robeson's concerts used the black congregational model and adapted it to an internationalist project. His process of performative reflexivity relied on the involvement of its audience members, each of whom could come to reflect on themselves when, picking up on the signals broadcast, they sensed the social flow "bending back on itself," creating new social composites or a previously unthinkable coalitional alliance, in the course of the performance.[112]

Attempting to shift the focus from the personal to the social and political contexts of Robeson's plight, from his public persona as a "Communist" to that of Negro community activist, the concerts also sought to achieve related goals that reflected the interests not simply of the singular image of Robeson but the larger material mechanisms behind him. These were the forces that created the product known as Robeson. This strategy apprehended the social in systemic terms, understanding that "each productive sphere at any moment is determined by and determining of other spheres," that grasped "how the division of labor . . . [is] related to patterns of production and consumption which are affected by and in turn shape political and ideological structures."[113] The importance of using the institutional apparatus around Robeson to alter the public "Paul Robeson" and likewise foment grassroots political activism is obvious. To this end, three organizational objectives were outlined in planning for the 1953 tour: *Freedom* magazine, the Othello Recording Corporation, and the Council on African Affairs.[114] Robeson's appearance was to "be used to stimulate a variety of activities (meetings, conferences, statements of leaders, fund-raising, petitions to the UN, etc.)" with the "specific form of activity to be determined by local conditions and relationships" (PRC, reel 4, frame 573). The employment of specific personnel in each case demonstrates the attention devoted to each facet of the Robeson cause. Without these persons acting together, and themselves contributing to the collective format of Robeson's concerts, crucial aspects of Robeson's purpose of public performance would be sacrificed to the single-minded focus on "celebrity" that he disdained.

To be sure, Robeson's concerts were, above all, attempts to rally interest and money for the cause of Robeson, but at the same time the cause was always larger than the man himself: John Gray and his associates had to work without major media avenues at their disposal, a cutting off from the public that they saw as intimately connected to the repression of Robeson's passport. Seeing the lack of major label backing, of large-scale concert funding support, of access to key concert venues, and the reluctance of mainstream press to cover Robeson in a positive light as part of a campaign to suppress Robeson's politics, Gray responded by emphasizing a need to create and disseminate media in order to build public pressure to support Robeson. These campaigns, which were integral parts of the concert tours, were not about making Robeson reap millions in revenues but about restoring his basic civic rights, his access to the institutions that historically were linked to public outcry, and contravening mainstream exclusion by fostering homegrown institutions such as *Freedom*, the African Council's *Newsletter*, and Othello Records. Thus, the promotion of Robeson can be seen as an organized battle waged against not only major institutional blacklisting but also a tendency toward growing public ambivalence toward Robeson's black radicalism and internationalism, as evidenced by *Freedom*'s dwindling subscription rates and the lukewarm success of Robeson's 1953 tour.

SEEING DOUBLE

In spite of the insistence on Robeson's physical presence as an antidote to obscurity in the United States, his drive toward internationalism in the USSR proved that embodiment could have its drawbacks, particularly when it came to Cold War cultural understandings of Africa. For when physical absence creates fuel for manipulation, presence is often forced to follow suit. As we know from McKay's experiences, the suit in this case is a Russian tradition of using black "Americans" in order to understand Africa. When in Russia, McKay delighted in the decimation of what he previously understood as the rigidities of nationality, embraced Leninist internationalism, and aware of the slipperiness of definitions his personage afforded on-lookers, declared himself a "black ikon in the flesh."[115] Soviet understanding of Africa was historically based in a long-standing czarist interest and activity in Africa. This relationship constituted the building blocks for the field of Soviet African studies that emerged after the Bolsheviks came into power, and by the 1950s, a large body of information and scholarship about African geography, ethnography, linguistics, culture, and politics had been amassed. In addition, although Soviet policy changed its opinion several times about its revolutionary uses, indigenous African nationalisms had held Soviet attention throughout the years, and the Soviets had made every effort to keep abreast of its various vicissitudes.[116]

As the McKay case shows, however, the efforts of the Communists in the 1920s to unite Africans with black Americans reflected little knowledge of the concrete conditions of disenfranchised peoples living in the United States. The Comintern drew assumptions that because of the popularity of Marcus Garvey's Back to Africa movement and George Padmore's Pan-Africanism, "this ideological kinship reflected a more basic similarity of political conditions and political attitudes."[117] Such logic set up a dichotomy of black/white that placed the Soviets in the position of whiteness in spite of their claims to the contrary vis-à-vis Western imperialism. These very same contrary claims also sometimes succeeded in winning over anticolonial African nationals who saw in the Soviet Union the antithesis of Euro-imperial states. If some African American intellectuals sensed in Russians a parallel duality stemming from a filiation to and difference from Western European standards, Russian bureaucrats were certainly not poised to reciprocate or grant any foundational commonality between Russians and African Americans as marginalized others. The notion of Russians as first among equals was not shaken by the internationalist rhetoric of Soviet anti-imperialism. A Soviet belief in a reducible race question continued to enable "Africa" to be seamlessly appointed to African Americans; the political volatility of particular African nations was representable by the more stable U.S. counterparts. Whereas in the 1920s McKay sensed that the Russian people were greeting Africa through him, that he was being used as a stand-in African, in the 1950s Robeson served as an itinerant icon in the USSR for the promise (and in the United States as the fear) of Soviet prowess in Africa.

At the same time, in the United States, popular denunciation of Robeson resounded with the phrase "black Stalin," a title with which Robeson had been labeled by Manning Johnson during his testimony before HUAC. As the *New York Times* reported it, according to Johnson, following his title role in the film *Emperor Jones,* Robeson " 'developed delusions of grandeur,' and set out to become a 'black Stalin.' "[118] According to the FBI report filed on the incident, "Robeson Wants to Be a Stalin, Party Backs Him," such accusations not only revealed the U.S. fear that black Americans *could* be used as surrogate Africans—ignited by Soviet dogma and poised for world takeover—but also distracted attention from cogent examples of the imperial attitudes toward Africa in the United States. This was all part and parcel of U.S. containment policy (outlined by George Kennan in the infamous long telegram from Moscow in 1946).[119] One of the results of this was to deflect recognition of U.S. expansionism by keeping Robeson within U.S. boundaries—attempts at detachment caricatured in the *Krokodil* cartoons.[120]

In order to register the full force of its ideological punch, this cartoon must be located in its proximity to the Robeson image. This is a literal and figural correspondence, for this image appeared as the back cover to *Krokodil* just previous to the issue with the Robeson cover.[121] Drawn by the same artist, K. Rotova, the two cartoons are bound to one another conceptually in the artist's emphasis on the performance of black identity as larger than life. When describing Robeson, it was not unusual for Soviet reporters and friends to comment on his physicality, in particular his size. For example, in an article for *Pravda*, Polevoi likens Robeson to "Prometheus."[122] Just as the most noticeable thing about the Robeson cartoon is his size in comparison with the puny committee members, the figure labeled "Colonialism" in this cartoon nearly jumps off the page.

This image presents both challenging critiques of European colonialism and reconfirms some of the more prevalent Soviet assumptions about racial difference. In this image, the apotheosis of colonialism wears a pith helmet, white shorts, and a white shirt—the stereotypical uniform of the British colonial. Behind whips, spurs, and handcuffs, alms, flowers, and perfume flasks appear with the aid not just of any lackey but carefully suited businessmen and farmers in the name of "economic aid." The most accommodating of the bunch places the white mask of a feminine facade onto the snarling features of a dark-skinned beast whose hands, arms, and chest hair must undoubtedly shrink during this transgendering charade. "They masquerade," reads the caption. Colonialism is presented as a campaign of transvestism and cross-gender identifications—the feminizing of black masculinity into docile coordinates. But the stamp of femininity here is particular—a white femininity appended onto black masculinity. In this sense, the image harkens back to McKay's elaboration of the contiguities between the gendering of white femininity and black masculinity. The visual details of both are intimately conjoined and confounded. Colonialism is presented as a suspect female, but the white feminization of

15. "They Masquerade." *Krokodil* cartoon, July 1956.

black masculinity also suggests the imposed correlation between (and denigration of) the two by white supremacy.[123] At the same time, however, by showing the process of the masquerade (as opposed to focusing only on its finished product), what this cartoon promotes is a stress on the seething native beneath the mask of the impostor. Seeing through this guise, one is encouraged to believe that the danger of colonialism lies within the nation temporarily mollified by outside, falsely benevolent forces financing the masquerade. Gainsaying Soviet Africanist scholarship that had roots in antiethnocentric, anti-Western sentiments, and that supported the merits of indigenous African populations, this cartoon reveals the sense of unreality that characterized much of the Soviet inability to fully grasp the ways in which racist imagery pervaded popular consciousness, in spite of policies meant to safeguard the contrary.[124] Although masterminds of propaganda, Soviet bureaucrats were seemingly uninterested in the ways racism was disseminated through state-sponsored media even as government policy was proclaiming the moral high ground against Western imperialism. Apparently, it would not seem unreasonable to cast in the role of representative native beastliness none other than "our hero," Robeson.

By the 1950s, the Soviet Union had hardly resolved the problems of racial and ethnic conflict. In fact, the timing of this pro-Robeson media blitz was severely ironic, if not suggestively calculated. Robeson's popularity as a hero of the downtrodden, colored world masses coincided with some of the most virulently anti-Semitic Soviet activities of that century. Throughout his life, however, Robeson refused publicly to denounce the Soviet Union for the purging of Jews. Still, it is clear that far from reflecting an ignorance on his part, Robeson felt it more important to reserve his right to charge the United States with genocide (as he and William Patterson did in 1951 with a petition to the United Nations titled "We Charge Genocide") than to focus on Soviet crimes.[125] A public denunciation of the USSR for Jewish genocide would have made his United Nations action more difficult, as such a gesture against the Soviets would have been used by the United States to highlight America's presumably superior racial policies. A Robeson statement vilifying Soviet racism would have been a field day for U.S. media, so identified with the question of racial justice in the United States was he. Although some might wish that Robeson had done otherwise, one cannot dismiss as patently naive the entirety of his experiences of acceptance and the identity-forming power of a Soviet-inspired internationalist rhetoric for Americans like Robeson. Robeson's relationship with the Soviet Union permitted him a status, sense of self-worth, ideological insights, and international agency unrealizable at the time in the United States. On the other hand, however unwittingly, Robeson played into a Soviet willingness to foment the merging of black and Red scares in the States. As exemplified in the *Krokodil* cover image and numerous media accounts, Soviets used depictions of U.S. racism to forward their own interests in decolonizing nations and embrace the cause of "Diadia Pol' " ("Uncle Paul").[126]

Before patently condemning Soviets for their naive conceptions, though, it should be noted that such infiltration of racist imagery into the popular imagination was aided and abetted by even the most sympathetic of Robeson supporters. Polevoi's story about Robeson, "Joe Hill Resurrected," published in the widely read magazine *Ogonek* in 1956, raises questions about the possibility of translating Robeson to a Russian readership without relying on a racist cultural lens through which to picture Robeson.[127] "Joe Hill Resurrected," as mentioned above, describes an evening in Robeson's Harlem home in which Paul and his son, Paul Jr., discuss the pros and cons of accepting an invitation to perform in the Canadian Peace Arch Concert. The course of their conversation is framed in the racialized terms of a chess game, black versus white, that Paul Jr. plays as Robeson paces the room. Polevoi then traces their affirmative decision over the course of their trip to the border between Washington State and British Columbia and through the concert performance itself.

The point of the story—to both portray Robeson as a kind of reincarnated Joe Hill and suggest that the experience of a Robeson concert can be revivifying—can be read in at least two ways. First, there is every indication that Polevoi is attempting to moralize about the shared experience of humanity expressed through workers' solidarity. In this sense, Robeson's blackness is read as reducible to his "worker's soul." It is this inclusive soul heard when Robeson sings Joe Hill's favorite song, "If I Become a Soldier"—a song that confirms Robeson's ability to "agitate with themes and feelings, to capture" his listeners. The effect of such a reduction, on the other hand, is to make Robeson's blackness incidental to the fact that he bears a white man's spirit. In other words, Joe Hill functions as the redeeming white figure through whom Robeson can be read as safely deracinated, made familiar, and therefore capable of connection with his hypothetical Russian audience. Both readings, in spite of their attempts to create an inclusionary space in which Robeson can be understood and accepted as a cultural hero, nonetheless, in order to create such a space, rely on a liberal use of conventional, racialized images of Robeson that portray blackness as something inherently inescapable and frightening.

In the opening sequence of the story, Robeson is pacing the room, back and forth on a diagonal, lost in deep thought. Soon after, readers are told that this pacing figure "reminds one of a lion in a cage. Yes, he is a caged lion—Paul Robeson."[128] This picture of the fiercely wild yet cruelly restrained animal who looms "larger than life" is accompanied by descriptive terms that struggle to grasp the complexity of Robeson's incarceration. His cage is "stronger than those that hold lions in a zoo. . . . Oh, this is a cage! It is particularly harsh because no one can see its railings. One can only touch these railings when you stumble into them. And thus, like an imprisoned lion, the big black man walks back and forth across the room."[129] Attempting to place Robeson's case in the hands of a government that refuses to deny anything forthright ("as always in America, there's no formal statement that it is forbidden"), while at the same time championing its own support of liberty for all, Polevoi sustains such insights with the equally stereotypical portrait of Robeson as one step removed from the wild kingdom.[130] In order to convey the accurate image of the United States as a place where "they love to talk about individual freedom and can't stand the very word 'forbidden' " ("liubiat pogovorit' o svobode lichnosti i ne vynosiat samo eto slovo 'zapretit' "), Polevoi resorts to descriptive terms that portray Robeson in a fashion familiar to Russians accustomed to thinking of black persons as unfairly disenfranchised, but nevertheless wild, earthy, sensual, and inferior beings.[131]

Perhaps mistaking Soviet racism for universalism, Robeson played into this correlation of himself with Africa. He describes his first visit to the Soviet Union in 1934 as evolving "through my interest in Africa" (*HIS,* 36). His chief interest once in Moscow was "to study the Soviet national minority policy as it operates among the peoples of Central Asia."[132] Robeson wanted to use Soviet treatment of Yakuts and Uzbeks as test cases for the Soviet management of ethnic diversity and constitutional antiracism. And his visits served as evidence, as they had for McKay, Hughes, and Du Bois before him, of Soviet superiority to U.S. policies. Key to these figures' interpretation of the "success" of Soviet intervention in these areas was the fostering of national self-determination and the promise of extending these tactics internationally. Intervention began with Lenin's assessment of the power of nationalism and the way self-determination, having been so successful as a domestic policy, could be used as a weapon against capitalism in colonial nations. In short, support for self-determination constituted a "costless gesture" that was driven, as Edward T. Wilson has argued, by two specific ideological needs. One, "the emotional urge to identify with the plight of downtrodden peoples," and two, a lack of suitable targets for world revolution that led Communist theoreticians to focus on colonial revolution.[133] Indeed, at the second and third meetings of the Comintern, it was suggested that colonial nations could use the Soviet proletariat to make up for the "sociological deficiency" of the less developed societies and thereby bypass the capitalist stage of the recipe for revolution. And it was this forwarding of the processes of modernization along with the purported "urge to identify" with the oppressed that so excited Hughes, Du Bois, and Robeson when they visited Soviet Central Asia in the 1920s and 1930s.[134]

But contrary to the impression of superior management by the Soviets, the cartoons reprinted from *Krokodil* suggest that African Americans were in spite of good intentions deeply misinterpreted by most Russians. In the same year, an article published in *Sovetskaia Rossiia* declared that Robeson was the "spokesman for the opinion of the majority of U.S. Negroes," and yet all evidence indicates that nothing could have been further from the truth.[135] In a similar gesture of miscalculation, Russians continued to view black Americans in the way Lenin had thirty years earlier—that is, as "an untapped resource of human labor power" ("neispol'zovannogo chelove-cheskogo truda"). As was the case when McKay found himself perceived as a "black ikon in the flesh," so too did Robeson achieve iconic status as representative of not only what the USSR had to offer black Americans but also what all Africans could and should aspire to be. In simultaneously containing singularity and multitudes in Soviet eyes, Robeson partook in the practical disembodiment of the African continent. He became the "voice of all Negroes." For Robeson, this kind of disembodiment was tantamount to betrayal, for in founding the Council on African Affairs he emphasized the organization's twofold purpose: "to provide a sound basis of accurate information" about decolonization and to serve as a lobbying force for African interests.[136] And yet, far from Robeson's desire to bring attention to the plight of African colonies, these cartoons use the image of Robeson to signify accurate information both about Robeson's role in the imaginative othering underwritten by Soviet policy and the way such othering was caught up in combating U.S. two-faced denunciation of the international.

The danger of Robeson became, like the threat of communism to the United States, framed as contagious, capable of permeating even the most robust of boundaries. U.S. containment policy was developed to block the flow, and did so by promoting exemplary African Americans as representative stand-ins and pathologizing those who refused to fit the bill. So concerned was the State Department about the international impact of Robeson that it encouraged negative reports of him to be disseminated in

16. U.S. press coverage plays up the "black Stalin" idea. UPI photo of
Robeson at Russian Embassy party in Washington, D.C., to mark the thirty-
third anniversary of the October Revolution, 1950. © Bettmann/Corbis.

the African Cold Coast during this period. As Penny Von Eschen has
helpfully pointed out, a memo to this end states that "a thorough-going,
sympathetic and regretful but straight-talking treatment for the whole
Robeson episode" is badly needed, and that "the universality of its usefulness to us in Africa ought to warrant whatever costs in time and money."
Directly linking "the U.S. Negro problem in general" and Robeson case "in
particular," the memo claims that "in answering the latter we go a long way
toward answering the former." Prescribing an article in which Robeson
would be portrayed as a consummate artist who had suffered "spiritual
alienation from his country and the bulk of his own people," as well as an
"illness of the mind and heart, . . . not easily recognized, yet contagious,

and thus a deadly danger," the author of this memo requested that the article be penned by "an American Negro devoted to his race" and that it be widely serialized.[137]

As the State Department's memo suggests, put to action was a reinvigoration of American national identity as explicitly "individual" over and against the defeated bodies of the "collectivized" and "contagious," who Robeson emblematized. In turn, the Soviet Union's "failure" to provide an adequate formulation for political and social equality only encouraged the self-righteousness of such claims. In spite of these competing stances, Robeson's stalwart refusal to abandon a Left politics can be read as at once a challenge to the pathologizing strategies of U.S. national security and a refusal to abandon ideologies that linked global liberation with civil rights agitation, the flow of U.S. capital to the flow of U.S. racisms. Exposing the hypocrisy of U.S. arms outstretched to back colonial interests while the State Department proclaimed racial injustice singularly a domestic issue, Robeson's performative politics sought to stem this flow. Through his singing, he invoked the selfhood of oppressed peoples through their capacity for national consciousness, the capacity to feel with others, and he hoped to transmute this feeling into an international ethos. His political attachment to the "liberation of all oppressed peoples" along with the responses of both the USSR and United States to Robeson's internationalism can thus be seen as exemplary of the complex and at times contradictory instrumentality of racial difference to the sustenance of Cold War ideologies on both sides of the globe. By neglecting the association of Robeson with the USSR and instrumentality of this association to his internationalism, one runs the risk of perpetuating the myth of Robeson's deadly contagion.

The Only Television Hostess Who Doesn't Turn Red

QUESTION: Am I a black who happens to have been born
in Russia, or a Russian who happens to have been born black?
ANSWER: Neither. Both.—Yelena Khanga, *Soul to Soul*

In 1997, the appearance of a new talk show, based exclusively on the topic of
sex, sent shock waves through Russian television circuits. The show, *Pro Eto*
(*About It*), boasted the first explicit discussion of sex in television's public
sphere.[1] *Pro Eto* also garnered attention because of its host, Yelena Khanga,
who quickly became a Russian celebrity. Known by millions of viewers as
Russia's first black female television host, the image of Khanga embodies
the routes of identification and transnational cultural flows that I have been
underscoring throughout this book. At the same time, as a Russian-born
and raised woman of American, Jewish, and African descent, Khanga
complicates the genealogy of African Americans in Russia. Rather than
reiterating the pattern in which a black American traveled to the Soviet
Union in order to experience firsthand the purported exhilarations of the
Soviet project, and then turned back to the United States, Khanga's story is
the adumbration of an American diaspora—a tale about Americans who
went to the Soviet Union and stayed.[2] Because of its proximity to them,
Khanga's embodiment of these unusual routings reads through the screen
of earlier black Americans in the USSR. But her Soviet upbringing in the
1970s and 1980s also shifts the image broadcast to new interpretive frames.
Khanga's placement as the star of one of the most popular (and controversial) shows in Russian television history opens up areas for further reflection on the lingering effects of encounters between black and red.[3]

Khanga's *Pro Eto* debut was not the first time she had appeared on the public stage. In 1988, Khanga participated in the first U.S.-Soviet journalist exchange program—she left her post at the *Moscow News* to work for the *Christian Science Monitor* for a year. In this prized position, she was one of the journalists in attendance at the first Reagan-Gorbachev summit, and while there attracted ample media interest of her own.[4] One result of this attention was a Rockefeller Foundation grant to research her family history. In 1992, Khanga published an English account of this history in a book titled *Soul to Soul: A Black Russian Jewish Woman's Search for Her Roots.* Her book, published by W. W. Norton, tried to explain what that title might mean, and traced the extensions of her family tree back to the emigration of her grandparents from the United States to Uzbekistan in 1931.[5] Khanga is the granddaughter of Oliver Golden, the African American who together with his Polish-born Jewish American wife, Bertha Bialek, left New York to help develop the nascent cotton industry in Uzbekistan. Their daughter, Lily Golden, married the Tanzanian political figure Abdullah Khanga, who she met while studying in the 1960s at Moscow State University. In 1963, Lily Golden and Abdullah Khanga had a daughter, Yelena. *Soul to Soul* maps out Khanga's attempt to trace and explain her family history before her grandparents met: Lily's paternal grandfather, a descendant of Mississippi slaves, surmounted enormous obstacles to become a successful landowning farmer in the post–Civil War South; Lily's maternal grandfather was an orthodox rabbi who brought his family to New York from Warsaw in 1905. And the book inspects Lily's, and in turn Yelena's, imbrications in the complex legacies of these crossings as they merged in Uzbekistan and Moscow in the 1930s. Because Khanga's father was the least-present figure in her life—he was assassinated in Tanzania shortly after her birth—he receives less attention than her other predecessors. Hence, the book emphasizes the connections between Khanga's Russian and African American genealogies, somewhat bracketing the location of "Africa" within these nexuses of identification.[6]

When Khanga became a Russian celebrity in 1997, her image built on recollections of black celebrities that had permeated the popular consciousness of post-Soviet viewers. Among such reverberating images were the imprint left by Robeson and his representative black masculinity as well as the appearance, in 1972, of Angela Davis in the USSR. On the heels of her acquittal for "conspiracy" to defend the Soledad Brothers, Davis

17. Angela Davis in Palace Square, Leningrad, the site where the October Revolution was launched in 1917.

toured the socialist nations that had supported her, those that had "exerted serious pressure on the [U.S.] government."[7] Davis's *Autobiography* dedicates only a few lines to her two-week journey through Moscow, Leningrad, Tashkent, and Samarkand, but it does state that she conceived of the tour as in part a thank you to "the people who had contributed to the fight for my freedom." Davis also notes that when she delivered her speeches, "rallies were attended by more people than I had ever before seen assembled in one place."[8] This is confirmed by Soviet accounts that indicate that wherever Davis spoke, she was greeted by thousands of adoring fans. Photographs of this visit depict Davis surrounded by throngs of curious and supportive Soviets who were fully versed in the political travails and hypocrisies of Davis's recent run-in with the U.S. judicial system. *Andzhela v SSSR* (*Angela in the USSR*), a book-length journalistic account of her trip, describes an enthusiastic reception for the woman who manifestly represented the ironies of "democracy's" racial inequities, and who symbolized an image of racial otherness with which the Soviets had throughout the years come to establish an (uneasy) alliance and (partial) identification.

18. Following in Hughes's footsteps, Davis observes the unveiled participation of women in the public sphere, in this case providing a lecture on the preservation of national treasures in Samarkand, Uzbekistan.

But the double consciousness with which Soviets in the 1970s might most strongly have identified was not necessarily limited to the earlier articulations of philosophical alienation from the West or a Leninist "urge to identify" with the internationally oppressed. By the 1970s, these dualisms had been reelaborated to include a sense of twin Soviet realities that necessitated a firm division between private and public displays of political sentiment and affiliation. Khanga identifies this sense of duality when she writes about the period in her youth when her mother spoke about Khrushchev in hushed tones. Ousted from power in 1964, Khrushchev had been expunged all but entirely from the public record. "My mother was careful to warn me that I should not repeat her favorable words about Khrushchev outside the house. For me this was the beginning of the dual consciousness all honest Russian parents instilled in their children. I learned at a very early age that there were two realities: one for home and one for school" (*SS*, 126). Khanga adopts and rephrases the terms associated with Du Bois's masculine selfhood and nineteenth-century Russian theoretizations of subjecthood to create another layer of duality. Thus, while Davis's image may have served the purpose of linking oppressed and marginalized racial groups across national spectrums in the interest of an international solidarity, this tumultuous show of support for Davis may also have been partly a reflection of the necessity of its public display. Mikhail Epstein has depicted just this simultaneity when he discusses a simulacra effect in Brezhnev-era Russian society in which the distance between "reality" and "idea" eroded. Borrowing from Herbert Marcuse, Epstein asserts, "In a totalitarian society ideology cannot but be a faithful reflection of reality because reality itself is a faithful reflection of ideology. . . . [T]otalitarian ideology is itself the only reality, the supersignified, to which all ideological signs and interpretations refer."[9] Ideas become detached not only from reality but from other ideas as well. The figure of a woman as representative of the global oppressed may have rubbed against the grain of previous exposure to male representativeness embodied from McKay to Robeson, and troubled Russian presuppositions about male universality. But to the extent that disidentification with Davis existed (and surely it did), it was subsumed within the larger dictates of "internationalism." Her warm reception was a "faithful reflection of ideology," engineered to meet mandatory expectations, and thus in Epstein's terms, the only possible reality. Epstein's formulations, however, do not completely accommodate the possibility that the very mandate that disidentification not be addressed publicly also provided a means for dissent to blossom within the confines of one's home, or one's soul, or wherever one could believe oneself to have escaped the supersignified. As Khanga describes, and as samizdat publications testify, it was more likely that alternative views were expressed in private, in the comfort of a kitchen where conversation blurred under the sound of running water.

While these layered vectors of identification, desire, and loathing may have been surging simultaneously throughout the Soviet era, during the post-Soviet 1990s, new avenues opened up for the expression of affiliations between white Russians and their nonwhite counterparts. More often than not, these links have been expressed in aggressive terms of disidentification. Khanga comments, "The explosion of ethnic hatred since the Soviet empire began to break up shows how thin the amicable layer was. . . . [I]ntelligent, well-educated people always knew this Soviet brotherhood was a fiction, but the public silence kept many of us from examining our personal convictions too closely" (SS, 285). To the extent that it is able, a post-Soviet crisis of legitimation has buttressed an erasure of the fragmenting aspects of a "dual consciousness"—for which the Brezhnev era was famous—and a demand for totality and unification against the West.[10] As the editors of *Russian Cultural Studies* note, in the 1995 Duma elections, "the government party, Our Home is Russia . . . called for the 'unity and integrity of the Russian state.'"[11] But the question remained unanswered: How to define a "national ideal" that could carry forth the newly wrought promise of a Russia based historically not on singularity but in tension between the East and West? In the wake of such unanswered dilemmas, certain notions of "unity" and "integrity" have been put into practice with some violent repercussions. Post-Soviet Russians are fully cognizant of the ideological stranglehold a state policy of antiracism held over the Soviet people for eighty years. Now that the hold has been lifted, it is, according to one report, the worst possible time to be other than white in Russia.[12] Without the stay of Cold War tensions to keep blatant race-based aggression in check, such animosities have manifested themselves in various and multiple arenas: a 1998 attack on a black U.S. Marine in Moscow; a sweep of nonwhite persons from the streets of Moscow prior to the 1998 World Youth Games; and the racial profiling of *chernye* (a word that means "blacks," but referred to Armenians, Georgians, and Central Asians in this case) after a series of explosions in Moscow in 1999 and 2000.[13] Khanga tries to explain the awkwardness of Russian racial terminology here: "When Russians refer to *chernye* (the blacks), they aren't normally talking about black Russians, Africans, or Americans. *Chyornyy* is a generic term for anyone with a darker complexion than the standard Slavic shade" (*SS*, 285).[14] These stereotypes, while sweeping to be sure, also embody masculinist tendencies—that is, a reduction of the question of racial otherness to a male representative.

The complexities housed within such affinities might be found on the menu of a trendy Moscow restaurant, called Petrovich, started by Andrei Bilzho and named after his famous cartoon character of the same name. A visitor to the faux-Soviet decor of Petrovich will find a menu full of dishes named to lampoon everything from Soviet cabinet members to five-year plans.[15] Sandwiched among these caricatures are two dishes named to catch the spirit of Soviet racial policies: a dish called the "Paul Robeson" and one labeled the "Bez Racizm" ("No Racism"). The dishes remind the patrons of Petrovich—for the most part, Moscow yuppies—that in spite of constitutional bylaws meant to safeguard the contrary, there was (and is) racism in Russia. If this is funny it is because these same patrons are aware of the ironies at mouth's reach, and perhaps even compliant in their production. The ingredients of the "Robeson" confirm the vexed cultural cachet of a figure dubbed one of Russia's cultural heroes: twenty grams of black caviar served with the usual accompaniments—a dollop of white *smetana* (or sour cream) and a stout stack of Russian pancakes called *blini*. An order of "Bez Racizm," on the other hand, brings a plate of dry toast and black caviar. So the question for a curious connoisseur is, "What's the difference between the 'Robeson' and 'No Racism?'" Whereas the "No Racism" lacks in cultural distinction—just some fish eggs on a plate—the "Robeson" is all about distinctiveness heightened by key components of the Russian national cuisine—in this case glaringly white components. If the obvious joke is that a Russia without racism is not characteristically Russia at all, then the more subtle interpretation is that there is also a degree of nostalgia for an era whose utopian aspirations for a racism-free society contrast starkly with the very racist present. Likewise, the Robeson dish asks ironically if Robeson was actually an integral part of Russian cultural identity: removed from the plate of the "Robeson," the black caviar would leave behind not only Russian culinary distinctiveness but also the utopian ideal of no racism. In this presentation, one is reminded that even if Robeson's representative masculinity measured up to Soviet demands for a universalizable masculine subject, his racial otherness removed him from constitutive terms of agency. Whatever ambivalences about the past these dishes summon, most Russians would agree that with the fall of the Soviet Union came the end of racial tolerance tout court.

If by some accounts it is a difficult time to be black in Russia, it is by other reports also a difficult time to be a woman.[16] Contemporary to the waves of race-based belligerence, a public reinforcement of strict divisions between masculine and feminine roles has emerged. Post-Soviet political and social instabilities have resulted in an unspoken consolidation of the universal subject as Russian, white, and male.[17] Khanga's words both confound and construct this logic when she writes, "Both black and white Americans talk a great deal about their 'identities.' This is an unfamiliar concept to Russians. In Russia, no one says 'I have a black identity' or 'I have a female identity.' You're black, you're a woman: It's taken for granted" (*SS*, 258). Khanga seems to be suggesting that without a firm sense of the society into which a subject is interpolated, it is difficult to articulate "identity" per se. In this sense, to posit a female or black identity, let alone a black female Jewish one, is seen as a luxury and not a historical necessity. But at the same time, the attempted eradication of identity as a relevant factor in Russian society also reinforces the prevailing terms of subjectivity. Khanga's ideas are suggestive of the prerogatives accorded white men as the standard-bearers of "common sense," universal subject-hood. These prerogatives make themselves known without qualification. In so doing, newspaper classifieds advertise for secretaries who are single, can meet physical specifications, and most important, are "without com-plexes"—signifying that they're willing to sleep with the boss or not complain about a grab or grope. It seems that Russian femininity, long since "liberated" from the bourgeois confines of domestic drudgery and streamlined emphatically into the Soviet workforce, has returned home to roost. And on stiletto heels no less.

Over the course of the bumpy terrain of the 1970s, 1980s, and 1990s, the terms, conditions, and format of female black popularity have clearly shifted. In order to serve as a kind of unifying and identificatory lightning rod for Russians of a post-Soviet state, the image of the black woman necessitated redressing. Leonid Parfyonov, the executive producer and mastermind behind the *Pro Eto* television show, believed he had the an-swers when it came to crafting Khanga's marketable look: "We didn't want to go with an Angela Davis Afro-American style."[18] Instead, he proposed a short blond wig and blue contact lenses. Khanga rejected the latter but donned the former. Thus, Davis's black Afro was replaced by Khanga's flaxen wig. As Hughes said in a different context, "New times demand new people."

What these news flashes reveal are not simply the complicities of racial and sexual oppressions under a white supremacist patriarchy, although they do certainly suggest something of that order. Rather, in the sedi-mented accretion of these values and measures of control, one also sees the emergence of a challenge to one's own conceptions of racially and sexually disciplined bodies. While to some eyes Khanga's *Pro Eto* blond wig and sassy shifts with plunging necklines might seem a scandalous concession to the worst of female stereotyping and racial erasure, there is no denying that Khanga as spokeswoman for *Pro Eto* embodies in this form an allur-ing depiction of female agency. Parfyonov admitted that "blacks have a

19. Yelena Khanga hosts the Russian television program *Pro Eto*. © Peter Blakely/ Corbis SABA 1997.

stronger sexual image in Russia" (a sentiment Khanga confirms in her book), but so too had Russians never heard terms like "fellatio" and "cunnilingus" uttered publicly.[19] The show's motto that Khanga is "the only television hostess who doesn't turn red," suggests to Russians her purportedly blush-defying skin tone and matter-of-fact presentation of volatile topics. With Khanga's stalwart help, the show has supplanted Russian prudery with fact-based discussions of sexually contracted diseases, AIDS, bisexuality, sadomasochism, masturbation, geriatric sex, and non-hetero identifications. The image of Khanga may rely on stereotypes, and an implicit depoliticization of Khanga's historical genealogy—why she emerged in Moscow and not in New York—but the show is also administering extremely new messages about sexual openness and permissibility.

Khanga's "difference," then, is marked as Western, perhaps even American, and merges with the U.S.-influenced impulses of the show.[20] The very openness of topics could be seen as an importation of love American-style: sex and sexual difference are welcomed into the fold in order to normalize sexual heterogeneity. Seen through this frame, Western-influenced Russian media entrepreneurs carry forth an "enlightening" project on the dim

Russian masses in order to serve a pluralistic ideal, but one that is tempered through the broad strokes of disciplinary control.[21] But at the same time, these elites remain within the masculinist lexicon of Enlightenment philosophies and thus outside the lexicon of racial heterogeneity. Hence, this complexly racialized representation of femininity challenges one to read her cosmetic choices as anything other than a refashioning of an already irreducible identity—a willful display of the female body that refuses to synchronize expectation with effect. One might ask, "Why not the blue contacts?" With different priorities intact, the Russian image of Khanga emerges with a shifted sense of allegiances and cultural dualities. As much as anything, she seems to bear the awkward legacy of a cohabitation among masculine dualities outlined by the Russian "doubles" of Dostoevsky and Brezhnev, and the African American double consciousness of Du Bois. But into these models she forcibly introjects woman's excentricity, the site of an erased difference within the paradigm(s) of national alienation. Finally, one hears in the statement that Khanga is "the only television hostess who doesn't turn red" not only insinuations about her skin tone and frank style but an anxiety about the totality of her removal from the political leanings and aspirations of her African American predecessors. Although she is the product of cultural crossings that have desisted, gone the way of the iron curtain, her image continues to conjure the miscegenating specter of those who arrived before her. These earlier intermixings between black and red may have been secured behind the locked doors of a reputedly regrettable past. Yet what's to stop a woman from reconfiguring a key?

NOTES

1 For a discussion of Claude McKay's relationship to the label "black American," see chapter 1.

2 In the pages that follow, I use the terms "Negro," "black," and "African American" to designate U.S. citizens who traced their ancestry to Africa and the peoples of the African diaspora. My use of "Negro" follows that of authors during specific periods in which the word was common parlance; "black" is employed in reference to peoples both within and outside American national identity; and "African American" corresponds to a contemporary locution for U.S. citizens who identify themselves as members or progeny of an African diaspora.

3 Paul Gilroy, *The Black Atlantic: Modernity and Double Consciousness* (Cambridge: Harvard University Press, 1993). Analyses of black Atlantic and U.S. cultures in dialogue with Gilroy, and to which I am indebted, include those by Hazel Carby, Michael Denning, Stuart Hall, Paul Jay, Ronald Judy, Eric Lott, Michael Rogin, David Roediger, and Werner Sollors.

4 There are a number of recent studies that address black American interest in communism, all of which focus primarily on the domestic aspect of this involvement. They include James Edward Smethurst, *The New Red Negro: The Literary Left and African American Poetry, 1930–1946* (New York: Oxford University Press, 1999); Bill Mullen, *Popular Fronts: Chicago and African-American Cultural Politics, 1935–1946* (Urbana: University of Illinois Press, 1999); Theodore Kornweibel Jr., *"Seeing Red": Federal Campaigns against Black Militancy, 1919–1925* (Bloomington: Indiana University Press, 1998); Keith P. Griffler, *What Price Alliance? Black Radicals Confront White Labor, 1918–1938* (New York: Garland, 1995); and Earl Ofari Hutchinson, *Blacks and Reds: Race and Class in Conflict, 1919–1990* (East Lansing: Michigan State University Press, 1995). Specific discussions of the travels to the Soviet Union of the men I discuss here have appeared in biographies by Wayne Cooper, Arnold Rampersad, and Martin Duberman. William J. Maxwell's *New Negro, Old Left: African-American Writing and Communism between*

the Wars (New York: Columbia University Press, 1999) provides an illuminating discussion of Claude McKay's *Negroes in America,* which I discuss in chapter 1. Maxwell engages this book in the context of his look at Left revisionist history, and while thorough in his use of U.S. sources, he does not work directly with Soviet archival materials. David Chioni Moore has been working independently on Langston Hughes and Soviet Central Asia. His essay "Local Color, Global 'Color': Langston Hughes, the Black Atlantic, and Soviet Central Asia, 1932" (*Research in African Literatures,* 27, no. 4 [winter 1996]: 49–70) pursues Hughes's memoir *I Wonder as I Wander* along with his Soviet-published pamphlet "A Negro Looks at Soviet Central Asia." Moore's interest is in Hughes as a theorist of global color, and he is editing an eagerly anticipated expanded edition of Hughes's Soviet-published group of essays. To broaden my sense of Hughes's journey through Soviet Central Asia, I was granted access to Louise Thompson Patterson's unpublished memoir, for which I thank Patterson's daughter, Dr. Mary Louise Patterson, and Hazel Carby.

5   Major exceptions to this would be the pioneering work of critics such as Nell Painter, Mark Naison, and David Kelley, all of whom are discussed below. Revisionist accounts of U.S. leftism and leftist cultural production that have shaped and motivated my own work include recent monographs by Michael Denning, Barbara Foley, David Roediger, and Alan Wald as well as articles by Kathryne V. Lindberg.

6   Claude McKay, *Negry v Amerike,* Russian trans. P. Okhrimenko (Moscow: Gosudarstvennoe Izdatel'stvo, 1923), 21. Retranslation is my own.

7   Mark Naison, *Communists in Harlem during the Depression* (Urbana: University of Illinois Press, 1983).

8   Smethurst, *The New Red Negro,* 10.

9   Liah Greenfeld, *Nationalism: Five Roads to Modernity* (Cambridge: Harvard University Press, 1992), 270.

10   Gilroy, *The Black Atlantic,* 127.

11   Ibid., 4.

12   Neil Lazarus, "Modernity, Globalization, and the West," in *Nationalism and Cultural Practice in the Postcolonial World* (Cambridge: Cambridge University Press, 1999), 61.

13   Dale Peterson alludes to what he calls a "distinguished history of mutual awareness between Russian and black American literary intellectuals" (*Up from Bondage: The Literatures of Russian and African American Soul* [Durham, N.C.: Duke University Press, 2000], 13), but does not explore the content of this history.

14   Whereas Gilroy focuses on the transnational routings of black consciousness, Peterson concentrates on the national and domestic aspects of both Russian and African American alternative consciousnesses. Unlike Gilroy's symbiosis of three modes comprising double consciousness (particularist, nationalist, and dias-

poric), Peterson's version centers on the racially particularist, nationalist, and (to a lesser extent) universal, peripheralizing the transnational and, more important, internationalism.

15 A version of this portion of the text appeared in my article "Soul Mates," *Diaspora* 9, no. 3 (winter 2000): 399–420.

16 Exceptions to the more standard account include those of Naison, Kelley, Moore, Kornweibel, Smethurst, and Maxwell, as well as Mark Solomon, *The Cry Was Unity: Communists and African Americans, 1919–1936* (Jackson: University of Mississippi Press, 1998). With the exception of Solomon, whose work is discussed in chapter 1, these books remain focused primarily on the domestic aspects (and source materials) of black radicalism and do not pursue its international dimensions.

17 This and the previous statistic are from Richard Brod and Elizabeth B. Welles, "Foreign Language Enrollments in the United States Institutions of Higher Education, Fall 1998," Modern Language Association, Online (www.adfl.org/resources/enroll.htm).

18 See my "The Color Line and Its Discontents: Passing through Russia and the United States" (Ph.D. diss., Yale University, 1995), which includes chapters on Nella Larsen's *Passing,* Anastasiia Verbitskaia's *Kliuchi Shastiia* (*The Keys to Happiness*), Langston Hughes's *A Negro Looks at Soviet Central Asia,* and John Howard Griffin's *Black Like Me.* See also my article on Mexican soap operas in Russia, "Montezuma's Revenge: Reading *los ricos tambien lloran* in Russia," in *To Be Continued: Soap Operas around the World,* ed. Robert C. Allen (New York: Routledge, 1995), 285–300, and "Black Like Who? Cross-Testing the 'Real' Lines of John Howard Griffin's *Black Like Me,*" *Cultural Critique* 40 (fall 1998): 103–44.

19 Michel-Rolph Trouillot, *Silencing the Past: Power and the Production of History* (Boston: Beacon, 1995), 48.

20 The phrase is McKay's from his *A Long Way from Home* (1937; reprint, New York: Harcourt Brace Jovanovich, 1970), 151. A different reading of a U.S. "pilgrimage" to the Soviet Union can be found in Sylvia R. Margulies, *The Pilgrimage to Russia: The Soviet Union and the Treatment of Foreigners, 1924–1937* (Madison: University of Wisconsin Press, 1968)—an account that overlooks the participation of African Americans.

21 For more information on the little-known Moscow residency of Arle Tietz, who married a Russian composer and became a Soviet citizen, see L. Nekrassova, "A Negro Artist and Citizen of the USSR," *Soviet Russia Today* (August 1943): 25.

22 A complete list of the group and detailed account of their trip can be found in Louise Thompson Patterson's unpublished memoir. Thompson lists the twenty-two as follows: "Laurence O. Alberga, agricultural worker; Matthew Crawford, insurance clerk; Sylvia Garner, singer; Leonard Hill, social service worker; Langston Hughes, poet; Katherine Jenkins, social worker; Mildred Jones, art student;

Juanita Lewis, singer; Mollie Lewis, student; Thurston McNairy Lewis, journalist; Allan McKenzie, salesman; Loren Miller, journalist; Frank C. Montero, student; Henry Lee Moon, journalist; Lloyd Patterson, paperhanger; Theodore R. Poston, journalist; Wayland Rudd, actor; George Sample, law student; Homer Smith, postal worker; Louise Thompson Patterson; Dorothy West, writer; Constance White, social worker" (Louise Thompson Patterson, "Louise Thompson Patterson Memoirs: Trip to Russia—1932," draft 2, October–November 1994, 7).

23   Although neither Rudd nor Patterson published accounts of their Soviet experiences, Smith's 1964 memoir of his experiences in the Soviet Union, *Black Man in Red Russia* (Chicago: Johnson Publishing, 1964), describes his later disillusionment with the Soviet Union and has, along with Robert Robinson's searing attack on Soviet policy toward blacks (*Black on Red: A Black American's Forty-Four Years inside the Soviet Union* (Washington, D.C.: Acropolis Books, 1988), come to serve for some scholars as exemplary of black American logical renunciation of the USSR. For an elaboration of this debate, see my discussion in chapter 1.

24   See *Challenge* 1, no. 1 (March 1934) and *Challenge* 1, no. 2 (September 1934). "A Room in Red Square" is accompanied by the following note: "Mary Christopher is, we believe, a pseudonym for a woman who went to Russia a year ago with an acting company. If she has written more, we hope she will send. . . ."

25   Audre Lorde, "Notes from a Trip to Russia," *Sister/Outsider* (Trumansburg, N.Y.: Crossing Press, 1984), 13. A guest of the Union of Soviet Writers, Lorde traveled to Russia to attend the African-Asian Writers Conference in 1976. A Soviet record of Davis's trip can be found in Olga Chetchetkina, *Andzhela v Sovetskom Soiuze* (Moscow: Molodaia Gvardiia, 1973). In addition to these more politically motivated journeys, there is the reflection of a graduate student's impressions provided by Andrea Lee's *Russian Journal* (New York: Vintage, 1979), which offers an account of Lee's stay in Russia from 1978 to 1979.

26   W. E. B. Du Bois, *Dusk of Dawn: An Essay Towards an Autobiography of a Race Concept* (1940; reprint, New Brunswick, N.J.: Transaction Publishers, 1997), 287.

27   See Ella Winter, *I Saw the Russian People* (Boston: Little, Brown and Co., 1945), 97, 244.

28   Discussed in the RGALI collection of files are possible translations of Wright's work into Russian, an exploratory query about Wright's intentions to visit the USSR, published Soviet criticisms of *Native Son* and *Black Boy,* and reports on the reaction of the U.S. Left press to *Native Son.* The last file is dated 1957 and is a Soviet critique of *White Man Listen!* Here and elsewhere, files from RGALI will be listed by *fond* (collection), *opis* (list), and *delo* (file). The files mentioned above can be found in 631–14–31, 631–14–67, 631–14–1070, 631–14–1101, 631–14–1067, and 631–26–3939.

29   See my discussions of their Soviet published articles in chapters 3 and 4. An intriguing corollary to the Soviet interest in Shirley Graham as it reflects on Du

Bois is the fact that when searching in RGALI for files on Du Bois, one is directed to "Grexem, Sherli" (Shirley Graham), under whose name the contents of the Du Bois file can be obtained.

30 Critics who, like Wiegman, have opened the doors to expose how querying black masculinity is a critical feminist project include Hazel Carby, Robin D. G. Kelley, Phillip Brian Harper, Robert Reid-Pharr, and Siobhan Somerville. My work is indebted to their own.

31 The term chelovek translates as "person," but the gender neutrality of the word person veils the masculine connotations of chelovek. For this reason, chelovek will be translated in the following pages as the somewhat cumbersome "person/man."

32 *The Wall Street Journal* (November 4, 1963), as cited in Gerald Horne, *Black and Red: W. E. B. Du Bois and the Afro-American Response to the Cold War, 1944–1993* (Albany: State University of New York Press, 1986), 357.

33 Trouillot, *Silencing the Past*, 16.

34 W. E. B. Du Bois, *The Autobiography of W. E. B. Du Bois: A Soliloquy on Viewing My Life from the Last Decade of Its First Century* (1968; reprint, New York: International Publishers, 1991), 34.

35 Paul Robeson, "Vyi zovoevali uvazheniu vsego mira" ("You Have Won the Respect of the Entire World"), *Pravda* 27 January 1960, 6.

36 Patterson, "Trip to Russia," draft 2, 47.

I. "NOT AT ALL GOD'S WHITE PEOPLE": MCKAY AND THE NEGRO IN RED

1 Claude McKay, *Home to Harlem* (1928; reprint, Boston: Northeastern University Press, 1987), 228.

2 As I will discuss at greater length below, this is an argument persuasively presented by Dale Peterson in *Up from Bondage: The Literatures of Russian and African American Soul* (Durham, N.C.: Duke University Press, 2000).

3 David Lloyd and Abdul JanMohamed, introduction to *The Nature and Context of Minority Discourse*, ed. David Lloyd and Abdul JanMohamed (New York: Oxford University Press, 1990), 16.

4 Peter Steiner, "Slavic Literary Studies Yesterday and Tomorrow," *Profession 87* (1987): 3.

5 For a wide-ranging discussion of the appeal to African American Left intellectuals of nationalist art based in the folk, see James Smethurst, "African-American Poetry, Ideology, and the Left during the 1930s and 1940s from the Third Period to the Popular Front and Beyond," in *The New Red Negro: The Literary Left and African American Poetry, 1930–1946* (New York: Oxford University Press, 1999), 16–59.

6 Claude McKay, *Negroes in America*, trans. Robert J. Winter (1923; Russian transla-

tion by P.F. Okhrimenko) London: National University, 1979); hereafter cited parenthetically as NA. Claude McKay, *Trial by Lynching: Stories about Negro Life in North America*, trans. Robert Winter (1925, Mysore, India: Centre for Commonwealth Literature and Research, 1977). Unless otherwise noted, citations of these texts are in accordance with these English translations of the Russian editions (which were based on McKay's now lost English manuscripts).

7   *A Long Way From Home* hereafter cited parenthetically as *ALWFH*. By focusing on the English-Russian nexus of McKay's archive, I do not mean to slight the importance of Jamaican dialect to McKay's work. Indeed, McKay's first two books of poetry were written in this dialect, and likewise comprise equally significant pieces of McKay's multilingual archive. My point is simply to reiterate the necessity of thinking of McKay's work outside the limiting parameters of "English only."

8   As I explore below, William J. Maxwell's discussion of *Negroes in America* is the most substantial exception to this tendency.

9   Werner Sollors's edited volume *Multilingual America: Transnationalism, Ethnicity, and the Languages of American Literature* (New York: New York University Press, 1998) recuperates and stresses the importance of the multilingual routes of U.S. literary history.

10 Claude McKay, *A Long Way from Home* (1937; reprint, New York: Harcourt Brace Jovanovich, 1970); hereafter cited parenthetically as *ALWFH*. Examining the earlier work enables us to see a less familiar, more internationalist, McKay. This internationalist frame raises the question of McKay's own national connections and allegiances: During his time in Russia, McKay carried a British passport. Yet despite being born in Jamaica, the United States was a major point of reference for his national self-understanding, as he had resided there for several years prior to his Russian journey. McKay explained his national filiations in the following way: "I said that I was born in the West Indies and lived in the United States and that I was an American, even though I was a British subject, but I preferred to think of myself as an internationalist" (*ALWFH* 300).

11 In this sense, my reading of McKay's Russian work is much in sympathy with the illuminating account of *Negroes in America* that William J. Maxwell provides in *New Negro, Old Left: African-American Writing and Communism between the Wars* (New York: Columbia University Press, 1999). Maxwell identifies McKay as a Marxian pre-critic (85) of black cultural studies' interrogation of whiteness on the basis of black cultural production. As a precursor to the dismantling of "whiteness" that occurred in the late 1980s and early 1990s, McKay in Maxwell's reading challenged "the intellectual borders of the Black Atlantic and rephrased Marxism's Negro question in the earshot of a receptive Kremlin" (93). Maxwell rightly sees the theses that came out of the 1928 congress—including the so-called

black belt thesis—as products of interracial theorizing. But his suggestion that it was McKay's theorizing that convinced Bolsheviks such as Leon Trotsky and Grigory Zinoviev that the U.S. South did indeed comprise an independent nation is countered by a more ambivalent position outlined in *Trial by Lynching* and the Comintern documentation surrounding McKay's visit. My analysis departs from Maxwell's in three key areas. First, I examine McKay's work in light of the Soviet departure from socialism and women's suffrage during the New Economic Policy. Second, I connect the Soviet welcome of McKay to Russia's own thorny relationship to Western European theories of subjectivity. Finally, I link my discussion of *Negroes in America* to the Comintern archives of McKay's visit and the stories this trip produced, *Trial by Lynching*.

12 In a letter to Max Eastman dated 19 December 1934, McKay wrote, "The CP of America has carried on its propaganda among Negroes from the very acute angle of my position" (cited in Wayne Cooper, *The Passion of Claude McKay* [New York: Schocken Books, 1973], 213).

13 On Soviet iconography in the 1920s, see Elizabeth Waters, "The Female Form in Soviet Political Iconography, 1917–1932," in *Russia's Women: Accommodation, Resistance, Transformation,* ed. Barbara Evans Clemets, Barbara Alpern Engel, and Christine D. Worobec (Berkeley: University of California Press, 1991), 225–42; and Victoria E. Bonnell, "The Representation of Women in Early Soviet Political Art," *Russian Review* 50 (July 1991), and her more general discussion of political iconography in "The Iconography of the Worker in Soviet Political Art," in *Making Workers Soviet: Power, Class, and Identity,* ed. Lewis H. Siegelbaum and Ronald Grigor Suny (Ithaca, N.Y.: Cornell University Press, 1994), 341–75.

14 See Katerina Clark, *Petersburg: Crucible of Cultural Revolution* (Cambridge: Harvard University Press, 1995), 143–161 and Jeffrey Brooks, *Thank You, Comrade Stalin! Soviet Public Culture from Revolution to Cold War* (Princeton, N.J.: Princeton University Press, 2000), 27–37.

15 For a discussion of women's suffrage movements before, during, and after the revolution, see Richard Stites, *The Women's Liberation Movement in Russia: Feminism, Nihilism, and Bolshevism, 1860–1930* (Princeton, N.J.: Princeton University Press, 1978).

16 Peterson, *Up from Bondage,* 6.

17 See Mark Naison, *Communists in Harlem during the Depression* (Urbana: University of Illinois Press, 1982); and Robin D. G. Kelley, *Hammer and Hoe: Alabama Communists during the Great Depression* (Chapel Hill: University of North Carolina Press, 1990).

18 Published after this chapter was researched and drafted, Mark Solomon's book, *The Cry Was Unity: Communists and African Americans, 1917–1936* (Jackson:

University of Mississippi Press, 1998), addresses portions of the archival material on which I draw to fill out the picture of McKay's Russian work.

19 Solomon, *The Cry Was Unity,* xxxiii–iv. See also my discussion of William J. Maxwell's important work in *New Negro, Old Left,* n. 11, this chapter.

20 Ibid., xxv.

21 See Judith Mayne, *Kino and the Woman Question: Feminism and Soviet Silent Film* (Columbus: Ohio State University Press, 1989), 20–27.

22 Jeffrey Brooks, "The Press and Its Message: Images of America in the 1920s and 1930s," in *Russia in the Era of NEP: Explorations in Soviet Society and Culture,* ed. Sheila Fitzpatrick, Alexander Rabinowitch, and Richard Stites (Bloomington: Indiana University Press, 1991), 237.

23 Connections between women's suffrage and black abolitionism had certainly been articulated by such prominent figures as Frederick Douglass and Susan B. Anthony. Conventionally, the representative woman was conceived of as "white," and the representative black as "male." For a discussion of Douglass's support for women's suffrage as well as the oversight in suffragette theory of nonwhite and working-class women, see Angela Davis, *Women, Race, and Class* (New York: Vintage, 1991), 46–86. On Douglass's idealized masculinity, see Richard Yarborough, "Race, Violence, and Manhood: The Masculine Ideal in Frederick Douglass's 'The Heroic Slave,'" in *Haunted Bodies: Gender and Southern Texts,* ed. Anne Goodwyn Jones and Susan V. Donaldson (Charlottesville: University of Virginia Press, 1997), 159–84.

24 The "woman question" was also a topic of heated debate, but was peripheralized in discussions of black self-determination. Male representativeness of the "Negro" in question was assumed. Because my discussion relies on Comintern records that ignore these concerns, it of necessity departs temporarily from the woman question in order to analyze the complexities and incongruities of the Soviet Negro question. In noting how Soviet records elide any mention of sexual difference when addressing race, I wish to draw attention to the importance of the connections between racial and sexual suffrage in McKay's Russian work as, in part, an attempt to rectify this oversight. For a general exploration of the Soviet woman question, see Mary Buckley, "Soviet Interpretations of the Woman Question," *Soviet Sisterhood,* ed. Barbara Holland (Bloomington: Indiana University Press, 1985), 23–53.

25 Cited in John Reed, "The World Congress of the Communist International," *Communist* 10 (1920): 3.

26 Rossiiskii tsentr khraneniia i izucheniia dokumentov noveishei istorii (Russian Center for the Preservation and Study of Documents of Recent History), Moscow, 495–155–1: 3–11; hereafter cited parenthetically as RTSKhIDNI.

27 Records of the Congress dispute the exact placement of Lenin's draft theses: Draper places the "Negroes in America" as fourteenth out of sixteen points,

whereas Harry Haywood places it first out of fifteen. See Theodore Draper, *American Communism and Soviet Russia* (New York: Octagon, 1977), 320; and Harry Haywood, *Black Bolshevik: Autobiography of an Afro-American Communist* (Chicago: Liberator Press, 1978), 217.

28 The Russian text reads "nametil podrobnuiu programmu deistvii dlia partii i revoliutsionnykh organizatsii Blizhnego i Dal'nego Vostoka . . . *differentsirovat'* resheniia 2-ogo Vcemirnogo Kongressa Kominterna." "Negry-Chernie sredi nas," *Pravda* 3 Dec. 1922:3 ("Negroes-Blacks Among Us").

29 "Negritianskii Vopros," *Kommunisticheskii internatzional v dokumentakh, 1919– 1932.* Moskva: Partiinoeizdatel'stvo, 1933, 367. (Unless otherwise noted all English translations are my own.)

30 Huiswood was an official delegate to the Comintern, and became the first black man to meet Lenin and later serve as a candidate member of the Executive Committee of the Communist International (see Haywood, *Black Bolshevik,* 147).

31 It should be noted that references to this speech as found in Draper, *American Communism,* and Haywood, *Black Bolshevik,* rely on a German rendition found in *Protokoll des Vierten Kongresses der Kommunistischen International;* Wayne Cooper uses the *International Press Correspondent* version of 5 January 1923 in both his anthology and biography of McKay. In discussing McKay's Russia trip, Cooper relies almost entirely on McKay's *A Long Way from Home* and Draper's *American Communism,* which he calls "the best analysis of the early history of the Communist Party in the United States" n. 5 (401). As I have indicated above and will further demonstrate, there are serious problems with Draper's account, particularly regarding his analysis of the Fourth Congress, the Negro question as discussed therein, and McKay's participation in this discussion. Furthermore, although Draper states quite bluntly that the Comintern in 1922 was "as yet lacking Negro delegates from Africa [and] substituted American Negroes in the leadership of African liberation" (326), Cooper does not link this telling fact to either the public reception of McKay nor its impact on McKay's own sense of his public image as connected to his feelings of representational responsibility. In my discussion, I use the *Pravda* version of McKay's speech (25 Nov. 1922) and my own English translation, along with the English version found in the *International Press Correspondent,* "Report on the Negro Question," Jan. 5, 1923, 16–17. Further citations noted parenthetically in text.

32 Because *Pravda* was the party paper, the translation was likely done without McKay's knowledge and by a translator unfamiliar with McKay. In the case of McKay's books, however, the translations from English to Russian were done by his friend P. F. Okhrimenko. Correspondence from McKay to Okhrimenko indicates that the two men were on quite friendly terms. In one letter McKay writes, "Thank you for all the help that you gave me while I was in Russia—a real gods-fate-send that I met you. And also be assured that you can always call on me at any

time wherever I may be located—in America or in England—to do any service for you that you may think me capable of doing" (RGALI, 1673-1–30). In addition, a note McKay appended to the chapter "Negroes in Art and Music" suggests that McKay and Okhrimenko were in contact during the translation of *Negroes in America* (94). Because of McKay's apparent closeness to Okhrimenko, it cannot be assumed that the discrepancies evident in the *Pravda* translation of McKay's speech serve as examples of the kinds of discrepancies that may have appeared between the English versions of McKay's books and the Russian translations done by Okhrimenko.

33 Andrew Wachtel, "Translation, Imperialism, and National Self-Definition in Russia," *Public Culture* 11, no. 1 (winter 1999): 72.

34 This poem may well be the one McKay refers to in *A Long Way from Home* (7), when he describes the general excitement surrounding his presence in Moscow.

35 "Negritanskii Vopros," 367.

36 Ibid.

37 Liah Greenfeld, *Nationalism: Five Roads to Modernity* (Cambridge: Harvard University Press, 1992), 271.

38 Ibid., 270.

39 "Negritanskii Vopros," 367.

40 Ibid.

41 Letter to McKay, cited in *Negroes in America, 7.*

42 Evidence of Comintern awareness of Du Bois's views is documented by a copy of the demands established at the Third Pan-African Congress, signed by Du Bois and located in the Comintern files, RTSKhIDNI, 495–155–18.

43 William F. Dunne, *Workers Monthly* 4, no. 6 (April 1925): 260; cited in Wilson Record, *The Negro and the Communist Party* (Chapel Hill: University of North Carolina Press, 1951), 24; and Edward T. Wilson, *Russia and Black Africa before WWII* (New York: Holmes and Meier, 1974), 134.

44 James Jackson was a pseudonym used by Lovett Fort-Whiteman, the first national organizer of the ANLC, the Party unit created to organize black Americans. In 1937, Fort-Whiteman was targeted for punishment under Stalin. The Comintern record of Whiteman's involvement with the CP has been documented in Harvey Klehr, John Earl Haynes, and Kiril Mikhailovich Anderson, *The Soviet World of American Communism* (New Haven, Conn.: Yale University Press, 1998), which uses Whiteman as the example of how poorly black Americans were treated by the Soviets. One of the first black American students to attend KUTVA, Fort-Whiteman arrived in Moscow in 1924; he spent the subsequent years working for the Party in Chicago, moving back to Moscow in 1933. Sentenced to five years of external exile for "anti-Soviet agitation" in 1937, Fort-Whiteman spent a year in Kazakhstan, whereupon his sentence was changed to five years of hard labor and he was sent to a gulag in northeastern Siberia, where he died within a year (see

Klehr, Haynes, and Anderson, *The Soviet World*, 218–27). Although *The Soviet World* claims that the records "do not say what Fort-Whiteman had done that displeased the Comintern and the CPUSA" (221), a Comintern file indicates that Fort-Whiteman was being viewed with suspicion from the onset of his Moscow career. A confidential "editorial note" appended to the file on one of Fort-Whiteman's Comintern essays ("Some Suggestions Pertaining to the Proposed Negro World Congress to Be Held in Moscow") reads, "Comrade Jackson is shifting from the Communist to the petty bourgeoisie nationalist point of view. He says 'antagonism is not so much class as racial antagonism.' Such arguments are superficial" (RTSKhIDNI, 495–155–25, 73). Further indication of displeasure with Fort-Whiteman can be found in a memo (dated 22 May 1927) that details criticisms of his work for the ANLC, including "failure to initiate concrete struggles," "work in South neglected," "insufficient effort toward building the ANLC," "failure to work with other left-wingers," and "vague and incompetent direction" as a leader (RTSKhIDNI, 495–155–39, 1). While the tragedy of Fort-Whiteman is undeniable, the suggestion in *The Soviet World* that Fort-Whiteman's case is representative and therefore answers definitively the Negro question for Soviets overlooks the equally undeniable experiences of liberation and heightened racial consciousness expressed by other black Americans such as McKay, Hughes, Paul and Eslanda Robeson, Du Bois and Shirley Graham, Harry Haywood, William Patterson, Louise Thompson, and Oliver Golden. Citing Robert Robinson and Homer Smith as sources, *The Soviet World* relies on the testimony of black Americans who forcefully rejected the USSR and communism, alleging that "like many accounts written by American leftists disillusioned with the Soviet system, these books have been ignored by most scholars" (220). But the evidence supplied by Robinson and Homer is, as the authors themselves admit, based "on second- or third-hand information" (220) and hardly foundational source material for accounts of the period.

45 Even Edward T. Wilson reflects the connection between all blacks as ontological, de-emphasizing the linking possibilities of the shared experiences of exclusion, histories of disenfranchisement, and marginality to Western cultural paradigms.

46 V. Lenin, "The Socialist Revolution and the Right of Nations to Self-Determination (theses)," *The Rights of Nations to Self Determination* (New York: International Publishers, 1951), 83–84.

47 Wayne Cooper, *Claude McKay: Rebel Sojourner in the Harlem Renaissance* (Baton Rouge: Louisiana State University Press, 1987), 176.

48 For more information about Soviet and African relations prior to World War II, see Wilson, *Russia and Black Africa before WWII*, which argues against the prevailing Sovietology opinion that the Soviet Union had no interest in or real relationship with Africa prior to the 1950s. For the conventional Sovietologist take, see Helen Desfosses Cohn, *Soviet Policy toward Black Africa: The Focus on*

National Integration (New York: Praeger, 1974); and David E. Albright, ed. *Communism in Africa* (Bloomington: Indiana University Press, 1980).

49 Prerevolutionary interest in Africa included the groundbreaking work of V. S. Golenishchev (1856–1947), Russia's first Egyptologist; B. A. Turaev (1868–1920), the founder of the Russian school of ancient Oriental history, whose work in Egyptology stressed the cultural and artistic value of indigenous Egypt; the publication of the *Comparative Dictionary of all [African] Languages and Dialects* in 1790–1791, which served as the basis for further linguistic studies of such scholars as O. B. Lemm and A. L. Pogodin; geographic surveys sponsored by the Russian Geographical Society (founded in 1845); the ethnographic texts of M. G. Kokovtsov, E. P. Kovalevsky, W. W. Junker, and A. K. Bulatovich; and the art criticism of V. I. Matvey, whose book *Iskusstvo negrov* (*The Art of Negroes*) in 1914 presented the first readings of African art from an aesthetic viewpoint. See N. P. Gubina, ed., *Izuchenie afriki v rossii (dorevoliutzionnii period)* (Moscow: Izdatel'stvo Nauka, 1977). It should be pointed out, however, that antiethnocentric and anti-Western sentiments did not reflect or identify antipatriarchal aspirations.

50 Christopher Miller, *Blank Darkness: Africanist Discourse in French* (Chicago: University of Chicago Press, 1985), 64.

51 Ibid.

52 Isaiah Berlin, *Russian Thinkers* (New York: Viking, 1978), 118. Of course, not everyone agreed on the exact configuration of such "duality." The pochvenniki, or "native soil" thinkers, were the most influential—they believed, following Grigor'ev's lead, that "nationality" could not be divided; that it embraced the hopes and ideals of all society in an organic whole. See Derek Offord, "Lichnost': Notions of Individual Identity," in *Constructing Russian Culture in the Age of Revolution: 1881–1940*, ed. Catriona Kelly and David Shepherd (Oxford: Oxford University Press, 1998), 13–25.

53 W. E. B. Du Bois, *The Souls of Black Folk* (1903; reprint, New York: Bantam, 1989), 8.

54 Paul Gilroy, *The Black Atlantic: Modernity and Double Consciousness* (Cambridge: Harvard University Press, 1993), 12.

55 Again, although these models could be conceived as "other" to the dominating paradigms of Western philosophies of identity, the presumption of male representativeness within these models went unchallenged, and should be noted.

56 The repeated delay in setting a concrete date and location for the Negro Congress outlined in the Fourth Comintern Congress's theses is documented in the Comintern files (RTSKhIDNI, 495–155–14).

57 In *A Long Way from Home*, McKay recalls that he met Katayama in the United States and that Katayama greeted him warmly when he arrived in Moscow in 1922. McKay describes Katayama as "my first Japanese friend" who "made me

think of a fearless and faithful little hunting dog." In continuing to display his own adeptness at stereotyping people by race, McKay goes on to say that his fascination with Katayama made it "exciting to contrast Chinese and Japanese by the types I had known." On the political front, Katayama was "*the* Japanese revolutionist. . . . [H]e was regarded as an authority on all colored peoples' affairs. He had more real inside and sympathetic knowledge and understanding of American Negroes than many of the white American Communists who were camping in Moscow" (*ALWFH*, 164–65).

58 As should be clear, McKay was not an official CPUSA delegate, but his membership in the Party remains uncertain. Although there is no documentation supporting an official membership, in an 18 May 1923 letter to his friend and translator Okhrimenko, McKay indicates his allegiance to the party by closing with the phrase, "With Communist Party and fraternal wishes, yours sincerely, Claude McKay" (RGALI, 1673–1–30).

59 Among those accounts that insist that the U.S. party was a mouthpiece for Moscow are Irving Howe and Lewis Coser, *The American Communist Party: A Critical History, 1919–1957* (Boston: Beacon, 1957); Theodore Draper, *The Roots of American Communism* (New York: Viking, 1957), and *American Communism and Soviet Russia: The Formative Period* (New York: Viking, 1960); Max Kampelman, *The Communist Party vs. the C.I.O: A Study in Power Politics* (New York: Praeger, 1957); Harvey Klehr, *The Heyday of American Communism: The Depression Decade* (New York: Basic Books, 1984); and Harvey Klehr and John Earl Haynes, *The American Communist Movement: Storming Heaven Itself* (New York: Twayne Publishers, 1992). Among those accounts that dissent from the assessment that the CPUSA was a Moscow puppet are Robert W. Griffith and Nathan Theoharis, eds., *The Specter: Original Essays on the Cold War and the Origins of McCarthyism* (New York: New Viewpoints, 1974); Maurice Isserman, *Which Side Were You On? The American Communist Party during the Second World War* (Middletown, Conn.: Wesleyan University Press, 1982); Ellen W. Schrecker, *No Ivory Tower: McCarthyism and the Universities* (New York: Oxford University Press, 1986); Michael Brown, Frank Rosengarten, Randy Martin, and George Snedeker, eds., *New Studies in the Politics and Culture of U.S. Communism* (New York: Monthly Review, 1993); Bill Mullen and Sherry Linkon, eds., *Radical Representations: Rereading 1930s' Culture* (Urbana: University of Illinois Press, 1996); Bill Mullen, *Popular Fronts: Chicago and African-American Cultural Politics, 1935–1946* (Urbana: University of Illinois Press, 1999); as well as the work of Mark Naison, Robin D. G. Kelley, Mark Solomon, William J. Maxwell, and James Smethurst discussed above.

60 Klehr, Haynes, and Anderson, *The Soviet World*, 106.

61 This quote is taken from an article titled "Soviets Spread 'Red' Doctrines among Negroes" by Donald Ewing that is located in the indicated Comintern file; al-

though the date is provided (1 April 1924), the article's provenance is not (RTSKhIDNI, 495–155–27, 6).

62 As time went on, Soviets became more suspicious of U.S. attitudes toward race, fearing that class concerns were not being given their due weight. Articulating distrust of U.S. Communists, one Comintern memo reads, "Negroes were not born with saddles on their backs, nor were whites born with spurs on their feet. Racial discrimination and persecution of Negroes only dates from the origin of class society, especially since the inception of capitalism. . . . That Negro antagonism is directed against Negro workers and Negro merchants alike does not by any means alter the bourgeois nature of this antagonism: for is not the oppression of the economically backward countries and colonies also directed to a certain extent against all the classes in these conditions. . . . Our American comrades do not yet know how to approach the Negro question. Instead of unmasking the class character of the racial antagonism, they simply ignore the racial problem. In our opinion American Communists must not only pay more attention to this problem in their work among Negroes but should devote more attention to the world Negro liberation movement in general. They must support it at the same time combating its petty bourgeois utopian features, especially its slogan 'Back to Africa'" (RTSKhIDNI, 495–155–25, 73).

63 For a lively discussion of the work of Kollontai in the context of NEP restructuring, see Eric Naiman, "Revolutionary Anorexia: NEP as Female Complaint," *Slavic and East European Journal* 37, no. 3 (fall 1993): 305–25. For a more general exploration of Kollontai's role as a feminist agitator, see Christine Faure, "The Utopia of the New Woman in the Work of Alexandra Kollontai, and Its Impact on the French Feminist and Communist Press," in *Women in Culture and Politics: A Century of Change,* ed. Judith Friedlander, Wiesen Cook Blanche, Alice Kessler Harris, and Carroll Smith Rosenberg (Bloomington: Indiana University Press, 1986), 376–89).

64 At the same time, McKay was also commissioned to gather materials on the Russian Revolution to be compiled into a book for U.S. readers, but this project was never completed.

65 As I mention above, the exception is William J. Maxwell's *New Negro, Old Left.* Whereas Maxwell's focus is on the instrumentality of McKay's proclamations to Comintern policy, I concentrate on McKay's Soviet archive and the way it reveals a more ambiguous relationship between party resolution of the Negro question in 1922 and McKay's own formulations of the interrelatedness between the Negro and woman questions.

66 Wachtel, "Translation, Imperialism," 71.

67 McKay's thoughts about social equality had an impact on his colleagues in Moscow. A memo addressed "For Comrade Radek" written by Sen Katayama

confirms McKay's influence on someone McKay called the "authority on all colored peoples' affairs" (*ALWFH*, 165). Dated 14 July 1923 and titled "Negro Race as Factor in Coming World Social Revolution," Katayama's essay states that "the American Negro question cannot be solved simply on the economic ground. [The problems] are above all racial, which involves social, political, and economic interwoven each and the other. Now what are the American Negro problems looked at from the Negro side? The American Negro demands among other things the recognition of his social equality first of all, and his political and economic equality" (RTSKhIDNI 495–155–17). Katayama then proceeds to quote a long section from McKay's *Negroes in America*. Of course, within the Comintern itself, there was dissent against the notion that the Negro problem was "above all racial." Another memo by Israel Ampter, a leading figure in the U.S. Communist Party in the 1920s, states, "The CI [Comintern] must point out to the 150,000,000 Negroes of Africa and America that their problem is merely a phase of the general problem of emancipation of the working class of the world (the Negro is 'doomed' to supply cheap labor). . . . In the final analysis it is a class problem and can only be solved when the working class as a whole unites in struggle for emancipation" (RTSKhIDNI, 495–155–17, 24–33).

68 Marian B. McLeod, "Claude McKay's Russian Interpretation: *The Negroes in America*," *College Language Association Journal* 23 (1980): 337.

69 Structurally this link is echoed by the placement at the end of *Negroes in America* of a short story, "Out of Texas." This story of a falsely accused, light-skinned black man who is programmatically condemned under the "lynch law" offers a thematic link to the focus of the collection. "Out of Texas" is made up of a series of stories that are versions of the same incident, or nonincident, and their intertwinement reveals not simply the intersecting dimensions of fact and fiction but that storytelling can be an act with material consequences. The lives depicted in "Out of Texas" are contained within stories that precede them. As a meditation on the power of collectively formed images and narratives to make and break lives, "Out of Texas" makes available an alternate narrative that by indicting white female collaboration in the persecution of black men, enjoins the reader to contemplate the smoke screen of sex. By including this story in *Negroes in America* McKay makes available to Russians a narrative that links his reiteration of communist dogma to his hopes for a different future, a pledge toward historical possibility that turns on the linked figurations of racial and sexual difference.

70 *Trial by Lynching*, hereafter cited parenthetically as *TBL*, 8.

71 See Mayne, *Kino and the Woman Question;* Stites, *The Women's Liberation Movement in Russia.*

72 For an invaluable elaboration of this kind of racial collusion, see David R. Roediger's analysis of Du Bois's idea of a "psychological wage" in order to discuss

the historical alliance of working-class whites along racial (and not class) lines in *The Wages of Whiteness: Race and the Making of The American Working Class* (London: Verso, 1991).

73 On the problematic coupling of "blacks and women," an often-used designation that seems at once to deny the existence of women of color and assume that there is no overlap between the two groupings, see Robyn Wiegman, *American Anatomies: Theorizing Race and Gender* (Durham, N.C.: Duke University Press, 1995).

74 Elena Kartseva omits the film in her catalog of "Amerikanskaie nemye fil'my v Sovetskom prokate" ("American Silent Films in Soviet Distribution"), in *Kino i vremya* 1 (Moscow, 1960): 193–225.

75 See Jay Leyda, *Kino: A History of the Russian and Soviet Film* (Princeton, N.J.: Princeton University Press, 1983), 236.

76 Sergei Eisenstein, *Film Form* (New York: Harcourt Brace Jovanovich, 1977).

77 Sergei Gerassimov, "Out of the Factory of the Eccentric Actor," in *Cinema in Revolution*, ed. Luda Schnitzer, Jean Schnitzer, and Marcel Martin (New York: Da Capo, 1973), 115.

78 Eisenstein, *Film Form*, 234.

79 Sergei Eisenstein, *Immoral Memories*, trans. Herbert Marshall (Boston: Houghton Mifflin, 1983), 5.

80 In addition to Michael Rogin's account, discussed below, instructive looks at the film can be found in Jane Gaines, "Birthing Nations," in *Cinema and Nation*, ed. Mette Hjort and Scott MacKenie (London: Routledge, 2000), 298–316; Amy Kaplan, "The Birth of an Empire," *PMLA* 114, no. 5 (October 1999): 1068–76; and Richard Dyer, "Into the Light: The Whiteness of the South in the Birth of a Nation," in *Dixie Debates: Perspectives on Southern Culture*, ed. Richard H. King and Helen Taylor (New York: New York University Press, 1996), 165–76.

81 Eisenstein, *Film Form*, 235.

82 For an illuminating discussion of the film in terms of the new woman, see Michael Rogin, *Ronald Reagan the Movie, and Other Episodes in Political Demonology* (Berkeley: University of California Press, 1987), 198–200. For a discussion of the representation of women in early Soviet film, see Maya Turovskaya, "Women and the 'Woman Question' in the USSR," in *Red Women on the Silver Screen: Soviet Women and Cinema from the Beginning to the End of the Communist Era*, ed. Lynne Attwood (London: Pandora, 1993), 133–40.

83 In this sense, McKay's revamping of the Negro folk idiom reflects a similar move in a Soviet reconstitution of peasant fiction during this period—a reconfiguration that endorsed the city over the village. This parallelism indicates a tendency on the part of Soviets to think of the Negro question along the lines of the peasant one—both were to become proletarian. Peasant writers, as Katerina Clark ("The City versus the Countryside in Soviet Peasant Literature of the Twenties: A Duel

of Utopias," in *Bolshevik Culture*, ed. Abbott Gleason, Peter Kenez, and Richard Stites [Bloomington: Indiana University Press, 1985]) has demonstrated, accommodated this demand by promoting the city and its role in modernization, parroting Marx's remark about the "idiocy of village life" (186).

84 Fears about interracialism were reflected in U.S. immigration policies of the 1920s and, as Werner Sollors has helpfully elaborated in his recent work, have to this day contributed to the difficulties in writing U.S. histories in languages other than English. To address the problem of multilingual radical factions in the early part of the twentieth century the CPUSA established special language sectors so that non-English speakers could participate in the Party.

85 This line of thinking is indebted to Thorstein Veblen's theories of self-ownership and the leisure class outlined in his *The Theory of the Leisure Class* (1899; reprint, New York: Penguin, 1979). Two essays that draw on Veblen's analysis have been formative to my thinking here. They are Walter Benn Michaels's analysis of Edith Wharton's *The House of Mirth* in *The Gold Standard and the Logic of Naturalism: American Literature at the Turn of the Century* (Berkeley: University of California Press, 1987); and Margit Stange, "Personal Property: Exchange Value and the Female Self in *The Awakening*," *Genders* (1989): 106–19.

86 The idea of woman as a conduit of homosocial exchange between men has been brilliantly elaborated by Eve Kosofsky Sedgwick in *Between Men: English Literature and Male Homosocial Desire* (New York: Columbia University Press, 1985).

87 Wiegman, *American Anatomies*, 84, 83.

88 Again, evidence that McKay's work was in dialogue with the Comintern can be found in the Comintern archives where one reads of the "obscene sex-consciousness of the American nation." An essay by Sen Katayama elaborates, "American Negroes are periodically lynched for any or no offense and the cause is generally attributed to the 'rape of a white woman.' But Negro women are lynched also and burnt at the stake for instance. And the Northern states also fully share with the Southern enjoyment of the exclusively American national sport. Indeed, the whole white American nation is strangely possessed of a Negro neurosis" (RTSKhIDNI, 495–155–17, 13–23).

89 Wiegman, *American Anatomies*, 82.

90 Maxwell, *New Negro, Old Left*, 87.

91 Rogin, *Ronald Reagan*, 207.

92 The scenes recall what Jean Toomer describes so vividly in *Cane:* the image of mutilated black flesh lingering in the image of the white female body. Toomer writes, "And her slim white body, white as the ash / of black flesh after flame" ("Portrait in Georgia," *Cane* [1923; reprint, New York: W. W. Norton, 1988], 29).

93 Wiegman, *American Anatomies*, 84.

94 "The Mulatto Girl" hereafter cited parenthetically as MG, 27.

95 Nancy Armstrong, "The Rise of the Domestic Woman," in *Ideology of Conduct: Essays in Literature and the History of Sexuality,* ed. Nancy Armstrong and Leonard Tennenhouse (New York: Methuen, 1987), 136.

96 "The Soldier's Return," hereafter cited parenthetically as SR, 38.

97 The Russian word "pomes" carries more of a pejorative sense than our current understanding of "hybrid." See *Negry v Amerike,* 93.

98 Cited in McKay, *Trial by Lynching,* vii.

99 Claude McKay, "Soviet Russia and the Negro," in *The Passion of Claude McKay,* by Wayne Cooper (New York: Schocken Books, 1977), 101.

100 Ibid.

101 Gilroy, *Black Atlantic,* 17.

102 McKay, "Soviet Russia," 100.

103 "Socialism and the Negro," in *The Passion of Claude McKay,* 54.

104 McKay, "Soviet Russia," 105. McKay relates an anecdote in "Soviet Russia" told to him by the much-respected literary critic Kornei Chukovsky. In brief, when in London lodging at a cheap inn, Chukovsky met a Negro preacher and suggested he board at the same inn. After the preacher had secured a room and been there for several days, he encountered a white American family in the communal dining room. The family protested the clergyman's presence, and the landlady decided to deny him dining room privileges to assuage their objections. Chukovsky was given the task of informing the preacher, "but the black man was not unduly offended: 'The white guests have the right to object to me,' he explained, anticipating Garvey, 'they belong to a superior race.' 'But,' said Chukovsky, 'I do not object to you, I don't feel any difference; we don't understand color prejudice in Russia.' 'Well,' philosophized the preacher, 'you are very kind, but taking the scriptures as authority, I don't consider the Russians to be white people'" (106).

105 On this point, McKay refers to the African ancestry of the Russian national poet, Alexander Pushkin. Pushkin served as a model for McKay, as he did for Hughes and Robeson after him, of a writer whose ancestry did not hinder the public perception of his achievements as an artist.

106 One of the writers McKay met while in Russia, Evgenii Zamiatin—best known for his antiutopian novel *We* (1924) in which a Negro poet, perhaps based on a fusion of McKay and Pushkin, is one of the main characters—composed complex black characters in his work. For example, in a story titled "Africa" (1916), the protagonist is a Russian Arctic fisherman who meets a young woman who speaks a language he doesn't understand, which turns out to be an African dialect, and he falls heedlessly in love with her only for her to disappear as part of an illusory dream. The protagonist attempts to realize his dream by raising the money to travel to Africa, but reaches his destination only in an implied afterlife. (Evgenii Zamiatin, *Sobrannie Sochinenii* [Moscow: Fedoratsiia, 1929]). In 1929–30 Zamiatin also wrote a play that addresses similar themes titled "Afrikanskii gost'" /

"The African Guest." The play, never performed, was only published in 1963. See *Novii zhurnal*, no. 73 (1963): 38–95.

2. BETWEEN HAREM AND HARLEM:
HUGHES AND THE WAYS OF THE VEIL

1   Letter from Bontemps to Hughes, 14 November 1939, in Arna Bontemps, *Arna Bontemps/Langston Hughes Letters, 1925–1967*, ed. Charles H. Nichols (New York: Paragon, 1990), 41.

2   Letter from Hughes to Bontemps, April 1956, in ibid., 343. Compare this statement to Du Bois's similar one in *Dusk of Dawn: An Essay Towards an Autobiography of a Race Concept* (1940; reprint, New Brunswick, N.J.: Transaction Publishers, 1997) in which he states that autobiographies "assume too much or too little: too much in dreaming that one's own life has greatly influenced the world; too little in the reticences, repressions and distortions which come because men do not dare to be absolutely frank" (xxix).

3   Langston Hughes, "In an Emir's Harem," *Woman's Home Companion* (September 1934): 12, 91–92; "Farewell to Mahomet," *Travel Magazine* (February 1935): 29–31; "Soviet Theater in Central Asia," *Asia: Journal of the American Asiatic Association* (October 1934): 590–93; "Tamara Khanum: Soviet Asia's Greatest Dancer," *Theatre Arts* (November 1934): 829–35; and "Boy Dancers of Uzbekistan," *Travel Magazine* (December 1934): 36–37, 49–50. Other works from this period are "Negroes in Moscow," *International Literature* 1 (1933): 78–81; "Going South in Russia," *Crisis* (June 1934): 162–63; and "Moscow and Me," *International Literature* 1 (1933): 61–66.

4   Arnold Rampersad, *The Life of Langston Hughes, Volume II: 1941–1967, I Dream a World* (New York: Oxford University Press, 1988), 216. See also Langston Hughes, "Langston Hughes Speaks," *Crisis* 60, no. 5 (May 1953): 279–80.

5   Arnold Rampersad, *The Life of Langston Hughes, Volume II*, 220.

6   On the subject of homophobia in the 1950s, see Robert Corber, *Homosexuality in Cold War America: Resistance and the Crisis of Masculinity* (Durham, N.C.: Duke University Press, 1997); Alan Nadel, *Containment Culture: American Narratives, Postmodernism, and the Atomic Age* (Durham, N.C.: Duke University Press, 1995); and Thomas Dumm, "The Trial of J. Edgar Hoover," in *Secret Agents: The Rosenberg Case, McCarthyism, and Fifties America*, ed. Marjorie Garber and Rebecca L. Walkowitz (New York: Routledge, 1995), 77–92.

7   In "The Trial of J. Edgar Hoover," Dumm provides an insightful reading of Cohn that suggests that it was indeed because of his empowered political position that Cohn was so adamantly against gay rights, that desire for Cohn had everything to do with political (and not sexual per se) brokering. He argues, correctly I think, that Cohn cannot be easily assimilated into the conventional definition of homosexual as "men who sleep with men," and in this conclusion draws on Tony

Kushner's extraordinary play *Angels in America, a Gay Fantasia on National Themes: Part One, Millennium Approaches* (New York: Theatre Communications Group, 1993), as well as earlier queer commentary on Cohn iconography, such as Robert Mapplethorpe's photo portrait and Ron Vawter's performance piece *Roy Cohn/Jack Smith* (1992). Dumm's essay also points to the connection to Klaus Theweleit's *Male Fantasies* discussed below in the context of Arthur Koestler. In addition to Dumm's account, see Michael Cadden, "Strange Angel: The Pinklisting of Roy Cohn," in *Secret Agents: The Rosenberg Case, McCarthyism, and Fifties America*, ed. Marjorie Garber and Rebecca L. Walkowitz (New York: Routledge, 1995), 93–106.

8   See U.S. Senate, "Employment of Homosexuals and Other Sex Perverts in the U.S. Government," in *We Are Everywhere: A Historical Sourcebook of Gay and Lesbian Politics*, ed. Mark Blasius and Shane Phelan (New York: Routledge, 1997), 241–51. I am indebted to Siobhan Somerville for bringing this directive to my attention.

9   Cited in Rampersad, *Life of Langston Hughes, Volume II*, 216.

10 James Smethurst writes, "Hughes's poems of the 1930s are almost always explicitly or implicitly in a male voice and often addressed to a male listener" (*The New Red Negro: The Literary Left and African American Poetry, 1930–1946* (New York: Oxford University Press, 1999), 57.

11 As I will discuss below, Soviet interpretation of its own intervention in this region as by definition anti-imperialist is, given compulsory de-Islamicization and reterritorialization, somewhat problematic.

12 Hughes, "Boy Dancers," 37; hereafter cited parenthetically as BD.

13 Hughes, "Tamara Khanum," 832; hereafter cited parenthetically as TK.

14 The interrelated productions of race and homosexuality in the United States are illuminated by Siobhan Somerville, *Queering the Color Line: Race and the Invention of Homosexuality in American Culture* (Durham, N.C.: Duke University Press, 2000).

15 An elaboration of homosocial anxiety, from which I draw the phrase, can be found in Eve Kosofsky Sedgwick's powerful and enormously influential *Epistemology of the Closet* (Berkeley: University of California Press, 1990). See also her collection of essays *Tendencies* (Durham, N.C.: Duke University Press, 1993).

16 Marjorie Garber, *Vested Interests: Cross Dressing and Cultural Anxiety* (New York: Routledge, 1992), 10.

17 This is undoubtedly a reference to the first chapter of Stein's *The Autobiography of Alice B. Toklas* (New York: Harcourt Brace and Company 1933), in which she writes, "I may say that only three times in my life have I met a genius and each time a bell within me has rang and I was not mistaken, and I may say in each case it was before there was any general recognition of the quality of genius in them" (9).

18   Homosexuality has, of course, also been theorized as a desire for difference. See Biddy Martin, "Sexualities without Genders and Other Queer Utopias," *diacritics* 24 (summer–fall 1994): 104–21.

19   Indeed, an interrelatedness between various geographic locales in Hughes's articulation of self appears in his "possible titles" for his autobiography: *Harlem to Samarkand, From Harlem to Samarkand, Around the World Home,* and *Harlem to Samarkand and Around the World Home.*

20   See Lynne Attwood and Catriona Kelly, "Programmes for Identity: The 'New Man' and the 'New Woman,'" in *Constructing Russian Culture in the Age of Revolution: 1881–1940,* ed. Catriona Kelly and David Shepherd (Oxford: Oxford University Press, 1998), 256–85.

21   Langston Hughes, *A Negro Looks at Soviet Central Asia* (Moscow: International Publishers, 1934), 40.

22   Langston Hughes, "One More 'S' in the USA," *The Collected Poems of Langston Hughes,* ed. Arnold Rampersad (New York: Knopf, 1995), 177.

23   *Liberator,* 14 November 1931; cited in Robin D. G. Kelley, *Race Rebels: Culture, Politics, and the Black Working Class* (New York: Free Press, 1994), 119.

24   Louise Thompson Patterson, "Louise Thompson Patterson Memoirs: Trip to Russia—1932," draft 2, October–November 1994, 3; hereafter cited parenthetically as LTP 2.

25   Because Thompson's record of the trip was never published, it has taken a backseat to other accounts, of which Hughes's is the best known. As Thompson asserts in her account, Hughes was in many ways the celebrity member of their group, and the Soviets were especially attentive to him. "Anything he wanted seemed to be available to him," she recalls. And yet, in spite of whatever imbalance in attention the Soviets may have fostered, Thompson remains sanguine about her own and the others' treatment: "We are just living like royalty," she writes. "Everywhere we go we are treated as honored guests, given enthusiastic ovations and offered the best." Louise Thompson Patterson, "Louise Thompson Patterson Memoirs: Trip to Russia—," draft 1, n.d., 51, 60–61; hereafter cited parenthetically as LTP 1.

26   Louise Thompson to Langston Hughes, 9 May 1932, Langston Hughes correspondence, James Weldon Johnson Collection, Beneicke Rare Book and Manuscript Library, Yale University, box 149.

27   Langston Hughes, *I Wonder as I Wander* (New York: Thunder Mouth Press, 1956), 76. For more information on *Black and White,* see Hughes, *I Wonder as I Wander;* Rampersad, *Life of Langston Hughes, Volume I,* 242–75; Faith Berry, *Langston Hughes: Before and Beyond Harlem* (Westport, Conn.: L. Hill, 1983), 154–71; and LTP Drafts 1–3.

28   Louise Thompson to Langston Hughes, 27 May 1932, Langston Hughes correspondence, box 149.

29 Possible reasons for the film's failure to reach completion are outlined in Berry, *Before and Beyond Harlem*, 160–71. In her memoir, Thompson supplies a first-hand account that, without contradicting Berry, provides some much-needed context for Berry's assertion that the group was used as a political pawn.

30 Rampersad, *Life of Langston Hughes, Volume I*, 256.

31 See, for example, "Howard and Virginia State Graduates as Specialists Help Russia Grow Cotton," an article that reports the "first black baby born in Middle Asia in Modern Days" in *Afro-American*, 12 November 1932, 6; "Russian Doesn't Give a Damn about Race," *Afro-American*, 19 November 1932, 2; and Chatwood Hall [Homer Smith], "New Jersey Youth Abroad Takes Russia Bride," *Afro-American*, 25 February 1933, 3.

32 See Yelena Khanga, *Soul to Soul: A Black Russian Jewish Woman's Search for Her Roots* (New York: W. W. Norton, 1992); Harry Haywood, *Black Bolshevik: Autobiography of an Afro-American Communist* (Chicago: Liberator Press, 1978); Homer Smith, *Black Man in Red Russia: A Memoir* (Chicago: Johnson Publishing, 1964); and Robert Robinson, *Black on Red: A Black American's Forty-Four Years inside the Soviet Union* (Washington, D.C.: Acropolis Books, 1988).

33 Khanga, *Soul to Soul*, 76.

34 Unlike Robeson, who had befriended Golden through mutual communist connections and traveled in 1934 to the region specifically to witness the successful contributions of African Americans to Soviet industry, Hughes was unaware of the African American presence there. The fate of many of the members of this U.S. outpost is unknown, but by 1934 most of the original workers returned to the United States or were sent to other Soviet areas in need of agronomists. By 1938, Khanga writes, "every non-Soviet citizen in the group was ordered to leave the country, sometimes on forty-eight hours notice, unless he was willing to give up his American citizenship" (*Soul to Soul*, 91). Golden remained with his family in the USSR until his death in 1940. Like many of the narratives connecting Russia and African Americans, Golden's instrumentality in the creation of Soviet "white gold" (cotton) as a literal U.S.-Uzbek hybrid has been elided from official histories.

35 The group covered six thousand kilometers and toured six republics. Thompson records that independent of Hughes the group toured the Black Sea, returning several days later to Moscow.

36 "Louise Thompson Patterson Memoirs: Trip to Russia—1932," Draft 3, October–November 1994, 33, hereafter cited parenthetically as LTP 3.

37 Attesting to the strength of the veil as a metaphor for black racial consciousness, there exists an extensive number of intellectuals who have addressed Du Bois's veil. They include James Weldon Johnson, Werner Sollors, Anthony Appiah, Gerald Early, Nathan Huggins, and David Levering-Lewis. The potency of this metaphor as a signifier for black male racial consciousness has been further

underlined by Rampersad, who comments, "The most striking device in *The Souls of Black Folk* is Du Bois's adoption of the veil as the metaphor of black life in America . . . If any single idea guides the art of [this book] it is this concept. . . . The veil unites black men." Arnold Rampersad, *The Art and Imagination of W. E. B. Du Bois* (New York: Schocken Books, 1976), 79.

38 Cited in Henry Louis Gates Jr., introduction to *The Souls of Black Folk*, by W. E. B. Du Bois (1903; reprint, New York: Bantam, 1989), xiv.

39 W. E. B. Du Bois, *The Souls of Black Folk* (1903; reprint, New York: Bantam, 1989), 2, 6.

40 See Paul Gilroy, *The Black Atlantic: Modernity and Double Consciousness* (Cambridge: Harvard University Press, 1993), 120–24.

41 See Robert Young, *Colonial Desire: Hybridity in Theory, Culture, and Race* (London: Routledge, 1995).

42 Robyn Wiegman, *American Anatomies: Theorizing Race and Gender* (Durham, N.C.: Duke University Press, 1995), 94.

43 Du Bois, *Souls*, 2.

44 In designating the relative irrelevance of female desire and/or subjectivity, Du Bois's veil thus codes itself in terms that Sedgwick has elaborated in her work on "homo-social" desire in *Epistemology of the Closet*.

45 Even as subtle a reading as Garber's discussion of Du Bois's veil in terms of its marking of the radical indeterminacy of gender—what she calls "gender as an effect of race"—fails to comment on the links between Du Bois's veil and its Orientalist predecessors or the heteronormative economy that his discussion of the veil subtends. See Garber, *Vested Interests*, 290–91.

46 Du Bois, *Souls*, 2, 187.

47 For example, Hughes's imaginary imposition of self onto other is enabled by a superficial association via skin color—an association that is itself the product of post-Enlightenment attempts to ontologize race, and thus his gesture is embedded in this semantic framework. In other words, this kind of "going native" embraces distance and impossibility as its foundation—an impossibility confessed through a relentless attack on the other, veiled woman not merely as backward but as outside representation. Then again, it is precisely such impossibility (the objectless identification) that enables a renunciation of the terms of "identity." My interest, however, is in the specific bodies that allow such renunciation, in this case exclusively *female* ones, and what happens to them.

48 By "traditional" I mean in terms of Friedrich Nietzsche's account of the veil as a surface through which he challenges the "reality" and "truth" of a philosophy of "depth," and his depiction of women as epitomizing such a fusion of seeming and being; readings of the Orient as mysterious, enigmatic, and exotic, thereby denying Western attempts to conquer and know it, while at the same time providing a

blank screen on which to project such inscrutable otherness; as well as psychoanalytic insights that place the veil at the center of debates about vision, delusion, distrust, and the seductive powers of the feminine.

49 Winifred Woodhull, *Transfigurations of the Maghres* (Minneapolis: University of Minnesota Press, 1993), 3, 4. See also Chandra Talpade Mohanty, "Under Western Eyes: Feminist Scholarship and Colonial Discourse," in *Third World Women and the Politics of Feminism*, ed. Chandra Talpade Mohanty, Ann Russo, and Lourdes Torres (Bloomington: Indiana University Press, 1991), 51–80.

50 Mohanty, "Under Western Eyes," 74.

51 See Malek Alloula, *The Colonial Harem* (Minneapolis: University of Minnesota Press, 1986); Lila Abu-Lughod, *Veiled Sentiments: Honor and Poetry in a Bedouin Society* (Berkeley: University of California Press, 1986); Fatima Mernissi, *Dreams of Trespass: Tales of a Harem Girlhood* (Reading, MA: Addison Wesley, 1994) and *Beyond the Veil: Male-Female Dynamics in Modern Muslim Society* (Bloomington: Indiana University Press, 1987); Leila Ahmed, *Women and Gender in Islam* (New Haven, Conn.: Yale University Press, 1992); Assia Djebar, *l'amour la fantasia* (Paris, 1995); and Inderpal Grewal, *Home and Harem: Nation, Gender, Empire, and the Cultures of Travel* (Durham, N.C.: Duke University Press, 1996).

52 Grewal, *Home and Harem*, 19.

53 Mernissi has further elaborated on this argument to demonstrate how, in Morocco, during the 1940s and 1950s of her youth, the harem was less a specific place than an intuited boundary, a way of structuring the world, for women who were its members. As a metaphor for the harem, then, the veil served as a reminder of this ordering principle. As a curtain of separation, the veil removes the woman from public commerce, shields her with perceivable but invisible boundaries that induct her into proper spatial coordinates; this "veil" then becomes a woman's assertion of social stability by operating as a private, intuited boundary around an integrated selfhood. At the same time, the veil acts as a protective shield from the occidental spectacle of the gaze, which seeks knowledge through visibility. See Mernissi, *Dreams of Trespass* and *Beyond the Veil*. See also Alloula, *The Colonial Harem*.

54 It should be noted here that the influx of British imperialists into Central Asia in the nineteenth century set the standard for the Russian imperialists who were to follow, and in the literature of colonial Russia the trope of the veil resembles that found in British tales. The choice, then, of Soviet revolutionaries to focus primarily on the "liberation" of women as a stand-in proletariat reflects the influence of Euro-imperial attitudes toward Islamic culture; the notion of Asian backwardness; and a firm belief in the barbarous traditions of Uzbek despotism as fundamentally lacking in "civil society," or a proper distance between the state and individual. The fact that Russia, having endured three centuries of Mongol rule, had long wondered where it sat in relation to the "East" made this config-

uration slightly more complicated: in the words of Stephanie Sandler, "When Russia contemplates 'Asia' it sees not only people who had once conquered it, but also peoples whose cultures have left their imprint on Russia's own" (*Distant Pleasures: Alexander Pushkin and the Writing of Exile* [Stanford, Calif.: Stanford University Press, 1989]), 180. Adopting standard colonial policy toward Islam provided Russia with the opportunity to impose a necessary distance from the imprint of Asia by appearing European, for Russia's own imperial rule had itself been depicted as despotic. Importing Orientalist paradigms about Islamic culture, Russia could portray Uzbeks as barbaric while ignoring their own treatment of serfs under the mandate of "civilization."

55 Langston Hughes, *I Wonder as I Wander*, manuscript, James Weldon Johnson Collection, Beneicke Rare Book and Manuscript Library, Yale University, folder 2.

56 Hughes, "Going South in Russia," 75, cited in Berry, *Good Morning Revolution*, hereafter cited parenthetically as GSIR.

57 Langston Hughes, "The Soviet Union and Color," *Chicago Defender*, 15 June 1946, 89, cited in Berry, *Good Morning Revolution*, 85. Hereafter cited parenthetically as *SUC*.

58 Hughes, "Farewell to Mahomet," 47.

59 Anna Louise Strong, *I Change Worlds: The Remaking of an American* (New York: Garden City Publishing, 1937), 280.

60 I am drawing on Edward Said's work in his landmark study *Orientalism* (New York: Pantheon, 1978).

61 Hughes, *I Wonder as I Wander*, 116.

62 Hughes, *I Wonder as I Wander*, manuscript. Here, as elsewhere, Hughes indicates a confusion over place-names. Turkmenistan, Tadjikistan, and Uzbekistan are not clearly differentiated from one another in his papers.

63 Hughes, *I Wonder and I Wander*, 115.

64 See Klaus Theweleit, *Male Fantasies, Volume One: Women, Floods, Bodies, Histories*, trans. Stephen Conway (Minneapolis: University of Minnesota Press, 1987).

65 Hughes, *I Wonder as I Wander*, 115.

66 Ibid., 119.

67 Louise Thompson Patterson, "With Langston Hughes in the USSR," *Freedomways* 8, no. 2 (spring 1968): 158.

68 Hughes, *I Wonder as I Wander*, folder 1.

69 David Spurr, *The Rhetoric of Empire: Colonial Discourse in Journalism, Travel Writing, and Imperial Administration* (Durham, N.C.: Duke University Press, 1993), 143.

70 I am, of course, here referring to Barbara Johnson's citation of Paul de Man's descriptive passage about Archie and Edith Bunker, but with one critical difference in mind. Hughes's question, "Is this me?" unlike Archie's "What's the difference?" puts terms of alterity within the self on the line: instead of "denying us the

possibility of asking," and thereby suspending subjective judgment, Hughes's question destabilizes the certainty of a totalizing language of selfhood, thereby placing himself in the position of being judged by the other (Barbara Johnson, *A World of Difference* [Baltimore, Md.: Johns Hopkins University Press, 1987]), 39.

71 Cited in Homer Smith, "Hughes Reaches Moscow after Island Tour," *Afro-American*, 25 February 1933, 2–3.

72 Hughes's deployment of the terms of abjection rephrases the emancipatory potential of a model that has been most fully elaborated by Julia Kristeva in her book *Powers of Horror: An Essay on Abjection*, trans. Leon Roudiez (New York: Columbia University Press, 1982). Kristeva's model for abjection can help elucidate this feeling of oddness to oneself that Hughes so clearly articulates when he writes, "Is this me?" In Kristeva's words, "The one by whom the abject exists is thus a deject who places (himself), separates (himself), situates (himself), and therefore strays instead of getting his bearings, desiring, belonging, or refusing. Situationist in a sense . . . he divides, excludes, and without, properly speaking, wishing to know his abjections is not at all unaware of them. . . . Instead of sounding himself as to his 'being,' he does so concerning his place: 'Where am I?' instead of 'Who am I?' For the space that engrosses the deject, the excluded, is never one, nor homogeneous, nor totalizable. . . . [T]he deject is in short a stray" (8). It is, in fact, precisely the promise of such straying that promotes Hughes's repeated interest in the project of unveiling set forth by the Soviets, as a model for an emancipated African American selfhood. As Kristeva closes this passage, "And the more he strays, the more he is saved" (8). By attempting to locate himself "way over here in Asia," and in place of certainty finding a question, "Is this me?" Hughes documents how a continued sense of internal dislocation was enabled by an encounter with otherness. Kristeva contends that such interior discord describes the abject, which is "neither the subject nor the object. . . . It is a question, then, of a precarious state in which the subject is menaced by the possibility of collapsing into a chaos of indifference" (39). According to Kristeva, whenever subsequent identifications arise, the abject designates the self's boundaries by consistently recalling a rupture in primary identification. Serving as a recollection of this lack of differentiation toward which there is always a temptation to return, the abject situates a tension that keeps the subject from merging into nondifferentiation, but also denies idealized identification with (and absorption of) one's self-image. The ways in which Hughes accustoms himself to the question mark of identity, to an overhauling of propriety and instead to an ease with the feminine/"abject," again recollects the work he performed in order to establish his difference from Koestler.

73 Hughes's poem "Let America Be American Again" expresses this hope, excavating nostalgia's underbelly (the "America" that never was) and depicting the violence

there. If Americans believed that the integrity of their social system relied on a fulfillment of the claims of "equality," then inasmuch as a condoned, institutionalized racial discrimination—which segregation obviated—persisted, the United States could never be true to itself.

74 Mary Douglas, *Purity and Danger: An Analysis of the Concepts of Pollution and Taboo* (London: Routledge and Kegan Paul, 1966), 35.

75 Hughes, "Farewell to Mahomet," 30.

76 I might note that in the United States in the 1930s, "white" orbits would not have included Central Asia at all. In fact, Central Asia has until very recently been perceived as largely irrelevant to the United States.

77 Gregory J. Massell, *The Surrogate Proletariat: Moslem Women and Revolutionary Strategies in Soviet Central Asia, 1919–1929* (Princeton, N.J.: Princeton University Press, 1974), 93.

78 For a history of the Soviet remapping of Russian Bukhara, see Shirin Akiner, "Uzbeks," in *The Nationalist Question in the Soviet Union*, ed. Graham Smith (London: Longman Group, 1990), 214–27; and F. H. Skrine and E. D. Ross, *The Heart of Asia: A History of Russian Turkestan and the Central Asian Khanates from the Earliest Times* (London: Methuen, 1989), 238–428. For a discussion of the complexities of nation formation, see Ronald Grigor Suny, *The Revenge of the Past: Nationalism, Revolution, and the Collapse of the Soviet Union.* Stanford: Stanford University Press, 1993.

79 Akiner, "Uzbeks," 217.

80 In its reconstruction of the Oriental narrative, Hughes's work is not unlike that of Pushkin, the Russian poet of African descent of whom Hughes speaks with great reverence: "Pushkin! Pride of the Negroes . . . equal of Shakespeare, Dante, Goethe, in the literature of all time" ("Negroes in Moscow," 78). Familiar with Pushkin's major poems translated into English, Hughes had undoubtedly run across Pushkin's most famous harem poem, "Bakhchisarai fontan," a tale in which two women, one from the West and one from the East, are constructed as equals.

81 Hughes, "In an Emir's Harem," 12; hereafter cited parenthetically as EH.

82 As if anxious that Hughes's words alone would not suffice to entice the U.S. reader, the editors cemented suggestive verbal imagery with drawings. Adorning the opening page are overlapping sketches, drawn by Andre Durenceau, of camels, sheiks, and veiled women—and not, significantly, tractors, hammers, and sickle-bearing workers.

83 Hughes, "Farewell to Mahomet," 29. Hereafter cited parenthetically as FM.

84 Hughes, "The Soviet Union and Women," *Chicago Defender*, 29 June 1946, 89.

85 Inasmuch as one can assert such assessments (as based on advertisements, circulation statistics, and so on), *Woman's Home Companion*, to which I refer here, was directed to a "white" readership, which is not to say that nonwhite women

were not included in the mandate to "stay at home." They were included in gender segregation differently. For example, nonwhite women made up a majority of domestic servants whose primary occupation was, of course, to be at home, although usually not their own.

86 For a largely white readership, Hughes may well have operated as a compelling authority on "colored" issues no matter what the geographic locale.

87 Langston Hughes, *The Ways of White Folks* (1933; reprint, New York: Vintage, 1990); hereafter cited parenthetically as *WWF.*

88 Although some scholars have indicated Hughes's indebtedness to Lawrence with respect to the social realism and modernist irony of his tales, commentators have been reluctant to elaborate on the connections between Hughes's preoccupation with the feminine in his stories and Lawrence's own depiction of the feminine. They have been more reluctant still to link Hughes's engagement with female-imbued issues of isolation, propriety, and longing in his U.S.-directed short stories to similarly imbued concerns in his Uzbek-directed essays (see Rampersad, *The Life of Langston Hughes, Volume 1,* Hans Ostrom, *Langston Hughes: A Study of the Short Fiction* (New York: Twayne Publishers, 1993); Maryemma Graham, "The Practice of a Social Art," in *Langston Hughes: Critical Perspectives Past and Present,* ed. Henry Louis Gates Jr. and K. Anthony Appiah (New York: Amistad, 1993), 213–35; and Joyce Ann Joyce, "Race, Culture, and Gender in Langston Hughes's *The Ways of White Folks,*" in *Langston Hughes: The Man, His Art, and His Continuing Influence,* ed. C. James Trotman (New York: Garland Publishing, 1995).

89 Cited in Rampersad, *The Life of Langston Hughes, Volume 1,* 269.

90 For a discussion of Lawrence's influence on African American authors, see Leo Hamalian, "D. H. Lawrence and Black Writers," *Reader* 16, no. 4 (spring 1990): 579–96.

91 D. H. Lawrence, *The Lovely Lady* (London: Martin Secker, 1932) 92, 97. Hereafter cited parenthetically as *LL.*

92 See Ostrom, *Langston Hughes*; and Joyce, "Race, Culture, and Gender." The one exception is Graham, "The Practice of a Social Art." Graham does discuss Hughes's relationship with and travels to the Soviet Union, but like the other scholars mentioned, she does not connect *The Ways of White Folks* specifically to Hughes's writing about his Soviet experiences.

93 Joyce, "Race, Culture, and Gender," 99.

94 George W. Stocking Jr., *The Ethnographer's Magic and Other Essays in the History of Anthropology* (Madison: University of Wisconsin Press, 1992), 282.

95 On the relationship between Boas and Du Bois, see Lee Baker, *From Savage to Negro: Anthropology and the Construction of Race, 1896–1954* (Berkeley: University of California Press, 1998). Tzvetan Todorov, " 'Race,' Writing, and Culture" (in *"Race," Writing, and Difference,* ed. Henry Louis Gates Jr. [Chicago: University of Chicago Press, 1986]) makes the argument that the movement of coding race in

terms of "culture" was part of "nineteenth-century racialism" and its desire to move away from the pseudoscience on which notions of racial purity were based (174).

96   Again, Hughes's interest in the folk (most famously stressed in his essay "The Negro Artist and the Racial Mountain") provided another inroad for Soviet Communism, under whose mantle the folk was actively being reconstructed as the carrier of Soviet culture's authenticity. For more on the Soviet investment in the folk, see chapter 4. For an assessment of the Party's essentializing of black culture, see Kelley, *Race Rebels*, 116–18.

97   Kelley, *Race Rebels*, 121.

98   Ibid.

99   See ibid. See also James Smethurst, who in *The New Red Negro* makes the argument that in the black radicalism of the 1930s, "to the degree that the folk is somehow feminine, this femininity is associated with passivity, accommodationism, and racial self-hatred" (52).

100   Hughes, "The Soviet Theater in Central Asia," 591. Hereafter cited parenthetically as ST.

101   While retaining the edge of Hughes's critique of white supremacist structures, it is important not to ignore the fact that Cora's indictment is not a vague denunciation. It is aimed specifically at the white women who are Mrs. Art's colleagues, the women of the "Woman's Club." By "struggl[ing] against them all the way, accusing their women," Cora articulates the artifice of white femininity. Of course, Cora is revealing something that these women already know. Indeed, she is pinpointing the hypocrisy of veiled knowledge, of pretending one thing over and against another, of the masquerade of whiteness. Her political consciousness arises out of an apprehension of this substitution, and the related fear of the foreign on which it rests, as all about the ways of white folks.

102   Angela Davis, "Women and Capitalism: Dialectics of Oppression and Liberation," in *The Angela Y. Davis Reader*, ed. Joy James (Malden, Mass.: Blackwell, 1998), 164.

103   Hughes's engagement with the Negro mother as a redemptive figure stems back to a poem of the same title that appeared in the collection Hughes published just prior to his departure for Moscow. *The Negro Mother and Other Dramatic Recitations* (1931), with illustrations by Prentiss Taylor, extols the black woman as, in the words of Arnold Rampersad, "the hope of the race" (*The Life of Langston Hughes, Volume 1*, 222).

104   Joan W. Scott, "Experience," in *Feminists Theorize the Political*, ed. Judith Butler and Joan W. Scott (New York: Routledge, 1992), 37.

105   Hughes's choice of "Claudina Lawrence" suggests a tribute to Lawrence, and the role of catalyst that the two Lawrences share in common—for Arnie and his developing race consciousness, and for Hughes and his.

106 In *When Harlem Was in Vogue* (New York: Oxford University Press, 1979), David Levering Lewis emphasizes the importance of the experiences of black American troops, particularly in Paris, during World War I. See his chapter "We Return Fighting" (a title taken from Du Bois's "Returning Soldiers"), 3–24.

107 Gilroy, *The Black Atlantic*, 19.

108 As Gilroy himself admits, the black Atlantic model also insufficiently addresses the place of women and/or the feminine in this configuration of black transnationalism and modernity.

109 In this sense, Hughes extends the idea of abjection and female shamelessness he explored in "Cora Unashamed" to supplant repudiation with desire. Although not commonly associated with one another, abjection and desire can cohabitate in the sense that whereas abjection is a condition correlated with disavowal, desire can be thought of embedded in the multiple and contradictory impulses in which repudiation, shamelessness, and disavowal can be found.

110 Hughes's description of the ballroom Arnie visits with Claudina's crowd indicates some degree of criticism of the monied nonchalance surrounding Ms. Lawrence. The ballroom, called "Martinique where a native orchestra would play rattles and drums" (*WWF*, 148), summons the image of empire, the French reliance on its colonial holdings for its own material well-being. In brief, in order for Paris to be so attractive and enticing to these young black Americans, a legacy of French colonial history and the disenfranchisement of colonial subjects is put under erasure. Hughes paints this picture with a few, brief strokes, gesturing toward the collusion of African Americans in the commodification of "natives" who entertain with "rattles and drums" in this circuit of colony-dependent capital.

111 See correspondence between Blanche Knopf and Hughes, especially Blanche Knopf to Langston Hughes, 3 August 1934, Langston Hughes correspondence, box 97. Knopf writes, "I have now read the nine chapters of the Russian book that you sent me, and . . . I am disappointed. What you have done is charming and plesant but it is not fresh and it is not new and I don't think it's the kind of book the public expects to come from you. I think what you say is all true but that everybody knows it by now: they know that the harems are gone, etc. At this moment it seems to me that a book by you has got to be important. You could be writing of your own love affairs with Russian women. . . . I can't see readers awaiting just a nice book about Russia from your pen. They would expect something more striking and new or powerful at least." The decision to not publish the Russia book impelled Hughes to write another book in order to fulfill his contract with Knopf of December 1929. This book became *The Ways of White Folks*.

112 In his letters to Hughes before, during, and following Hughes's trip to Russia, Van Vechten does not even mention Hughes's trip but rather addresses him as if Hughes had never left the comfort of Carmel, California, where Hughes resided

prior to and just following his journey. Van Vechten's messages, rather, convey encouragement to move away from the "political" topics Hughes approached in his writing following Russia. A letter regarding Hughes's newly finished book of poetry *Good Morning Revolution* states, "The whole book of poems, which I find, as art, as propaganda, as anything, you can care to mention, Very Very Weak" (Carl Van Vechten to Langston Hughes, 20 March 1934, Langston Hughes correspondence, box 159.)

3. DU BOIS, RUSSIA, AND THE "REFUSAL TO BE 'WHITE'"

1 Gwen Bergner, "Politics and Pathologies: On the Subject of Race in Psychoanalysis," in *Frantz Fanon: Critical Perspectives*, ed. Anthony C. Alessandri (New York: Routledge, 1999), 221.

2 W. E. B. Du Bois, *Russia and America: An Interpretation*, in *The W. E. B. Du Bois Papers*, University of Massachusetts Amherst, reel 85, page 14, hereafter cited parenthetically as *RA*. The manuscript for *Russia and America: An Interpretation* can be found in reel 85, frames 395–527. Page numbers for *RA* are cited here and elsewhere as they appear in the manuscript. *The Du Bois Papers* will hereafter be cited parenthetically as W.E.B. Du Bois Papers, followed by reel and, where available, frame numbers. Here as elsewhere Du Bois refers to the Soviet Union as Russia. For clarification sake, when citing Du Bois, I will use his terminology but as elsewhere in the book, I will generally use Russia only when referring to that specific republic and otherwise the Soviet Union when referring to the inclusive nation of the Union of Soviet Socialist Republics.

3 Indeed, the title of his book, *Russia and America*, indicates Du Bois's usage of Russia and the Soviet Union as if they were interchangeable.

4 W. E. B. Du Bois, *Dusk of Dawn: An Essay Towards an Autobiography of a Race Concept* (1940; reprint, New Brunswick, N.J.: Transaction Publishers, 1997), 285–87; hereafter cited parenthetically as *DD*.

5 Critical assessments of Du Bois by Francis Broderick and Elliot Rudwick as well as anthologies edited by Meyer Weinberg, Andrew Paschal, and Nathan Huggins are early examples of such oversight. See Francis L. Broderick, *W. E. B. Du Bois: Negro Leader in a Time of Crisis* (1959; reprint, Stanford, Calif.: Stanford University Press, 1982); Elliot Rudwick, *W. E. B. Du Bois: Voice of the Black Protest Movement* (1960; reprint, Urbana: University of Illinois Press, 1982); Meyer Weinberg, ed., *W. E. B. Du Bois: A Reader* (New York: Harper and Row, 1970); Andrew G. Paschal, ed., *A W. E. B. Du Bois Reader* (New York: Macmillan, 1971); and Nathan Huggins, ed., *Du Bois Writings* (New York: Library of America, 1986). Because my argument is concerned with the current reception and perception of Du Bois, my focus here is on single-volume collections that are currently in print. There are other multivolume collections of Du Bois's oeuvre, which in addition to his

microfilmed papers, include Julius Lester, ed., *The Seventh Son: The Thought and Writing of W. E. B. Du Bois*, 2 vols. (New York: Random House, 1971); and the collected published works edited by Herbert Aptheker (4 vols.).

6 On the specific relationship between Du Bois and the Soviet Union, Horne is by far the most thorough, and his analysis has been critical to my own. Like Horne, Robinson and Marable recognize the significance of Russia to Du Bois and refrain from criticizing this connection. Rampersad, Cain, and Sundquist are somewhat less forgiving. Reed's book is discussed below. See Gerald Horne, *Black and Red: W. E. B. Du Bois and the Afro-American Response to the Cold War, 1944–1963* (Albany: State University of New York, 1986); Cedric Robinson, *Black Marxism: The Making of the Black Radical Tradition* (Chapel Hill: University of North Carolina Press, 2000); Manning Marable, *W. E. B. Du Bois: Black Radical Democrat* (Boston: G. K. Hall, 1986); Adolph Reed, *W. E. B. Du Bois and American Political Thought* (New York: Oxford University Press, 1997); Arnold Rampersad, *The Art and Imagination of W. E. B. Du Bois* (Cambridge: Harvard University Press, 1976); William E. Cain, "W. E. B. Du Bois's Autobiography and the Politics of Literature," *Black American Forum* 24 (1990): 299–313, and "From Liberalism to Communism: The Political Thought of W. E. B. Du Bois," in *Cultures of United States Imperialism*, ed. Amy Kaplan & Donald Pease (Durham, N.C.: Duke University Press, 1993), 456–73; and Eric J. Sundquist, "Introduction: W. E. B. Du Bois and the Autobiography of a Race," in *The Oxford W. E. B. Du Bois Reader* (New York: Oxford University Press, 1996), 3–36. Recent examples of extended focus on the early Du Bois include Keith E. Byerman, *Seizing the Word: History, Art, and Self in the Work of W. E. B. Du Bois* (Athens: University of Georgia Press, 1994); Shamoon Zamir, *Dark Voices: W. E. B. Du Bois and American Thought, 1888–1903* (Chicago: University of Chicago Press, 1995); and Bernard W. Bell, Emily Grosholz, and James B. Stewart, ed., *W. E. B. Du Bois on Race and Culture: Philosophy, Politics, and Poetics* (New York: Routledge, 1996).

7 In her illuminating work on Du Bois ("W. E. B. Du Bois's *Dusk of Dawn* and James Yate's *Mississippi to Madrid* or 'What Goes around comes around and around and around' in Autobiography," *Massachusetts Review* 35, no. 2 [summer 1994]), Kathryne V. Lindberg asserts that he "never abandoned what he called his 'German education'" (283). This is a point with which I agree, but in this chapter I am seeking to underline the extent to which his Hegelianism was modified (and failed to be modified) by the important intervention of a "Soviet education."

8 Even though he doesn't provide any sustained analysis of the book, Gerald Horne is the exception. In his discussion of Du Bois's intellectual involvement with the Soviet Union, he mentions an earlier draft of the manuscript, titled *Russia and America: An Attempt at Interpretation* (*Black and Red*, 315).

9 The terms here are Cain's, who asserts that Du Bois "set himself on a tragic

course" by identifying with the Soviet Union and "connecting its fate to his own" ("From Liberalism to Communism," 467).

10 W. E. B. Du Bois, "World Changer," *Mainstream* 10, no. 1 (January 1957): 3.

11 Michael Denning, *The Cultural Front: The Laboring of Culture in the Twentieth Century* (New York: Verso, 1996), xix.

12 Sundquist, "Introduction," 4.

13 Paul Gilroy, *The Black Atlantic: Modernity and Double Consciousness* (Cambridge: Harvard University Press, 1993), 115.

14 For a compelling elaboration of this point, see Kenneth Mostern, who in providing a sustained analysis of *Dusk of Dawn*, acknowledges that he omits attention to the Soviet Union ("Three Theories of the Race of W. E. B. Du Bois," in *Autobiography and Black Identity Politics: Racialization in Twentieth-Century America* [Cambridge: Cambridge University Press, 1999], n.64, p. 236).

15 Du Bois likewise anticipated the systematic debilitation of links between those movements that ensued in the 1960s—a severing of ties sponsored by a rhetoric of racial equality based in *national* citizenship, the presupposition that the autonomous U.S. subject existed, and the assumption that the United States should protect its citizens from contamination by communists at home and abroad.

16 For an elaboration on these parallel histories, see my discussion in the introduction and chapter 1.

17 Although the political situation has greatly changed, there is a contemporary resuscitation of (an inadequate) binary logic to differentiate between good and evil, freedom and tyranny, and so on, to substantiate the war in Afghanistan. Evidencing a perilously proximate logic, the Red threat seems to have been recycled rhetorically into a Green one.

18 Olaudah Equiano (1745–1797) has been called the creator of the slave narrative genre. *The Interesting Narrative of the Life of Olaudah Equiano, or Gustavus Vassa, the African,* is one of the first-known autobiographies to combine the Augustian tradition with social protest. See Angelo Costanzo, *Surprising Narrative: Olaudah Equiano and the Beginnings of Black Autobiography* (New York: Greenwood, 1987).

19 Henry Louis Gates Jr., "Bad Influence," *New Yorker,* 7 March 1994, 94.

20 I am thinking in particular of Zora Neale Hurston's *Dust Tracks on the Road* and Richard Wright's *Black Boy,* autobiographies that sought to remove themselves from the burden of representativeness. It should be noted, however, that Hurston's autobiography, which appeared in 1942, and Wright's, which was published in 1945, had politically motivated reasons for asserting the priority of the individual over the communal. Hurston was an avowed critic of African American involvement with communism, and Wright had also by this time renounced his affiliations with the movement. See Zora Neale Hurston, "Why the Negro Won't Buy Communism," *American Legion* 50 (June 1951): 55–60; and Richard Wright,

"I Tried to Be a Communist," originally published in *Atlantic Monthly* in 1944, and reprinted in *The God That Failed*, ed. Richard H. Crossman (Washington, D.C.: Gateway, 1949), 115–64. Du Bois's assertions of a particular (although somewhat different) "communalism" in 1940, I believe, must be read in the context of these denunciations of communism.

21 Gilroy, *The Black Atlantic*, 111, 117, 18.

22 As George Lipsitz has argued in challenging the British-centered metaphors of the black Atlantic, there is also a black Pacific. See his " 'Frantic to Join . . . the Japanese Army': The Asia Pacific War in the Lives of African American Soldiers and Civilians," in *The Politics of Culture in the Shadow of Capital*, ed. Lisa Lowe and David Lloyd (Durham, N.C.: Duke University Press, 1997), 324–53.

23 In addition to Du Bois and his wife, Shirley Graham, passports had been denied Paul and Eslanda Robeson—since each refused to declare in writing that they were not communists.

24 As elucidated by the case of Robeson, the inability to speak out against injustices abroad was a blow to Du Bois. Martin Duberman explains that "to deny black Americans the right to disclose their grievances abroad was tantamount to denying them one historic means they had always employed for winning their struggle at home" (*Paul Robeson: A Biography* [New York: Ballantine, 1989], 436). But although unable to leave the country, Du Bois was not deterred from political action and spoke whenever possible, even going so far as to run for the Senate in New York in order to make his platform heard.

25 W. E. B. Du Bois, *The Autobiography of W. E. B. Du Bois: A Soliloquy on Viewing My Life from the Last Decade of Its First Century* (1968; reprint, New York: International Publishers, 1991), 11; hereafter cited parenthetically as *A*.

26 Louis A. Renza, "A Theory of Autobiography," in *Autobiography: Essays Theoretical and Critical*, ed. James Olney (Princeton, N.J.: Princeton University Press, 1980), 286.

27 The primary exceptions are Horne (*Black and Red*), who expertly addresses Du Bois's political affiliations, retrieving the bulk of Du Bois's considerable written work from this period (excluding the autobiographies, however), and Reed, who in *W. E. B. Du Bois and American Political Thought* takes to task those who read Du Bois's defining terms in the idea of double consciousness he forwarded in *The Souls of Black Folk*. Echoing Reed's important critique, I point out below how Du Bois abandoned this trope in his later years. Unlike Reed, though, I see in Du Bois's rejection of this existential paradox not only a trenchant maintenance of its elitist terms but also a politically minded reformulation of the terms of the color line that corresponds to his rearticulation of the genre of autobiography. More recently, Timothy Brennan has provided a refreshing counter to the trend of overlooking the late Du Bois, asserting that "it is rarely noted that as the century

wore on, he revised that view [of the color line] by expanding and enriching his understanding of the problem of race. Almost nothing is said about the last decades of his life around the Communist Party—an enormously fruitful period of his mature thinking" (*At Home in the World: Cosmopolitanism Now* [Cambridge: Harvard University Press, 1997], 28).

28 W. E. B. Du Bois, *The Correspondence of W. E. B. Du Bois: Volume 3, Selections, 1944–1963*, ed. Herbert Aptheker (Amherst: University of Massachusetts Press, 1978), 340. Du Bois repeated this sentiment in an interview with Ralph McGill in 1965. " 'Washington,' he said, a smile softening the severe, gaunt lines of his face, 'died in 1915. A lot of people think I died at the same time' " (*Atlantic Monthly* 216, no. 5 [1965]: 78–81). This was Du Bois's last interview.

29 W. E. B. Du Bois Papers, reel 65, frame 78.

30 Ibid., reel 84, frame 124; published in the *National Guardian* as "Du Bois Reports on Moscow Peace Congress," 26 September 1949.

31 Du Bois's assessment of enforced collectivization was edited, in part, by Jessica Smith, the editor of *Soviet Russia Today,* a periodical in which Du Bois published several articles about Russia, including "Russia: An Interpretation," which was adapted from the *Russia and America* manuscript. In correspondence with Du Bois on his rendition of collectivization, Smith says, "You telescope so much into a brief paragraph that it seemed to me the impression of compulsory collectivization comes through a little too strongly. Of course there was force and violence in that period, which was tantamount to a second revolution, but this has to be understood in the whole historical setting of the period. . . . Stalin made a speech called 'Dizziness from Success,' condemning local officials for using compulsion, and insisting that joining collectives must be a voluntary affair, following which earlier abuses were corrected" (cited in W. E. B. Du Bois Papers, reel 64, frame 330). The letter is dated 11 October 1949. Du Bois's article can be found in *Soviet Russia Today* 17 (November 1949): 14–15, 32. For an example of another woman's influence over Du Bois's analyses of Russia, see also Du Bois's review of Anna Louise Strong's *The Stalin Years* in which Du Bois sides with Strong's opinion that not "anyone anywhere knows the full story of the excesses that occurred in the USSR in 1936–38," and Stalin "did more to change the world" than any other person in the first half of the twentieth century ("World Changer," 3, 5).

32 W. E. B. Du Bois: *The Fight for Equality and the American Century, 1919–1963* (New York, Henry Holt, 2000) 557.

33 Compare this statement to the poem that closes chapter 1 of *Russia and America* in which Du Bois imagines the rebirth of the utopian nation. The imagery of this poem uses miscegenation, hybridity, and improper crossings, which together recollect the formative spurn of *Souls*—the rejection of the young Du Bois by a white girl discussed in chapter 2. Although Du Bois moved beyond his 1903

formulation of the color line, the question of female acquiescence remained primary. One of the first things Du Bois notes about Russia is that "women sit beside me quite confidentially and unconsciously" (*RA*, 27). Because of the over-determined connection between black men and white women brought together by the specter of lynching, Du Bois's adherence to this image as the one that most potently fixes his imaginary identification with other blacks also returns one to the transitional figure of the white woman.

34   In eerie anticipation of his own arrest, which would follow shortly in 1951, Du Bois denoted the increased curtailing of civil liberties in the United States, including the ratification of the Smith Act, under which Du Bois eventually would be indicted and tried: "At the center of all red-baiting today stands the charge that all Communism and all Communists are agents of a foreign power" (*RA*, 243).

35   W. E. B. Du Bois Papers, reel 64, frame 375.

36   W. E. B. Du Bois Papers, reel 84, frame 165.

37   Of course, not all African Americans were willing to join the communist movement. See, for example, Josh White, "I Was a Sucker for the Communists," *Negro Digest* 9, no. 2 (1950): 26–31; and Hurston, "Why the Negro Won't Buy Communism."

38   Horne, *Black and Red,* 9.

39   Cited in W. E. B. Du Bois Papers, reel 72, frame 39; letter dated 28 February 1956.

40   For an instructive account of the black American activism on behalf of the "international" during the postwar years, see Penny M. Von Eschen, *Race against Empire: Black Americans and Anticolonialism, 1937–1957* (Ithaca, N.Y.: Cornell University Press, 1997).

41   W. E. B. Du Bois, "Color Lines," *National Guardian*, 12 February 1953, 7.

42   W. E. B. Du Bois, "The Africans and the Colonialist Tactic," *New Times* 7 (1959): 19.

43   "The New Negro Liberation Movements," W. E. B. Du Bois Papers, reel 84.

44   It is along the lines of double consciousness that I differ from Nahum Chandler's argument about Du Bois's autobiographical "example." Chandler contends that the prevailing paradigm of the entirety of Du Bois's autobiography is that of double consciousness, whereas I am alleging that it is precisely such color-bound consciousness that Du Bois seeks to unravel and expose as having enabled the black liberal response to anticommunism in his later autobiography. It is just such a fissure in his earlier formulation that Du Bois makes when he writes of the Soviets' refusal to be white. See Nahum Chandler's "The Figure of the X: An Elaboration of the Du Boisian Autobiographical Example," in *Displacement, Diaspora, and Geographies of Identity,* ed. Smadar Lavie and Ted Swedenburg (Durham, N.C.: Duke University Press, 1996). There has, of course, been excellent work that challenges this limited notion of U.S. national identity. In addition to

the work of John Carlos Rowe, the notion of continuities (and asymmetries) between U.S. imperialism and domestic militarism, racisms abroad and at home, has been pursued by such scholars as Von Eschen, Amy Kaplan and Donald Pease, Brenda Gayle Plummer, and in Janice Radway's address to the American Studies Association in 1998, published as "What's in a Name?" *American Quarterly* 51, no. 1 (March 1999): 1–32.

45 See, for example, Martin Duberman's description of *Life* magazine's praise of the "Yale football squad's election of a black captain, Levi Jackson, as proof that the American Way 'worked' and that the 'extremist' tactics of a Paul Robeson were as unnecessary as they were misguided" (*Paul Robeson: A Biography*, 337).

46 For a fascinating tale of this kind of color play, see Angela Calomiris, *Red Masquerade: Undercover for the F.B.I.* (Philadelphia: J. B. Lippincott, 1950). Calomiris's "passing" narrative makes no attempt to deny common misconceptions about life behind "enemy lines." Her story thus delineates passing's presuppositions, confirming an essential difference between "us" and "them."

47 For more information on Soviet policies on race and nationality, see Vladimir Ilyich Lenin, *The Right of Nations to Self Determination* (New York: International Publishing, 1951); Joseph Stalin, *Marxism and the National and Colonial Question* (London: Lawrence and Wishar, 1936); Ronald Grigor Suny, *Revenge of the Past: Nationalism, Revolution, and the Collapse of the Soviet Union* (Stanford, Calif.: Stanford University Press, 1993); Gerhard Simon, *Nationalism and the Policies toward the Nationalities in the Soviet Union: From Totalitarian Dictatorship to Post-Stalinist Society*, trans. Karen Forster and Oswald Forster (Boulder, Colo.: Westview Press, 1991); and Alexander J. Motyl, ed., *Thinking Theoretically about Soviet Nationalities: History and Comparison in the Study of the USSR* (New York: Columbia University Press, 1992).

48 W. E. B. Du Bois Papers, reel 63.

49 The most thorough and sophisticated account of the final ratification of this thesis, and the participation of African Americans in the process, is provided by Harry Haywood, *Black Bolshevik: Autobiography of an Afro-American Communist* (Chicago: Liberator Press, 1978).

50 In *Black and Red*, Horne provides an excellent analysis of the political climate surrounding Du Bois's trial.

51 W. E. B. Du Bois, *In Battle for Peace: The Story of My Eighty-third Birthday* (New York: Masses and Mainstream, 1952), 77; hereafter cited parenthetically as *IBP*.

52 Du Bois's earlier ruminations about his contemporaries, however, suggest that he could not have been overly surprised by this revelation. For example, in *Dusk of Dawn* he writes, "My colored colleagues especially were deeply American with the old theory of individualism" (290).

53 Alan Nadel (*Containment Culture: American Narratives, Postmodernism, and the*

Atomic Age [Durham, N.C.: Duke University Press, 1995]) suggests the ease with which Du Bois may have moved from his pronouncements about double consciousness to warnings about U.S. militarism. Nadel observes that the masculine component of the African American cultural narrative exemplified by double consciousness "identifies a duality that antedates America's nuclear supremacy and, more importantly, that reflects disempowerment rather than power. Within this narrative, nuclear supremacy becomes just one manifestation of white supremacy" (226). Seeing in both double consciousness and containment a constitutive duality, Nadel directly contrasts what he interprets as containment's excesses with the deprivations on which double consciousness was based. Nadel's comments provide a useful framework for understanding the complexities of Cold War rhetoric in which containment was based, and yet Nadel relies on Du Bois's 1903 formulations in the context of a discussion of 1950s' Cold War culture. See his chapter "My Country Too: Time, Place, and African-American Identity in the Work of John A. Williams," esp. 227–29.

54 Emphasizing the correlation between action and intellect, Du Bois's text also reveals the ways in which the physical aspect of intellectual work, structured through feeling, was key to his own analytic development.

55 Nadel, *Containment Culture*, 227.

56 By "exemplary black masculinity" I am referring to the paradigm of blackness as representatively masculine laid out in Hazel Carby's illuminating analysis of *The Souls of Black Folk* in her book *Race Men* (Cambridge: Harvard University Press, 1998), 9–41.

57 This is Graham's (mis)translation.

58 For example, in describing her first contact with Du Bois, she emphasizes his influence on the African American community. Her poem "Black Man's Music," to which she credits Du Bois's inspirational vision, names him as "the symbol of our hopes and aspirations; the one who from a high place described the vision . . . a song, so irresistible with charm / That straight into the soul it sinks / And breaking down all bars of prejudice and pride, / There it remains" (*IBP,* 14).

59 See Carby, *Race Men*.

60 Gerald Horne's biography of Graham, *Race Woman: The Lives of Shirley Graham Du Bois* (New York: New York University Press, 2000) offers a groundbreaking and instructive account of Graham's contributions to racial and sexual emancipation in concert with and independently of Du Bois. But a critical analysis of her work has not yet been endeavored.

61 Du Bois also indicates that Rogge was instrumental in the conviction of the Rosenbergs, entering the trial as counsel for one of the chief witnesses against the couple. Rogge arranged for the witness and his wife to sign statements implicating the Rosenbergs in exchange for which the husband received a light sentence, the wife was acquitted, and the Rosenbergs convicted (*IBP,* 118).

62 Readers learn from Graham that among Du Bois's more "practical" characteris-
tics are his penchant for gold rings from Cartier's and "French restaurants,"
which "are always high in W. E. B.'s favor. And he is loved by the waiters because
he consults with them in French, giving his undivided attention" (*IBP,* 57).

63 See Catriona Kelly, "The Retreat from Dogmatism: Populism under Khrushchev
and Brezhnev," in *Russian Cultural Studies: An Introduction,* ed. Catriona Kelly
and David Shepherd (Oxford: Oxford University Press, 1998), 249–73; and Ella
Winter, *I Saw the Russian People* (Boston: Little, Brown and Co., 1945), 62–98.

64 Louise Thompson Patterson, "Louise Thompson Patterson Memoirs: Trip to
Russia," Draft 123.

65 "The Peace Congress at Moscow," W. E. B. Du Bois Papers, reel 84, frame 126.

66 The complexity of gender construction in the USSR is outside the parameters of
this chapter.

67 A sampling of these articles includes "Nevidannyi skachok" ("An Unprecedented
Leap"), *Literaturnaia Gazeta,* 5 November 1957, 5; "Bor'ba Polia Robsona" ("The
Battle of Paul Robeson"), *Literaturnaia Gazeta,* 10 April 1958, 4; "Vseobshchii mir i
sovetskii semiletii plan" ("Universal Peace and the Soviet Seven Year Plan"),
Pravda, 25 November 1958, 5; "Amerikanskie negry dob'iutsia polnogo osvobo-
zhdeniia ("American Negroes Will Obtain Full Freedom"), *Pravda,* 17 July 1959, 4;
"Triumf sotsializma" ("The Triumph of Socialism"), *Izvestiia,* 7 November 1959, 5;
"V soedinennykh shtatakh neobkhodimo vosstanovit' demokratiiu ("In the
United States It Is Necessary to Reconstruct Democracy"), *Pravda,* 23 May 1960,
3–4; "Kommunizm pobedit!" ("Communism Will Triumph!"), *Pravda,* 24 November 1961, 6; and "Utro novogo dnia" ("The Morning of a New Day"), *Pravda,*
22 April 1963, 3.

68 For correspondence between Du Bois and M. F. Nesturkh, editor of *Soviet Anthropology,* see W. E. B. Du Bois Papers, reel 73, frames 904–5. *Autobiography* was
published in the USSR six years prior to its publication in the United States.

69 "Bortsy za mir" ("Fighters for Peace"), *Ogonek,* 10 May 1959, 1, 6–8.

70 "V Zashchitu Mira" ("In Defense of Peace"), *Literaturnaia Gazeta,* 25 September
1951, n.p.

71 In addition to the coverage of Du Bois and Robeson, see, for example, the
coverage of Moscow's Youth Festival in September 1957. The magazine *Ogonek*
pictured three girls on its cover—one Chinese, one Russian, and one Indian. As
Catriona Kelly has argued, this festival marked a "watershed in East-West relations as the threat of real war was replaced by propaganda conflict. [It was a] key
experience of the Khrushchev thaw; among other things, it was marked by a large
exhibition of work by young foreign painters," although I disagree with her
contention that Soviet artists had been "starved of contact with artists outside the
Soviet bloc for more than twenty years" ("Creating a Consumer: Advertising and
Commercialization," in *Russian Cultural Studies: An Introduction,* ed. Catriona

Kelly and David Shepherd [Oxford: Oxford University Press, 1998], 231). In 1955, as I discuss in chapter 4, the U.S. cast of *Porgy and Bess* toured Moscow and Leningrad.

72　See *Voprosy Istorii* 8 (1951): 158–59. The letter is quite long, sketching out a brief history of Du Bois's career, and positioning him as an esteemed scholar-historian as well as "active fighter for peace" (*"aktivnogo bortsa za mir"*). The letter opens with the modest assertion that "all of honest humanity is troubled by the recent crime of American inflammatory agitators" ("Vse chestnoe chelovechestvo voz-mushcheno novyim prestupleniem amerikanskikh podzhigatelei").

73　Horne, *Black and Red,* 9.

74　W. E. B. Du Bois Papers, reel 73, frame 942.

75　W. E. B. Du Bois, "Lenin I Afrika" ("Lenin and Africa"), *Sovremennyi Vostok* 4 (1959): 5–6.

76　The correspondence between Du Bois and Potekhin can be found in the W. E. B. Du Bois Papers, reel 74, frames 10–15.

77　For example, Graham and Du Bois attended the first Conference of Asian and African Writers, in Tashkent, in 1958. The conference, according to Graham "extending as it did from Japan and China to Egypt and Ghana, and from Central Asia to Indonesia, was a continuation of a purpose—to tumble the walls and burst the fetters of colonialism" ("Letter from Tashkent"). *Mainstream,* Vol. II: 12 (1958), 17.

78　This section is indebted to the insights of Avery F. Gordon's stunning theoriza-tions in *Ghostly Matters: Haunting and the Sociological Imagination* (Minne-apolis: University of Minnesota Press, 1997).

4. BLACK SHADOWS ACROSS THE IRON CURTAIN: ROBESON'S STANCE BETWEEN COLD WAR CULTURES

1　[Patricia Blakely], "Russians Lionize 'Porgy' Cast," *Life* 9 (January 1956): 17.

2　Cited in Hollis Alpert, *The Life and Times of Porgy and Bess* (New York: Knopf, 1990), 211.

3　Ibid., 211.

4　"*Porgy* in Leningrad," *Time,* 9 January 1956, 51.

5　[Blakely], "Russians Lionize 'Porgy' Cast," 17.

6　Cited in Alpert, *Life and Times of Porgy and Bess,* 221.

7　James Standifer, "The Tumultuous Life of Porgy and Bess," *Humanities* 18, no. 6 (November/December 1997), 53. Standifer also notes that Harold Cruse criticizes the opera for portraying "the seamiest side of Negro life—presumably the image of black people that white audiences want to see. . . . [It] belongs in a museum and no self-respecting African American should want to see it, or be seen in it" (11).

8　Truman Capote, "Porgy and Bess in Russia I: When the Cannons Are Silent," *New*

Yorker 32, no. 35 (20 October 1956): 80; see also Truman Capote, "Porgy and Bess in Russia II: The Muses Are Heard," *New Yorker* 32, no. 36 (27 October 1956): 41–106. These pieces later appeared in his group of essays *The Dogs Bark: Public People and Private Places* (New York: Plume, 1957).

9 Cited in Alpert, *Life and Times of Porgy and Bess*, 229.

10 Paul Robeson, "Moi novogodnie nadezhdy" ("My New Year's Wishes"), *Pravda*, 3 January 1956, 3.

11 *New York Times*, 25 April 1949, as cited in Martin Duberman, *Paul Robeson: A Biography* (New York: Ballantine, 1989), 349.

12 Even in the 1950s, there were voices that resisted this kind of political whitewashing. In a letter to the editor of *Novoe Vremia*, William L. Patterson commented on the reviews of Robeson's revival of his Othello role at Stratford-on-Avon: "For Paul Robeson, the road that led to Stratford was a long and torturous highway. Yet [a reporter] asks us to 'Forget Paul Robeson's politics for the moment and consider instead the whole complex emotional background against which this eminent Negro faced the opening night.' . . . Is this 'eminent Negro' to lose his eminence if his politics are found distasteful? . . . How can we forget or submerge what has contributed so much to the making of a world renowned figure? Can Paul Robeson's devotion to the freedom struggles of his people, to the liberation struggles of all men, to respect for human dignity be forgotten? Can we forget his deathless devotion to the cause of peace? All this is indissolubly linked with that Othello" ("Paul Robeson's Latest Success," *Novoe Vremia* 20 (1959): 31.

13 Peter Applebome, "From the Valley of Obscurity, Robeson's Baritone Rings Out," *New York Times*, 25 February 1998, E1, 4.

14 Martin Duberman, "A Giant Denied His Rightful Stature in Film," *New York Times*, 29 March 1998, sec. 2, 1. The U.S. Postal Service was taking no chances: a movement to get Robeson's image on a commemorative stamp was derailed, despite the signatures of over ninety thousand Americans on petitions and the endorsement of nearly sixty congressional members. See "Robeson Put Stamp on America," *Daily News* (New York), 19 April 1998, 42; Maitland Zane, "A Robeson Centennial Concert in Oakland Honors Gifted but Controversial Singer," *San Francisco Chronicle*, 26 March 1998: A19; and "A Robeson Stamp," *Boston Globe*, 3 January 1998, A10.

15 Paul Von Blum, cited in Applebome, "From the Valley of Obscurity," E1.

16 Paul Robeson, *Here I Stand* (New York: International Publishers, 1958), 48; hereafter cited parenthetically as *HIS*.

17 See, for example, Alan Wald, *The New York Intellectuals: The Rise and Decline of the Anti-Stalinist Left from the 1930s to the 1980s* (Chapel Hill: University of North Carolina Press, 1987) and *Writing From the Left: New Essays on Radical Culture and Politics* (London: Verso, 1994); Elaine Tyler May, *Homeward Bound: American*

Families in the Cold War Era (New York: Basic Books, 1988); and Alan Nadel, *Containment Culture: American Narratives, Postmodernism, and the Atomic Age* (Durham, N.C.: Duke University Press, 1995).

18 Martin Duberman, "Remembering Paul Robeson," *Newshour with Jim Lehrer*, PBS, 9 April 1998, transcript.

19 Hazel Carby, *Race Men* (Cambridge: Harvard University Press, 1998), 83.

20 For a critical take on Robeson's anti anticommunism, see Stephen Whitfield Jr., *The Culture of the Cold War*, 2d ed. (Baltimore, Md.: Johns Hopkins University Press, 1996), 192–96. Particularly surprising is how Whitfield condemns Robeson for "professing concern only about his own country" when Robeson's efforts to raise awareness over global racial injustice was primary to his politics, and the reason for his founding the Council on African Affairs (CAA). Whitfield lambastes Robeson for Robeson's inattention to Stalinist purges, saying that Robeson's response "constituted a macabre libel on millions of Soviet political prisoners" (192). Robeson's response to such a line of questioning, however, was based in a genealogy of being used as a poster boy for the successful American black male and his refusal to testify according to State Department strictures must be read within this context of combative Cold War cultures. For an example of the National Association for the Advancement of Colored People's (NAACP) and popular black rejection of communism, see Herbert Hill, "The Communist Party—Enemy of Negro Equality," *Crisis* 58, no. 6 (June–July 1951): 365–71; and Alfred Baker Lewis, "The Problem of Communist Infiltration," *Crisis* 61, no. 10 (December 1954): 585–87.

21 Paul Robeson, "To You Beloved Comrade," *New World Review* 21, no. 4 (April 1953): 11–13.

22 Eslanda Robeson, FBI Files on Paul Robeson, reel 1, section 2, frame 234. Although there is a wealth of material on Eslanda Robeson's relationship to the Soviet Union, particularly regarding her advocacy both of her husband and African peoples, a thorough discussion of her significant contributions remains outside the scope of this chapter. I have used the advisory term "reportedly" because this quote is taken from a confidential field report submitted to the FBI in 1947. In general, when using quotes from the FBI's Robeson files, I will indicate the dubious nature of accuracy, placing this question within the larger context of the contingencies at play in the particular selection of materials (and reported speech) represented in these files.

23 Helen Desfosses Cohn, *Soviet Policy toward Black Africa: The Focus on National Integration* (New York: Praeger, 1974), 19.

24 Michelle A. Stephens, "Black Transnationalism and the Politics of National Identity: West Indian Intellectuals in Harlem in the Age of War and Revolution," *American Quarterly* 50 (September 1998): 605.

25 "Extracts from a Resolution of the Executive Committee of the Communist International Political Secretariat on the Negro Question in the United States" (26 October 1930) in *The Communist International, 1919–1943, Documents,* ed. Jane Degras (London: Oxford University Press, 1956–1965), 3:133–34.

26 As early as 1952, Stalin recognized that the Soviets had to create a "new approach toward nationalism if it [the Soviet Union] were to gain any influence over the developing nations" (Cohn, *Soviet Policy,* 25). And based on the success of the Bandung Conference in April 1955, Khrushchev later inaugurated polices toward third world nationalism "based on a pragmatic assessment of the power of these movements" that recognized their ability not only to "diminish the power of the West but also to affect the course of world politics through its foreign policy variant, neutralism or non-alignment" (ibid., 25–26). It is crucial to remember, however, as Edward T. Wilson notes, that although Soviet Policy toward Africa changed in 1928, and the Soviets remained thereafter largely self-interested in Africa, "even if we charge the Soviets with unrealistic, inefficient methods and insignificant actual efforts taken; clearly the Communists were committed to carrying revolution" into Africa (*Russia and Black Africa before WWII*) (New York: Holmes and Meier, 1974), 155.

27 On the promise of early Soviet rhetoric as distinct from the later failures of Stalinism, see Steven F. Cohen, *Rethinking the Soviet Experience: Politics and History since 1917* (New York: Oxford University Press, 1985).

28 Ronald Grigor Suny, *Revenge of the Past: Nationalism, Revolution, and the Collapse of the Soviet Union* (Stanford, Calif.: Stanford University Press, 1993). For more information on Soviet policies on race and nationality, see Vladimir Ilyich Lenin, *The Rights of Nations to Self Determination* (New York: International Publishers, 1951); Joseph Stalin, *Marxism and the National and Colonial Question* (London: International Publishers, 1936); Gerhard Simon, *Nationalism and the Policies toward the Nationalities in the Soviet Union: From Totalitarian Dictatorship to Post-Stalinist Society,* trans. Karen Forster and Oswald Forster (Boulder, Colo.: Westview Press, 1991); and Alexander J. Motyl, ed., *Thinking Theoretically about Soviet Nationalities: History and Comparison in the Study of the USSR* (New York: Columbia University Press, 1992).

29 On the difference between "internationalism" and "transnationalism," see Stephens, "Black Transnationalism."

30 Richard Wright, *American Hunger* (New York: Harper and Row, 1944), 63.

31 Ibid.

32 See W. E. B. Du Bois Papers, 1926–1961, University of Massachusetts, Amherst, 9 March 1949, reel 63.

33 On the participation of black liberals in U.S. foreign affairs during the postwar period, see Brenda Gayle Plummer, *Rising Wind: Black Americans and U.S. For-*

eign Affairs, 1935–1960 (Chapel Hill: University of North Carolina Press, 1996); and Penny M. Von Eschen, *Race against Empire: Black Americans and Anti-colonialism, 1937–1957* (Ithaca, N.Y.: Cornell University Press, 1997).

34   Von Eschen, *Race against Empire*, 145.

35   Duberman, *Paul Robeson*, 431. For an example of the NAACP's and popular black rejection of communism see Hill, "The Communist Party—Enemy of Negro Equality," 365–71; and Lewis, "The Problem of Communist Infiltration," 585–87.

36   See Plummer's discussion in *Rising Wind*, 198–216.

37   In addition to Von Eschen, *Race against Empire*, see also Robin D. G. Kelley, *Race Rebels: Culture, Politics, and the Black Working Class* (New York: Free Press, 1994).

38   Cited in B. Mikleburg, "Interv'iu Polia Robsona" ("Interview with Paul Robeson"), *V Zashchitu Mira* (May 1956): 31.

39   Sandra L. Richards makes the argument that although much of the criticism of African American literature emphasizes a folk tradition in written texts, scant critical attention is paid to the arena in which folk discursive traditions were most dominant: those of performance ("Writing the Absent Potential: Drama, Performance, and the Canon of African-American Literature," in *Performativity and Performance*, ed. Andrew Parker and Eve Kosofsky Sedgwick (New York: Routledge, 1995), 64–88.

40   Ibid., 73.

41   David Lloyd and Abdul JanMohamed, "Introduction: Towards a Theory of Minority Discourse: What Is to Be Done?" in *The Nature and Context of Minority Discourse*, ed. David Lloyd and Abdul JanMohamed (New York: Oxford University Press, 1990), 1–16. See my discussion in chapter 1.

42   Ibid., 10.

43   A thorough discussion of Robeson's gender politics is outside the purview of this book. Robeson's occlusion of gender as a schematic of subject differentiation integral to the racial and national exclusions on which his internationalism was based is significant, and offers a point of differentiation from McKay's reworking of sex into the question "What is to be done?" At the same time, Robeson repeatedly made a point of including women in his discussions of global liberation, and in his messages to the Soviet peoples, often addressed women directly. Robeson also unfailingly promoted the feminist work of his wife. For examples of Robeson's inclusion of women in his proposed united community of spirit and soul, see *Here I Stand*, 99–100, 105. (Interestingly, this attention to women is in the chapter of *Here I Stand* that was removed from the Russian version.) For Robeson's greetings to Soviet women, see A. Sofronov, "My poem c Polem Robsonom" ("We Sing with Paul Robeson"), *Ogonek* 1 (1956): 19. Instances of Eslanda's attention to women's, race, and gender issues can be found in the articles she wrote for such Soviet publications as *Sovetskaia Zhenshchina, Novoe*

Vremiia, Mezhdunarodnaia Zhizn', Sovetskii Pechat', Druzhba Narodov, Izvestiia, and *Literaturnaia Gazeta.*

44 Paul Gilroy, *The Black Atlantic: Modernity and Double Consciousness* (Cambridge: Harvard University Press, 1993), 127.

45 Neil Lazarus, "Modernity, Globalization, and the West," in *Nationalism and Cultural Practice in the Postcolonial World* (Cambridge: Cambridge University Press, 1999), 61.

46 Duberman, *Paul Robeson,* 434.

47 Ibid., 433. A version of this portion of the text appeared in my article "Soul Mates," *Diaspora* 9, no. 3 (winter 2000): 399–420.

48 V. Gorokhov, "C pesnii v bor'be" ("Into the Struggle with Songs"), *Sovetskaia Muzika* 4 (1953): 99.

49 See K. Kudrov, "Artist, Borets" ("Artist, Fighter"), *Izvestiia,* 9 April 1963, 4.

50 Antonio Gramsci, *Selections from the Prison Notebooks,* trans. Quintin Hoare and Geoffrey Nowell Smith (New York: International Publishers, 1971), 418.

51 Neil Lazarus, "Transnationalism and the Alleged Death of the Nation State," in *Cultural Readings of Imperialism: Edward Said and the Gravity of History,* ed. Keith Ansell-Pearson, Benita Parry, and Judith Squires (New York: St. Martin's Press, 1997), 46.

52 Andrew Parker and Eve Kosofsky Sedgwick, "Introduction," in *Performativity and Performance,* 3.

53 On the asymmetrical relationships between nation and gender, see Norma Alcaron, Caren Kaplan, and Minoo Moallem, "Introduction: Between Woman and Nation," in *Between Woman and Nation: Nationalisms, Transnational Feminisms, and the State,* ed. Norma Alcaron, Caren Kaplan and Minoo Moallem (Durham, N.C.: Duke University Press, 1999), 1–16.

54 See Jeffrey C. Stewart, ed., *Paul Robeson: Artist and Citizen* (New Brunswick, N.J.: Rutgers University Press, 1998), xxviii; and Duberman, *Paul Robeson,* 175.

55 Cited in Duberman, *Paul Robeson,* 178.

56 Cited in Ibid., 173, 175.

57 Cited in Ibid.

58 Cited in Ibid., 178.

59 Paul Robeson, foreword, *Favorite Songs of the Red Army and Navy* (1941), in Philip S. Foner, ed., *Paul Robeson Speaks: Writings, Speeches, Interviews, 1918–1974* (New York: Carol Publishing Group, 1978), 136.

60 Paul Robeson, "Pesni moego naroda" ("Songs of My People"), *Sovetskaia musika* 7 (1949): 100.

61 Robeson, foreword to *Favorite Songs,* 137.

62 Cited in Anatol Schlosser, "Paul Robeson's Mission in Music," in *Paul Robeson the Great Forerunner,* ed. editors of *Freedomways* (New York: International Publishers, 1985), 87.

63 See, for example, how Robeson changed the words to "Old Man River" over the years to make varying statements based on the moment and place of performance (Foner, *Paul Robeson Speaks*, 482). See also the discussion of his performance of "Zog Nit Keynmol" ("Song of the Warsaw Ghetto Rebellion") in Moscow in 1949 (David Levering Lewis, "Paul Robeson and the U.S.S.R.," in *Paul Robeson: Artist and Citizen*, 224–26).

64 Paul Robeson Jr., *Paul Robeson: The Legendary Moscow Concert* (1949), (New York: Fenix Entertainment, 1995); statement made by Robeson in Russian (my translation).

65 Robeson's exalted expression was furthered by the use of transnational motifs— such as he described in Antonín Dvořák's use of the theme from "Swing Low Sweet Chariot" in his *New World Symphony*.

66 Cited in B. Mikelburg, "Interv'iu Polia Robsona" ("Interview with Paul Robeson"), 26.

67 Cited in Duberman, *Paul Robeson*, 173. The invocation of Shakespeare also complicates Robeson's insistence on the significance of recuperating folk performance as legitimate art. For although certainly "theater," and in that sense performative, Shakespeare undoubtedly is the canonical author par excellence for the English-speaking world. Therefore, the arguments about performance as a degraded, suspect mode do not apply to Shakespeare's work in the same way they do to U.S. drama in general and African American oral traditions in particular.

68 A request from a Soviet audience member for a reading from Shakespeare, in lieu of a folk song, as an encore was reported in *Pravda*'s coverage of Robeson's triumphal 1958 concert in Moscow (D. Zarapin, "Poet Pol' Robson" (Paul Robeson Sings"), *Pravda*, 18 August 1958, 4). According to the report, Robeson recited the title character's final monologue from *Othello*. The *Othello* reading was also reported by Lev Nikulin, "Dva kontserta Polia Robsona" (Two Paul Robeson Concerts), *Literaturnaia Gazeta*, 19 August 1958, 3.

69 See Liah Greenfeld, "The Scythian Rome: Russia," in *Nationalism: Five Roads to Modernity* (Cambridge: Harvard University Press, 1992), 189–274.

70 See Maureen Perrie, "Narodnost': Notions of National Identity," in *Constructing Russian Culture in the Age of Revolution: 1881–1940*, ed. Catriona Kelly and David Shepherd (Oxford: Oxford University Press, 1998), 28–36.

71 For a wide-ranging discussion of the appeal to African American Left intellectuals of nationalist art based in the folk, see James Smethurst, "African-American Poetry, Ideology, and the Left during the 1930s and 1940s from the Third Period to the Popular Front and Beyond," *The New Red Negro: The Literary Left and African American Poetry, 1930–1946* (New York: Oxford University Press, 1999), 16–59.

72 Cited in Lynne Attwood and Catriona Kelly, "Programmes for Identity: The 'New

Man' and the 'New Woman,'" in *Constructing Russian Culture in the Age of Revolution: 1881–1940*, 285.

73 Ibid., 286. See also F. J. Miller, *Folklore for Stalin: Russian Folklore and Pseudofolklore of the Stalin Era* (Armonk, N.Y.: M. E. Sharpe 1990); Richard Stites, *Russian Popular Culture: Entertainment and Society since 1900* (Cambridge: Harvard University Press, 1992); and Svetlana Boym, *Common Places: Mythologies of Everyday Life in Russia* (Cambridge: Harvard University Press, 1994).

74 Catriona Kelly and David Shepherd, "Introduction: Why Cultural Studies?" in *Russian Cultural Studies: An Introduction*, ed. Catriona Kelly and David Shepherd (Oxford: Oxford University Press, 1998), 9.

75 Attwood and Kelly, "Programmes for Identity," 287.

76 See my discussion of Hughes's reverence for Pushkin in his essay "Negroes in Moscow" in *The Color Line and Its Discontents: Passing through Russia and the United States*. (Ph.D. dissertation, Yale University, 1995).

77 "Ia chital Pushkina eshche zadolgo do togo, kak v pervye otvedal khleba v vashei strane. I khotia ia vyros v Amerike i vospitan na angliiskoi kul'ture, russkuiu poeziiu i literaturu ia inogda chuvstvuiu luchshe, chem angliiskuiu. Mozhet byt', eto potomu . . . chto russkaia literatura glubzhe peredala chuvstva i stradaniia ugnetennykh" (cited in L. Tiurina, "Ia Eshche pobyvaiu v Moskvei privezu mnogo novikh pesen!" ("I will visit Moscow Again and Bring Many New Songs!"), *Ogonek* 2 (1957): 25.

78 Paul Robeson, "Serdechnyi Privet Sovetskomu narodu!" ("Sincere Greetings to the Soviet People"), *Pravda*, 1 January 1956, 5. In fact, it is difficult to find a Soviet article about Robeson that does not in some way refer to Robeson's love of Pushkin. A fine example can be found in Boris Polevoi's "Zdravstvuite, dorogoi drug!" ("Greetings Dear Friend!"), (*Pravda*, 15 August 1958, 4) in which the author describes visiting Robeson in his Harlem home in 1956 and finding him reciting the first lines of Pushkin's epic poem "Eugene Onegin," which according to Polevoi, Robeson was translating into English. Polevoi retells this story in *Amerikanskie Dnevniki* (Moscow: Detskaia Literatura, 1957) and in a letter to Robeson dated 9 May 1956 (RGALI, fond 631, opis 26, ex. 3882; here and elsewhere ex, edinista khrahenia, denotes an individual collection within a fond.

79 For a sampling of the extensive Soviet coverage of Robeson, see the following: "Nashi druz'ia" ("Our Friends"), *Ogonek* 18 (1951): 25; Dzh. Roberts, "Narodny Tribun" ("The People's Stand"), *Molodezh' Mira* 6 (1952): 18–19; G. Avenarius, "Pol' Robson—Kinoakter" ("Paul Robeson—Film Actor"), *Ogonek* 35 (1955): 23; "U Polia Robsona" ("At Home with Paul Robeson"), *Pravda*, 4 December 1956, 4; Cedric Belfridzh, "Moi drug Pol' Robson" ("My Friend Paul Robeson"), *Literaturnaia Gazeta*, 5 July 1956, 1; "Pol' Robson v Londone" ("Paul Robeson in London"), *Literaturnaia Gazeta*, 29 July 1958, 4; "Vydaiushchiĭsia artist i borets"

("Outstanding Artist and Fighter"), *Literaturnaia Gazeta*, 8 April 1958, 4; "V Gostiiakh u Polia Robsona" ("At Home with Paul Robeson"), *Pravda*, 7 April 1958, 3; I. Karev, "Vstrecha c Robsonom" ("A Meeting with Robeson"), *Izvestiia*, 8 April 1958, 3; I. Kurdiumov, "Vstrecha s Polem Robsonom" ("A Meeting with Paul Robeson"), *Sovetskaia Kul'tura*, 8 April 1958, 5; I. Kozlovskii, "Nash Pol' Robson" ("Our Paul Robeson"), *Izvestiia*, 9 April 1958, 5; I. Martynov, "Nash Dorogoi gost' " ("Our Dear Guest"), *Izvestiia*, 15 August 1958, 2; Evg. Dolmatov-skii, "Dobro pozhalovat'!" ("A Warm Welcome!"), *Literaturnaia Gazeta*, 16 August 1958, 4; Lev Nikulin, "Dva kontserta Polia Robsona" ("Two Concerts by Paul Robeson"), *Literaturnaia Gazeta*, 19 August 1958, 3; Mikhail Dolgopolov, "Pol' Robson—pochetnyi professor Moskovskoi konservatorii" ("Paul Robeson—Honored Professor of the Moscow Conservatory"), *Literaturnaia Gazeta*, 14 September 1958, 3; Gerbert Marshall, "Moi vstrechi s Robsonom" ("My Meetings with Robeson"), *Teatr* 8 (1960): 182–84; "Pol' Robson: Cherez vsiu zhizn' " ("Paul Robeson: Throughout His Life"), *Teatralnaia Zhizn'* (1960): 4–5; I. Kurdiumov, "Pevets svobody i druzhby narodov" ("Singer of Freedom and Friendship among Peoples"), *Pravda*, 9 April 1963, 4; K. Kudrov, "Artist, Borets" ("Artist, Fighter"), *Izvestiia*, 9 April 1963, 4; and "Pozdravliaem vas, Pol' Robson!" ("Congratulations, Paul Robeson!"), *Kul'tura I Zhizn'* 4 (1963): 42. Unless otherwise noted, all translations here and elsewhere are my own.

80 See, for example, I. Lapitskiia, "Pol' Robson" ("Paul Robeson"), *Ogonek* 15 (1949): 23; Robeson, "Pesni moego naroda"; Robeson "Pesni svobody" ("Songs of Freedom"), *Inostrannaia Literatura* 5 (1955): 249–50; "Pol' Robson obviniaet" ("Paul Robeson is Prosecuted"), *Izvestiia*, 15 June 1956; "Ia vsegda s sovetskim narodom" ("I Am Always with the Soviet People"), *Sovetskaia Rossiia*, 4 December 1956; Vladimir Zimianin, *Pol' Robson* (Moscow: Molodaia Gvardiia, 1985). Interestingly, the FBI confidential field report depicts Robeson's initial reaction to the Soviet Union in the following manner: "How can I describe my feelings upon crossing the Soviet border. All I can say is that the moment I came there I realized that I had found what I had been seeking all my life. It was a new planet—a new constellation. It filled me with such happiness as I have never before known in my life" (FBI Files, reel 1, section 1, frame 105).

81 L. Glazkova, "Pevets-tribun" ("The Singer's Stand"), *Sovetskaia muzika* 7 (1949): 78. Similar positive reactions and praise for Robeson's inclusive concert repertoire can be found in the following biographies, articles, and poems: I Kulikova, Pol Robson—Borets za mir i demokratiia ("Paul Robeson—Fighter for Peace and Democracy"), Moscow: Izdatel'stvo Znanie, 1952; Zimianin, *Pol' Robson* (Moscow: Molodaia Gvardia, 1985), I. Lapitskii, "Pol' Robson" ("Paul Robeson"), *Ogonek* 15 (April 1949): 23; N. Grebnev, "Pesnia Mira" ("Songs of Peace"), *Smena* 9 (1950): 14; A. Pidsukha, "Slovo o nashikh druz'iakh" ("Words about Our

Friends"), *Druzhba Narodov* 4 (1950): 8–12; "Nashi Druz'ia" ("Our Friends"), *Ogonek* 18 (April 1951): 25; Dzh. Roberts, "Narodnii tribun" ("The People's Stand"), *Molodezh' Mira* 6 (1952): 18–19; Mark Maksimov, "Robson v Moskve" ("Robeson in Moscow"), *Novy Mir* 1 (1952): 7–8; Dzhozef Starobin, "Robson poet" ("Robeson Sings"), *Inostrannaia Literatura* 2 (1952): 253–56; as well as an undated, unauthored memo, "Pol' Robson, kontserti v Moskve/Paul Robeson, the Concerts in Moscow," RGALI, fond 631, opis 26, ex. 3857.

82 I. C. Kulikova, "Soldat armii mira" ("Soldier in the Army of Peace"), *Teatr* 3 (1951): 102.

83 Paul Robeson, *Na Tom Ia Stoiu* (Moscow: Uzdatel'stvo Pravda, *Moskva* 1958), 28; hereafter cited parenthetically as *NTIS*.

84 L. T. Kosmodem'ianskaia, "Pesni mira" ("Songs of Peace") *Sovetskaia Zhenshchina (Soviet Woman)* (1951): 44.

85 This was reported in the *L.A. Evening Herald*, 1 October 1953: "The Soviet Alpinist Society today honored the American Negro singer Paul Robeson by naming a mountain peak the 'Paul Robeson Peak.' The mountain is in the Tan range on the northern border of the republic of Kazakhstan." The location and mountain range is corrected in an article by Thelma Dale Perkins in which she reports that the Robeson peak is the highest in the Ala-Tau range in the Kirghiz republic ("A Letter to Paul Robeson on Our Visit to Mt. Robeson," *New World Review* 4 (1973); also cited in Duberman, *Paul Robeson*, n.8, p. 717.

86 A telepress release dated 21 December 1950 indicates that the showpieces of the opening of the 1950 Soviet art exhibition at Moscow's Tretiakov Gallery were a sculpture inspired by Robeson's message (depicting international peace and the peoples of the world) and a painting portraying Robeson specifically (Paul Robeson Collection, Schomburg Center for Research in Black Culture [Bethesda, Md.: University Publications of America, 1991], reel 2, frame 809; hereafter cited parenthetically as PRC). A press release dated 24 November 1954 from the Provisional Committee to Restore Paul Robeson's Passport indicates that the Soviet author Boris Polevoi "has written a play about Robeson which has been produced in Moscow and other centers of the Soviet Union" (PRC, reel 6, frame 954). I have found no such play in Polevoi's collected works, but in a letter from Polevoi to Robeson (2 November 1954), the author does mention the short story "entitled 'Joe Hill Resurrected' where I tell of your concert given to the workers of the district where Joe Hill lived and heroically died." According to this letter, Robeson had written some introductory "notes" for the book in which the story was to be published (PRC, reel 1, frame 416). Yet this is somewhat contradicted by a later letter (14 December 1956) sent by Polevoi to Robeson that casts doubt over Robeson's familiarity with Polevoi's Joe Hill story, its appearance in book form, and its provenance. In the later letter, Polevoi states that the story was "somehow pub-

lished in *Ogonek.*" He writes, "The story is about you" ("rasskaz o tebe"), that he is sending another copy to Robeson (the previous copy presumably never arrived), and that he is anxious to hear Robeson's reaction (RGALI, fond 631, opis 26, ex. 3882). Indeed, "Joe Hill Resurrected" did appear in *Ogonek* in November 1956 (and only later in book form, in the collection *Dalekie druz'ia* (*Distant Friends*) (Moscow: Pravda, 1959). Polevoi also makes no reference to a play about Robeson in the articles (describing their warm relationship) he wrote for *Pravda* that appeared in 1958 ("Pol' Robson: K 60-letiiu so dnia rozhdeniia" ("Paul Robeson: On His Sixtieth Birthday"), *Pravda,* 9 April 1958, 5; and "Zdravstvuite, dorogoi drug!")

87   D. B. Skobel'tsin, "Laureaty Stalinskikh premii mira" ("Laureates of the Stalin Peace Prize"), *Pravda,* 21 December 1952, 1. Although he was one of seven to receive the prize, Robeson took center stage in the coverage of recipients, as evidenced by *Pravda*'s placing his photograph as the centerpiece of those of the seven awardees.

88   Letter from Sergei Yutkevich to Paul Robeson, 15 March 1955 (PRC, reel 6, frame 199). On the same topic, see Robeson correspondence with the Union of Soviet Writers, April–May 1955 (RGALI, fond 631, opis 26, ex. 3849).

89   As indicated by the Robeson File holdings at RGALI, Robeson also corresponded with numerous Russians, both friends and functionaries. The most substantial of these holdings are from the file of the Foreign Commission of the Union of Soviet Writers (Inostrannaia komissiia Soiuza pisatelei SSSR), fond 631. They include his correspondence with Polevoi (fond 631, opis 26, ex. 199, 258, 246, 3882, 3840); with Fadeev (fond 631, opis 26, ex. 38); with Mikola Bazhan (fond 631, opis 26, ex. 199, 246); and telegrams and invitations from the Union of Soviet Writers as well as correspondence with the editors of *Freedomways* (fond 631, opis 28, delo 11, 27; and fond 631, opis 26, ex. 246, 3820, 3840, 3790, 3960, 4275). The other notable collection can be found in the Eisenstein file, fond 1923, and includes correspondence between Robeson and Eisenstein, who together hoped to make a film (*Black Majesty*) describing the Haitian rebellion led by Henri Christophe against Napoleon's troops and starring Robeson (fond 1923, opis 1, ex. 1118, 1509, 2074); and numerous photographs of the two men (fond 1923, opis 1, ex. 2900, 2974; and fond 1923, opis 2, ex. 2163, 2244, 2646, 2647). Some of the Eisenstein-Robeson correspondence, which took place in the 1930s, was published in the magazine *Inostrannaia Literatura* 1 (1958): 242–51.

90   See correspondence between Paul Robeson and the Union of Soviet Writers, 18 September 1954 to 31 December 1954 (RGALI, fond 631, opis 28, delo 11). Letter of invitation to the congress from Alexander Fadeev and Boris Polevoi to Paul Robeson (20 October 1954) also in Robeson Papers, reel 6, frame 678; this invitation is also mentioned in a letter from Boris Polevoi to Paul Robeson dated 22 August 1955 (RGALI, fond 631, opis 26, ex. 3840). Robeson's subsequent request

for permission to add a visit to Moscow to his itinerary delineated in his passport application of 1954 is found in a letter from Paul Robeson to Mrs. R. B. Shipley dated 5 November 1954 (PRC, reel 6, frame 679). The press release announcing the refusal of his passport can be found in PRC, reel 6, frame 954.

91   RGALI, fond 631, opis 26, ex. 3840.

92   "Trudno, ochen' trudno inostrantsu, priekhavshemu nenadolgo v vashu velikuiu i svoeobraznuiu stranu, napisat' o nei, da tak, chtoby bylo i zhivo i interesno, i ne bylo v nei 'razvesistoi kliukvy'—kak u nas govoriat" (letter from Boris Polevoi to Paul Robeson, 9 May 1956 [RGALI, fond 631, opis 26, ex. 3882]). Again indicating the partiality of his perspective, Polevoi goes on in his letter to request that Robeson offer his critical comments and advice about how to improve the *Diaries.*

93   Polevoi was also well aware of the limitations imposed by censorship in getting a "true" message across national boundaries. An extended footnote in *American Diaries* reveals that a falsified account of Polevoi's trip to the United States appeared in an article in *Reader's Digest.* In response, Polevoi wrote an outraged letter first to *Reader's Digest* and subsequently to the editor of the *New York Times.* He received no reply from either publication. As he concluded, so much for the "very popular American myth of a free press" (Polevoi, *Amerikanskie Dnevniki,* 294).

94   Ibid.

95   PRC, reel 1, frame 428. Polevoi repeats this story in a later letter to Robeson in which he thanks Robeson for the signed photo of the singer: "Helen is finally convinced that You are a person, not a mythological one but a real one" ("Alena okonchatel'no ubedilas', chto vy figura ne mifologicheskaia, a realnaia") (RGALI, fond 631, opis 26, ex 3840).

96   Kosmodem'ianskaia, "Pesni mira," 44.

97   I. Martynov, "Nash dorogoi gost.'"

98   See especially the following articles published in June and July of 1956: C. Belfredge, "Moi drug Pol' Robson" ("My Friend Paul Robeson"), *Izvestiia,* 14 June 1956; C. Belfredge, "Presledovanie Polia Robsona" ("The Persecution of Paul Robeson"), *Pravda,* 14 June 1956; C. Belfredge, "Pol' Robson obviniaet" ("Paul Robeson Accuses"), *Izvestiia,* 15 June 1956, 2; as well as others from earlier in the year, including the New Year's greetings from Paul Robeson, "Idet novii den'" ("A New Day Is Coming"), *Pravda,* 3 January 1956, 3; and F. Orekhov, "U Polia Robsona" ("At Home with Paul Robeson"), *Pravda,* 4 December 1956, 4.

99   See Andrew Parker and Eve Kosofsky Sedgwick, "Introduction" *Performativity and Performance,* 9.

100   In a wry commentary on his own predicament in a letter to the editor of *New York Amsterdam News,* Robeson suggested another book to reference the hypocrisy of

the court. "Let others go abroad and 'praise' the treatment of Negroes in Mississippi, if that is what they are moved to do, but tell me: Where in the Bible does it say that the Commandment, 'Thou shalt not bear false witness,' does not apply to Negro Americans who travel abroad?" Letter from Paul Robeson to *New York Amsterdam News* editor, 15 September 1955 (PRC, reel 6, frame 71).

101   See Lloyd L. Brown, "State Department Says African Freedom 'Against Best Interests of U.S.,'" *Freedom* (April 1952): 5. As the *Spotlight on Africa* newsletter, published by the Council on African Affairs, points out, Robeson was not the only prominent figure denied passport privileges. In addition to Robeson, Du Bois and Dr. George Shepherd (executive director of the American Committee on Africa) had their passport privileges revoked. The newsletter notes that "several other persons engaged in African affairs who have been critical of existing colonial policies from a liberal non-Communist viewpoint have had difficulty entering the United States. Our Passport and Immigration Department seems to be open to suggestion from colonial powers that 'critics' be kept out or restricted. . . . An alarming curtain of silence is descending between the U.S. and the colonies cutting our people off from basic sources of information about important events in Africa" (PRC, reel 7, frames 207–8).

102   Unsigned letter to Dr. Alphaeus Hunton, 14 February 1952 (PRC, reel 6, frame 178).

103   About his disappointment with the film *Tales of Manhattan,* in which he played a sharecropper, Robeson told the *New York Times,* "I thought I could change the picture as we went along . . . but in the end it turned out to be the same old thing—the Negro solving his problem by singing his way to glory. This is very offensive to my people" ("Hollywood's 'Old Plantation Tradition' is 'Offensive to My People,'" *New York Times,* 24 September 1942; reprinted in Philip S. Foner, ed., *Paul Robeson Speaks: Writings Speeches, Interviews, 1918–1974* [New York: Carol Publishing Group, 1978], 142).

104   My understanding of performativity is indebted to discussions by Jacques Derrida, "Signature Event Context," in *Margins of Philosophy,* trans. Alan Bass (Chicago: University of Chicago Press, 1992); Judith Butler, *Gender Trouble: Feminism and the Subversion of Identity* (New York: Routledge, 1988), and *Bodies That Matter: On the Discursive Limits of "Sex"* (New York: Routledge, 1993), and Parker and Sedgwick, "Introduction." As Butler writes, "Performativity describes [a] relation of being implicated in that which one opposes, this turning of power against itself to produce alternate modalities of power, to establish a kind of political contestation that is not a 'pure' opposition, a 'transcendence' of contemporary relationships of power, but a difficult labor of forging a future from resources inevitably impure" (*Bodies That Matter,* 241).

105   Jeffrey C. Stewart, "The Black Body: Paul Robeson as a Work of Art and Politics," in *Paul Robeson: Artist and Citizen,* 160.

106   The history of handling goes back to the management of Robeson's concert schedule by Max Yergan during the 1940s. The specificities of this handling are well documented in the FBI reports, sec. 1. Of particular interest is the transcript of a conversation between Yergan and Robeson (sec. 1, 103–4), and Yergan's reporting of the conversation in a subsequent transcript (sec. 1, 108–9).

107   Victor Turner, *The Anthropology of Performance* (New York: PAJ Publications, 1988), 24.

108   As Gerald Horne has pointed out, although Robeson "was no doubt a brilliant individual . . . he did not grow to political and intellectual maturity alone." He may have been the " 'tallest tree in our forest,' but he was far from being the only tree in that forest" ("Comrades and Friends: The Personal/Political World of Paul Robeson," in *Paul Robeson: Artist and Citizen*, 215.

109   Turner, *The Anthropology of Performance*, 91.

110   In chapter 3 I discuss a similar strategy of Du Bois's—that is, the attempt to bring to life the "excluded and illegible domain that haunts the [intelligible] domain as the spectre of its own impossibility, the very limit to intelligibility, its constitutive outside" (Butler, *Bodies That Matter*, xi).

111   Ibid.

112   On the use of opposition to foment creative dynamics in the black church, see Gerald L. Davis, *I Got the Word in Me and I Can Sing It, You Know: A Study of the Performed African-American Sermon* (Philadelphia: University of Pennsylvania Press, 1985), 11.

113   Rosemary Hennessy, *Materialist Feminism and the Politics of Discourse* (New York: Routledge, 1993), 32.

114   The FBI took great interest in the attempts of Robeson et al. to resist mainstream blacklisting. See, for example, FBI, reel 1, section 7, frame 986.

115   At the same time, McKay supported a "Communist definition of self-determined blackness which would affix black nationalist sentiment to actual geographic territory in America by identifying the southern black belt of the US as an oppressed nation" (Stephens, "Black Transnationalism" 602). Thus McKay, like Robeson, desired to see a simultaneous emerging of the international and national. In this sense, although the political climate had changed dramatically by the 1950s, McKay's sense that he was received like a "black ikon" by the Soviets offers a prism through which to see Russian reaction to Robeson more clearly. See McKay's recollections of his 1922 trip to Russia in *A Long Way from Home* (1937; reprint, New York: Harcourt Brace Jovanovich, 1970). As I state elsewhere, McKay's 1937 memories of his visit diverge greatly from the descriptions and impressions he penned in 1922–1923.

116   For more information about Soviet and African relations prior to World War II, see Wilson, *Russia and Black Africa before WWII*, which argues against the prevailing Sovietology opinion that the Soviet Union had no interest in or real

relationship with Africa prior to the 1950s. A more conventional Sovietologist take can be found in Cohn, *Soviet Policy toward Black Africa;* and David E. Albright, "Moscow's African Policy of the 1970s," ed. David E. Albright, *Communism in Africa* (Bloomington: Indiana University Press, 1980), 35–66.

117   Cohn, *Soviet Policy toward Black Africa,* 23.

118   " 'Black Stalin' Aim is Laid to Robeson," *New York Times,* 15 July 1949, n.p.

119   FBI files, sec. 12, reel 2, frame 16. For more on Kennan's interesting relationship with the Soviet Union, see Frank Costigliola, " 'Unceasing Pressure for Penetration': Gender, Pathology, and Emotion in George Kennan's Formation of the Cold War," *Journal of American History* 83, no. 4 (March 1997): 1309–60. Kennan's nostalgia for the Russian people as "unforgettable . . . [t]hey really are in a great many ways a new type of human being," reflects the excitement even a diplomat such as Kennan felt at the prospect of the novi Sovetskii chelovek (new Soviet person/man). It was this sense of a reformulated citizen that resonated even more strongly with African Americans such as Hughes and Robeson in Russia during these same years (1933–1934).

120   See Thomas J. Noer's discussion of how the United States attempted to negotiate a "middle position" between anticolonialism and white supremacy in *Cold War and Black Liberation: The United States and White Rule in Africa, 1948–1968* (Columbia: University of Missouri Press, 1985), 17–56.

121   *Krokodil,* no. 21, 30 July 1956, 1455.

122   Polevoi, "Zdravstvuite, dorogoi drug!" Of course, such liberties were often taken with the understanding that there was a U.S. precedent at hand. In a *Literaturnaia Gazeta* article, the author writes, "Big Paul, as he is called here [in the United States] by his close friends" (L. Grigor'ev, "Ia vsegda budu vashim drugom" ("I Will Always Be Your Friend"), *Literaturnaia Gazeta,* 7 April 1958, 4). (The fact that such "bigness" referred to age—the younger Paul Jr. was called "Little Paul"— was likely lost on Russians.) But even Du Bois portrayed Robeson as "magnificent in height and breadth," an indication that Robeson's physical presence encouraged descriptive terms that played into conventional, racialized understandings of blacks as physically anomalous, as fundamentally different from whites ("Tribute to Robeson," in *The Autobiography of W. E. B. Du Bois: A Soliloquy on Viewing My Life from the Last Decade of Its First Century* [1968; reprint, New York: International Publishers, 1991], 397).

123   By designating Western colonialism as a process by which beastly black men are turned into pliant white women, this cartoon also suggests (and reproduces) the evisceration of black women.

124   See discussion of prerevolutionary interest in Africa on page 274 note 49.

125   For the details concerning Robeson's knowledge of these activities, his friendships with key Jewish figures, and his reaction to the Khrushchev revelations, see Paul

Robeson, Jr. "How My Father Last Met Itzik Feffer," *Jewish Currents* (November 1981): 4–8; Arie L. Eliav, *Between Hammer and Sickle* (New York, New American Library, 1969); Nora Levin, *The Jews in the Soviet Union since 1917: Paradox of Survival,* Vol. II (New York, New York University Press, 1990), 503, 593, 915n.63, 932n.64; Louis Rapoport, *Stalin's War against the Jews: The Doctor's Plot and the Soviet Solution* (New York, Free Press, 1990), 66–67, 91–93, 115–117, 172–173, 260–261n.78–80; Paul Robeson Jr., liner notes to *The Legendary Moscow Concert* (New York: Fenix Entertainment, 1995); and M. Geizer, *Mikhoels: Zhuzn' i smert'/ Mikhoels: Life and Death* (Moscow: Zhurnalistkoe Agentstvo "Glasnost'" Soiuz Zhurnalistov, 1998), 234–235; and Duberman, *Paul Robeson* 352–353, 417, 690n.42, 711–712n.29. For a more general account of the party line during the same period, see Howard Fast, *Being Red* (New York: Dell, 1990), 217–221; 322–324; 330–331; 346–347. See also William L. Patterson *The Man Who Cried Genocide* (New York, International Publishers 1951); Paul Robeson, "Genocide Stalks the U.S.A.," *New World Review* (February, 1952): 24–29; and Duberman, *Paul Robeson,* 397–399, 705n.41.

126 See the article by V. Strel'nikov in which the author depicts Soviet concert-goers reacting with positive enthusiasm to Robeson's performances and chanting "Diadia Pavel!" This article also underlines the familiarity of Soviets with Robeson, "it's pointless for me to describe him . . . you readers know Robeson well / Mne nezachem opisyvat' ego . . . chitateli khorosho znaiut Robsona," "V Gostiiakh u Polia Robsona," 3.

127 Boris Polevoi, "Voskresenie Dzho Hilla" ("Joe Hill Resurrected"), *Ogonek* 44 (November 1956): 20–24.

128 Ibid., 20. The Russian text reads, "On napominaet l'va v kletke. Da on i est' lev v kletke—Pol' Robson."

129 Ibid.

130 Ibid., 21. This is likely as far as Polevoi was permitted to go in terms of suggesting Soviet willingness to be quite explicit about what was not permitted Soviet citizens, particularly when it came to movement both within and outside national borders. Unlike Robeson's cage, the boundaries surrounding Soviets were, as Polevoi was well aware, quite visible and "formal."

131 See, for example, a fairly straightforward article about desegregation in the previous month's *Ogonek* by L. Tiurina, "V iuzhnykh shtatakh" ("In the Southern States"), *Ogonek* 44 (1956): 14. In this article, a caustic exposé of race-based inequalities, a familiar tactic of associating black Americans with the rural South adheres to the sensualized depiction.

132 Quoted in Duberman, *Paul Robeson,* 186.

133 Wilson, *Russia and Black Africa Before WWII,* 97.

134 Wilson contends that, "For Africans, exposure to Russia had both a modernizing

and politicizing effect. . . . On a practical level, Africans learned from Communists the importance of propaganda and the utility of establishing newspapers
and organizing international conferences to further their political ends. . . .
[T]he Comintern contributed valuable psychological conditions for the independence movement. ("Russia's Historic Stake in Africa," in *Communism in Africa*,
ed. David E. Albright (Bloomington: Indiana University Press, 1980), 91). For a
Soviet perspective on these issues, see A. A. Ozadovskiĭ, *Ssha i Afrika: Problemy
Neokolonializm* (Moscow: Izdatel'stvo Mysl', 1997).

135   V. Chernishov, "Ia Vsegda c Covetskim narodom ("I Am Always with the Soviet
People"), *Sovetskaia Rossiia*, 4 December 1956, n.p.

136   Quoted in Duberman, *Paul Robeson,* 257.

137   This and previous quotes cited in Von Eschen, *Race against Empire,* 127.

EPILOGUE: THE ONLY TELEVISION HOSTESS
WHO DOESN'T TURN RED

1   With the repeal of antipornography laws in the era of glasnost and the burgeoning of a popular porn industry by the 1990s, sex was very much out of the Soviet
closet by the time *Pro Eto* appeared. See M. Levitt and A. Torpokov, eds., *Eros and
Pornography in Russian Culture* (Moscow: Ladomir, 1999). It should be noted that
the title of the show, *Pro Eto,* is borrowed from a cycle of poems by Vladimir
Mayakovsky in which the "it" in *About It* is meant to signify sex.

2   There are an estimated fourteen thousand "Afro-Russians" living in Russia today,
a majority of whom are the descendants of African men (who came to study in
Russia in the 1960s and 1970s) and Soviet women. See Marisa Robertson-Textor,
"Russia's Few Blacks Find an Uneasy Home in Their White Motherland," *Los
Angeles Times,* 13 June 1999, A3.

3   For a discussion of the controversies over new, Western-style television shows in
Russia, in particular the alleged licentiousness of *Pro Eto,* see Andrei Zolotov,
"NTV Scolded by Duma for Low Moral Standard," *The Moscow Times,* 1 February
1998. ⟨http://www.moscowtimes.ru/stories/1998/02/07/004.html⟩.

4   As Khanga mentions in *Soul to Soul: A Black Russian Jewish Woman's Search for
Her Roots* (New York: W. W. Norton, 1992), she was interviewed by *Jet* magazine
and was the topic of a *20/20* segment on ABC. *Soul to Soul* is hereafter cited
parenthetically as *SS.*

5   An in-depth review of Khanga's book can be found in Joshua Rubenstein, "Black
in the U.S.S.R.," *Nation* 14, December 1992, 750–63.

6   According to *Soul to Soul,* Bertha Bialek's renunciation of her Jewish upbringing
was reflected in the largely nonreligious rearing of Yelena. Thus, the "Jewish"
element of Khanga's genealogy receives less focus, although she does describe her
encounter in the 1990s with the U.S. Bialeks as a family reunion. Jewishness, then,

is far from renounced; it is simply not a focus of her genealogical excavations. Interestingly, Khanga locates "soul" in Russian and African American cultures, but not in Africa.

7   Angela Davis, *An Autobiography* (1974; reprint, New York: International Publishers, 1988), 398.

8   Ibid.

9   Mikhail Epstein, *After the Future: The Paradoxes of Postmodernism and Contemporary Russian Culture,* trans. and ed. Anesa Miller-Pogacar (Amherst: University of Massachusetts Press, 1995), 155.

10 For a discussion of Russian responses to post-Communist changes and an elaboration of what it means to "be" Russian, see Catriona Kelly, David Shepherd, and Stephen White, "Conclusion: Towards Post-Soviet Pluralism? Postmodernism and Beyond," in *Russian Cultural Studies: An Introduction,* ed. Catriona Kelly and David Shepherd (Oxford: Oxford University Press, 1998), 387–400. As Stephen F. Cohen explains, the reasons for firm disillusionment with and resentments against the West include: the expansion of the North Atlantic Treaty Organization to Russia's borders; U.S. policy toward Iraq; the buildup of U.S. military bases in Uzbekistan; a refusal to pardon Russia's immense foreign debt; and a general sense that "Russia no longer matters" ("Second Chance with Russia," *Nation,* 5 November 2001, 7, 23).

11 Kelly, Shepherd, and White, "Conclusion," 394.

12 See Kester Klomegah, who writes, "If you are black in Russia, hardly a day goes by without having to confront racism" ("Victims of Racism in New Russia Defenseless," *The Moscow Times,* 26 November 1997.

13 See Michael R. Gordon, "Black U.S. Marine Assaulted in Wave of Racism in Moscow," *New York Times,* 5 May 1998, A5.

14 Transliteration appears here as it does in *Soul to Soul.*

15 For a discussion of the Soviet era as a kind of "postmodern pastiche," see Epstein's provocative analysis in *After the Future.*

16 See, for example, Helen Womack, "Russian Dolls: They May Know Their D&G from Their Versace, but after Ten Years of Capitalism, the Lives of Russian Women Are Still in the Dark Ages," *Independent,* 3 October 1999, Features, 1–2.

17 It should be noted that Western feminism is often pilloried for its perceived lack of relevance to the Russian context, and used as an example of the difference between Russians and the West. In this sense, it is not at all difficult to be a woman in Russia: the delineations between masculinity and femininity make it quite easy for a woman to know her place, and thus, if she is so inclined, to challenge it. This view of women and women's issues, however, does not preclude the existence of women in Russia who confound stereotypes and refuse the reduction of sex to gender (and vice versa). For a range of Russian women writers' views on women's

issues in Soviet and post-Soviet society, see Christine Tomei, ed., *Russian Women Writers*, vols. 1 and 2 (New York: Garland, 1999).

18 Cited in Alessandra Stanley, "On Russian TV, Suddenly the Screen is Steamy," *New York Times*, 11 November 1997, A4. See also Jennifer Younger, "Daughter of Greenwich Village," *Village Voice* 43, no. 10 (10 March 1998): 46–49; and Chrystia Freeland, "Sex, Talk, and Allusion," *Financial Times*, 1 July 1998, 17.

19 Cited in Stanley, "On Russian TV"; see also Khanga, *Soul to Soul*, 160.

20 For a look at the emergence and mutations of a Western-style televisual circuit of desire and identification in a post-Soviet Russia, see my article, "Montezuma's Revenge: Reading *los ricos tambien lloran* in Russia," in *To Be Continued: Soap Operas Around the World,* ed. Robert C. Allen (London, New York: Routledge, 1995), 285–300.

21 I am indebted to Kevin Platt for his multiple, insightful comments on this epilogue, in particular his interpretation of the missionary zeal with which (the political line on) *Pro Eto* seeks to redeem sexual differences and the ways this reflects an "enlightening" project carried out by Westernized Russian media moguls on behalf of the Russian masses.

SELECTED BIBLIOGRAPHY

MICROFILM AND ARCHIVAL SOURCES

FBI Files on Paul Robeson. 2 Reels (1941–1978). Wilmington: Scholarly Resources, 1987.

James Weldon Johnson Memorial Collection of Negro Arts and Letters. Beinecke Rare Book and Manuscript Library, Yale University.

Paul Robeson Collection. 9 reels (1949–1956). Schomburg Center for Research in Black Culture. Bethesda, Md.: University Publications of America, 1991.

Rossiiskii gosudarstvennyi arkhiv literatury i iskusstva (RGALI) (Russian State Archive of Literature and Art). Moscow.

Rossiiskii tsentr khraneniia i izucheniia dokumentov noveishei istorii (RTSKhIDNI) (Russian Center for the Preservation and Study of Documents of Recent History). Moscow.

W. E. B. Du Bois Papers. 89 reels (1926–1961). University of Massachusetts, Amherst. Sanford, N.C.: Microfilming Corporation of America, 1980–1981.

UNPUBLISHED MANUSCRIPTS

Hughes, Langston. *I Wonder as I Wander.* Manuscript. James Weldon Johnson Collection. Beinecke Rare Book and Manuscript Library, Yale University.

——. Selected correspondence. James Weldon Johnson Collection. Beinecke Rare Book and Manuscript Library, Yale University.

Patterson, Louise Thompson. "Louise Thompson Patterson Memoirs: Trip to Russia." Draft 1. n.d. Special collections and Archives. Robert W. Woodruff Library, Emory University.

——. Louise Thompson Patterson Memoirs: Trip to Russia—1932." Draft 2. October–November 1994. Special Collections and Archives. Robert W. Woodruff Library, Emory University.

——. "Louise Thompson Patterson Memoirs: Trip to Russia—1932." Draft 3. October–November 1994. Special Collections and Archives. Robert W. Woodruff Library, Emory University.

——. Interview by Margaret Wilkerson, 21 January 1986. Special Collections and Archives. Robert W. Woodruff Library, Emory University.

Albright, David E. ed. *Communism in Africa*. Bloomington: Indiana University Press, 1980.

Aptheker, Herbert, ed. *The Correspondence of W. E. B. Du Bois, Vol. III, Selections 1944–1963*. Amherst: University of Massachusetts Press, 1978.

Attwood, Lynne, and Catriona Kelly. "Programmes for Identity: The 'New Man' and the 'New Woman.'" In *Constructing Russian Culture in the Age of Revolution: 1881–1940*, edited by Catriona Kelly and David Shepherd. Oxford: Oxford University Press, 1998.

Baker, Lee. *From Savage to Negro: Anthropology and the Construction of Race, 1896–1954*. Berkeley: University of California Press, 1998.

Benjamin, Walter. *Reflections*. Translated by Edmund Jephcott. New York: Schocken Books, 1978.

Berlin, Isaiah. *Russian Thinkers*. New York: Viking, 1978.

Berry, Faith. *Langston Hughes: Before and Beyond Harlem*. Westport, Conn.: L. Hill, 1983.

Blakely, Allison. *Russia and the Negro: Blacks in Russian History and Thought*. Washington, D.C.: Howard University Press, 1986.

Bontemps, Arna. *Arna Bontemps/Langston Hughes Letters, 1925–1967*. Edited by Charles H. Nichols. New York: Paragon, 1990.

Brooks, Jeffrey. "Official Xenophobia and Popular Cosmopolitanism in Early Soviet Russia." *American Historical Review* 97, no. 5 (1992): 1431–48.

———. "The Press and Its Message: Images of America in the 1920s and 1930s." In *Russia in the Era of NEP: Explorations in Soviet Society and Culture*, edited by Sheila Fitzpatrick, A. Rabinowitch, and Richard Stites. Bloomington: Indiana University Press, 1991.

Butler, Judith. *Bodies That Matter: On the Discursive Limits of "Sex."* New York: Routledge, 1993. ·

Carby, Hazel. *Race Men*. Cambridge: Harvard University Press, 1998.

Chernishov, V. "Ia vsegda c Covetskim narodom." *Sovetskaia Rossiia*, 4 December 1956. n.p.

Cohn, Helen Desfosses. *Soviet Policy toward Black Africa: The Focus on National Integration*. New York: Praeger, 1974.

Cooper, Wayne. *Claude McKay: Rebel Sojourner in the Harlem Renaissance*. Baton Rouge: Louisiana State University Press, 1987.

———. *The Passion of Claude McKay*. New York: Schocken Books, 1973.

Davis, Angela. "Women and Capitalism: Dialectics of Oppression and Liberation." In *The Angela Y. Davis Reader*, edited by Joy James. Malden, Mass.: Blackwell, 1998.

Denning, Michael. *The Cultural Front: The Laboring of Culture in the Twentieth Century*. New York: Verso, 1996.

Douglas, Mary. *Purity and Danger: An Analysis of the Concepts of Pollution and Taboo.* London: Routledge and Kegan Paul, 1966.

Draper, Theodore. *American Communism and Soviet Russia.* New York: Octagon, 1977.

Duberman, Martin. *Paul Robeson: A Biography.* New York: Ballantine, 1989.

Du Bois, W. E. B. "The Africans and the Colonialist Tactic." *New Times* 7 (1959): 18–19.

———. "Afrika-god 1958." *Sovetskii Vostok* 3 (1959): 13–15.

———. "Amerikanskie negry dob'iutsia po polnogo osvobozhdeniia." *Pravda,* 17 July 1959, 4.

———. *The Autobiography of W. E. B. Du Bois: A Soliloquy on Viewing My Life from the Last Decade of Its First Century.* 1968. Reprint, New York: International Publishers, 1991.

———. "Bor'ba Polia Robsona." *Literaturnaia Gazeta,* 10 April 1958, 4.

———. "Color Lines." *National Guardian,* 12 February 1953, 7.

———. *The Correspondence of W. E. B. Du Bois: Volume 3, Selections, 1944–1963.* Edited by Herbert Aptheker. Amherst: University of Massachusetts Press, 1978.

———. *Dusk of Dawn: An Essay Towards an Autobiography of a Race Concept.* 1940. Reprint, New Brunswick, N.J.: Transaction Publishers, 1997.

———. "Etapy izucheniia negrov v SSHA." *Voprosy Antropologii* 6 (1961): 92–99.

———. *In Battle for Peace: The Story of My Eighty-third Birthday.* New York: Masses and Mainstream, 1952.

———. "Kommunizm pobedit." *Pravda,* 24 November 1961, 6.

———. "Kul'turnye sviazi neobkhodimy." *Inostrannaia Literatura* 5 (1958): 213–14.

———. "Nevidannyi skachok." *Literaturnaia Gazeta,* 5 November 1957, 5.

———. *The Souls of Black Folk.* 1903. Reprint, New York: Bantam, 1989.

———. "Triumf sotsializma." *Izvestiia,* 7 November 1959, 5.

———. "Utro novogo dnia." *Pravda,* 22 April 1963, 3.

———. "Vseobshchii mir i sovetskii semiletii plan." *Pravda,* 25 November 1958, 5.

———. "V soedinennykh shtatakh neobkhodimo vosstanovit' demokratiiu." *Pravda,* 23 May 1960, 3–4.

———. "World Changer." *Mainstream* 10, no. 1 (January 1957): 1–5.

Eisenstein, Sergei. *Film Form.* New York: Harcourt Brace Jovanovich, 1977.

———. *Immoral Memories.* Translated by Herbert Marshall. Boston: Houghton Mifflin, 1983.

———. "Extracts from a Resolution of the Executive Committee of the Communist International Political Secretariat on the Negro Question in the United States" (26 October 1930). In *The Communist International, 1919–1943, Documents,* edited by Jane Degras. 3 vols. London: Oxford University Press, 1956–1965.

Fast, Howard. *Being Red.* New York: Dell, 1990.

Foley, Barbara. *Radical Representations: Politics and Form in U.S. Proletarian Fiction, 1929–1941.* Durham, N.C.: Duke University Press, 1993.

Foner, Philip S., ed. *Paul Robeson Speaks: Writings, Speeches, Interviews, 1918–1974.* New York: Carol Publishing Group, 1978.

Freud, Sigmund. "Findings, Ideas, Problems" (1938). In *The Standard Edition of the Complete Psychological Works of Sigmund Freud,* Vol. XXIII, translated by James Strachey. London: Hogarth Press, 1964.

Gates, Henry Louis, Jr. "Introduction: Darkly as through a Veil." In *The Souls of Black Folk,* by W. E. B. Du Bois. New York: Bantam, 1989.

Gerassimov, Sergei. "Out of the Factory of the Eccentric Actor." In *Cinema in Revolution,* edited by Luda Schnitzer, Jean Schnitzer, and Marcel Martin. New York: Da Capo, 1973.

Gilroy, Paul. *The Black Atlantic: Modernity and Double Consciousness.* Cambridge: Harvard University Press, 1993.

Glazkova, L. "Pevets-tribun." *Sovetskaia muzika* 7 (1949): 78–80.

Gorokhov, V. "C pesnii v bor'be." *Sovetskaia muzika* 4 (1953): 96–99.

Graham, Maryemma. "The Practice of a Social Art." In *Langston Hughes: Critical Perspectives Past and Present,* edited by Henry Louis Gates Jr. and K. A. Appiah. New York: Amistad, 1993.

Graham, Shirley. "Liudi Akkry." *Sovetskii Vostok* 3 (1959): 16–19.

Greenfeld, Liah. *Nationalism: Five Roads to Modernity.* Cambridge: Harvard University Press, 1992.

Grewal, Inderpal. *Home and Harem: Nation, Gender, Empire, and the Cultures of Travel.* Durham, N.C.: Duke University Press, 1996.

Grigor'ev, L. "Ia vsegda budu vashim drugom." *Literaturnaia Gazeta,* 7 April 1958, 4.

Gubina, N. P., ed. *Izuchenie afriki v rossii (dorevoliutzionnii period).* Moscow: Izdatel'stvo Nauka, 1977.

Haywood, Harry. *Black Bolshevik: Autobiography of an Afro-American Communist.* Chicago: Liberator Press, 1978.

Hennessy, Rosemary. *Materialist Feminism and the Politics of Discourse.* New York: Routledge, 1993.

Horne, Gerald. *Black and Red: W. E. B. Du Bois and the Afro-American Response to the Cold War, 1944–1993.* Albany: State University of New York, 1986.

———. "Comrades and Friends: The Personal/Political World of Paul Robeson." In *Paul Robeson: Artist and Citizen,* edited by Jeffrey C. Stewart. New Brunswick, N.J.: Rutgers University Press, 1998.

Hughes, Langston. "Boy Dancers of Uzbekistan." *Travel Magazine* (December 1934): 36–37, 49–50.

———. "Democracy and Me." In *Good Morning Revolution,* edited by Faith Berry. New York: Citadel, 1973.

———. "Farewell to Mahomet." *Travel* (February 1935): 29–31.

———. "Going South in Russia." *Crisis* (June 1934): 162–63.

———. "In an Emir's Harem." *Woman's Home Companion* (September 1934): 12, 91–92.

———. *I Wonder as I Wander.* 1956. Reprint, New York: Thunder Mouth Press, 1986.

———. "Moscow and Me." *International Literature* 3 (1933): 61–66.

———. *A Negro Looks at Soviet Central Asia.* Moscow: International Publishers, 1934.

———. "Negroes in Moscow." *International Literature* 4 (1933): 78–81.

———. "The Soviet Theater in Central Asia." *Asia: Journal of the American Asiatic Association* (October 1934): 590–93.

———. "The Soviet Union and Color." *Chicago Defender,* 15 June 1946, cited in *Langston Hughes and the Chicago Defender: Essays on Race, Politics, and Culture, 1942–1962,* ed. Christopher C. De Santis (Urbana: University of Illinois Press, 1995), 170–72.

———. "The Soviet Union and Women" *Chicago Defender,* 29 June 1946, cited in *Langston Hughes and the Chicago Defender,* 172–74.

———. "Tamara Khanum: Soviet Asia's Greatest Dancer." *Theatre Arts* (November 1934): 829–35.

———. *The Ways of White Folks.* 1933. Reprint, New York: Vintage, 1990.

Huiswood, Otto. "Speech to the Third International." *International Press Correspondent* 3, 5 January 1923, 14–16.

James, C. L. R. "Paul Robeson: Black Star." *Black World* XX no. 1 (November 1970): 106–115.

Jay, Paul. "The Myth of 'America' and the Politics of Location: Modernity, Border Studies, and the Literature of the Americas," *Arizona Quarterly* 54, no. 2 (summer 1998): 165–92.

Johnson, Barbara. *A World of Difference.* Baltimore, Md.: Johns Hopkins University Press, 1987.

Joyce, Joyce Ann. "Race, Culture, and Gender in Langston Hughes's *The Ways of White Folks.*" In *Langston Hughes: The Man, His Art, and His Continuing Influence,* edited by C. James Trotman. New York: Garland Publishing, 1995.

Judy, Ronald A. T. "Paul Gilroy's Black Atlantic and the Place(s) of English in the Global," *Critical Quarterly* 39, no. 1 (spring 1997): 22–29.

Kaplan, Amy, and Donald Pease, eds. *Cultures of United States Imperialism.* Durham, N.C.: Duke University Press, 1993.

Kelley, Robin D. G. *Race Rebels: Culture, Politics, and the Black Working Class.* New York: Free Press, 1994.

Kelly, Catriona, and David Shepherd, eds. *Constructing Russian Culture in the Age of Revolution: 1881–1940.* Oxford: Oxford University Press, 1998.

———. *Russian Cultural Studies: An Introduction.* Oxford: Oxford University Press, 1998.

Khanga, Yelena, *Soul to Soul: A Black Russian Jewish Woman's Search for Her Roots.* New York: W. W. Norton, 1992.

Khrushchev, Nikita. "Doktoru Uil'iamu Diubua." *Pravda,* 23 February 1963, 1.

Klehr, Harvey. *The Heyday of American Communism: The Depression Decade.* New York: Basic Books, 1984.

Klehr, Harvey, and John Earl Haynes. *The American Communist Movement: Storming Heaven Itself.* New York: Twayne Publishers, 1992.

Klehr, Harvey, John Earl Haynes, and Kiril Mikhailovich Anderson. *The Soviet World of American Communism.* New Haven, Conn.: Yale University Press, 1998.

Kommunisticheskii internatzional v dokumentakh, 1919–1932. Moscow: Partiĭnoeizdatel'stvo, 1933.

Kosmodem'ianskaia, L. T. "Pesni mira." *Sovetskaia Zhenshchina* 2 (1951): 44.

Kristeva, Julia. *Powers of Horror: An Essay on Abjection.* Translated by Leon Roudiez. New York: Columbia University Press, 1982.

Kudrov, K. "Artist, Boretz." *Izvestiia,* 9 April 1963, 4.

Kulikova, I. C. *Pol' Robson—Borets za mir i demokratiiu.* Moscow: Izdatel'stvo Znanie, 1952.

——. "Soldat armii mira." *Teatr* 3 (1951): 96–102.

Lawrence, D. H. *The Lovely Lady.* 1930. Reprint, London: Martin Secker, 1932.

Lazarus, Neil. *Nationalism and Cultural Practice in the Postcolonial World.* Cambridge: Cambridge University Press, 1999.

Lewis, David Levering. "Paul Robeson and the U.S.S.R." In *Paul Robeson: Artist and Citizen,* edited by Jeffrey C. Stewart. New Brunswick, N.J.: Rutgers University Press, 1998.

——. *W. E. B. Du Bois: The Fight for Equality and the American Century.* New York: Henry Holt, 2000.

——. *When Harlem Was in Vogue.* New York: Oxford University Press, 1979.

Lindberg, Kathryne V. "W. E. B. Du Bois's *Dusk of Dawn* and James Yate's *Mississippi to Madrid* or 'What Goes around Comes around and around and around' in Autobiography." *Massachusetts Review* 35, no. 2 (summer 1994): 283–308.

Lipsitz, George. " 'Frantic to Join . . . the Japanese Army': The Asia Pacific War in the Lives of African American Soldiers and Civilians." In *The Politics of Culture in the Shadow of Capital,* edited by Lisa Lowe and David Lloyd. Durham, N.C.: Duke University Press, 1997.

——. " 'Swing Low, Sweet Cadillac': White Supremacy, Antiblack Racism, and the New Historicism." *American Literary History* 7, no. 4 (winter 1995): 700–725.

Litoshka, E. "Bol'shaia iarkaia zhizn.' " *Pravda,* 28 February 1958, 6.

Lott, Eric. "After Identity, Politics: The Return of Universalism." *New Literary History* 31 no. 4 (fall 2000): 661–80.

Lloyd, David, and Abdul JanMohamed, eds. *The Nature and Context of Minority Discourse.* New York: Oxford University Press, 1990.

Marable, Manning. *Race, Reform, and Rebellion: The Second Reconstruction in Black America, 1945–1990.* 2d ed. Jackson: University Press of Mississippi, 1991.

Marshall, Herbert, and Mildred Stock, eds. *Ira Aldridge: The Negro Tragedian.* Washington, D.C.: Howard University Press, 1993.

Martynov, I. "Nash dorogoĭ gost.'" *Izvestiia,* 15 August 1958, 2.

McKay, Claude. *Home to Harlem.* 1928. Reprint, Boston: Northeastern University Press, 1987.

——. *A Long Way from Home.* 1937. Reprint, New York: Harcourt Brace and Jovanovich, 1970.

——. *Negroes in America.* English translation by Robert J. Winter. 1923. Reprint, London: National University, 1979.

——. *Negry v Amerike.* Russian translation by P. Okhrimenko. Moscow: Gosudarstvennoe Izdatel'stvo, 1923.

——. "Report on the Negro Question." *International Press Correspondent* 3 (5 January 1923): 16–17.

——. "Soviet Russia and the Negro." In *The Passion of Claude McKay,* by Wayne Cooper. New York: Schocken Books, 1973.

——. *Sudom Lincha.* Russian translation by P. Okhrimenko. Moscow, Izdatel'stvo Ogonek, 1925.

——. *Trial by Lynching: Stories about Negro Life in North America.* English translation by Robert Winter. 1925. Reprint, Mysore, India: Centre for Commonwealth Literature and Research, 1977.

Mikelburg, B. "Interv'iu Polia Robsona." *V Zashchitu Mira* (May 1956): 25–32.

Miller, Christopher. *Blank Darkness: Africanist Discourse in French.* Chicago: University of Chicago Press, 1985.

Nadel, Alan. *Containment Culture: American Narratives, Postmodernism, and the Atomic Age.* Durham, N.C.: Duke University Press, 1995.

"Negritianskii vopros. Doklad T. Billingsa (Negr)" ("The Negro Question. The Paper of Comrade Billings [a Negro]"). *Pravda,* 29 November 1922, 6.

Nichols, Charles H. ed. *Arna Bontemps/Langston Hughes Letters, 1925–1967.* New York: Paragon House, 1980.

Noer, Thomas J. *Cold War and Black Liberation: The United States and White Rule in Africa, 1948–1968.* Columbia: University of Missouri Press, 1985.

Obradovich, O. "Negr v Moskve." *Pravda,* 18 November 1922, 4.

Offord, Derek. "Lichnost': Notions of Individual Identity." In *Constructing Russian Culture in the Age of Revolution: 1881–1940,* edited by Catriona Kelly and David Shepherd. Oxford: Oxford University Press, 1998.

Ostrom, Hans. *Langston Hughes: A Study of the Short Fiction.* New York: Twayne Publishers, 1993.

Ozadovskii, A. A. *Ssha u Afrika: Problemy Neokolonializm.* Moscow: Izdatel'stvo Myisl', 1997.

Patterson, William L. "Paul Robeson's Latest Success." *Novoe Vremia* 20 (1959): 31.

Perrie, Maureen. "Narodnost': Notions of National Identity." In *Constructing Russian Culture in the Age of Revolution: 1881–1940,* edited by Catriona Kelly and David Shepherd. Oxford: Oxford University Press, 1998.

Peterson, Dale. *Up from Bondage: The Literatures of Russian and African American Soul.* Durham, N.C.: Duke University Press, 2000.

"Pis'mo v redaktziiu." *Voprosy Istorii* 8 (1951): 158–59.

Plummer, Brenda Gayle. *Rising Wind: Black Americans and U.S. Foreign Affairs, 1935– 1960.* Chapel Hill: University of North Carolina Press, 1996.

Polevoi, Boris. *Amerikanskie Dnevniki.* Moscow: Detskaia Literatura, 1957.

———. "Pol' Robson: K 60-letiiu so dnia rozhdeniia." *Pravda,* 9 April 1958, 5.

———. "Voskresenie Dzho Hilla." *Ogonek* 44 (November 1956): 20–24.

———. "Zdravstvuite, dorogoi drug!" *Pravda,* 15 August 1958, 4.

Prince, Nancy. *A Narrative of the Life and Travels of Mrs. Nancy Prince Written by Herself.* 1856. Reprint, *A Black Woman's Odyssey through Russia and Jamaica,* edited by Ronald G. Walters, New York: Markus Wiener Publishing, 1990.

Rampersad, Arnold. *The Art and Imagination of W. E. B. Du Bois.* Cambridge: Harvard University Press, 1976.

———. *The Life of Langston Hughes, Volume I: 1902–1941, I, Too, Sing America.* New York: Oxford University Press, 1986.

———. *The Life of Langston Hughes, Volume II: 1941–1967, I Dream a World.* New York: Oxford University Press, 1988.

"Rech' T. Mak-keia" ("Speech of Comrade McKay"). *Pravda,* 29 November 1922, 4.

Record, Wilson. *The Negro and the Communist Party.* Chapel Hill: University of North Carolina Press, 1951.

Reed, John. "The World Congress of the Communist International." *Communist* 10 (1920): 3.

"Remembering Paul Robeson." *Newshour with Jim Lehrer,* PBS, 9 April 1998.

Renza, Louis A. "A Theory of Autobiography." In *Autobiography: Essays Theoretical and Critical,* edited by James Olney. Princeton, N.J.: Princeton University Press, 1980.

Richards, Sandra L. "Writing the Absent Potential: Drama, Performance, and the Canon of African-American Literature." In *Performativity and Performance,* edited by Andrew Parker and Eve Kosofsky Sedgwick. New York: Routledge, 1995.

Robeson, Eslanda. "Afrika rvet okovyi." *Druzhba Narodov* 6 (1959): 189–94.

———. "Amerikantsy na Afrikanskoi Konferentzii." *Sovetskii Vostok* 3 (1959): 20–21.

———. "Lui Armstrong vyiskazyivaet svoe mnenie." *Literaturnaiা Gazeta,* 5 December 1957, 4.

———. "The Negro in American Life." *Novoe Vremiia* 25 (June 1963): 14–18.

———. "Net inogo vyibora, krome bor'by." *Mezhdunarodnaia Zhuzn'* 3 (1957): 54–56.

———. "The New General Assembly." *Novoe Vremiia* 2 (1956): 8–10.

———. "Pochemu ia drug Sovetskogo Soiuza." *Sovetskaia Zhenshchina* 1 (1954): 42.

———. "Pokhod negrov za svobodu." *Mezhdunarodnaia Zhuizn'* 8 (1957): 135–56.

———. "Triumf sotzializma." *Izvestiia,* 25 April 1961, 2.

———. "V bor'be za svoiprava." *Mezhdunarodnaia Zhuzn'* 1 (1957): 92–95.

Robeson, Paul. "The Battleground Is Here." In *Paul Robeson: The Great Forerunner,* edited by the editors of *Freedomways.* New York: International Publishers, 1985.

——. "Chekhov liubim vo vsem mire." *Izvestiia*, 31 January 1960, 4.

——. Foreword to *Favorite Songs of the Red Army and Navy* (1941). In *Paul Robeson Speaks: Writings, Speeches, Interviews, 1918–1974*, ed. Philip S. Foner, New York, Citadel Press, 1978.

——. "Genocide Stalks the U.S.A." *New World Review*, February 1952, 24–29.

——. *Here I Stand*. New York: International Publishers, 1958.

——. "Ia privetstvuiu vas." *Literaturnaia Gazeta*, 19 October 1957, 4.

——. "Idet novyii den'. " *Pravda*, 3 January 1956, 3.

——. "Moĭ novogodnie nadezhdyi." *Pravda*, 3 January 1956, 3.

——. "Nadezhda budushchego." *Pravda*, 16 November 1957, 4.

——. *Na Tom Ia Stoiu*. Moscow: Uzdatel'stvo Pravda, 1958.

——. "Pesni moego naroda." *Sovetskaia musika* 7 (1949): 100–104.

——. "Pesni svobody." *Inostrannaia Literatura* 5 (1955): 249–50.

——. "Pis'ma k Sergeiu Mikhbilovichu Eisenshteinu" *Inostrannaia Literatura* 1 (n.d.): 242–51.

——. "Serdechnyi Privet Sovetskomu narodu!" *Pravda*, 1 January 1956, 5.

——. "Slovo druga." *Molodaia Gvardiia* 3 (1960): 12–15.

——. "Vo imia nuzhd chelovechestva." *Literaturnaia Gazeta*, 15 July 1958, 1.

——. "Vy zavoevali uvazhenie vsego mira." *Pravda*, 27 January 1960, 6.

Robeson, Paul, Jr. "Paul Robeson's Censored Moscow Concert." In *Paul Robeson: The Legendary Moscow Concert*. New York: Fenix Entertainment, 1995.

Robinson, Cedric. *Black Marxism: The Making of the Black Radical Tradition*. Chapel Hill: University of North Carolina, Press, 2000.

Roediger, David R. *Towards the Abolition of Whiteness: Essays on Race, Politics, and Working-Class History*. New York: Verso, 1994.

Rogin, Michael. *Ronald Reagan, the Movie, and Other Episodes in Political Demonology*. Berkeley: University of California Press, 1987.

Romanova, Elena. "Svet chernogo plameni." *Literaturnaia Gazeta*, 23 February 1963, 4.

Rowe, John Carlos. *Literary Culture and U.S. Imperialism: From the Revolution to World War II*. New York: Oxford University Press, 2000.

Said, Edward. *Orientalism*. New York: Pantheon, 1978.

Sandler, Stephanie. *Distant Pleasures: Alexander Pushkin and the Writing of Exile*. Stanford, Calif.: Stanford University Press, 1989.

Sawyer-Lauçanno, Christopher. "The Chosen Exile of Richard Wright." In *The Continual Pilgrimage: American Writers in Paris, 1944–1960*. New York: Grove Press, 1992.

Schlosser, Anatol. "Paul Robeson's Mission in Music," in *Paul Robeson the Great Forerunner*, edited by the editors of *Freedomways*. New York: International Publishers, 1985.

Scott, Joan W. "Experience." In *Feminists Theorize the Political*, edited by Judith Butler and Joan W. Scott. New York: Routledge, 1992.

Sedgwick, Eve Kosofsky. *Between Men: English Literature and Male Homosocial Desire*. New York: Columbia University Press, 1985.

——. *Epistemology of the Closet*. Berkeley: University of California Press, 1990.

Smith, Homer. "Hughes Reaches Moscow after Island Tour." *Afro-American*, 25 February 1933, 5.

Sofronov, A. "Myi poem c Polem Robsonom." *Ogonek* 1 (1956): 17–19.

Sollors, Werner, ed. *Multilingual America: Transnationalism, Ethnicity, and the Languages of American Literature*. New York: New York University Press, 1998.

Somerville, Siobhan. *Queering the Color Line: Race and the Invention of Homosexuality in American Culture*. Durham, N.C.: Duke University Press, 2000.

Spivak, Gayatri Chakravorty. "The Political Economy of Women as Seen by a Literary Critic." In *Coming to Terms: Feminism, Theory, Politics*, edited by Elizabeth Weed. New York: Routledge, 1989.

Spurr, David. *The Rhetoric of Empire: Colonial Discourse in Journalism, Travel Writing, and Imperial Administration*. Durham, N.C.: Duke University Press, 1993.

Starobin, Dzhozef. "Robson Poet." *Inostrannaia Literatura* 2 (1955): 253–56.

Stein, Gertrude. "This One Is Serious." In *Painted Lace and Other Pieces, 1914–1937*. New Haven, Conn.: Yale University Press, 1955.

Stewart, Jeffrey C. "The Black Body: Paul Robeson as a Work of Art and Politics." In *Paul Robeson: Artist and Citizen*, edited by Jeffrey C. Stewart. New Brunswick, N.J.: Rutgers University Press, 1998.

Stocking, George W., Jr. *The Ethnographer's Magic and Other Essays in the History of Anthropology*. Madison: University of Wisconsin Press, 1992.

Strel'nikov, B. "V gostiiakh u Polia Robsona," *Pravda*, 7 April 1958, 6.

Strong, Anna Louise. *I Change Worlds: The Remaking of an American*. New York: Garden City Publishing, 1937.

——. *Red Star in Samarkand*. New York: Coward-McCann, 1929.

Sundquist, Eric J., ed. *The Oxford W. E. B. Du Bois Reader*. New York: Oxford University Press, 1996.

Suny, Grigor. *Revenge of the Past: Nationalism, Revolution, and the Collapse of the Soviet Union*. Stanford, Calif.: Stanford University Press, 1993.

Svirin, Nikolai. "Russkaia kolonial'naia literatura." *Literaturnyi kritik* 9 (1934): 51–79.

Tiurina, L. "Pol' Robson: 'O, ia eshche pobyvaiu v Moskve i privezu mnogo novikh pesen!'" *Ogonek* 2 (1957): 25.

Todorov, Tzvetan. " 'Race,' Writing, and Culture." In *"Race," Writing, and Difference*, edited by Henry Louis Gates Jr. Chicago: University of Chicago Press, 1986.

Trouillot, Michel-Rolph. *Silencing the Past: Power and the Production of History*. Boston: Beacon, 1995.

Turner, Victor. *The Anthropology of Performance*. New York: PAJ Publications, 1988.

Von Eschen, Penny M. *Race against Empire: Black Americans and Anticolonialism, 1937–1957*. Ithaca, N.Y.: Cornell University Press, 1997.

Wachtel, Andrew. "Translation, Imperialism, and National Self-Definition in Russia." *Public Culture* 11, no. 1 (winter 1999): 49–73.

Wald, Alan M. *Writing from the Left: New Essays on Radical Culture and Politics.* New York: Verso, 1994.

——. *The New York Intellectuals: The Rise and Decline of the Anti-Stalinist Left from the 1930s to the 1980s* (Chapel Hill, N.C. and London: University of North Carolina Press, 1987).

Wiegman, Robyn. *American Anatomies: Theorizing Race and Gender.* Durham, N.C.: Duke University Press, 1995.

Wilson, Edward T. *Russia and Black Africa before WWII.* New York: Holmes and Meier, 1974.

——. "Russia's Historic Stake in Africa." In *Communism in Africa,* edited by David E. Albright. Bloomington: Indiana University Press, 1980.

Woodhull, Winifred. *Transfigurations of the Maghreb.* Minneapolis: University of Minnesota Press, 1993.

Young, Robert. *Colonial Desire: Hybridity in Theory, Culture, and Race.* London: Routledge, 1995.

Zarapin, D. "Poet Pol' Robson: Pervoe Vystuplenie v Luzhnikakh." *Pravda,* 18 August 1958, 4.

Zimianin, Vladimir. *Pol' Robson.* Moscow: Molodaia Gvardiia, 1985.

Zinoviev, G. "Negri-Chernie sredi nas." *Pravda,* 3 December 1922, 3.

INDEX

Bandung Conference, 159, 213, 229, 304 n.26

Beardon, Bessye, 96

Bergner, Gwen, 149

Berlin, Isaiah, 52

Big Jim McLain, 213

Birth of a Nation, 64–66, 278 nn.80, 82

Black and White, 15, 96–99, 283 n.25, 284 n.29

Black Atlanticism, 8–11, 140, 161–62, 216–17, 267 n.11, 291 n.108, 295 n.22

Black belt thesis, 29–30, 36, 110, 126, 131, 181, 268 n.11, 315 n.115

Black intellectuals, 16, 27, 67–68, 130, 186–87, 278 n.83, 299 n.52

Boas, Franz, 130, 290 n.95

Bontemps, Arna, 86, 147, 166

Borders and boundaries: of citizenship, 113; in "Cora Unashamed," 126, 132–38, 291 n.101; Du Bois on travel, 161–63; of gender and sexual difference, 90–94, 118; harem, 119–25, 126–27, 286 n.53, 289 nn.80, 85; in Hughes's Uzbek pieces, 128–30; Jim Crow as, 4, 56, 79, 89, 99–101, 114–16, 122–23; in "Poor Little Black Fellow," 142–45

"The Boy Dancers of Uzbekistan" (Hughes), 90–94, 125, 128

Brennan, Timothy, 296 n.27

Broderick, Francis, 293 n.5

Brooks, Jeffrey, 34, 66

Butler, Judith, 10, 314 n.104

Cain, William, 150, 293 n.6, 294 n.9

Capitalism, 110, 135, 179–81, 185; Du Bois on, 158; Negroes and, 45; and racism, 41, 275 n.62

Capote, Truman, 204

Carby, Hazel, 18, 192, 209, 263 n.4, 267 n.30, 300 n.56

Carver, George Washington, 101

Central Asia, Soviet: compared to the U. S. South, 113–14; Hughes and, 96, 108–16; Louise Thompson's visit to, 96–99; racial equality in, 89, 99, 108; Sovietization of, 109, 289 n.78; Uzbek women in, 86, 88, 90–94, 102, 118, 128, 286 n.54; the veil in, 86, 88–93, 102–8, 284 n.37, 285 n.47, 286 n.53

Chandler, Nahum, 298 n.44

Chelovek (novyi Sovetskii chelovek), 18, 30, 35, 95, 267 n.31, 315 n.119

Cherneshevsky, Nikolai, 11, 26–27

Chernye, 258

Christopher, Mary. See West, Dorothy

Citizenship: African Americans and, 139, 167, 172–74, 189, 209, 213–14; *Chelovek* (novyi Sovetskii chelovek), 18, 30, 35, 95, 267 n.31, 315 n.119; and harem life, 125; and racial equality, 158, 295 n.15; Robeson the performer and, 237–38; sexual desire and, 141–42, 146; and whiteness, 70, 126

Citron, Alice, 193

The Clansman (Dixon), 64, 65

Clark, Katerina, 269 n.14, 278 n.83

Class: and belonging, 144–45; and black struggle, 186–87; and gender, 184–85; and race, 185, 215, 275 n.62; in *Trial by Lynching*, 62–64, 67–71, 128. See also Race and racism

Clifford, James, 107

Cohen, Steven, 305 n.27, 319 n.10

Cohn, Roy, 87, 281 n.7

Cold war, 3–4, 176, 206, 208

Collectivization, Soviet, 170–71, 297 n.31

Colonialism: colonial territory as feminine space, 107, 286 n.53; denigration of white femininity and black masculinity by white supremacy, 244–45, 316 n.123; and Jim Crow, 79; in Soviet Union *(korenizatsiia)*, 195; and the

United States economy, 179; the veil and, 104–6, 285 n.47

The Color Curtain (Wright), 159

The color line: in autobiography, 160, 165; in *Dusk of Dawn*, 180–81; racial politics and, 147, 158–60, 165, 174, 177, 182–83, 296 n.27; in *Souls of Black Folk*, 161; Talented Tenth theory, 185–86, 188

Comintern: African Americans and Pan-Africanist movement and, 45–46; Africans and African Americans and, 243–44, 315 n.19; on black belt in U. S. South, 131, 315 n.115; on class and racism, 275 n.62; on colonialism, 248–49; Communist Party of America (CPUSA) relations with, 56–57, 276 n.59; Communist University of the Toilers of the East (KUTVa), 14–15, 272 n.44; Fourth Congress, 37, 54–55, 181, 275 n.58; and the Negro question, 34, 210–11; Sixth Congress, 210–11

Communism: African Americans and, 2–3, 34, 209–11, 263 n.4; anti-communism, 22, 41, 168, 295 n.20, 298 n.37; anti-racism and communist threat (1950s–1960s), 159–61, 295 n.17; black culture and, 131, 137–38, 291 n.96; and black masculinity, 18, 267 n.30; Du Bois on, 153–58, 166, 168, 171, 182, 297 n.31; McKay's influence on, 29–30, 269 n.12; post-Communist responses in Russia, 258–59, 319 n.10; and racism in America, 41, 53

Communist Party of America (CPUSA): black American participation in, 5, 19, 35–36; Comintern relations with, 56–57, 276 n.59; racism in, 41, 53–54, 57, 68, 182, 183; and white chauvinism, 32, 53, 54, 58–59

Communist University of the Toilers of the East (KUTVa), 14–15, 272 n.44

Cooper, Wayne, 50, 263 n.4, 271 n.31

Cooperating Committee for the Production of a Soviet Film on Negro Life, 96

"Cora Unashamed" (Hughes), 126, 132–37, 291 n.101

Council on African Affairs, 241–42, 249, 315 n.114

Cowley, Malcolm, 96

Crawford, Matt, 15, 100

Cruse, Harold, 302 n.7

Culture, black: autobiography and, 158, 295 n.18; communism and, 131, 137–38, 291 n.96; exile and, 130, 290 n.95; as folk-based culture, 27, 67–68, 130–31, 278 n.83

Davis, Angela, 15, 135, 254–57

Davis, William H., 96

Dell, Floyd, 96

Denning, Michael, 155

Derrida, Jacques, 314 n.104

Desire: and black internationalism, 141; cross-racial desire and unveiling, 124, 137, 144–46; female agency and racial liberation, 127–28, 132, 135–36, 141–42, 145–47, 292 n.109; Hughes on, 89–94; male desire and female identification, 92–94, 102–4; reproduction of whiteness and costs of aborted desire, 133–34; sexual, and citizenship, 143–44. *See also* Veiling/unveiling

Dixon, Thomas, 64

Djebar, Assia, 107, 286 n.51

Domingo, W. A., 96

Dostoevsky, Fyodor, 26, 27

Double consciousness: black Atlanticism and, 8–11, 141, 161–62, 216–17, 268 n.11, 292 n.108, 296 n.22; and black internationalism, 141; and black masculinity, 113, 188–98, 257–58, 299 n.53, 300 nn.56, 62; Du Bois on, 9, 116, 149–

Double consciousness (*cont.*)
51, 166, 175–76, 296 n.27, 298 n.44,
299 n.53; Gilroy on, 216–17, 264 n.14;
and Hughes' identification with Soviet
Central Asia, 108–17; in 1970s Soviet
Union, 256–58
Douglas, Mary, 117
Douglass, Frederick, 270 n.23
Draper, Theodore, 32, 36, 271 n.31,
275 n.59
Dreiser, Theodore, 95
Duberman, Martin, 206, 207, 220,
263 n.4, 298 n.45, 303 n.14
Du Bois, W. E. B.: his autobiographies,
152–53, 155–61, 163–66, 189–90, 199–
201, 294 n.20; *In Battle for Peace*, 152,
161, 184–86, 189–90, 300 n.54; black
intellectuals and, 186–87, 299 n.52; on
the color line, 148, 158–61, 165, 174, 177,
182–83, 296 n.27; on communism, 153–
58, 166, 168, 171, 182, 297 n.31; double
consciousness and, 9, 116, 149–50, 166,
175–76, 296 n.27, 298 n.44, 299 n.53;
Dusk of Dawn, 155, 156, 157, 161, 162–63,
180–82, 200; *Encyclopedia Africana*, 151,
198–99; espionage trial of, 159, 161,
184–89, 298 n.34, 299 n.53, 301 n.72;
Graham's relations with, 190–93,
300 n.58; on historiography, 153–59,
167–68, 183; Lenin Prize, 151, 196–97;
Marxism and, 10, 154, 167, 181, 182–
83; on masculinity, 188–98, 300 n.62;
media coverage in Russia of, 196–98,
301 n.71; *The Ordeal of Mansart*, 176–
77; passport denied, 163–65, 199, 296
nn.23, 24, 313 n.100; Peace Information
Center (PIC), 184–85, 187; *Russia and
America*, 154–56, 161, 165, 167, 168, 172–
74, 186; *The Souls of Black Folk*, 102–6,
117, 115, 142, 149–50, 284 n.37, 296 n.27;
Soviet Africa Institute, 198–99; and

Soviet Union, 21, 169–71, 170, 175–
76, 293 n.6, 297 nn.31, 33; on Stalin,
154, 171, 173, 175, 297 n.31; travels
to Soviet Union, 150–58, 161–63,
296 n.23; on veiling/unveiling, 102–6,
117, 123–24, 141–42, 149, 284 n.37; on
women, 190–93, 297 n.33, 300 n.58;
World Peace Congress (1949), 168, 169,
197–98
Dubose, Heyward, 202
Dunne, William, 45
Duranty, Walter, 95
Dusk of Dawn (Du Bois), 155, 156, 157, 161,
162–64, 180–82, 200
Dust Tracks on the Road (Hurston),
295 n.20

Early, Gerald, 284 n.37
Eastman, Max, 269 n.12
Eisenstein, Sergei, 65, 66, 94
Ekk, Nikolai, 95
Ellison, Ralph, 16–17, 266 n. 28
Encyclopedia Africana, 151, 198–99
Engels, Friedrich, 62
Epstein, Mikhail, 257
Equiano, Olaudah, 295 n.18
Erskine, Caldwell, 95
Espionage, 159, 161, 184–85, 187–89,
298 n.34, 299 n.53, 301 n.72
Europe: African Americans in, 139–48;
and colonialism, 244–45; race con-
sciousness and European travel, 80–82,
139–46, 161–63; and Russian national
identity, 31–32, 43–44, 51–52, 81–84,
158–59, 224–25; 280 nn.104, 105
Experience: and African American autobiography, 157–61, 163–65, 295 nn.18,
20; Du Bois' experience of racism and
the Soviet Union, 157–59, 174; Hughes
on the African American experience in
Europe, 140–45

Fadeev, Alexander, 231, 312 n.89, 90
"Farewell to Mahomet" (Hughes), 122–23, 125
Femininity: colonial territory as feminine space, 107, 286 n.53; female agency and racial liberation, 126–27, 132, 134–35, 141–42, 145–46, 292 n.109; Muslim women and, 118–21, 289 n.78; *Trial by Lynching* and black femininity, 75–77, 104, 128; in *The Ways of White Folks*, 126–28, 290 n.92; white femininity and black masculinity, 104–5, 285 nn.47, 48. *See also* Women
Film: *Big Jim McLain*, 213; *Birth of a Nation*, 64–66, 278 nn.80, 82; *Black and White*, 15, 96–101, 283 n.25, 284 n.29; blacks in American film, 96; *The Clansman*, 64, 65; Cooperating Committee for the Production of a Soviet Film on Negro Life, 96; Meschrabpom Film, 15, 96–101, 283 n.25; *The Red Menace*, 213. *See also* Media
Fischer, Louis, 95
Folk culture: black radicalism and, 6, 88, 282 n.10, 308 n.71; Negro folklore, 67–68, 131, 225, 278 n.83; Robeson's songs, 204, 214–23, 240–41, 307 nn.63, 65, 308 n.68; and Russian literature, 25–27, 274 n.52, 291 n.96; in Soviet Union, 210–12, 224–27, 304 n.26
Folklore, Negro, 67–68, 131, 278 n.83
Ford, James, 96
Fordism, 35
Foreign Commission of the Union of Soviet Writers, 17, 20, 266 n.28
Fort-Whiteman, Lovett, 14, 47, 53, 56, 65–66, 272 n.44
Frank, Waldo, 95, 96
Freedom (magazine), 239, 241–42, 315 n.114

Friendship Society with the Soviet Union, 96

Garber, Marjorie, 92
Garvey, Marcus, 96, 243
Gates, Henry Louis, Jr., 160, 285 n.38
Gender: "The Boy Dancers of Uzbekistan," 90–94, 125, 128; class and, 185–86; colonialism, gendering of, 107–8, 286 n.53; Du Bois and, 190–93, 300 n.58; female agency and racial liberation, 126–27, 132, 134–35, 141–42, 145–46, 292 n.109; gender integration in teahouses, 122; Hughes on, 90–94, 102, 117–24, 289 n.80; male desire and feminine identification, 92–94, 102–4; Robeson on, 306 n.43; sexism in post-Communist Russia, 259–60, 319 nn.16, 17; Soviet Union and gender equality, 196; and unveiling, 90–93, 102–8, 118–24, 144, 284 n.37, 285 n.47, 286 n.53, 289 n.80
Gerassimov, Sergei, 65
Gershwin, Ira, 202
Gilroy, Paul: black Atlantic model, 8–11, 141, 160–62, 216–17, 263 n.3, 292 n.108; double consciousness, 216–17, 264 n.14; on Du Bois, 157
Giroux, Robert, 167
Golden, Oliver, 15, 101, 284 n.34
Goode, Paul, 15
Gordon, Avery, 302 n.78
Gorky, Maxim, 225
Graham, Shirley, 17, 18, 265 n.29, 290 n.92; *In Battle for Peace* and, 185, 190; Du Bois' relations with, 190–93, 300 n.58; on United States censorship of Du Bois, 176–77
Gramsci, Antonio, 218–19, 307 n.50
Gray, John, 239, 241–42
Greenfield, Liah, 7–9, 43–44

Grewal, Inderpal, 107, 286 n.51
Griffith, D. W., 64

Harem, 120–25, 133, 139, 286 n.53, 289
    nn.80, 85, 290 n.86
Harlem, 3, 76, 131, 137
Harper, Phillip Brian, 267 n.30
Hayes, John Earl, 56, 275 n.59
Haywood, Harry, 14, 271 n.31, 299 n.49
Hegel, Georg, 7, 20, 116
Here I Stand (Robeson), 228–31
Heterosexuality, 115–16, 124, 128, 142
Himes, Chester, 16
Hindus, Maurice, 95
Historiography: Du Bois and, 153–59,
    167–68, 183; and multilingualism, 29;
    Russian translation of McKay's speech
    on the Negro question, 37, 39–42,
    271 n.32
"Home" (Hughes), 138
Homophobia and homosocial culture,
    87–88, 114, 281 nn.6, 7
Horne, Gerald, 152, 176, 193, 198, 293 n.6,
    294 n.8, 296 n.27, 314 n.108
House Un-American Activities Commit-
    tee (HUAC), 87–88, 213–14, 235–38,
    243–44, 313 n.100
Howe, Irving, 275 n.59
Huggins, Nathan, 284 n.37, 293 n.5
Hughes, Langston: on African American
    selfhood, 110, 114–18, 122–23, 287 n.70,
    288 n.72; on the African American
    experience in Europe, 140–45; Black
    and White (film), 15, 96–99, 283 n.25;
    "The Boy Dancers of Uzbekistan," 90–
    94, 125, 128; and Central Asia, 86, 88–93,
    101–2, 108–17, 134, 284 nn.34, 35; "Cora
    Unashamed," 126, 132–37, 291 n.101; on
    desire, 89–93, 140; "Farewell to
    Mahomet," 122–23, 125; on gender, 90–
    93, 102, 118, 120–24, 289 n.80; Good

Morning Revolution, 292 n.112; on
    harem life, 123–25, 289 n.85, 290 n.86;
    "Home," 138; homophobia and homo-
    social culture, 87–88, 114, 281 nn.6, 7;
    HUAC interrogation, 87–88; "In an
    Emir's Harem," 120–25, 133, 139,
    289 n.80; internationalism, 3–4, 21–22,
    118, 126; The Lovely Lady and, 126–27,
    291 n.105; "The Negro Artist and the
    Racial Mountain," 291 n.96; on the new
    Soviet person (chelovek), 95; "Poor Lit-
    tle Black Fellow," 126, 138–46; Ramper-
    sad on, 87, 127, 152, 284 n.37, 291 n.103,
    293 n.6; Russian language proficiency,
    4; "Slave on the Block," 126, 137–38;
    on Uzbek women, 86, 88, 90–94, 102–3,
    118–19, 128; on the veil, 86, 88–94, 102–
    9, 118–19, 284 n.37, 285 n.47, 286 n.53;
    The Ways of White Folks, 126–30,
    290 n.92
Huiswood, Otto, 14–15, 37, 49–50, 54,
    271 n.30
Hurston, Zora Neale, 130, 295 n.20,
    298 n.37

Identity, black: and African American
    selfhood, 117–18, 123, 135–36, 287 n.70,
    288 n.72; in "Cora Unashamed," 136–
    37; Du Bois' identification as a black
    American intellectual, 157; and
    Hughes' Uzbek pieces, 129–30; race
    consciousness and, 136, 139–40, 141;
    Russian cultural imagination of, 81–85,
    280 nn.104, 105; whiteness as national
    identity in United States, 129–30, 144–
    45
"In an Emir's Harem" (Hughes), 120–25,
    133, 139, 289 n.80
In Battle for Peace (Du Bois), 152, 161,
    184–86, 189–90, 300 n.54
Internationalism: American exception-

New Economic Policy (NEP), 31, 34,
276 n.63
New Masses, 17
Nietzsche, Friedrich, 285 n.48

Ogonek, 5, 196–98, 247–48, 301 n.71
Okhrimenko, P. F., 271 n.32
The Ordeal of Mansart (Du Bois), 176–
77
Othello Recording Corporation, 241–42,
313 n.114
Other and Otherness: as abjection, 117,
288 n.72; of African Americans, 114–
16, 172–74; black artists as, 138–39; of
Muslim women, 119–21, 289 n.78; the
Negro and the Russian as, 52, 274 n.55;
orientalism and, 110, 116–17, 123; and
the perception of self, 110–11, 115–19,
122, 287; Uzbek women as, 86, 88, 90–
94, 102–3, 118; the veil and, 89–94, 102–
9, 118, 284 n.37, 285 n.47
"Out of Texas" (*Negroes in America*),
277 n.69

Padmore, George, 243
Painter, Nell, 5
Pan-Africanism, 45–46, 243
Parker, Andrew, 219
Patterson, Lloyd, 15
Patterson, William, 246, 302 n.12
Peace Information Center (PIC), 184–85,
187
Pease, Donald, 293 n.6, 298 n.44
Peterson, Dale, 11, 31–32, 224–25, 264
nn.13, 14
Platt, Kevin, 320 n.21
Pochvenniki, 25–26, 274 n.52
Polevoi, Boris, 231–33, 244, 247–48,
309 n.78, 312 nn.90, 92, 313 nn.93, 95,
316 n.122, 317 n.130
"Poor Little Black Fellow," 126, 138–46

Porgy and Bess, 202–5
Potekhin, Ivan, 198–99
Powell, Adam Clayton, Jr., 213
Pravda, 5, 37, 39–42, 60, 204, 271 n.32
Pro Eto, 253, 254, 260–61, 320 nn.20, 21
Pudovkin, Vsevolod, 65, 95
Pushkin, Alexander, 226–27, 280 n.105,
289 n.80, 309 n.78

Race and racism, 108–9; and American
identity, 3, 33, 163, 167, 288 n.73; anti-
communism and, 22, 41; anti-racism
and communist threat (1950s–1960s),
159–60, 295 n.17; assimilation and,
178, 298 n.45; *Birth of a Nation*, 64–67;
and black culture, 131, 290 n.95; black
identity and, 135–40; capitalism, 41,
275 n.62; *chernye*, 258; in Communist
Party of America (CPUSA), 41, 53–55,
57, 68, 182, 183; interracialism, taboo of,
69, 128, 278 n.84; Jim Crow, 4, 56, 79,
89, 100–102, 114–15, 122; lynching, 71–
73, 78, 171, 279 n.88, 297 n.33; McKay
and, 49–50, 53–55, 79; Negro caricatures in Soviet Union, 65–66, 236, 244–
49, 258–59, 316 n.123; in *Porgy and Bess*,
203, 302 n.7; racial emancipation and
female unveiling, 89–94, 102–5, 107,
116, 118, 284 n.37, 285 n.47; and skin
color, 50, 54, 78–79, 114–15, 133, 145,
258; Soviet race relations compared to
United States, 5, 100–102, 108, 109–13,
167, 175–80, 299 n.46; in Soviet Union,
48–49, 53–54, 110–13, 245–49, 258–59,
274 n.56; in *Trial by Lynching*, 60–64,
70–71, 77–79, 104, 128; the veil and
black racial consciousness, 89–94, 101–
8, 118–19, 284 n.37; women and, 126–
28, 133–34, 147, 291 n.101. *See also*
Other and Otherness; The South
(United States); Whiteness

depiction of blacks in film, 96–99; desegregation in, 213–14; Du Bois and post-World War II United States, 155; in *Here I Stand,* 228–29; homophobia and homosocial culture in, 87–88, 114, 281 nn.6, 7; House Un-American Activities Committee (HUAC), 87–88, 213–14, 235–38, 243–44, 313 n.100; Jim Crow and, 4, 56, 79, 89, 99–101, 114–15; myth of America in, 34–35; *Porgy and Bess,* government support for, 202–5; and racial equality in Central Asia, 109–13; racism in *Trial by Lynching,* 60–64, 70–71; Robeson and, 208–9, 217–18, 249–51; Russia's image in, 167–68; Soviet Union race relations compared to, 5, 100–102, 108, 167, 175–80, 299 n.46; the veil and social boundaries in, 107; whiteness as national identity in, 129, 146

Uzbek women: empowerment of, 128; the harem and, 120–25, 286 n.53, 289 nn.80, 85; Hughes' Uzbek essays on, 86, 88, 90–94, 102–3; Muslim women in, 118–20, 289 n.78; racial equality and, 99–100; the veil and, 86, 88–94, 102–8, 118–19, 284 n.37, 285 n.47, 286 nn.53, 54

Van Vechten, Carl, 147, 292 n.112

Veblen, Thorstein, 279 n.85

Veiling/unveiling: Du Bois and, 102–6, 117, 123–24, 141–42, 149, 284 n.37; gender and, 90–94, 102–8, 118–24, 144, 284 n.37, 285 n.47, 286 n.53, 289 n.80; harem, 120–25, 286 n.53, 289 nn.80, 85; Khanum's unveiling, 92, 94, 128, 134–36; paranja, 123; whiteness and, 103–5, 113, 132–34, 144, 291 n.101

Vertov, Dziga, 95

VOKS (All-Union Society for Overseas Cultural Links), 168, 174

Von Eschen, Penny, 213, 298 nn.40, 44, 305 n.33

Wachtel, Andrew, 8, 38–39, 60

Wald, Alan, 208

Washington, Booker T., 166–67

The Ways of White Folks (Hughes), 126–30, 290 n.92

West, Dorothy, 15

White chauvinism, 32, 53, 54, 58–59

Whiteness: and Americanization, 182–83; in *Birth of a Nation,* 64–67; in black cultural studies, 268 n.11; and black intellectuals, 186, 299 n.52; and black masculinity, 71–72, 117–18; in "Cora Unashamed," 126, 132–37, 291 n.101; European v. Russian paradigm of, 51–52; immigration and, 64–65; as national identity in the United States, 129, 146; normativity of, 115; in "Poor Little Black Fellow," 141–42; relations between African Americans and white Americans, 52, 72–73, 110–13, 138–40; and Russian national identity, 81–84, 280 nn.104, 105; skin color and racial identity, 78–79; in Soviet Union, 81–82, 161, 177–78, 183, 212, 230–31, 280 n.104; the veil and, 103–5, 113, 132–34, 144, 291 n.101; white chauvinism in Soviet Union, 32, 53, 54, 58–59; white femininity and racism, 134, 146, 291 n.101; women's representations and, 69–70, 73–74, 270 n.23, 279 n.92

White supremacy: denigration of white femininity and black masculinity by, 244–45; economic basis of, 158; and social reproduction, 135–37; in *Trial by Lynching,* 62, 71–72, 74–76, 277 n.69, 279 n.88; white femininity as complicit in, 134, 146, 291 n.101

Whitfield, Stephen, 303 n.20

Wiegman, Robyn, 18, 71–72, 104, 267 n.30
Wilson, Edward, 248, 304 n.26, 318 n.134
Winter, Ella, 17, 95
Women: domesticity and, 124–25,
289 n.85, 290 n.86; Du Bois on, 190–
93, 297 n.33, 300 n.58; female agency
and racial liberation, 126–27, 132, 134–
35, 141–42, 145–46, 292 n.109; the
harem and, 120–25, 133, 286 n.53, 289
nn.80, 85; labor of, 69–70, 277 nn.85,
86; Muslim women, 118–20, 280 n.78;
Negro mother as redemptive figure,
136, 291 n.103; and "The Negro Question," 62–63, 68, 70, 270 n.24; the "new
woman" in *Trial by Lynching*, 67–74,
279 nn.85, 86; as represenative of global
oppression, 257; Robeson on, 306 n.43;
sexual control in *Trial by Lynching*, 62,

277 n.69; Soviet patriotism and, 195–
96; Uzbek women, 86, 88, 90–94, 102–
3, 118, 286 n.54; and whiteness, 69–70,
73–77, 138, 140, 270 n.23, 279 nn.88, 92;
women of color, 64, 277 n.73, 297 n.33;
in works of D. H. Lawrence, 127–28
Women's suffrage, 17–18, 30, 34–35, 59,
60, 122–23, 269 n.15, 270 nn.23, 24
Woodhull, Winifred, 106, 107, 286 n.49
World War II, 7, 170, 177, 298 n.40
Wright, Richard, 16–17, 159, 210, 295 n.20

Yergan, Max, 314 n.106
Young, Robert, 102–3

Zamiatin, Evgenii, 280 n.106
Zhenotdel (Women's Department), 34
Zinoviev, Aleksandr, 37, 53, 56

Kate A. Baldwin is Assistant Professor of English
at the University of Notre Dame.

Library of Congress Cataloging-in-Publication Data
Baldwin, Kate A.
Beyond the color line and the Iron Curtain : reading
encounters between Black and Red, 1922–1963 / by Kate A. Baldwin.
p. cm.—(New Americanists)
Includes bibliographical references and index.
ISBN 0-8223-2976-X (alk. paper)
ISBN 0-8223-2990-5 (pbk. : alk. paper)
1. African Americans—Intellectual life—20th century. 2. African
American intellectuals—Travel—Soviet Union. 3. African American
authors—Political and social views. 4. African American arts—20th
century. 5. Communism—United States. I. Title. II. Series.
E185.61 .B224   2002   810.9′3247′08996073—dc21   2002003974